OXFORD MONOGRAPHS ON MUSIC

THE MUSIC OF HANS PFITZNER

The Music of
Hans Pfitzner

❧❧

JOHN WILLIAMSON

CLARENDON PRESS · OXFORD
1992

Oxford University Press, Walton Street, Oxford OX2 6DP
Oxford New York Toronto
Delhi Bombay Calcutta Madras Karachi
Petaling Jaya Singapore Hong Kong Tokyo
Nairobi Dar es Salaam Cape Town
Melbourne Auckland
and associated companies in
Berlin Ibadan

Oxford is a trade mark of Oxford University Press

Published in the United States
by Oxford University Press, New York

British Library Cataloguing in Publication Data
(Data available)
ISBN 0–19–816160–3

Library of Congress Cataloging in Publication Data
Williamson, John.
The music of Hans Pfitzner/John Williamson.
Includes bibliographical references (p.   ) and index.
1. Pfitzner, Hans Erich, 1869–1949—Criticism and interpretation.
I. Title.
ML410.P32W5   1992
780'.92—dc20
ISBN 0–19–816160–3

Typeset by Best-set Typesetter Ltd., Hong Kong
Printed in Great Britain by
Biddles Ltd, Guildford and King's Lynn

Preface

꧁꧂

THIS is not a conventional study of Pfitzner's life and works. The first chapter is a biographical overture to a study of Pfitzner the composer. The second chapter is an overture of a different kind. Pfitzner left three volumes of collected papers, which have recently been augmented by a fourth. These provide considerable insight into the creative process as he imagined it. In recent years, the possibility of extracting a coherent system from these has led to several important books and essays. My second chapter aims to condense many of their insights into a picture of Pfitzner's intellectual life sufficient to throw some light on the music, to which the remainder of the book is devoted. Broadly, the approach is chronological by genre. Chapter 3 considers chamber music to the Violin Sonata, Chapter 4 stage music up to and including *Das Christ-Elflein*, while Chapter 5 is the longest, dealing with *Palestrina*. The genre of greatest sustained significance in Pfitzner's career was song, and this is the subject of Chapter 6. Chapter 7 breaks with the generic pattern in considering the music of the 1920s, a decade that marks Pfitzner's furthest advance towards a 'modern' position. Events conspired to give Pfitzner's last period a character that cannot be considered apart from political matters, in particular the question as to whether a composer can legitimately separate his art from the claims of a totalitarian state. Pfitzner's admirers and detractors divide over this, seemingly beyond hope of reconciliation. Rather than giving analytical descriptions of little-known works (which would be meaningless to an English-speaking readership), I have tried here to give a general picture of Pfitzner's style in the 1930s and 1940s, while considering the extent to which this represented a retreat into a private sphere beyond the reach of the Nazi leaders, many of whom were known to Pfitzner.

In general, I have not tried to provide 'programme notes' for each and every work by Pfitzner, which would make for a tedious book. My objective has been rather to place works within general trends, themes, and genres. That Pfitzner was a conservative in musical matters seems to me a fundamentally trivial generalization. In several works, his music embraces extremes of twentieth-century style, albeit with a firm bedrock in German tradition. There are places where analysis according to a rigorous system might produce insights of greater depth than mine. It is my hope that what I have to say about Pfitzner may indeed some day lead to analysis of Pfitzner's music by system. For that, however, there must be a twofold change in opinion. Pfitzner's music must acquire a wider audience, and analysis must acquire a broader repertory. What is presented here as analysis is not uninfluenced in places by system but is more an attempt at what Adorno called 'eine musikalische Physiognomik': a profile of Pfitzner, to which analysis inevitably contributes.

The impulse to study Pfitzner came from my supervisor, Dr Egon Wellesz, and his successor in that role, Dr F. W. Sternfeld, also showed an interest in my questions about Pfitzner that deserves recognition. Amongst others who have helped towards this book, there is Professor Arnold Whittall, who gave me the opportunity to try out the substance of Chapter 2 at a seminar in the Faculty of Music, King's College, London. Of my colleagues in Liverpool, Professor Michael Talbot should be mentioned, not only for reading the whole book in typescript and making many suggestions as to content and style, but also for the encouragement which he gave me to write a study of Pfitzner in the first place. Alongside him I must thank Bruce Phillips (and his readers at Oxford University Press) who gave my vague plans a firmer shape; without his suggestion of a short study of Pfitzner, this longer study would never have occurred. Among Pfitzner scholars, my greatest debts are to Dr Hans Rectanus, who has provided information and tapes, and to Professor Wolfgang Osthoff, who has pointed out misconceptions with great tolerance, and afforded me the opportunity to study important sketches in Würzburg. By reading a draft typescript of the whole book, he not merely saved me from numerous errors, he also gave me the benefit of his deep insight into both musical and literary matters. Dr Johann Peter Vogel, Pfitzner's most recent biographer, has also replied to some questions about material in Vienna. The staff of the Österreichische Nationalbibliothek (which today holds Pfitzner's *Nachlass*) and the Bayerische Staatsbibliothek, in particular Dr Günter Brosche and Dr

Robert Münster, have answered several queries and provided me with access to unpublished letters and various sketches and fair copies of Pfitzner's music; in addition to them, I must thank Pfitzner's stepdaughter, Frau Annelore Habs, and Walter Abendroth's widow, Frau Hilda Abendroth, for permission to quote from this material. Finally I have to acknowledge the tolerance of my wife and children, all of whom discovered the existence of Pfitzner through me. I can only hope the process was not too painful.

Grateful acknowledgement is due to the following for permission to reproduce extracts from the works cited:

Max Brockhaus Verlag of Bonn-Bad Godesberg: *Der arme Heinrich*; String Quartet, Op. 13; *Das dunkle Reich*; *Kleine Sinfonie*, Op. 44; Fünf Lieder, Op. 9; Fünf Lieder, Op. 22; Fünf Lieder, Op. 26.

Schott & Co., Ltd.: *Palestrina*.

Richard Schauer and Alfred Lengnick & Co., Ltd.: Trio in F major, Op. 8.

B. Schott's Söhne, Mainz, and Boosey and Hawkes Music Publishers Ltd.: Concerto for Violin in B minor, Op. 34; Quartet in C sharp minor, Op. 36; *Das Herz*.

Hans Schneider Verlag, Tutzing: *Gesammelte Schriften*; *Sämtliche Schriften*.

Contents

❖❖❖

Abbreviations

FHP	*Festschrift aus Anlass des 100. Geburtstags am 05. Mai 1969 und des 20. Todestags am 22. Mai 1969 von Hans Pfitzner,* ed. Walter Abendroth and Karl-Robert Danler (Munich, 1969).
Jl.	*Jugendlieder* (see Worklist).
MPG	*Mitteilungen der Hans Pfitzner-Gesellschaft.*
PLZ	*Hans Pfitzner und die musikalische Lyrik seiner Zeit,* ed. Wolfgang Osthoff (Tutzing, forthcoming).
PVB	*Hans Pfitzner, Vierteljahreshefte des Bühnenvolksbundes,* 3/4 (1921).
RSB	Hans Pfitzner, *Reden, Schriften, Briefe,* ed. Walter Abendroth (Berlin, 1955; this volume is cited only for letters).
SPB	*Symposium Hans Pfitzner Berlin 1981: Tagungsbericht,* ed. Wolfgang Osthoff (Tutzing, 1984).
SS I/II	Hans Pfitzner, *Gesammelte Schriften,* vols. 1 and 2 (Augsburg, 1926; these are to be reprinted as *Sämtliche Schriften,* vols. 1 and 2, Tutzing).
SS III	Hans Pfitzner, *Werk und Wiedergabe,* 2nd edn., afterword by Walter Abendroth (Tutzing, 1969; an annotated reprint of *Gesammelte Schriften,* vol. 3, Augsburg, 1929).
SS IV	Hans Pfitzner, *Sämtliche Schriften,* vol. 4, ed. Bernhard Adamy (Tutzing, 1987). (All works published by Pfitzner after 1939, including *Über musikalische Inspiration* and *Meine Beziehungen zu Max Bruch,* and all material published posthumously by Abendroth in *RSB* are cited as in this volume. An annotated catalogue of Pfitzner's literary works and their rather complicated publication history can be found in *SS IV* 754–849. In the present study, bibliographical details of Pfitzner's literary works will only be provided where necessary.)

Tb   Hans Pfitzner, *Palestrina: Musikalische Legende in drei Akten: Textbuch* (Mainz, 1951).

Library sigla are as in *Grove VI*, with the exception of

D-WÜim   Germany, University of Würzburg, Institut für Musikwissenschaft.

Scale degrees are indicated by the conventional caret (ˆ) above the appropriate numeral. Indications of pitch register are given as C_1, C, c, c^1, c^2, etc., in accordance with standard analytical practice.

The texts of Pfitzner's vocal compositions occasionally pose problems, in that the versions set diverge slightly from the originals. Such divergences seldom alter the sense, and I have usually cited the original, save in cases (such as the song 'Abbitte') where Pfitzner's word-setting would be distorted. Pfitzner's own comments on the reproduction of his song texts would seem to sanction a pragmatic approach (*SS IV* 467).

Chronological Summary

❖❖

1869	Hans Pfitzner born in Moscow.
1872	Pfitzner family settles in Frankfurt am Main.
1878	Pfitzner attends the Klingerschule in Frankfurt; meets Cossmann.
1886–90	Attends the Hoch Conservatory in Frankfurt.
1890–1	Private teacher.
1892	Teaches in the Conservatory in Koblenz.
1893	Returns to Frankfurt.
1894–5	Employed in the Stadttheater, Mainz.
1896	Returns to Frankfurt.
1897	Teaches composition and conducting in the Stern Conservatory, Berlin.
1899	Elopes to Canterbury with, and marries, Mimi Kwast.
1903	Birth of son, Paul.
1903–5	Conductor at Theater des Westens.
1904	Foundation of *Süddeutsche Monatshefte*.
1905	*Die Rose vom Liebesgarten* in Vienna; beginnings of Vienna circle.
1906	Birth of son, Peter.
1907	Leaves Berlin.
1908	Moves to Strasbourg as director of the Conservatory and conductor. Birth of daughter, Agnes.
1910	Honorary Doctor of Philosophy at the University of Strasbourg. Director of the Opera, Strasbourg.
1911	Birth and death of son, Johannes.
1917	Member of the Royal Swedish Academy of Arts.

1918   Foundation of the Hans-Pfitzner-Verein für deutsche Tonkunst, Munich.
Leaves Strasbourg for Munich.

1919   Settles in Schondorf am Ammersee.
Severe illness of Paul Pfitzner.

1920–1 Takes a masterclass in composition at the Hochschule, Berlin.

1922   Foundation of Hans-Pfitzner-Gemeinde, Vienna.

1923   Meets Hitler in Schwabing Hospital.

1924   Further ill-health; death of Pfitzner's mother.

1925   Senator of the German Academy.

1926   Death of Mimi; death of Willy Levin.

1928   Death of James Grun.

1929   Honorary member of the University of Munich.
Lives in Munich and receives life membership of Academy of Music.

1932   Beginning of attachment to Lilo Martin.

1933   Appointed to the Reichsmusikkammer; withdrawal from Salzburg Festival.
Signs the protest against Thomas Mann's Wagner lecture.
Imprisonment of Cossmann; Pfitzner protests on his and others' behalf.

1934   Pensioned off by the Academy of Music in Munich.

1935   Personal confrontation with Goering; Pfitzner submits.

1936   Appointed Reichskultursenator.
Death of Paul Pfitzner.
Beginning of long feud with the psychologist Julius Bahle.

1937–8 Estrangement from his other children.

1939   Seventieth birthday celebrations (without official support).
Suicide of Agnes; breach with Cossmann.
Marries Mali Soherr (née Stoll).

1940   Begins his autobiography.

1941   Cossmann imprisoned again.

1942   Death of Cossmann in Theresienstadt.
        First visit to Cracow on Hans Frank's initiative.

1943   Destruction of his house in Munich.

1944   Takes up residence in Rodaun suburb of Vienna.
        Death of Peter in Russia.
        Receives honorarium from Goebbels.

1945   Flees from Vienna to Garmisch-Partenkirchen.
        Compositions banned by occupation forces of the
        United States.

1946   Enters an old people's home in a suburb of Munich.
        Ban on compositions lifted.
        Sends telegram of condolence to Hans Frank in
        Nuremberg.

1947   Beginning of Denazification procedure.
        Testimony on his behalf by (*inter alia*) Bruno Walter,
        Schoenberg, and Alma Mahler-Werfel.

1948   Classified as a *Mitläufer* ('fellow traveller').

1949   Death of Pfitzner in Salzburg.

1

Friends, Enemies, Teachers

IN effect there are three composers in Hans Pfitzner. Pre-eminent is the composer of opera and music-drama, though music for the stage does not fill so permanent and regular a place in his career as other genres. Then there is the composer of instrumental music in the traditional genres: symphony, concerto, string quartet, and piano-led ensembles. Finally there is the master of the Lied, less versatile than Wolf, less ample in invention than Strauss, but none the less a setter of German lyric poetry as scrupulous as any of his predecessors. It would hardly seem necessary to draw attention to such many-sidedness had not Pfitzner lived in Wagner's aftermath. The latter's highly specialized output, with its overpowering concentration on music-drama, stands in stark contrast to the career of Brahms, and it was within their twin shadows that Pfitzner and his contemporaries began their careers. Examples of specialization comparable to Wagner's spring to mind among his successors, notably the Lieder of Wolf and the symphonies and songs of Mahler. Rather more composers, however, saw a virtue in restoring that general competence and mastery that Wagner seemed to override with his all-embracing concept of musical drama. Pfitzner here belongs with those such as Busoni, Schoenberg, and Zemlinsky, company that otherwise he would have shunned from circumstances that made his career controversial in his own lifetime. Thomas Mann paid his greatest tribute to Pfitzner and his masterpiece, *Palestrina*, in his *Betrachtungen eines Unpolitischen*, but it is nowadays the fate of the non-political man that his politics are deduced from refusals, denials, and evasions if positive gestures are lacking. In this context it is hardly possible to consider Pfitzner as a socio-political animal separately from the vexed question of his relationship with the Nazis. A study of Pfitzner the composer can hardly ignore the issue, though it may sidestep it until the character of the music makes it urgent and unavoidable. For it is a paradox of Pfitzner's career that much of his most vital and deeply imagined music was composed during the Great War and the *Systemzeit* of the Weimar Republic, which he hated, while the thirties brought a partial atrophy which may be related, albeit with many qualifications, to Pfitzner's state of mind in the Nazi period.

If the controversial nature of Pfitzner's politics is passed over for the moment, there is still the narrower but perhaps more relevant question of the personal conflicts which he aroused. In his career strong opinions rarely went unspoken. He was no enemy of polemics which in part flowed from his character. Bruno Walter perhaps knew the best and worst of Pfitzner as well as any of his contemporaries among musicians:

Pfitzner was a powerful fighter, able to formulate his thoughts poignantly and discuss them imaginatively. To call him a brilliant conversationalist would be going too far, because he was given too little to listening and was too passionately ruled by his own views. What he lacked in breadth of views, though, he made up for by intensity. I doubt that anyone ever conversed with him who did not feel enriched by the experience.[1]

The nature of Pfitzner's temperament perhaps most easily offended the worldly and urbane, frequently cracking the carapace offered to the world at large. No more trenchant and negative an appraisal of Pfitzner's character exists than that which Richard Strauss addressed to Franz Schalk in 1919, shortly after the latter had directed the first Viennese performance of *Palestrina*.

I am heartily pleased for you in particular that *Palestrina* was so successful. But if you want to please me, don't bring Pfitzner to the Academy in Vienna! The perpetual sight of him could wither all the joy in Vienna for me and he is in such good keeping in Munich amidst his own community!! I left Munich for that very purpose. Moreover Pfitzner takes absolutely no interest in the Conservatory and we only create one more camp-follower for ourselves! Weingartner and Gregor right and left are quite enough for the moment—Bruno Walter in the distance; thanks for nothing. And the good Pfitzner is so dreary and so 'ideal'! We would do everything for him and his works—except have him near us![2]

---

[1] Bruno Walter, *Theme and Variations*, trans. James A. Galston (London, 1947), 135–6.
[2] *Richard Strauss-Franz Schalk: Ein Briefwechsel*, ed. Günter Brosche (Tutzing, 1983), 103–4 (all translations by myself unless otherwise stated).

Strauss was moved at least in part to this outburst by an article written by the Viennese critic Ludwig Karpath in which Strauss *and* Pfitzner had been yoked together; 'That damned sweet little word', fumed Strauss in parody of Act II of *Tristan*. But amid the flood of invective, signs of Pfitzner's character emerge if we interpret 'dreary and ideal' with knowledge of Strauss's own temperament. For all Strauss's insistence on remaining apart from 'the eternal journalists' scrawl—*the moderns*', Pfitzner probably felt the greater temperamental need to isolate himself from contemporary trends 'amidst his own community'. This was certainly apparent to those officials of a later period who suspiciously assessed his trustworthiness in wartime Germany:

Prof. Dr Pfitzner keeps himself very much to himself and for this reason is little known; also he is away very often. He is described as a surly man who treats his staff and musicians roughly. His two stepchildren of ten and twelve years old belong to no division of the National-Socialist Youth Movement. He does not belong to the N[ational] S[ocialistische] V[olkswohlfahrt] which does not preclude the possibility that he might be a member in one of his other places of dwelling.[3]

The ideality of middle age seemed to have degenerated into the churlishness of old age.

This is hardly the whole story. Pfitzner had his friends and biographers who bear witness to deeper qualities. The reserve and suspicion which surrounded him became a barrier behind which an intense and difficult personality locked his real feelings. Henry-Louis de La Grange has drawn attention to Pfitzner's 'habitual awkwardness' in his condolences to Alma Mahler on the death of her elder daughter: 'Permit me to say nothing about it to you for everything must seem banal to you'; but Alma had always sensed something substantial behind the *maladresse*.[4] In her case, sympathy for Pfitzner teetered on the brink of something deeper and perhaps more passionate, but in spite of this she discerned qualities which made something resembling an objective judgement possible. 'I saw Pfitzner and Schoenberg standing as stylites on either side of [Strauss] and he as the worldling in between.'[5] Like

[3] Joseph Wulf, *Musik im Dritten Reich: Eine Dokumentation*, pbk. edn. (Frankfurt am Main, 1983), 341.

[4] Henry-Louis de La Grange, *Gustav Mahler*, 3 vols. (Paris, 1979–84), iii. 88–9.

[5] Alma Mahler, *Gustav Mahler: Memories and Letters*, trans. Basil Creighton, ed. Donald Mitchell and Knud Martner, 4th edn. (London, 1990), 28.

Schoenberg, Pfitzner was a difficult character. Schoenberg too could lash out against his critics, though his gift for invective was less developed and exercised more frequently in private; in some of Pfitzner's polemics, Schoenberg hovers as a generally unspoken antagonist but somehow beyond the immediate conflict. Alma sensed an affinity between them if only in their unlikeness to Strauss and the worldly. As far as Pfitzner was concerned, she spotted an artist 'in his very first words', words that could hardly have had a more sympathetic unseen listener than Alma the composer, opposed as they were by Mahler, 'coldly, calmly, tersely'.[6] Alma was to be instrumental in opening Mahler's eyes to the qualities of Pfitzner's music; as to his character, that touched a chord in her but she perceived a limitation in his nationalism, particularly in the way that he 'writhed like a worm and left in mortification' when his equation of nationalism and truth in Wagner was challenged by Mahler and Gerhart Hauptmann.[7]

Nationalism was one of Pfitzner's touchstones. His birthplace, somewhat incongruously, was Moscow, but his parents were German; at a time when such things could be a matter of life and death, his unimpeachably German and Aryan background was proved by a biographer, Erich Valentin.[8] He left Moscow too young for the expatriate's sense of nationalism to develop in him. Like so many non-political Germans, he acquired his nationalism as he absorbed influences surrounding him, German landscape and German music. Music in particular was 'the passion of my youth', 'the cantus firmus of my life' (*SS IV* 562–3). 'You followed blithely the power of love', noted Thomas Mann to Pfitzner (quoting the third act of *Die Walküre*), as he defended his own 'deliberate self-disciplining' which was to lead to exile,[9] and there is something unresisting in the way Pfitzner followed a somnambulistic course from the intimacies of domestic music such as existed in German middle-class households to a reverence for all things German: poets, thinkers, and especially the composers who transcended the banalities of the real world. The other-worldly devotion, calm but cheerful and above all serious and withdrawn, which settles over Palestrina in the closing bars of the opera, is an ideal towards which Pfitzner's stormy personality at

---

[6] Ibid. 42.
[7] Ibid. 81.
[8] *Hans Pfitzner: Werk und Gestalt eines Deutschen* (Regensburg, 1939), 25–39.
[9] Thomas Mann, *Pro and Contra Wagner*, trans. Allan Blunden (London, 1985), 79.

times aspired, perhaps as a 'last stone' such as Palestrina seeks in Pfitzner's masterpiece, and which is scarcely to be separated from the 'deutsch und wahr' and 'deutsch und echt' which Wagner hymned in the closing pages of *Die Meistersinger*. The enemy was the 'wälsche Dunst' and 'wälsche Tand' against which Wagner had also warned in Sachs's final monologue. As a result there is an untimeliness about Pfitzner in the context of twentieth-century music which explains the zeal of many contemporaries in depicting him as a final bloom of German Romanticism.[10] This was not pleasing to Pfitzner himself, whose values seemed permanent, nor does it take account of all of the facts. The poets he set were not confined to Goethe, Heine, and Eichendorff; Dehmel and Ricarda Huch were there as well. The 'real' world (which he satirized in Act II of *Palestrina*) could also espouse his values on occasion, if ultimately as a grotesque *Totentanz* such as Pfitzner himself had envisaged when he led his defender of the teutonic *Liebesgarten* into the bizarre kingdom of the Nacht-Wunderer; it was his tragedy that the analogy was not immediately apparent to him.

In Pfitzner's own account of his upbringing, nature and music are discussed cheek by jowl, but there is a surprising note in the discussion:

The following observations also belong here in the sphere of the conflict between pleasure in fantasy and in reality: I could never dwell long in the contemplation of nature. I know well the feeling, 'One can easily see too much of woods and fields.' A friend accordingly concluded on one occasion in earlier years that feeling for nature had passed me by. This is loudly contradicted in my consciousness by the frequently indescribable delight which I can experience in viewing nature ... But I can never do what so many people can, sit for hours and quietly drink in a beautiful landscape; as I mulled this over for the first time, I discovered that it was precisely the passionate, longing, greedy type of feeling which didn't permit me to linger long in quiet pleasure. One can't rush right into the heart of the evening, one can't devour, kiss, drink, or embrace the landscape, so one goes home. (*SS IV* 561)

The tone is characteristic. There are elements of the Romantic in Pfitzner's view of nature, but held firmly in check by a coldly observing eye directed inwards towards the feelings.

---

[10] See, for example, Conrad Wandrey, *Hans Pfitzner: Seine geistige Persönlichkeit und das Ende der Romantik* (Leipzig, 1922).

The Danish musicologist Ulrik Skouenborg would see the essence of Pfitzner and his historical position in the modern, disillusioned eye which Pfitzner turned on romantic themes.[11] Passion and longing, however, were there too and strongest when it came to the contemplation of the fruits of the mind, poetry, philosophy, and primarily music. One may view this sober intensity as the characteristic tone, the austerity (*Herbheit*) which numerous German commentators have noted (not always with the composer's approval) in Pfitzner's musical style.

This style did not crystallize easily. It was one thing to acquire a feeling for music from his father, a professional violinist who had studied at the Leipzig Conservatory with David and played under Mendelssohn. Tales of Schumann and Lortzing, and of the superior smile with which Mendelssohn conveyed his judgement of the *Tannhäuser* Overture to David (while Robert Pfitzner sat 'as if he had passed out' from inspiration; *SS IV* 565), formed a taste which was not easily satisfied. Pfitzner faced problems in his own family. He was squeezed between a father possessed by 'lethargic indifference' (how different from Julius Korngold, Pfitzner noted), his mother Wilhelmine, whose dilettantish gift for the piano was scarcely adequate for the son whom she had determined to teach, and an elder brother Heinrich who also chose music as a career, thereby creating a 'Kampf um den Klavierstuhl' even after Pfitzner had entered the Hoch Conservatory (1886) in his home city of Frankfurt am Main (*SS IV* 574, 576–8). (Heinrich Pfitzner also studied there in preparation for a composer's career; some of his compositions may be seen in the Österreichische Nationalbibliothek.) There is a constant undercurrent of self-justification in Pfitzner's memoirs, written in his disillusioned old age. To read of his compelling his father to instruct him 'by virtue of my innermost will' is to feel some sympathy for Robert in the face of his formidably determined son (*SS IV* 574). But the tuition and Pfitzner's individual studies brought considerable understanding of traditional harmony. A Piano Trio in B flat (of which three movements, possibly all that were written, have survived Pfitzner's hurried departure from Strasbourg in 1918[12]) reveals

---

[11] *Von Wagner zu Pfitzner* (Tutzing, 1983), 35.

[12] Hans Pfitzner, *Trio in B-Dur für Violine, Violoncello und Klavier (1886)*, ed. Hans Rectanus (Mainz, 1982).

numerous clearly apparent faults in form, phrase construction, and sense of balance, but does display a firm grasp of harmony, albeit in a style that goes little beyond the mid-nineteenth century in daring. Melodic major ninths recalling Weber and Schubertian augmented sixths are handled with precision, even if contrapuntal episodes tend to be grafted on. Pfitzner was obviously thinking big, even if he equated growth with repetition and sequence (especially in the second subject of the opening Allegro molto) and probably failed to write his finale. The *Romanze*, like the published *Jugendlieder*, has pleasantly Schumannesque moments and real feeling for chromatic harmony. What remained to be seen was whether Pfitzner would acquire an individual voice.

Pfitzner has left a record of his tastes in music when he entered the Conservatory: Wagner and Schumann, then Weber, Marschner, and Schubert. Of his shortcomings as a Mozartian he is quite candid; *Don Giovanni* and other related works he liked for their 'romantic' tone, but the symphonies he thought inferior to those of Haydn. Although his tastes were subsequently modified in various ways, he remained remarkably consistent in his devotion to German romantic opera, including the faded star of Marschner; in later years he would make arrangements of *Der Templer und die Jüdin* and *Der Vampyr* for his own use, as well as a revised piano reduction of E. T. A. Hoffmann's *Undine*. His development is distinct from that of Richard Strauss in that Pfitzner's respect for Brahms was acquired after his taste for Wagner. In Strauss's case, it is correct to speak of Wagner supplanting Brahms in his affection; Pfitzner came to admire both, though Wagner remained the greater figure in his eyes.

Brahms was hardly to be avoided in Frankfurt's premier Conservatory.[13] Its first director, Joachim Raff, had been a close associate of Liszt in Weimar, but by the time of his appointment in Frankfurt (1877) he had perceptibly distanced himself from the 'New German School'. In choosing a staff for the new Conservatory, he attempted to strike a balance between the principal musical camps of the day. Lisztians such as Bernhard Cossmann and Anton Urspruch were employed alongside friends of Brahms such as Clara Schumann

---

[13] Apart from Pfitzner's own memoirs, the principal source of information on the Hoch Conservatory in Pfitzner's time is the official history by Peter Cahn, *Das Hoch'sche Konservatorium in Frankfurt am Main, 1878–1978* (Frankfurt am Main, 1979), 97–120.

and Julius Stockhausen. The effort of controlling a divided staff, in particular the problems of handling Stockhausen, may well have contributed to Raff's death in 1882. His successor, Bernhard Scholz, was no believer in balance. It was a condition of his accepting the post that the 'moderns' would have to go (thus leading to the foundation of a second Frankfurt Conservatory named after Raff). Scholz was a friend of Brahms and one of the signatories of the manifesto of 1860 against the 'New German School' (along with Brahms, Joachim, and Julius Otto Grimm). The tone which Scholz set within the Conservatory was accentuated by the traditionalist bias of the counterpoint teacher, Iwan Knorr, another (discriminating) advocate of Brahms. Pfitzner was too shrewd a musical thinker to equate Brahms with academic conservatism (which was just as well, since Scholz's institution paraded its conservatism and its partisanship for Brahms in unison); indeed he hoped at one point that Brahms might give him composition lessons. But his opinion of Scholz was quite distinct from his attitude towards Scholz's idol. Pfitzner seems to have needed his enemies and liked them to be Goliaths. Scholz was the first of these, and whatever humiliations Pfitzner suffered, he paid Scholz back in his memoirs, where the refrain, 'the friend of Brahms and Dilthey', ironically deflates the man 'more fit to be in charge of a barracks than an artistic institution' (*SS IV* 578). The works by Pfitzner which were performed at the Conservatory in open rehearsals were in safe genres, more movements for piano trio, songs, and a Scherzo in C minor. Several works from Pfitzner's Conservatory days were published, in some cases years after their composition; the rather feeble Scherzo bears a dedication to the Berlin Philharmonic Orchestra, which performed it at an important concert (for Pfitzner) on 4 May 1893. One work which did not see the light of day (at least in Pfitzner's lifetime) was an early Cello Concerto which Scholz would not allow to be performed; his ban also fell on a *Ballade* after Freiligrath, *Der Blumen Rache*, for alto solo, women's chorus, and orchestra, which was later published.

The tuition which produced these early compositions must to some extent be inferred, since the Conservatory did not boast a composition teacher in the modern sense of the term. Knorr as counterpoint teacher provided tuition in note manipulation of a highly formal kind. The sketches for Pfitzner's incidental music to Ibsen's *Feast at Solhaug* contain various comments from (presumably) Knorr's pencil, which relate more to forbidden parallel intervals than to the substance of the work.[14] From Pfitzner's respectful account of Knorr's teaching, it may be gathered that Knorr also taught the elements of traditional *Formenlehre* together with aural training of a kind familiar to all music students of the present day. More fruitfully, he introduced Pfitzner to the music of Brahms in a humane and informed way (*SS IV* 581–6). Brahms is the only composer mentioned as a model in the critical comments on the sketches for the Ibsen music. It is hardly surprising that under these circumstances one of the most successful of Pfitzner's early compositions should have been prompted by the friendship of an outstanding fellow pupil rather than the insight of a teacher. The friend was the cellist Heinrich Kiefer and the work, Pfitzner's Opus 1, was the Cello Sonata in F sharp minor.

Something of the impact Kiefer made at the Conservatory may be deduced from the fact that his teacher, Bernhard Cossmann, wrote a fantasy on Schubert's 'Erlkönig' for his pupil's sole use (*SS II* 291). According to Pfitzner, Kiefer had a soloist's temperament, and cared less for chamber music. The forbidden Cello Concerto was written first for him, and the account which Pfitzner wrote of its birth-pangs in his obituary of Kiefer gives a flavour of the Conservatory, its tyrannical director, and his rebellious students:

We two very quickly formed a friendship; when and on what occasion the first advances took place I no longer know. Admittedly we must have been drawn together more by our talent and our ambition than by the example of our director, Bernhard Scholz, who had an unconquerable aversion to everything talented. So we two were not held in high regard in this place and thus became sympathetic companions; as free scholars, moreover, we were encouraged to be modest. The tiresome orchestral practices, which took up half the day, and which Kiefer attended unwillingly—or willingly did not attend—because it cost him practice time, afforded material for conflict. On the other hand I, who was robbed of years of study by obediently passing the accompanying of the singing lessons (to which I was ordered), I was more unpopular because of my seditious compositions, which were never even heard at the examination concerts of this institution. Among other works treated thus was a Cello Concerto, which I wrote for Kiefer as the fruit of our friendship. The work, accepted by my teacher Iwan Knorr for an examination

---

[14] *D-Mbs*, Tresor Mus. mss 9693.

concert, aroused the enthusiasm of Kiefer and the well-intentioned interest of his teacher, the celebrated cellist and Nestor of the Conservatory professors, Bernhard Cossmann. Kiefer made the difficult cello part his own with amazing speed. The concert had to receive the approval of the ears of the director. With consummate virtuosity, it was performed to the mighty one under my accompaniment in the presence of Professor Cossmann. Already this performance should have earned the work a hearing in the examination concert; it would have been a high point of the performances and an incitement and a wonder to the young, struggling artists. Instead the effect was an outburst of rage from Scholz. As I had feared, because it contained a few augmented triads, he found it 'Wagnerized' (the worst heresy for him); but his scorn was most aroused by the scandalous use of three trombones. 'Three trombones in a cello concerto!!' With this cry of indignation, he left the locale, thundering from the distance. The concerto, a strong indication of talent for a student work, was never performed; two young men were richer by one bitterness and there was one more injustice in the world. Kiefer and I later left the institution without recommendation and advancement, and had to make our way alone. (*SS II* 293–4)

Pfitzner and Kiefer remained close friends and later taught together at the Stern Conservatory in Berlin. The Cello Sonata was also included in the Berlin concert of 4 May 1893, played by Kiefer and the pianist Ernst Jedliczka. Yet although it was the fruit of a rebellious friendship, it also represents the consummation of Pfitzner's study of Brahms under Knorr. It stands as a counterweight to the incidental music to *Das Fest auf Solhaug*, as Ibsen's *Gildet på Solhaug* was known in Emma Klingenfeld's translation. Pfitzner's acute sense of resentment over his Frankfurt training emerges in his account of the problems he experienced in showing this work to Knorr. Whereas the latter could appreciate much of Pfitzner's writing in orthodox forms, he seems to have stumbled over the incidental score with its mixture of idioms, its motivic apparatus suggestive of Wagner, and its prominent use of melodrama. The unhelpful nature of his comments on the work brought home afresh to Pfitzner his lack of a patron in 1890 as the doors of the Conservatory closed on him. His feeling of grievance was compounded by a series of farcical adventures relating to *Das Fest auf Solhaug* (which Pfitzner invests in his memoirs with some humour). These dragged in a formidable cast, including Emma Klingenfeld, Possart (the Intendant of the Munich Court Theatre), no less a person than Ibsen himself, and Hans von Bülow, whom Pfitzner (who must later have reflected on Bülow's assistance to Strauss and Mahler) dearly wanted as a patron.[15] Pfitzner wrote his incidental music from enthusiasm for the great Scandinavian writer rather than for a fixed commission. Only then did he approach Klingenfeld for permission to use her translation. This had been granted to the Danish composer Peter Lange-Müller (except in Vienna, where a new score was commissioned from Hugo Wolf; his dealings with the play and the management of the Burgtheater would require a chapter to themselves). To overcome the obstinate Fraülein Klingenfeld, Pfitzner approached Ibsen who lived then in Munich, confident that Ibsen, the fighter for truth and scourge of conventions, would appreciate a struggling fellow-artist of a similar temperament:

... before I entered the lion's den, I had to see him first. This was easily done, for Ibsen, like Kant, passed his time like clockwork. He was always to be seen at the same hour of the afternoon on the Maximilianstrasse, then he went into the (at that time) Café Maximilian, drank first a glass of beer, then a glass of punch, and read many newspapers. He wore a top-hat in which a mirror was fixed, dressed in black, and carried himself stiff and bolt-upright.... One day I plucked up courage, put on my best clothes, took my score under my arm, and rang at his house door. As it was opened to me, I presented my card very modestly and announced myself to Herr Henrik Ibsen. But I was not led into a chamber, instead Ibsen himself came out and asked what I wanted. I said that I had written a score for his *Feast at Solhaug*, which I would be happy to play him and with which I had experienced great difficulties as to possible performance. He plucked indecisively at the newspaper in which the score was wrapped, looked at me through his spectacles with sea-blue eyes as if weeping and said that he didn't feel well and 'didn't dare listen to music' but didn't doubt that it was beautiful and, on account of the problems of performance, that I should address myself to Fraülein Emma Klingenfeld, and so bowed me out. So that was the merry berserker I had imagined—but I could add a new item to the Leporello's list of my disappointments. (*SS IV* 592–3)

The tone of the final clause echoes the mood of that 'bitterness' and 'injustice' caused by the Cello Concerto episode. A direct attempt to enlist the help of Bülow (whose second wife was a distinguished Meiningen actress and thus no stranger to the

---

[15] A fuller account of the composition and history of *Das Fest auf Solhaug* may be found in John Williamson, 'Pfitzner and Ibsen', *Music & Letters*, 67 (1986), 127–46.

works of Ibsen) also miscarried. It was part of Pfitzner's temper that subtle approaches and careful preparation were ruled out, either from the start or from accidents due to impulsiveness. Thus a parcel of compositions (including the banned Cello Concerto) sent to Max Bruch in an unsolicited attempt to gain a hearing was returned because it was unfranked; Bruch accompanied it with a sharp note to the effect that Pfitzner should not expect a potential judge of his compositions also to pay for them (*SS IV* 503–4). On such incidents Pfitzner's later sense of grievance was nourished. Disillusionment and suspicion became a way of life; the world was always against him. It took five years to bring the incidental music to performance at Mainz, and a few years later he had to revise the whole carefully when a new translation appeared from the pen of Christian Morgenstern. However disastrous the experience, Pfitzner emerged from Frankfurt with two works, the Cello Sonata and the Ibsen music, which showed that he would not belong simply to one camp; his career as a composer would follow paths which led from Wagner and from Brahms (with the additional deep knowledge of their forebears, Weber and Marschner, and Schubert and Schumann, who at times would loom larger than Pfitzner's immediate predecessors).

It is characteristic of Pfitzner that his career should have been conducted under the aegis of friendship rather than patronage. Kiefer was a prime example of this. Frankfurt has its crucial place in Pfitzner's biography because it was there that he met several figures who formed the intellectual environment in which he could develop as an artist. One was a fellow student called James Grun, the son of a German father and an English mother. Like Pfitzner, he came from beyond Germany's borders to reside in Frankfurt. According to Grun's sister, the poet Frances Grun, Pfitzner attended their house almost every day and was inseparable from James.[16] Superficially, Pfitzner's attachment to the Grun household resembles a traditional musical coterie out of the world of early Romanticism (Grun's sisters also studied music at the Conservatory). But Grun and his family helped to open a wider world to Pfitzner.

---

[16] *Hans Thoma und Frances Grun: Lebenserinnerungen von Frances Grun*, ed. Walter Kreuzburg (Frankfurt am Main, 1957), 22; the idyllic scenes depicted by Frances Grun should be qualified by Pfitzner's own account of the wrangling with the whole Grun family over the contract for *Der arme Heinrich* (*SS IV* 606–8).

Grun was an individual character and intellect. His education was very patchy and he stood on bad terms with the German language; but he had nevertheless acquired a certain educational background from reading and from his frank outlook on the world. His mind sought out everything great and significant in the areas which interested him, art, religion, and socialism. (*SS IV* 587)

Pfitzner's description is mildly humorous in its depiction of a man who attended the Conservatory out of love of music 'without music loving him in return'. 'More ethical than aesthetical', Grun drew his disciples from his character as 'a sectarian, a penitent, a wandering monk, and followed his trade of a world reformer and benefactor'. Grun provided Pfitzner with a sympathetic spirit attuned to the cloudier areas of German aspiration in the late nineteenth century, medieval, intense, and Wagnerian in its approach to the ethical, with a strong mixture of primitive symbolism. It is Grun's character which explains why Pfitzner the non-religious man should have set operatic texts of such persistently re-ligiose hue. It is almost true to say that the image of spiritual ascetic which came to irritate Pfitzner when glibly repeated by critics first arose from Grun's libretto for *Der arme Heinrich*. Not that the spiritual ethos of Pfitzner's first opera was the personal property of Grun. Through Grun, Pfitzner entered an artistic circle which surrounded the painter Hans Thoma, with whom Frances Grun was to form a deep friendship. She provides valuable evidence of the intimacy of the young composer and librettist with the distinguished painter (whose reputation, painfully won in his lifetime, has hardly spread much beyond Germany and even there has faded sadly).

My brother James in this Frankfurt period wrote the text for Hans Pfitzner's music-drama, *Der arme Heinrich*. Hans Pfitzner impetuously set off composing straight away even before the text was ready. We all listened enraptured when he was with James and presented what had just been composed on the piano while gently intoning the vocal parts.

Hans Thoma, who interested himself very much in the text for *Der arme Heinrich*, repeatedly sketched my brother. He made a portrait of James in watercolour for the book of poems, *Glocken von Eisen und von Gold*, which James edited at that time in Frankfurt. Thoma also reproduced James in his celebrated lithograph, *Der blinde Geiger*. My brother sat playing his violin with closed eyes for this picture. Later James again wrote a text for Hans Pfitzner's music-drama, *Die Rose vom Liebesgarten*. A painting by Hans Thoma, entitled *Der Wächter vor dem Liebesgarten,* provided James with the first inspiration. This picture, painted in 1890, is very well known and of richly coloured beauty. Before the dark columns of the entrance stands tall and solemn the armour-clad figure of the guardian, a mighty lion lying near him in the shadows. . . . My brother inserted the guardian like the lion and the love-garden into his text.[17]

Pfitzner's memoirs serve to remind us how tightly knit his circle was, embracing figures from the Conservatory and Frankfurt's wider artistic life. An important focus was the house of Bernhard Cossmann, where Grun, Pfitzner, Knorr, and Thoma met on such occasions as the first reading of the libretto of *Der arme Heinrich* at some point in 1891/2. The reception was not unanimously warm. Some of the more critical comments led to the rumour, 'The young Pfitzner has written an opera which is set entirely in bed' (*SS IV* 608); admittedly the hero does outdo the Tristan of Act III in resting on his bed of pain, finally stirring his knightly limbs in Pfitzner's Act III. Pfitzner remembered that the criticism was led by his piano teacher from the Conservatory, James Kwast, with his first wife Antonie (a daughter of Ferdinand Hiller). This was an indication that relations were not to be smooth with the man who later became his father-in-law. Whether Bernhard Cossmann's son was present on this occasion Pfitzner does not say. But Paul Nikolaus Cossmann was the most important figure whom Pfitzner met and befriended in Frankfurt. Like Pfitzner, Cossmann had been born in Moscow, then returned to Frankfurt where he attended the same school. This friendship thus antedated the connections with Grun and Kiefer, and surpassed them in significance. The younger Cossmann was a man of 'enthusiasm . . . deep artistic understanding and . . . exceptional mental power', according to Bruno Walter, all of which he put at Pfitzner's service.[18] It was he who made the ill-fated approach to Hans von Bülow, who knew the Cossmann family well. Cossmann further provided Pfitzner with innumerable services connected with *Das Fest auf Solhaug* and subsequent works, receiving the reward of the dedication of *Der arme Heinrich.* More than this, however, Pfitzner was fortunate in his friend, since he had seemingly found a star of the first magnitude.

[17] Ibid. 26; as yet unpublished research by Wolfgang Osthoff suggests that more than one painting by Thoma lay behind the themes of the opera.
[18] Walter, *Theme and Variations,* 136.

A wealthy man, brought up in a house which frequently received guests such as Liszt, Cossmann turned his formidable intellect to journalism, founding the *Süddeutsche Monatshefte* in 1903 and acting as its editor-in-chief until 1933; after the Great War, he became political consultant and director of the *Münchner Neueste Nachrichten*. Cossmann was Jewish but highly assimilated. In Bavaria he came to move in the highest circles, especially after converting to Catholicism in 1905. Neither fact seems seriously to have affected his friendship with Pfitzner, whose anti-Semitism, acquired long after meeting Cossmann, was always prepared to make exceptions according to certain well-defined criteria and could be described as theoretical, at least until after 1933, when the distinction rather lost its point. If anything, Pfitzner found Cossmann's conversion harder to understand than his Jewishness. But Cossmann himself provides yet another chapter in the history of that phenomenon so tendentiously entitled Jewish self-hate.

Even the *völkische* element did not lack its Jewish spokesmen. Its most notorious representative was Paul Nikolaus Cossmann, who converted in 1905 in his mid-thirties, to Catholicism; he had founded a literary-political journal, *Süddeutsche Monatshefte*, in Munich just a year before. Stridently conservative, virulently nationalistic, Cossmann and his chosen contributors gave wide circulation to the stock slanders about Jewish 'corrosiveness', 'materialism', 'hatred of tradition'; the *Süddeutsche Monatshefte* is a vivid, if depressing, reminder of how far some German Jews could go in escaping from their past.[19]

The verdict of Peter Gay does not do justice to the full complexity of Cossmann's political position, though it is fully aware of the irony of the Jewish anti-Semite who fought for right-wing causes, opposed the Nazis, and died of typhus in Theresienstadt. During the war, his journal stood on Tirpitz's side over the question of unrestricted submarine warfare. After Versailles, he flung himself into ceaseless battle against the war-guilt clause of the Treaty and backed the military-led government which succeeded the suppression of the Soviet Republic in Bavaria. He was rumoured to have written (with two friends) the speech of Gustav von Kahr which Hitler dramatically interrupted on the night of 8 November 1923; most of the guests at the Bürgerbräukeller that evening were

---

[19] Peter Gay, *Freud, Jews and Other Germans*, paperback edn. (Oxford, 1979), 156.

invited on his recommendation.[20] Possibly his activity in this affair, together with his advocacy of Bavarian separatism, did more than anything else to earn him his spell in Dachau in 1933.

If Grun helped shape the ethos of Pfitzner's music-dramas, Cossmann provided both financial help and political colouring. Pfitzner was one of the co-founders of the *Süddeutsche Monatshefte*, along with Friedrich Naumann, Hans Thoma, and the journalist and essayist Josef Hofmiller. Karl Alexander von Müller, the noted historian who moved in the same set, provided a group-portrait of Cossmann, Hofmiller, and Pfitzner, under the heading, 'Ein Freundestrio'.[21] The journal operated virtually out of Cossmann's study, in which the others would gather to edit the contributions on art, culture, and politics from a wide and distinguished cast of contributors: Richard Dehmel, Hofmannsthal, Alfred Hugenberg, Thomas Mann, Helene Raff, Max Reger, Ulrich von Hassel, Konstantin Balmont, Oswald Spengler, Ricarda Huch, and Tirpitz himself are a random selection of names from its pages.[22] Müller suggests that it was music which held the strong personalities of his trio together, but that is to ignore the extent of the common outlook that Cossmann and Pfitzner shared. Sometimes compositions by Pfitzner would appear as supplements in the journal. Many of his early essays and the books formed by gathering them together were published by the journal, while such critics as Alexander Berrsche and Rudolf Louis wrote on Pfitzner's behalf. But in addition to finance, publicity, and moral support, Cossmann helped in the elopement of Pfitzner and Maria (Mimi) Kwast which led in 1899 to their marriage at Canterbury. Another major service was to publish his own pamphlet on Pfitzner in 1904, which remains of interest to the student of Pfitzner's early years.[23] No man had a greater influence on Pfitzner's career.

Like many another student emerging from a Conservatory of music, Pfitzner was forced to make his way as teacher and performer, which, for a good if not virtuoso pianist, often meant conducting. If this meant that composition was thrust

---

[20] Harold J. Gordon, Jr., *Hitler and the Beer Hall Putsch* (Princeton, NJ, 1972), 281.

[21] Karl Alexander von Müller, *Am Rand der Geschichte*, 2nd edn. (Munich, 1958), 46–55.

[22] Wolfram Selig, *Paul Nikolaus Cossmann und die Süddeutschen Monatshefte von 1914–1918* (Osnabrück, 1967), 199–203.

[23] Paul Nikolaus Cossmann, *Hans Pfitzner* (Munich and Leipzig, 1904).

into the margins of Pfitzner's life, it did not check his productivity in the 1890s, which saw the composition of a steady stream of major works, including his first opera, the most formally ambitious of all his chamber works (the Piano Trio in F, Opus 8), a *Ballade* for baritone and orchestra on Herder's *Herr Oluf*, and, at the decade's end, another opera, *Die Rose vom Liebesgarten*. In this period was also planted the seed of *Palestrina*. That this was a 'by-product' of reading Ambros's *Geschichte der Musik* is an indirect tribute to Pfitzner's desire to remedy such deficiencies in his musical education as remained from his Conservatory days. Perhaps for a similar reason, he turned for a testimonial to Hugo Riemann at a time when *Der arme Heinrich* had just received its first performance. It is hard at this date to estimate how much good Riemann's testimonial did Pfitzner, nor indeed what precisely he learned or hoped to learn from Riemann. There is no mention of the subject in Pfitzner's memoirs. What Riemann had to say after perusing *Der arme Heinrich* was simply that 'the freedom and daring of your treatment of harmony is astonishing, but awakens no trace of discomfort, because you are sustained by a strong feeling of strict logic, so that I entertain the conviction that you are one of the most competent followers of Richard Wagner'.[24] According to Abendroth, a few lessons followed but there is little indication of what these comprised, an omission which is to be regretted in view of the fact that Pfitzner himself contributed few later hints as to his views on music theory, particularly in its harmonic and contrapuntal aspects; the only clue comes in a letter from Riemann to Pfitzner of 20 April 1897:

I have followed the fate of your 'Arme Heinrich' with interest . . . I am . . . curious to see your Trio. I have as you know a high opinion of your talent, but naturally that will not lead me to prejudge your Trio since it deals with a quite different genre. . . . I should be delighted . . . if you came to me once again for a while, and I make only one condition, namely . . . that you be in a condition to reduce all . . . music . . . to tonic, dominant, and subdominant.[25]

The cities in which Pfitzner began his career as teacher and conductor were Koblenz and Mainz, close enough to Frankfurt

---

[24] Ibid. 40.
[25] Walter Abendroth, *Hans Pfitzner* (Munich, 1935), 86; Riemann's letter is cited from *Katalog Nr. 288: Hans Pfitzner (1869–1949)* (Tutzing: Musikantiquariat Hans Schneider, 1986), 30.

to maintain contact with his friends and roots. He taught in the Conservatory at Koblenz in 1892/3, but this pedagogical work paled into insignificance beside the important concert in Berlin on 4 May 1893, at which the best of his early works were performed by friends such as Kiefer, and also by the Berlin Philharmonic Orchestra. The concert made enough of an impact to bring Pfitzner's name to a wider public, earning the praise of, amongst others, the critic Wilhelm Tappert.[26] Pfitzner, then, was not unknown when he was appointed Kapellmeister at the Stadttheater in Mainz. It was here that both *Der arme Heinrich* and a staged version of *Das Fest auf Solhaug* received their first performances, on 2 April and 28 November 1905 respectively. Reviews were generally favourable, particularly those by Engelbert Humperdinck, who was to be a supporter of Pfitzner's music as a whole, and by Max Steinitzer, the future biographer of Richard Strauss. The conductor of the opera's first performance was Pfitzner himself, but the work's success was mainly guaranteed by the Heldentenor who sang the title-role, an import from Cologne called Bruno Heydrich, whose family (including his son, the notorious Reinhard of a later period) Pfitzner came to know well. Of other musicians whom Pfitzner encountered at this time, some were to disappoint him, notably Hermann Levi, who refused his first opera in Munich. But other great names came to his support. Eugen d'Albert approached Pfitzner on behalf of the Allgemeiner Deutscher Musikverein for compositions to be performed by the society; Pfitzner suggested the Piano Trio, Opus 8, which d'Albert later recommended to the publisher Simrock. He met Max von Schillings in 1896 at a Bayreuth performance of the 'Ring'. With Bayreuth itself, he was less than impressed, mainly because of the dictatorial management of Cosima; he noted and regretted the attitude towards Schumann and Brahms which she fostered.

It was now apparent that Pfitzner was ready to walk on a wider stage. In 1897 he moved to Berlin to teach composition, theory, piano, and conducting at the Stern Conservatory, a post later supplemented by conducting at the Theater des Westens from 1903. This prestigious move was quickly followed by an arrangement with the publishing firm of Max Brockhaus, which was to handle many of Pfitzner's compositions. The circle that surrounded Pfitzner in Berlin has been

---

[26] Cossmann, *Hans Pfitzner*, 25–9.

described in some detail by Walter Abendroth.[27] It included distinguished performers and numerous figures from the world of letters and the stage. Of the latter, Arthur Eloesser, Richard Voss, and Ilse von Stach were all to be involved briefly in the history of *Palestrina*. Stach was also the poet of *Das Christ-Elflein*, Pfitzner's one venture into *Spieloper*, and of 'An die Mark', arguably Pfitzner's most beautiful song. On a more personal level, she was almost certainly the cause of a temporary separation between Pfitzner and his wife in 1907.[28] A prominent figure in this group was Willy Levin, one of the most discriminating of cultural patrons with a wide range of friends in artistic circles. His importance to Strauss was rewarded with the dedication of *Elektra*, his assistance to Pfitzner with that of *Das Christ-Elflein*. A portrait of Pfitzner at Levin's house has been set down by Willy's son Kurt, the impartiality of which is remarkable, given that it originated in a lecture to Jewish emigrants in wartime Belfast. The tenor Julius Liban first brought Pfitzner to the Levins' house; the composer immediately became an object of attention:

At that time, [he was] a man of around thirty years, small, slender, with a delicate, interesting head, very short-sighted eyes, an untidy blond shock of hair, no beard at first, later for a time with a pointed beard. He was unprecedentedly nervous, on many occasions completely silent for a whole evening, but on many others, after a successful performance and a good glass of wine, enormously lively, wise, witty, and frequently somewhat malicious. When he was in a good mood, he sat at the piano and played indefatigably for his own and the listeners' pleasure, best of all his greatly beloved Schumann. I have heard no-one accompany the Eichendorff *Liederkreis* or *Dichterliebe* more sweetly and beautifully than him; many times with freely improvised transitions from one song to another. Pfitzner was fanatical in his opinions about true art, and German art in particular. Each of the great masters' notes was sacred to him, but just as much each note and scene-direction of his own works. For that reason, he became a feared man, hated by many theatrical conductors and singers. He particularly revered and loved (apart from the great classics) the romantics, Weber, Schumann, and Marschner. His first act as conductor at the Theater des Westens in Berlin was to bring out with moderate means a masterly performance of *Der Freischütz*. Works which he loved he conducted and

---

[27] Abendroth, *Hans Pfitzner*, 112–14.
[28] Johann Peter Vogel, *Hans Pfitzner mit Selbstzeugnissen und Bilddokumenten* (Reinbek bei Hamburg, 1989), 44; this was not the only temporary estrangement between Pfitzner and Mimi, nor was he always the erring party.

directed incomparably; but as a routine orchestral conductor, who had to be fair to different styles, he was not up to much. On those occasions, his movements on the rostrum were hasty, unclear, and lacking in suggestion, and I know that we children laughed at him without respect. In pianissimo passages he sank low on bended knee, and in forte he looked up as if he wanted to fly in the air. After each performance of a symphony, the little man was physically exhausted, but rallied quickly with a glass of wine. For every organizational, administrative, and social activity he was unsuited; he created countless difficulties for himself by his inflexibility and touchiness.[29]

The difficulties which Pfitzner created were often resolved with the aid of Levin, who also helped him out with money in much the same way as Cossmann. Pfitzner thus was greatly indebted to what Peter Gay has described as 'the Berlin-Jewish spirit'.[30] On all sides of him were artistic enterprises financed, directed, and organized by Jewish men of business and letters. Among his intimates Levin and Eloesser were both Jewish. The great Ibsen director, Otto Brahm, whose productions Pfitzner frequently attended, was Jewish, as was Max Reinhardt, with whom Pfitzner was to collaborate in 1905 on Kleist's *Das Kätchen von Heilbronn*. In these surroundings, Pfitzner became a confirmed anti-Semite. As Bernhard Adamy has shown, the reasons for this are complex, nor should Pfitzner's anti-Semitism be regarded as of the virulent Nazi variety.[31] But it is striking evidence of a mentality similar to that noted in Theodor Fontane by Gay, an attitude that took what was offered and returned a friendship which potentially excluded much that was fundamental to the individual Jew. A Jew was always welcome to such a mind if he or she proved to be German and nationalist in thought (here Cossmann was the supreme paradigm). All the evidence suggests that when the Nazis seized power, Pfitzner did intercede for Cossmann, Eloesser, and others, though to little effect. That in itself is some evidence to support the idea that his anti-Semitism was of a theoretical nature for the most part. But it still remained a stick with which to beat the individual, should he fail to meet the theoretical requirements, as in the later case of Paul Bekker. The spectacle

[29] Kurt Levin, 'Erinnerungen', *FHP* 58–9.
[30] Gay, *Freud, Jews and Other Germans*, chs. 2 and 3.
[31] Bernhard Adamy, *Hans Pfitzner: Literatur, Philosophie und Zeitgeschehen in seinem Weltbild und Werk* (Tutzing, 1980), 304.

remains remarkable, an anti-Semitic conductor and teacher surrounded by Jewish friends and colleagues, accepting the devotion of the Jewish Bruno Walter in 1900, teaching the Jewish Otto Klemperer, and married to a wife whose mother was part-Jewish; but it was not unique and cannot have seemed so to contemporaries. Rather it was part of a social nexus in which many anti-Semites followed Karl Lueger, the famous Viennese mayor, and made up their own minds about who was Jewish and acceptable. Given that this was the era of such ardently German Jews as Schenker and Siegbert Tarrasch, Pfitzner's distinction between national and international Jews, one of the cornerstones of his theory, must have seemed tenable to many.

In spite of his many activities in Berlin, Pfitzner did not fail to produce a number of substantial compositions. Perhaps even more important than his three large-scale works for the theatre (*Die Rose vom Liebesgarten, Das Christ-Elflein*, the Kleist incidental music) and his first String Quartet was the resumption of song-writing which had dried up on leaving the Conservatory. Germinating throughout the period was the idea of *Palestrina*, though it still lacked a libretto. Pfitzner was gradually becoming known beyond his immediate environs. The acquaintance with Walter developed into friendship with Alma Mahler and the support of her husband. With the first Viennese performance of *Die Rose vom Liebesgarten*, a circle of admirers started to grow in that city from 1905, of whom Victor Junk, Margaritta Fischer, and Therese Rie would have parts to play in his career. In Munich, Cossmann's chosen place of residence, he already had a champion of standing. His relations with both cities were to be stormy, however, leading to charges of boycotts and prejudice which were only partly the products of a sense of persecution and neglect.

The city which was to see the full range of Pfitzner's talents deployed was Strasbourg. He went there in 1908 as director of the Conservatory and conductor of the orchestra, and later became director of the opera house. Here he was to write his Piano Quintet and many fine songs as well as *Palestrina*. These were considerable achievements in view of the strife which Pfitzner stirred up around him and which has been so graphically portrayed by Peter Heyworth in the first part of his monumental biography of Otto Klemperer (who contributed not a little to the tensions that arose in the later

Strasbourg years).[32] As the chief figure in the city's musical
life, he was in a position to pay old debts; Mahler's work for
Die Rose vom Liebesgarten in Vienna was repaid with a performance of the Second Symphony (though the work was
painfully uncongenial to Pfitzner). Old wounds were sometimes healed, as when he invited the aged Max Bruch to his
staging of *Die Loreley* in 1916 (*SS IV* 505–51). But fundamentally Pfitzner remained the intransigent figure of old, emerging
in the war as rather less 'non-political' by composing the song
'Klage', dedicated to Tirpitz, who was finally to politicize
German Nationalism unequivocally by the founding of
the Fatherland Party with the approval of the *Süddeutsche
Monatshefte*. It is characteristic that Pfitzner should have
created the spiritual triumph of *Palestrina* at a time when
strife raged both within the cultural life of his adopted city
and in the real world outside. By this time his temper was
fixed, and his targets identified. What remained was to direct
his energies towards his two principal activities, the theatre
and composition. For some time, however, he had in addition
been defining his attitudes towards artistic matters in essays
mostly published in Cossmann's journal. This led willy-nilly
to a gradual clarification of his views on aesthetics as they
related in particular to the stage; in a sense this clarification
grew out of his operas and the protracted creation of the
libretto for *Palestrina*, which circumstances finally forced him
to write himself. Pfitzner's Strasbourg years, in addition
to beginning his most creative period, became the testing-
ground for the polemical campaigns which he launched with
Futuristengefahr in 1916. As Germany became more externally
embattled, Pfitzner stepped forward as new defender of
German tradition and German musical inspiration from
internal enemies.

[32] Peter Heyworth, *Otto Klemperer: His Life and Times*, vol. 1, *1885–1933*
(Cambridge, 1983), 87–119.

2

Inspiration

❦

In the aesthetic literature of the nineteenth century, the term 'genius' is something of a beacon.

> Mit dem Genius steht die Natur in ewigem Bunde,

proclaimed Schiller in *Kolumbus*, and it was this poem that Pfitzner chose to set for unaccompanied chorus in 1905 to commemorate the hundredth anniversary of the poet's death. Perhaps no one definition catches the full essence of what effectively was a talisman as much as a concept. Had Pfitzner been called to define this term in abstract, he might have answered in words like those of Schopenhauer in *Parerga und Paralipomena*:

A genius is a man in whose head the *world as representation* has attained a greater degree of clarity and stands out with the stamp of greater distinctness; and as the more important and profound insight is furnished not by a careful observation of details, but only by an intensity of apprehension of the whole, so mankind can look forward to the greatest instruction from him. If he develops and perfects himself, he will give this now in one form and now in another. Accordingly, we can also define genius as an exceedingly clear consciousness of things and thus also of the opposite, namely of our own self. Mankind, therefore, looks up to one so gifted for information about things and about its own true nature.[1]

To Pfitzner, this would have been an ideal definition, subject, however, to certain qualifying factors. Among the sayings he included in his study of 1940, *Über musikalische Inspiration*, are the lines,

> The world is dead. Were it alive,
> It would give fame's place to genius. (*SS IV* 306)

'Mankind *should* look up to one so gifted', might then be Pfitzner's answer to Schopenhauer.

---

[1] Arthur Schopenhauer, *Parerga and Paralipomena*, 2 vols., trans. (with slight modification) E. F. J. Payne (Oxford, 1974), ii. 76.

A consequence of Pfitzner's subscription to the value of genius was a constant interest in the possessors of genius. Among his writings are parodies of writers, sonnets to writers and composers, and a curious *Halbtraum* (to use his subtitle), 'Totengespräch', in which a variety of great men utter 'characteristic' remarks as mankind attempts to escape from its prison. Pfitzner's heroes are present, Schopenhauer and Kant among philosophers, Goethe, Schiller, Kleist, Eichendorff, Hebbel, and (more surprisingly) Gutzkow among writers, Beethoven and Wagner to represent the composers, and Luther and Bismarck as world-historical figures. Others are less obviously sympathetic to Pfitzner's outlook, such as Nietzsche and Napoleon, and there are few non-Germans (apart from Napoleon and Giordano Bruno), but Shakespeare is given a place of honour, responding to Hebbel's 'If only I could see something' with 'I see enough to depict the whole company in the meantime' (*SS IV* 63). The childish conceit merely serves to illustrate the company Pfitzner kept in his dreams. The parodies of Bürger, Hoffmann, and Wilhelm Busch are more substantial, and that of a chapter by Hoffmann is a particularly effective evocation of the characters and atmosphere of a fantastic tale such as *Die Brautwahl* or *Rat Krespel*. Both Bürger and Hoffmann are among the dedicatees of Pfitzner's six sonnets, the others being Schopenhauer, Lortzing, Schumann, and Wagner. Although the list is quite unashamedly German, to be German is not necessarily an advantage. Bürger's case is striking, in that 'Had the tragedy of your life been half myth and you a Spaniard from the Middle Ages, how full of praise, then, the German psalter of glory would have glowed, how full of pity all posterity!'

Doch Du warst nur ein Deutscher. (*SS II* 301)

That to be German condemned an artist and genius to neglect in his own homeland became a constant theme in Pfitzner's thinking. This was the single most important example in Pfitzner's eyes of the dishonour which the world inflicted on genius. It was the factor which decided that Pfitzner would become a polemicist.

It would be untrue to suggest that Pfitzner's journalism and its implications for politics and culture have obscured interest in his career as a composer. But in the English-speaking world it has sometimes seemed as if Pfitzner were a one-work composer, and that work, *Palestrina*, a mere adjunct to a series of propaganda campaigns against assorted rivals from Busoni to Thomas Mann that have assumed the status of touchstones in the march of musical progress. This is particularly marked in the case of the dispute between Busoni and Pfitzner, where the speculative, innovatory, and (in Nietzsche's sense) Mediterranean qualities of the former's *Entwurf einer neuen Ästhetik der Tonkunst* stand opposed to Pfitzner's picture of the potential decay of traditional Western musical values. To refuse to take sides on such an issue is difficult even for those who share Schoenberg's view, 'Were party standpoints relevant for me, Pfitzner *and* Busoni would be my party, since they seem to me two of the few estimable musical characters of our time.'[2] To read Pfitzner's *Futuristengefahr* after Busoni's pamphlet is still to catch the clash of arms, but with this important difference: Busoni's *Entwurf* is futuristic in a sense quite other to that which Pfitzner implied. It reads as a supplement to Busoni's own career, suggesting avenues that others were to follow with more persistence. Inasmuch as *Futuristengefahr* is essentially a celebration of one positive, inspiration, it functions mainly as a footnote in Pfitzner's career; as Peter Franklin has noted, it can be read as a marginal gloss on *Palestrina*.[3] But it is also a polemical appendix to ideas which Pfitzner elaborated at greater length in other contexts. The resulting contentiousness of *Futuristengefahr* is also marked in the later controversy with the psychologist Julius Bahle, a controversy at once more fundamental and sterile.[4] That Bahle wished to formulate a general theory of musical creation on the basis of

---

[2] Pfitzner attacked the second edition of Busoni's *Entwurf* (Leipzig, 1916); the standard English translation by Dr Th. Baker is reprinted in *Three Classics in the Aesthetic of Music* (New York, 1962), 73–102. *Futuristengefahr* (Munich and Leipzig, 1917) has never been translated into English, though it was reprinted in *SS I* (in which form it is cited in this book). Busoni replied in an open letter to the *Vossische Zeitung* which is translated by Rosamond Ley in Ferruccio Busoni, *The Essence of Music and Other Papers* (New York, 1965), 17–19. Schoenberg's verdict is given in H. H. Stuckenschmidt, *Schönberg: Leben, Umwelt, Werk* (Zurich, 1974), 211 (the English translation of this study is seriously flawed).

[3] Peter Franklin, *The Idea of Music: Schoenberg and Others* (London, 1985), 124–30.

[4] The main texts of the Bahle–Pfitzner controversy are Bahle's *Eingebung und Tat im musikalischen Schaffen* (Leipzig, 1939; 2nd edn., Hemmenhofen, 1982), Pfitzner's *Über musikalische Inspiration* (Berlin-Grunewald, 1940, but always cited here as in *SS IV*), and Bahle's *Hans Pfitzner und der geniale Mensch* (Konstanz, 1949), though there were numerous other publications by both men and by Pfitzner's friends which preceded Bahle's intemperate final study.

psychological experiment seems naïve; that he should have attacked Pfitzner on the issue of the mystical nature of inspiration seems tactless. Bahle's writings have had little or no influence on aesthetic discourse; Pfitzner's response added little to his aesthetic position. The little book which resulted, *Über musikalische Inspiration*, promises more than it delivers. One chapter-heading, 'Das Reich des Unbewussten: der Schoss der Inspiration', seems to say more about Pfitzner's view of inspiration than much of the contents (*SS IV* 282).

The controversy which involved Pfitzner with the critic Paul Bekker and with Alban Berg seems less urgent now than the polemics over Busoni's aesthetic. In opposing the emphasis on explication of music according to poetic ideas as practised by Bekker, Pfitzner seemed to subscribe to the aesthetic of the purely musical that had been preached by Hanslick. Pfitzner's major contribution to the controversy, *Die neue Ästhetik der musikalischen Impotenz*, thus has a historical significance in the growing ascendancy of Hanslick's theories over rival views such as those of Hausegger, but more through the fact of its existence than through the details of its argument. It attracts more attention today because Berg saw an opportunity to counter with a defence of the analytical, the view that melodic inspiration was some irreducible and mystical unknown; his contribution gave the debate its dignity, revealing a deeper issue than was apparent behind Bekker's study of Beethoven which had caused the initial trouble.[5] The nature of inspiration is the dominant question in all of Pfitzner's controversies, however much personalities and abuse cloud the issue, and inspiration was the prerogative of genius. This had been the main theme of Pfitzner's writings even before he felt obliged to campaign against its enemies. Had genius and inspiration not seemed in need of defence, it is likely that much of Pfitzner's work for the *Süddeutsche Monatshefte* would have consisted of supplementary songs. Instead he published several essays which are characteris-

---

[5] Paul Bekker's *Beethoven* (1st edn., Berlin, 1911, reprinted in 1912 and 1918) provoked Pfitzner's *Die neue Ästhetik der musikalischen Impotenz* (1st edn., Munich, 1920, 2nd edn., with a preface, Munich, 1920, and reprinted with a second preface in *SS II*, the form in which it is cited here; this preface is referred to as the preface to the third edition). Berg entered the controversy with 'Die musikalische Impotenz der "neuen Ästhetik" Hans Pfitzners', published in *Musikblätter des Anbruch*, 2 (1920); it is translated by Cornelius Cardew in Willi Reich, *The Life and Work of Alban Berg* (London, 1965), 205–18.

tically defensive (albeit through counter-attack on an often invisible enemy), but more exclusively devoted to purely aesthetic questions than the later polemics.

In defining the difference for him between poetic and musical inspiration in the essay 'Zur Grundfrage der Operndichtung' (1908), Pfitzner set forth his basic tenets. Some of these were already apparent in earlier essays on 'Bühnen-Tradition' (1905), where 'a *truth* in the highest sense' is unequivocally lodged in 'the intuition occurring directly in the head of the genius, the idea of genius, the inspiration' (*SS I* 8). There is a cautionary note, however, in the blunt admission that 'the greatest work of poetry cannot be of genius throughout and in every part' (*SS I* 9). The essay on opera poetry expands this and other passing insights into the notion of poetry as formed by a single governing idea; in this sense Pfitzner accepted Wagner as a poet, though it ought to have been clear to him after the writing of the *Palestrina* libretto that, as a versifier, Wagner was mediocre in a way that he himself happily avoided. Musical inspiration on the other hand reflected the presence of smaller entities, specific small inspirational ideas as opposed to a governing concept. The antithesis between poetry and music was particularly relevant to Pfitzner in that the essay was an overture to the writing of the libretto for *Palestrina*, a form of intellectual discipline before attempting to invoke inspiration in a medium not naturally congenial to him. As a result, such sentiments were spaced out for emphasis:

The great elemental difference between all poetry and all composition resides in this: that each work of poetry according to its essence only depicts in its course a unity impalpable in itself (conception, action) from the first to the last word, a unity from which it has set out; while each composition, according to its essence, sets out from a sensuously perceptible unity complete in itself (inspiration, theme), on which the process draws or to which it must bring something new. (*SS II* 19)

One consequence of Pfitzner's characterization of music has been drawn with pardonable exaggeration by Ulrik Skouenborg, a playing-down of that organic image of form so widespread in thinking about music in Pfitzner's own time. Pfitzner himself seems to deal in a notion of form that depends on successions of ideas rather than something more complex.

A musical composition is nothing more (how unimportant it sounds like that) than a 'compound' of pure moments in the present, tangible unities, which fill a form of no essence in itself, whether a small form (a little piece, a folksong) be completely filled by one unity (melody), or purely independent small unities (melodies) be placed side by side (lower art-forms: dance music, potpourri), or a unity (theme) be repeated again in a fixed order (fugue), or others be shaped from a unity (melody, theme, motive) until this is used up in a manner of speaking and a new one becomes necessary (higher art-forms: double fugue, sonata form, etc.), and whatever more may be thinkable from the same possibilities. (*SS II* 21–2)

Inasmuch as the motive still has a role in Pfitzner's conception of musical forms, the organic has not been completely thrust aside; nevertheless, Pfitzner stands as far from Mahler's notion of the musical cell as he stands from the Schenkerian *Ursatz*. Form is accidental beside the primacy of the *Einfall*.

The term, *Tondichtung*, so beloved in our time when applied to musical works, is not only meaningless but unsympathetic for this reason: it wants to rob poetry of its highest prerogative, to concentrate *one* idea. The proper *Tondichtung* (if one wishes for once to define the word in its true sense) is the musical *inspiration* of genius, which concentrates all the elements of music, melody, harmony, and rhythm, in indivisible unity as in a chemical compound. (*SS II* 22)

'Zur Grundfrage der Operndichtung' reads in part like a blast directed against Bekker and Berg before the controversy began. Although Pfitzner concedes that his definition may seem to belittle music beside the grand working-out of an idea in poetry, his vision of music in reality contains a weighty imperative. Whereas poetry may have its troughs where tradition may see poet and actor through, music demands consistency of inspiration, ideas informed by inspiration to such an extent that they override mere working-out; the great musical work for Pfitzner was not simply the drawing of consequences from an initial motive that bore the whole work within itself in embryo. Hence the acuteness of the clash with Berg, who saw the genesis of Schumann's 'Träumerei' in its opening fourth and in the subsequent neighbouring-note motion, f^1–e^1–f^1. To Pfitzner, 'Träumerei' did not grow from small cells but was a whole inspirational idea, hence an intuition from the realm of the unconscious. In 'Träumerei', the inspiration was the whole piece. Since this was not always the case, the accidental nature of musical continuity was reflected in a further contrast with poetry that introduced a new dimension. Whereas the forms of poetry were sanctified by long tradition,

...the history of musical forms is the chronic embarrassment of accommodating the material of musical inspiration. We see forms taking shape, becoming established, used up, new forms arising, old forms being transformed, we see music leaning on the other arts, copying their forms, and repeatedly growing weary of what it found...

Inborn feeling for form in the individual is always a matter of talent, a cultural inheritance, so to speak; the born melodist is a genius. (*SS II* 24–5)

Berg challenged Pfitzner specifically on the third chapter of *Die neue Ästhetik*, the section which contained the core of Pfitzner's thinking on the history and philosophy of music. In Pfitzner's eyes, music, unlike the other arts, was the product of human reflection. Poetry and the visual arts took their point of departure directly from the world, a point of view that reflects on the type of poetry and painting which appealed most strongly to Pfitzner. (In painting, symbolism and realism of a type represented in the works of Hans Thoma was an ideal which he never went beyond.) Music required something more than the material of the surrounding world. In tone and rhythm resided potential for expression of feeling and structure, but it was not until history had created harmony, 'a labour many centuries long of an entire group of peoples, achieved only once in the existence of the world', that music achieved its essence. With the creation of harmony, rhythm and melody were emancipated. In the history of music, two streams were to be discerned, the creation of a contrapuntal art by the Church, 'stone upon stone', and a popular melodic culture which included troubadour and minnesinger.

In this remarkable period [the Middle Ages and early Renaissance], we see the two *capabilities* of music which we designated the only possible expressed historically in tolerably neat division on the largest scale: the free art of the heart in the antique fashion with Orpheus as ancestor, which enchanted man and beast by song and lyre, with the *tone* as essential and the will to stir feeling: *music as expression of feeling*. And the polyphonic art from the first singing schools, from the first two-part writing to the most complicated finesses of mensural technique: *music as architecture*, with the will to measure, design, and build. (*SS II* 178–9)

In a sense, Pfitzner is glossing the conflict between Palestrina and his pupil Silla in the opera; the metaphor of the stone harks back to the opera with particular clarity. Here the conflict is reconciled.

The two streams merged in the seventeenth century to produce the 'intellectual material' of music, the *Tongestalt*, a synthesis carried in microcosm within the composer; Pfitzner here follows a favoured practice of converting a historical argument into an internal state. The *Tongestalt* is not so much defined as rendered rhapsodical in Pfitzner's prose. Terms such as 'small unity', theme, motive, melody, and figure are all drawn into the argument, but what Pfitzner is fundamentally discussing is contained in the possibilities opened up by 'the synthesis tone-line', or as he more amply describes it, 'the union of *harmony* (note plus note) and *movement of the same* (line plus line)'. Thus a cadence could be envisaged as a simple example of a 'small unity'. Such precompositional formulas were the composer's raw material, and it was distinguished from that of the other arts in that it was already an intellectual human achievement. Whereas other artists arranged, the composer truly created from within by 'projection of the heart into the world'. But the *Tongestalt*, as preformed material, was without value in itself. Value came with the inspiration of genius which enabled music to escape from the image and the representational.

Although Pfitzner seems at this point to have subscribed totally to a vision of music as movement of shapes, in reality he has no intention of denying himself the possibility of music as expression. The capacity for expression which existed in the primary *Ton* did not disappear with the creation of the *Tongestalt*. An inspiration such as the G major march in Act II of *Tannhäuser* (the entrance of the singers) was far from tone-painting but evoked feeling which could only be described in an image: 'I have the direct feeling of a definite German medieval period; it is as if the idea of a former courtly German way of life were captured here in these few bars' (*SS II* 190). Pfitzner admits that words are powerless to say exactly what this march conveys and how it conveys it. The image thus is the inadequate tool of the explicator but not the prompter of the inspiration. In his preceding paragraph on 'Träumerei', he faces a similar dilemma. His technical analysis is as superficial as Mosco Carner suggests.[6] But he is forced once again

---

[6] Mosco Carner, 'Pfitzner v. Berg, or Inspiration v. Analysis', *Musical Times*, 118 (1977), 380.

to enter territory bounded by the image if only because he feels it necessary to point out that 'Träumerei' 'is not the reverie of a child (and thus does not properly belong in *Kinderszenen*...)'; technical analysis is overridden, the image is used to define what 'Träumerei' is not; what remains is the invocation of 'quality of melody', for which quality of inspiration might be substituted (*SS II* 189). Pfitzner seems to stand awestruck before 'Träumerei' like Hans Sachs before the 'Preislied'. Yet awe is not a quality to which so disputatious a nature as Pfitzner's could submit for long, and elsewhere he clarifies some aspects of inspiration that suggest that there is still a role for the critical faculties.

In *Über musikalische Inspiration*, Pfitzner turned to the question of the composition process as it related to Beethoven's sketchbooks and his own experiences.

I remember that the very first inspiration for the song, 'An die Bienen', originally went differently from that finally published. I believe it simply went through the notes of the F♯ major triad on the words, 'Wollt ihr wissen, holde Bienen', something like this: c♯–c♯–f♯–f♯–c♯–c♯–a♯–a♯ (no sketchbook now exists in which it might be found); that didn't really please me, and I gave the melody more flexibility by reshaping the voice part to c♯–c♯–f♯–f♯–e♯–d♯–c♯–b. Naturally that 'improved' the inspiration but it was only possible because this inspiration was nothing special but summoned up instead by the rhythm of the poem and thus no 'inspiration of the first rank'. In spite of this, it became quite a charming little song which I had no need to be ashamed of, but not to be compared with numerous other creations of my song output where the stream of music flowed 'autonomously'. (*SS IV* 298)

Thus there are shades to the quality of melody whose highest level is to be discerned in 'Träumerei', and they may depend on genre, if not in any absolute sense. Furthermore, his speculations on sketches for the 'Eroica' Symphony make it clear that alterations and improvements to inspirations are to be expected in any serious composition, particularly where such factors as historical innovation and extended form are concerned (as in the 'Eroica', 'the birth-pangs of the new symphonic style'); but it is still an article of faith that 'a meaningful musical construction cannot possibly be developed from an insignificant theme' (*SS IV* 297). The small unities that lie behind inspirations in any case may well be conceived as suitable to specific types. *Die neue Ästhetik* surveys a few motives from works admired by Pfitzner to

demonstrate variation in the character of inspiration. First
there is Siegfried's horn call (Ex. 2.1), 'born to remain as it is':

Ex. 2.1

becomes

Antecedent of a period

. . . what it expresses as it stands is immediately lost if it is taken up
in the flux of a large form, a development [*Verlauf*], and has to be
transformed to this purpose; first it must be killed, so to speak; this
is illustrated most clearly in the interlude of the first transformation
in *Götterdämmerung*, 'Siegfried's Rhine Journey', where the motive
is divided in two by harmony in order to build form and period.

Pfitzner thus views the original call harmonically as a prolongation of I by arpeggiation ($\hat{1}-\hat{3}-P-\hat{5}$). The second example
is from Beethoven's Fifth Symphony (Ex. 2.2). 'A fine feel-
ing for quality finds in these six notes the most authentic
musicality, a full musical life; untranslatable, analogous
with nothing; music in itself, symphonic in character' (*SS II*
218–19). This character is linked to the motive's adaptability
to varying harmonic circumstances by contrast with the
major triad of the horn call.

In these examples, Pfitzner found the continuing presence of
expression and 'movement of shapes' in music even after the
meeting of streams in the seventeenth century. And it is the
question of music as expression that caused Pfitzner to orien-
tate himself most clearly with the philosophical model that
influenced him deeply from the moment that James Grun
gave him a copy of *Die Welt als Wille und Vorstellung*, the
system of Schopenhauer. The roots of Pfitzner's aesthetic are
clear enough in Schopenhauer, as he noted when he cited:
'The invention of melody, the disclosure in it of all the deepest

Ex. 2.2

secrets of human willing and feeling, is the work of genius, whose effect is more apparent here than anywhere else, is far removed from all reflection and conscious intention, and might be called an inspiration.'[7] Equally, Pfitzner's belief in the unconscious as the breeding-ground of inspiration must have been buttressed by Schopenhauer's likening of the composer to 'a magnetic somnambulist' giving 'information about things of which she has no conception when she is awake'.[8] But Pfitzner felt that refinements were required in Schopenhauer's picture of music before it could serve his own purpose. Schopenhauer's ideal of melody, after all, was bound up with 'the playfulness of the *galant* period', with Rossini and Mozart (*SS II* 203–4). There was no serious evaluation of Weber, Schubert, or Schumann. In spite of the frequent mention of music's expressive qualities, Schopenhauer's ideal exhibited a concern with one strand, 'movement of shapes'.

Chapter 3 of *Die neue Ästhetik* accordingly settles into an exposition and critique of Schopenhauer's doctrine of music as proceeding from the metaphysical Will itself (in opposition to the representational nature of the other arts). It was Schopenhauer's contention that in music, 'We do not recognize the copy, the repetition, of any Idea of the inner nature of the world'. But Pfitzner sensed an 'open door' in the statement, 'Thus music is as *immediate* an objectification and copy of the whole Will as the world is, *indeed as the [Platonic] Ideas are*' (Pfitzner's emphasis).[9]

If one is willing to take Schopenhauer further sharply at his word, one can also pick at the place where he says that music depicts *everything* 'which the faculty of reason embraces under the wide and negative concept of "feeling"'; because 'feeling' by his definition is simply everything present in the consciousness which is *not concept*, not abstract perception of reason, my province, which I assign to music, truly has absolute foundation and splendidly agrees with the eternal truth on this score, that precisely *only concepts, abstract*

[7] Arthur Schopenhauer, *The World as Will and Representation*, 2 vols., trans. E. F. J. Payne (New York, 1969), i. 260 (cited in *SS II* 195).

[8] Ibid. i. 260.

[9] Ibid. i. 256–7 (*SS II* 207).

perceptions of reason are excluded from any imaginable music. (*SS II* 207–8)

Through this open door, Pfitzner drove his own picture of expression, exhibited in 'Träumerei' and the *Tannhäuser* march, a quality of remembrance, 'the feeling of *recognition*, admittedly in the widest sense, not merely contingent on things within the course of life, but wide over time and space, tying the bonds round past and present'.

This recognition, taken in the cosmic sense, illustrates what I call in this case *understanding* music; it has nothing to do with specialism. It is possible that one musician can completely fail to agree with another equally well educated about the beauty and expression of a piece of music—and thus moreover about an entire creative vision; to a third it will speak just as clearly as to that one of the [original] two to whom it says something. There are feelings by which one knows for absolutely no reason, only a priori, but with the most extreme certainty that others must also have them; to these belong the recurrence of many dreams, for instance, the succession of irrelevant impressions known in advance which one has apparently once experienced. There is a similar feeling with a whole class of musical inspirations, indeed a side of music as a whole... (*SS II* 206)

The possibilities of musical expression are thus as much a matter of unconscious intuition as the sources of inspiration. Pfitzner sensed that his open door in reality was a space left by Schopenhauer in anticipation of his formula.

...if the Ideas are creations of the Will at first hand, 'immediate objectifications', and music just as immediate and therefore on the same level as the Ideas, that is *movements* of the Will directly expressed, why are *creations* of the Will not also on the same level? And if Schopenhauer rediscovered on hearing music clearly and distinctly those impulses of the Will in music on which he built his profound and correct aesthetic, it is equally a matter of feeling that I (and in my case the more surely in this period of human existence) have with music the sensation of images and experienced impressions, not the vague ones I talked of above which loosely accompany listening to a symphony and in connection with which the listener 'can show no similarity between that play of sound and the things which drifted before him' (*Die Welt als Wille und Vorstellung*), but of such a type whose connection with music is of the most thrilling clarity, of the certainty of an experience, much more distinct than the feelings of joy, sorrow, boredom, etc. can be. (*SS II* 206–7)

Thus Pfitzner's aesthetic proceeds from the unconscious through inspiration to the specific inspirational ideas which may shape the course of a composition or create expression through the presence or possession of a *Stimmung*. So heavily are his ideas infiltrated by Schopenhauer that it is difficult at times to say for certain who is speaking. His grasp of the broad outlines of Schopenhauer's thought is convincing enough. In effect he articulates the same interpretation of Schopenhauer's aesthetic as Bryan Magee, who proceeds from the fact that music in Schopenhauer 'is an *alternative* to the Ideas', which is tantamount to calling music 'an alternative to the world'.[10] If there is a sense at a definite point of Schopenhauer being hijacked for Pfitzner's view of the history of nineteenth-century music, it reflects the feeling expressed again by Magee that Schopenhauer's aesthetic is hardly to be comprehended as romantic in the sense of 'expression of emotion, or indeed as self-expression of any kind'.[11] But Schopenhauer's writings were not quite adequate to suggest how the factor of recognition and remembrance might operate. The words from *Parerga und Paralipomena* which Pfitzner placed before *Palestrina* provide the clue:

To that purely intellectual life of the individual, there corresponds just such a life of the whole of mankind whose *real* life is likewise to be found in the Will ... This purely intellectual life of mankind consists in its advance in knowledge by means of the sciences and in the perfection of the arts, both of which progress slowly throughout the ages and centuries and to which each generation furnishes its contribution as it hurries past. Like an ethereal addition, this intellectual life hovers, as a sweet-scented air that is developed from the ferment over the stir and movement of the world, that real life of nations which is dominated by the *Will*. Along with the history of the world, there goes innocent and unstained with blood the history of philosophy, the sciences and the arts.[12]

Here is clear confirmation if not explanation of the fact noted by Magee that the Will which brutalizes the real world and is to be overcome and renounced in human existence, in music does not have that 'uniquely *terrible*' character which logically would seem to follow.[13] The explanation presumably lies in the unconscious roots of artistic creation; music which is an

[10] Bryan Magee, *The Philosophy of Schopenhauer* (Oxford, 1983), 182.
[11] Ibid. 169.
[12] Schopenhauer, *Parerga and Paralipomena*, ii. 75.
[13] Magee, *Philosophy of Schopenhauer*, 240.

immediate product of the Will flows through the Will-less channel of the intuitive genius. At any rate, it is the purely intellectual life which Pfitzner's quality of remembrance taps. The question remains to what extent this whole process is also to be equated with the folk-memory to which Pfitzner's esoteric and élitist view of art claimed access.

Pfitzner's aesthetic rests on a gospel of conservatism, 'a labour many centuries long', 'stone upon stone', drawing on a tradition of intellectual life which is by implication 'un-political' in its freedom from the stains of the real world. He follows a particular German tradition which places the intel-lectual life beyond the merely political, and which at the same time is part of the apologia of German nationalism as expressed from 1870 onwards; indeed nationalism of the kind extolled by Thomas Mann in the period of the Great War was scarcely thought compatible with politics by its advocates. Even in the relatively circumscribed field of musical aesthetics this tradition has its dark side in the anti-Semitic ideas with which Pfitzner assailed Bekker's theories. It is a problem with Pfitzner that his writings are often at their most trenchant at the point where they are most unpleasant in their cultural implications. This emerges clearly in the address, 'Was ist uns Weber?' (1926). Weber's essence lies in his 'deep, consecrating sense of belonging to his own land and folk, a sense of home-land above time and place, which is a metaphysical matter through and through'. Music 'speaks out of the inner self (*Ansich*) of a people as it sounds from the inner self of the world, according to Schopenhauer' (*SS I* 88). Weber in this context was the dawn to Wagner's midday. But Pfitzner, in this speech delivered from the heart of the Weimar period, could not help dragging in 'the sweeter natures of Luther and Bismarck', the metaphysical power which founded the German Empire and its symbol, Bayreuth, and pointing out the contrast between the cultural tradition of which Weber was part and 'negro rhythms and aboriginal noises'. As the preface to the third edition of *Die neue Ästhetik* makes clear, Pfitzner could equally well have substituted atonality for the jazz band without distorting his basic viewpoint. The choice of jazz rhythms, however, is also given point by comparison with the preface to the third edition. The hate figure of that least agreeable of Pfitzner's literary works is, as Pfitzner takes great trouble to point out, not the individual Jew (that would have been strange from the friend of Cossmann, Willy Levin,

Bruno Walter, and Arthur Eloesser). Rather it is the hydra of international Jewry, which had already been attacked in the first edition of *Die neue Ästhetik* as the embodiment of the antagonist to Pfitzner's concept of *Volk*. 'The dividing-line in Germany runs not between Jew and non-Jew but between German-national and international sentiments' (*SS II* 244). As ammunition for this distinction between the individual Jew and the mythical *Judentum*, Pfitzner brings forward that most ambivalent witness in this context, Otto Weininger. In the preface to the third edition, Pfitzner makes it quite clear that 'soulless internationalism' is linked to 'pseudo- and a-national Americanism', for which the jazz band is one symbol (*SS II* 113). The combination of anti-Semitism and anti-Americanism is sufficient to make one wonder if Pfitzner's cultural place is not with old-fashioned German conservatism (whose elegy was already being sung by Thomas Mann) but with the con-servative revolutionaries whom Jeffrey Herf has characterized as 'reactionary modernists'.[14] This is a question which cannot be adequately answered without extensive consideration of Pfitzner's own music. The Weber essay does give off a nostalgic glow for a lost past for which the German people longed in the aftermath of the *Diktat* of Versailles. But Pfitzner was not a blind devotee of the German past. The contemporary piece on 'Marschners *Vampyr*' (1925) illustrates a secondary aspect of his nationalism. As much to be feared as futuristic innovations of the present was denigration of the values of the past by musical archaeology in the form of resurrecting worthless composers. This too was a symptom of decline, and Pfitzner imagined the prospect of a 'Zelter–Hába evening organized by a new Society to promulgate International Culture in Germany' (*SS I* 126). In general, Pfitzner's aesthetic refused to bow to the merely fashionable, the product of the age, but special scorn was reserved for the revival of forgotten masters, especially if they were German; if 'German' was a term with positive significance when applied to 'Träumerei', it could only be devalued in relation to Zelter.

To Pfitzner, his values and his inspirations were permanent

[14] Jeffrey Herf, *Reactionary Modernism: Technology, Culture, and Politics in Weimar and the Third Reich* (Cambridge, 1984); the vital element necessary to enrol Pfitzner among the 'reactionary modernists', a positive outlook on technology (specifically German technology), is virtually impossible to measure—Pfitzner seems to have been more fascinated by the negative aspects of the work of Oswald Spengler than by its Nietzschean positives.

and German. This did not preclude appreciation of other cultures. He simply could not enter into them with the reverence he bestowed on German poets and thinkers. In part this was a product of his deficiencies as a linguist. Although he recognized the influence of Plato on Schopenhauer, his philosophical taste was almost exclusively German, embracing Kant besides Schopenhauer (*SS IV* 471–2); Hegel he dismissed as much for his German as for his dialectic (*SS IV* 45–6). He recognized fully that his grasp of philosophy was that of a layman, but literature was a different matter. His reading in poetry and prose was wide and embraced most of the German classics. Inasmuch as Shakespeare had been domiciled by August Wilhelm Schlegel and Tieck, he belonged in Pfitzner's pantheon. Much the same applied to Ibsen, whose plays Pfitzner encountered in the early translations by Emma Klingenfeld and others; later he collaborated with Christian Morgenstern in adapting the latter's translation of *Das Fest auf Solhaug* to Pfitzner's incidental music.[15] Shakespeare and Ibsen became touchstones for Pfitzner, who liked to quote them when appropriate. A motto for one of the chapters of *Die neue Ästhetik* was taken from *Macbeth*: 'Schön ist hässlich, hässlich schön', a thought which he developed in another famous quotation in the preface to the third edition, 'Kinder, macht Scheussliches' (the source this time being Wagner). With Shakespeare he could be quite a purist. Although he had some sympathy for Verdi, he deplored the Shakespearian operas (and, for similar reasons, *Don Carlos*). Ibsen is perhaps a more interesting love, since it does offer an indication of what Pfitzner sought on the modern stage. Naturalism was a subject about which he had at best mixed feelings; his appreciation of Ibsen suggests strongly that his ideal was a combination of symbol and reality (natural but not naturalistic) in a clear, cold-eyed perspective. One might expect Pfitzner to have had a particular preference for the 'problem plays', *Brand*, *Peer Gynt*, and *Emperor and Galilean*, but this was not so. An English critic divided the German appreciation of Ibsen into four phases, Classic, Romantic, Neoclassic, and Expressionist, with a different group of plays as the focus of each new trend.[16] Pfitzner seems to have been oblivious to such divisions; he embraced even the social plays and *Rosmersholm*, 'one of the greatest love stories of world litera-

---

[15] John Williamson, 'Pfitzner and Ibsen', *Music & Letters*, 67 (1986), 140–3.
[16] David E. R. George, *Henrik Ibsen in Deutschland* (Göttingen, 1968).

ture' (*SS IV* 473–4). He could also speak charitably of Dante, of French writers, notably Molière, Balzac, and Maupassant, and of Lesskov and other Russians. Where intellectual matters and the pure intellectual life were concerned, Pfitzner was no chauvinist; he simply felt that German composers, authors, and performers should stick to what they did best, their own tradition (Caruso didn't sing Wagner).

The tradition of German intellectual life brought Pfitzner most frequently into contact with German verse, and here his standards and tastes reflected his reverence for those poets who stood closest to the history of the Lied. By far the best-represented poet among Pfitzner's song output is Eichendorff, the poet also of the cantata *Von deutscher Seele*, which was originally to be called *Eichendorffiana*. In a sense Pfitzner and Eichendorff were made for each other. The sections of the cantata have titles which suggest those areas of Eichendorff's output which appealed most strongly to Pfitzner: 'Mensch und Natur', 'Leben und Singen', and 'Liederteil'. It is in this final section that Pfitzner comes closest to the 'reactionary' side of the poet. The cantata was written in 1920/1 at a time when Pfitzner was still licking his wounds at his enforced departure from Strasbourg. It is easy to draw a parallel between Eichendorff after the Treaty of Tilsit and the humiliation of Prussia (and Germany in general), and Pfitzner after Versailles. Eichendorff saw the Tilsit system overturned within a decade; the parallel cannot have been lost on Pfitzner. Idyllic visions lead to dreams of liberation. The crucial song is the last but one.

Der Friedensbote (1814)

Schlaf ein, mein Liebchen, schlaf ein,
Leis durch die Blumen am Gitter
Säuselt des Laubes Gezitter,
Rauschen die Quellen herein;
Gesenkt auf den schneeweissen Arm,
Schlaf ein, mein Liebchen, schlaf ein,
Wie atmest du lieblich und warm!

Aus dem Kriege kommen wir heim;
In stürmischer Nacht und Regen,
Wenn ich auf der Lauer gelegen,
Wie dachte ich dorten dein!
Gott stand in der Not uns bei,
Nun droben bei Mondenschein,
Schlaf ruhig, das Land ist ja frei!

Fall asleep, my sweetheart, the trembling of the leaves rustles softly
through the flowers by the trellis, the streams rush in; sunk on the
snow-white arm, sleep on, my sweetheart, how sweetly and warmly
you breathe!
  We come home from the war; when I stood on guard in stormy
night and rain, how I thought of you there! God stood by us in need,
now sleep peacefully up there in the moonlight, the land is indeed
free!

  The poem's imagery seems carefully divided between the
two stanzas. The first is the familiar Eichendorff, the imagery
a counterpoint of love and nature, an idyll imbued with a
standard pathetic fallacy. The second stanza replaces this
with a no less characteristic Eichendorff episode, perhaps less
familiar in the Lied, a scene from military life. But it is not a
simple contrast of stanzas. The war is past as the first line of
the second stanza makes clear. The sentry and the beloved are
balanced in lines three and four. Like a good song-writer,
Pfitzner found a figure which would convey both the rocking
motion of the first stanza and the more robust tones of the
second. After a halt for the evocation of moonlight, the rhythm
grows in a crescendo towards the end. As recent critics have
noted, Pfitzner's setting aims for the last five words at the
expense of the return to the image of sleep with which the
poem opened;[17] the end is C major, fortissimo, as Eichendorff's
statement of fact becomes Pfitzner's hoped-for reality. It is an
additional curiosity that this climax is one of the only two
points in the sketches for *Von deutscher Seele* at which Pfitzner
marked a date, '5. Juli 1921' (the other, '12. Juli 1921', being
at the end of the short score of the final chorus).[18] The date
itself seems to have no significance outside of the composition-
process of the cantata, and does not seem to be the conservative Pfitzner's equivalent of the excited greeting of a 'German-
Austrian Republic' at the close of the autograph of Schreker's
Der Schatzgräber.[19] None the less, the date may be indicative
of the sense of achievement felt by Pfitzner at this of all points

[17] Gottfried Eberle, 'Hans Pfitzner: Präfaschistische Tendenzen in seinem
ästhetischen und politischen Denken', *Musik und Musikpolitik im faschistischen
Deutschland*, ed. Hanns-Werner Heister and Hans-Günter Klein (Frankfurt am Main,
1984), 136; Peter Franklin also pays close attention to this setting in his essay,
'Audiences, Critics and the Depurification of Music: Reflections on a 1920s
Controversy', *Journal of the Royal Musical Association*, 114 (1989), 87–8.
[18] *A-Wn*, S.m. 30,423, Hans Pfitzner, Opus 28, Skizzen zu den Eichendorff-
Sprüchen, fols. 84ᵛ and 92ʳ.
[19] Matthias Brzoska, *Franz Schrekers Oper 'Der Schatzgräber'* (Wiesbaden, 1988),
157–8.

in the work. It is naïve, perhaps, to claim that Pfitzner does violence to the poem. The climax is at least as much a question of preparing a jubilant orchestral transition to the final song as a patriotic effusion. It does, however, establish a sense of continuity with earlier works by Pfitzner. It was another of Eichendorff's 'Zeitlieder' that had caused him to break off the composition of *Palestrina* at a crucial point in 1915. 'Klage' (1809) contrasted the stupidity of the present (in the year of Wagram) with 'princely works and deeds, ancient honour and splendour'. When Pfitzner published his setting as part of his Opus 25 in 1916, it bore a dedication to Tirpitz, who had recently resigned in protest at Bethmann-Hollweg's attacks on him for the Grand Admiral's advocacy of unrestricted submarine warfare. The topicality of the theme disguises the fact that it was not new in Pfitzner's song output. In 1810, Eichendorff had continued the theme of 'Klage' with 'Zorn':

> Seh' ich im verfallnen, dunkeln
> Haus die alten Waffen hangen,
> Zornig aus dem Roste funkeln,
> Wenn der Morgen aufgegangen,
>
> Und den letzten Klang verflogen,
> Wo im wilden Zug der Wetter,
> Aufs gekreuzte Schwert gebogen,
> Einst gehaust des Landes Retter;
>
> Und ein neu Geschlecht von Zwergen
> Schwindelnd um die Felsen klettern,
> Frech, wenn's sonnig auf den Bergen,
> Feige krümmend sich in Wettern,
>
> Ihres Heilands Blut und Tränen
> Spottend noch einmal verkaufen,
> Ohne Klage, Wunsch und Sehnen
> In der Zeiten Strom ersaufen;
>
> Denk' ich dann, wie du gestanden
> Treu, da niemand treu geblieben:
> Möcht' ich, über unsre Schande
> Tiefentbrannt in zorn'gem Lieben,
>
> Wurzeln in der Felsen Marke,
> Und empor zu Himmels Lichten
> Stumm anstrebend, wie die starke
> Riesentanne, mich aufrichten.

As I see the old weapons hanging in the dark, ruined house, flashing angrily with rust at daybreak, and the last sound flown away, where, in the wild course of the storm, bowed over the crossed sword, once lived the land's saviour;

and a new race of dwarfs climbing dizzily about the rocks, cheekily if it's sunny in the mountains, cringing like cowards in the thunder,

selling their saviour's blood and tears once again with a joke, without complaint, desire, or longing to be drowned in the stream of the times,

then I think how you stood true when no one remained true: would that I, deeply inflamed in wrathful love about our shame,

rooted in the rocks' core and mutely striving up to the light of heaven, might stand up like the strong giant fir-tree.

Pfitzner composed 'Zorn' in 1904, the year in which the *Süddeutsche Monatshefte* first appeared. Unlike the dedication of 'Klage' or the ending of 'Der Friedensbote', there does not seem to have been a cause for setting so fiercely critical a song. It suggests that Pfitzner's later tirades against a-national Germans were part of his uncompromising character long before the war and Weimar. The musical style adopted is no less fierce than the poem. The manner seems to ape such models as Wolf's 'Prometheus' with abrupt modulations, dissonance of both chromatic and diatonic kinds, declamatory outbursts, and an emphatically overwritten accompaniment. Pfitzner's feelings come close to bursting the limits of the artistically acceptable. 'Zorn' suggests that polemics and composition in Pfitzner's case may not stand in a fruitful relationship. One of its most striking features is the defiant and rhetorical manner in which he handles the central religious metaphor which the 'Christian patriot' Eichendorff wove into his illustration of degenerate times.[20] Both at 'einst gehaust des Landes Retter' and 'denk' ich dann, wie du gestanden treu', Pfitzner uses a heavily dotted climactic motive (an interesting pointer to the angry Borromeo's departure for Trent in Act I of *Palestrina*). That these images join in 'Zorn' to the image of the saviour is not caught in the song, and while the climax falls on 'Lieben', the tone is still set by 'zorn'gem'. A dimension of the poem is thus lost to the song's relative impoverishment; it becomes more of a tirade, though potentially a magnificent one in the hands of a bass such as Hans Hotter. Pfitzner's love of Eichendorff is thus decidedly

---

[20] Eckart Busse, *Die Eichendorff-Rezeption im Kunstlied: Versuch einer Typologie anhand von Kompositionen Schumanns, Wolfs und Pfitzners* (Würzburg, 1975), 123.

two-edged. In general, however, he responded best to the romantic, idyllic side of the poet.

This leads naturally to an important question, how far may Pfitzner himself be termed romantic. Bernhard Adamy, in his survey of Pfitzner's literary tastes, has noted that romantic authors in the strict sense, such as Tieck, Novalis, or the authors of *Des Knaben Wunderhorn*, are not represented in Pfitzner's output.[21] But this is not necessarily a valid yard-stick. Pfitzner never set Shakespeare, E. T. A. Hoffmann, or the mature Ibsen, yet felt himself spiritually close to all three. In any case, the musician has a somewhat different perspective on Romanticism from the literary historian. Romanticism in music, vague enough as a label, in the form of the Lied cannibalized the works of not a few who, properly speaking, stand apart from Romanticism, notably Goethe and Heine, both of whom Pfitzner revered and set. Adamy gauges accurately Pfitzner's feeling for Eichendorff when he writes: 'Pfitzner's relationship to (literary) Romanticism is narrower than at first appears; it is determined by fixed figurative ideas, mood pictures (wood, bird, night, wind, trees), by the feeling of "freedom", timelessness, stillness.'[22] Others had more thoroughgoing ideas of Pfitzner's relationship to Romanticism.

For Conrad Wandrey, Pfitzner, the soul-mate of Eichendorff to a degree unknown in Wolf or even Schumann, spoke the authentic language of Romantic *Sehnsucht*, from the Cello Sonata through the early operas to *Palestrina*, a tone compounded of sorrow, renunciation, and sacrifice, of knightliness and Christianity; this is a tempting picture, given the medieval tableau of renunciation concocted in *Der arme Heinrich*, the divine inspiration of *Palestrina*, and even Margit's path from carnal love to a convent in *Das Fest auf Solhaug*. From all of this, Pfitzner emerges bathed in a mystical flood of inspiration, representing with Thomas Mann 'the final notes and end of the bourgeois era, the beginning and end of the more extensive Romanticism'.[23]

Although Wandrey's book displeased Pfitzner, there was much in it which could hardly have offended. The author spoke of art's secret origin and insisted that the artist was indivisible from his people, being a purer form of its idea. He

---

[21] Bernhard Adamy, *Hans Pfitzner* (Tutzing, 1980), 198.
[22] Ibid.   [23] Conrad Wandrey, *Hans Pfitzner* (Leipzig, 1922), 83.

also restated certain theories of Romanticism, from its essentially Germanic nature to its finding of its ideal in music, with which Pfitzner was familiar along with most of his contemporaries. As a crowning compliment, he bracketed Pfitzner with his beloved Schumann. But Wandrey offended when he implied that the artist was a tragic figure, subject to the laws of time along with his race and people. There was no sorrow comparable to that which 'darkens the noblest descendants of a declining epoch if their nature is burdened with creative impetus'.[24] Furthermore, there is just a hint that Wandrey is providing not so much appreciation as a Nietzschean critique. 'It was an instinct of genius that let Nietzsche rediscover the tempo of great passion in andante after one had falsely sought it so long only in allegro.'[25] Taken with Wandrey's rhetorical surprise at Cossmann's ascription of cheerful inspirations to the young Pfitzner, this contributed to the creation of an image that Pfitzner disliked at all times, that of an ascetic.[26] It did not take much imagination to see that Wandrey's study of 1922 was written in the intellectual shadow of Thomas Mann's *Betrachtungen eines Unpolitischen* (published four years earlier), which contained a celebrated response to *Palestrina*. There came a time when this too would be held against Wandrey.

Pfitzner responded to Wandrey's description with the complaint that he had been cast in the role of the ghost who 'buried himself scratching his own grave' in Eichendorff's 'Nachtwanderer' (*SS IV* 261). He rattled off a series of adjectives commonly applied to him, linear, austere, hard, etc., which produced the picture of a musical ascetic. He recognized elements of this in the heroes and heroines of his operas, but complained that Wandrey had mistaken a theme for the whole. This is consistent with things that Pfitzner wrote elsewhere. He did not take Wandrey's view as anything more than part of a critical climate.

I repeat . . . that it is his vanity which has infatuated him in the revelation of his Pfitzner portrait, and I repeat that this entire slander, whether original or copied, has caused me endless harm. For such aesthetic errors, as I shall indulgently take them, lead naturally to malicious and crude coarsening and intensification. The 'asceticism' is carried over to the musical invention, the sympathy with death and the past as the transitoriness and death of my music, etc. (*SS IV* 263)

---

[24] Ibid. 18.   [25] Ibid. 44.   [26] Ibid. 69.

This is a slightly curious response. At least in part it may have arisen from the circumstances in which Pfitzner felt moved to answer. He replied (by open letter) not to Wandrey's original booklet but to a later article in *Völkische Kultur* of May 1934; by that year, asceticism and sympathy with death were hardly acceptable manifestations of *Kraft durch Freude*, as Pfitzner discovered in 1933, when 'Klage' and 'Zorn' proved unacceptable on several counts for a programme to accompany a meeting of lawyers. However much Pfitzner viewed his music *sub specie aeternitatis*, the temporalities of history in this case took their revenge; conceived in one set of circumstances, the songs were simply inappropriate in another. 'Sympathy with death', though Pfitzner forbore from placing it in quotation marks, had been the very quality singled out in *Palestrina* by Pfitzner himself which struck so resounding a chord in Thomas Mann in the days when they had been intimate.[27] Certainly he was right to emphasize that his music was of wider range than this, even within *Palestrina*, where the doings of the Council of Trent are depicted with such gleeful malice. Behind the petty front of his open letter, Pfitzner quite possibly kept a more general objection to Wandrey's book in barely suppressed reserve. In the folk-memory of his own people resided one of Pfitzner's positives. His polemics were aimed at reawakening the German people's awareness of their culture as he interpreted it. It was with the implications of the *last* Romantic that Pfitzner took such great exception.

In *Die neue Ästhetik*, Pfitzner had revealed some thoughts on Romanticism. After all, his two streams, the great edifice of contrapuntal church music and the melodic culture, might seem to be another way of making the old distinction, classic or romantic. But he shied away from the terms; classical meant a composer, regularly performed, 'in the first place dead, in the second long dead, and in the third very long dead ... But I dare say the works of our classicists were termed romantic' (*SS II* 193). What Pfitzner objected to was not the term Romanticism but its coupling with Classicism. In such a loaded context, he preferred to contrast expression, fantasy, and *Tonbeflügelung* (lending wings to notes) with structure, technique, and *Tonbezwingung* (mastering the notes). Both types were present in Beethoven but Schumann encapsulated as no other the expressive and the lyrical. In this

---

[27] Jon Newsom, 'Hans Pfitzner, Thomas Mann and *The Magic Mountain*', *Music & Letters*, 55 (1974), 141.

context he was quite prepared to speak of Romanticism: 'it is no accident that all romanticists and lyricists who now followed, after Beethoven gave music every freedom of movement and opened up every possibility of expression, were intimate children of the land, German—I name only Weber, Schubert, Schumann, Wagner, who could, so to speak, give themselves up luxuriously to expression in its entirety' (*SS II* 233). Furthermore, the essence of such romantic achievement lay in music's alliance with the spoken word. As a consequence, the figure of Brahms who had been thrust before him as a model in Frankfurt is a relatively infrequent visitor to the pages of *Die neue Ästhetik*; of the monstrosities that followed him there is little mention in the book, other than the celebrated juxtaposition, '*Veni creator spiritus . . .* But if it doesn't come, what then?', assumed by Adorno and others to allude to Mahler's Eighth Symphony.[28] (In the fourth chapter, Pfitzner broadened his attack to include Bekker's book, *Die Sinfonie von Beethoven bis Mahler*.)

If Pfitzner had a fear for his own time, it perhaps lay in these words: 'In life, in the "life of nations which is dominated by the Will", one can abolish aristocracies, kill, banish, and extradite kings and emperors, but one cannot kill and abolish the aristocracy of nature, art; one can only say, it's not there; and in Germany one can well believe it' (*SS II* 229). The message of Pfitzner's polemics was a doubtful, muted variant of Hans Sachs's final address.

Yet if Romanticism in Pfitzner's outlook was scarcely different from the tradition of German music in the nineteenth century, in opposing Wandrey he merely found another way of declaring the potential of that tradition in seemingly unpropitious circumstances. As with music, so with literature. Questions of Romanticism were always broadened. Pfitzner found the appropriate tone in Goethe or Conrad Ferdinand Meyer whether the history books recorded them as Romantic or not. Admittedly he liked a strong streak of the irrational, mystical, knightly, and medieval. He shared greedily in his age's revaluation of Kleist, both in its nationalistic aspects (as

[28] Theodor W. Adorno, *Mahler: Eine musikalische Physiognomik* (Frankfurt am Main, 1960), 182; another sally at Mahler arises from an appraisal of the feeling for nature in Schumann's 'Auf einer Burg': the depth of feeling in the song is not simply a matter of nature itself since 'a thousand variations on "Pan schläft", or "l'après midi [*sic*] d'un faune" or "d'un vieux chevalier" with all possible respect leave me sincerely cold' (*SS II* 210).

in *Die Hermannsschlacht*, for which he wrote a chorus), and in its gentler side (as in *Das Käthchen von Heilbronn*, for which he wrote a complete set of incidental music). Among his contemporaries, he surprisingly singled out Gerhart Hauptmann, whose naturalism might have seemed alien to Pfitzner's nature. Only seven years, however, cover the writing and appearance of *Der arme Heinrich* and Hauptmann's play on the same subject. There is too an odd affinity between *Palestrina*, *Das Christ-Elflein*, and *Hanneles Himmelfahrt*, with their intrusions of angelic beings into the real world. In judging literature and music, Pfitzner's separation of the world and the intellectual life was scrupulously maintained. Anti-Semitic passions may have raged in his denunciation of Jewish corruption, but Mendelssohn had his place within the German tradition, even if it was not so prominent as that of Schumann or Wagner. The hallmark of Pfitzner's thinking on such matters was iron consistency which with the passage of time became virtually indistinguishable from blindness. If he ever learned that art too could be contaminated by the blood-stains of the world, he buried it deep within his conscience.

3

In the Footsteps of Schumann

✵✵

IN 1936, Pfitzner looked back at the puzzling relationship which existed between the two composers whose careers had most helped to shape his own. The mutual incomprehension with which Schumann and Wagner had regarded each other was a historical conundrum which Pfitzner was not the man to shirk. He chose to interpret it as a *Sternenfreundschaft*, a term that had been applied by Nietzsche to his relationship to Wagner (in *Die fröhliche Wissenschaft*), and that might have been applied by the misguided, Pfitzner noted, to Wagner and Liszt. In his definition, the term stood for

... the deep inner fellowship existing between two human beings, better between two men, but which cannot make itself felt during their lifetime; a higher solidarity which is not visible in itself and which only too often turns into the opposite of friendship in the falsifying light of this world, whereby the very idea in itself suggests that the true relationship might only find its expression somewhere else in the universe on another better star ... (*SS IV* 119)

For so 'cosmic' a friendship, neither the uncreative Nietzsche nor the cosmopolitan (and also uncreative) Liszt lacked the credentials. Wagner's praise of Liszt's symphonic poems ranked as one of the most puzzling and unmusical mistakes of his career, as Pfitzner on several occasions attempted to point out (*SS I* 204; *IV* 93–4). The accounts of his friends bear further witness to the low opinion in which he held Lisztian 'symphonic poetry', in particular its predilection for the pause as substitute for real musical linkage.[1]

Schumann on the other hand possessed the correct attributes for such a relationship. To Pfitzner, Schumann and Wagner were like the 'geliebte Götter' addressed by Palestrina in Act I, the spirits of the great tradition to which he himself belonged, the encapsulation respectively of the lyric and the dramatic strands in German music (*SS IV* 123). Their inability to appreciate one another (which was far from total incom-

[1] E.g. Josef Hofmiller, *Revolutionstagebuch 1918/19*, 2nd edn. (Leipzig, 1937), 94.

prehension, as Pfitzner fully recognized) he was inclined to attribute to musico-political issues (for example, the polarization of Weimar and Leipzig and the dogma of the Bayreuth circle), which in turn stemmed from Wagner's view of the symphony. Wagner must have seen, Pfitzner felt, a threat in Schumann the symphonist to his own claim to have inherited and appropriated Beethoven's symphonic legacy for the orchestra of the music-drama. This is a remarkable statement, given the low esteem in which the Schumann symphonies were often held in Pfitzner's lifetime. But it was Pfitzner's belief that the criticism of Schumann's orchestration had not yet begun at the time of Schumann's death (*SS IV* 131). In his account, Schumann's symphonies should have been accepted masterpieces. The claim is remarkable also in the light of Pfitzner's declared sympathies in this matter, for he 'was committed in broad essentials to Wagner's music-historical and philosophical opinion on the symphonic question . . . even though I too have allowed myself to write a symphony'. Pfitzner could concede that much with tongue perhaps in cheek, since the symphony in question was in truth an odd affair, a transcription of a string quartet. Two points emerge from this. Pfitzner's claims for Schumann extended beyond the lyricist to his symphonies and to his chamber music. And here also is the reason for the curious role that the symphony plays in Pfitzner's own career; the youthful creator of chamber music, a concerto, songs, and music-dramas avoided the genre central to German music since Haydn from broad acquiescence in Wagner's view that the genre had been perfected as far as instrumental music was concerned by Beethoven. Even in spite of this, however, Wagner and Schumann were to be understood as the two subjects of a sonata-form movement which 'must be in opposition in order to permit the form of the whole . . . to become a unity', and that unity a higher one (*SS IV* 133).

The example of Schumann had been apparent in Pfitzner's first instrumental music; the Scherzo for orchestra written in Frankfurt and later published has usually been explained as written under the influence of Schumann and Mendelssohn.[2] That is a natural reflection of tastes in the Hoch Conservatory. Schumann was complemented rather than replaced by the influence of Scholz's much-admired Brahms. The latter hardly

---

[2] Erwin Kroll, *Hans Pfitzner* (Munich, 1924), 93.

represented for Pfitzner, chronologically or stylistically, that higher unity for which Schumann and Wagner prepared the way. But the nature of that higher unity in any case remains obscure. Did Pfitzner see the possibility of it in his own generation? Hardly, given the low opinion of Strauss and Mahler that he would form with the passage of time. Yet the libretto for Act I of Palestrina provides this much of a clue, that the hero sustained the great tradition in a period otherwise marked by dilettantism and decadence. The example of Brahms must have seemed at the very least a respectable continuation of Schumann. Pfitzner's instrumental output after the Scherzo (little more than a student exercise) and the unhappy Cello Concerto was a string of chamber works, each in a different genre, but each genre represented in the output of Brahms, and all but one in that of Schumann: Cello Sonata, Piano Trio, String Quartet, Piano Quintet, and Violin Sonata. Even before this impressive assault on the chamber music repertory began, Pfitzner had written a String Quartet, subsequently lost but recently recovered. Clearly he felt that he had found a genre that had not been exhausted like the symphony, yet which had a firm tradition. His approach to it is solidly within that Brahmsian tradition. That Pfitzner's chamber music was to be considered as 'absolute music' is almost self-evident. Only in placing a quotation from a poem by Heine that Schumann had set in *Dichterliebe* over the Cello Sonata did Pfitzner suggest that fondness for recondite, hermetic allusion characteristic of Schumann and to a lesser degree Brahms:

> Das Lied soll schauern und beben . . .

It may only be a 'poeticized' performance indication, though Constantin Floros has made a potentially bigger claim for it. 'This motto impressively documents not only Pfitzner's affinity to German Romanticism, but also that he, who later championed so energetically the cause of "absolute music", in early years wrote music more poetically experienced than absolute.'[3] In the lack of more substantial evidence, however, it may be better to consider the inscription more as a form of dedication (which is the general character of Heine's poem) than as a pointer to hidden programmatic depths. Pfitzner

[3] Constantin Floros, 'Gedanken über Brahms und Pfitzner', *MPG* 49 (Jan. 1988), 72–3.

remained content that the work be experienced as abstract music.

All of the works concerned are in four movements, with the exception of the Violin Sonata, which, like one of Schumann's and two of Brahms's works in that genre, has three movements. Pfitzner's later interest in single-movement form is already evident in the various devices he employs to ensure connections between movements, most obviously in the three later works, whose finales are all designed to follow the slow movements without a perceptible break. But formal experimentation is subordinate to traditional generic expectations. There is no particularly favoured succession to the inner movements; the two String Quartets and the Piano Quintet prefer to place the scherzo before the slow movement, while the Cello Sonata and the Trio place the scherzo third. Pfitzner did not particularly favour the description 'scherzo', usually preferring a tempo indication or the designation 'Intermezzo' (in the Piano Quintet). These essentially humorous movements favour duple time after the Cello Sonata (2/4 in the Quartet in D and the Quintet, 6/8 in the Trio). The humour is sometimes overt, as in the Quartet in D ('Kräftig, mit Humor'), occasionally mysterious as in the Cello Sonata ('So schnell als möglich, beinahe durchweg pp'), and often rather improvisatory: the Quintet's 'Mit ruhiger Grazie' is a more 'elegant' (Pfitzner's description in a footnote) version of the 'etwas frei im Vortrag' of the Trio. The heart of each work is metaphorically in the slow movement. 'Sehr langsam' is very much the dominant tempo indication here, and the mood tends to vary between the austere (of which the intricate counterpoint of the String Quartet is the most characteristic example) and the improvisatory. The two later works, the Quintet and the Violin Sonata, show this aspect of Pfitzner's style most clearly. The viola, which opens the Quintet's Adagio, is directed, 'mit tiefer Empfindung, aber bei aller Genauigkeit im Rhythmus gleichsam improvisierend vorzutragen'; the Violin Sonata's slow movement is an 'Adagio, quasi fantasia'. Such rhythmic freedom is the counterpart to the often obsessively repeated rhythms of the opening movements, as in the Quartet in D, the most extreme example of this rather Schumannesque trait. After the intensity of the slow movements, Pfitzner usually permits his audience to relax, either in one of his seldom robust scherzi, or in a finale which is often committed to the notion of the last movement as romp. The idea of a Beethovenian apotheosis is seldom employed. In the two sonatas the major mode is employed from the outset of the finale, and terms such as 'mit Humor' and 'schwungvoll' emphasize the open mood. The Quintet goes furthest in surrendering to an easy-going mood, though the Rondo ('Im heiteren Reigentempo') of the Quartet is not far behind. Such intellectually unstrenuous endings are not unknown in Brahms. Only the Trio attempts more, by plunging into the tonic minor from the outset and holding it to the end. In form this is also the most obscure of Pfitzner's finales. Not that he is uninventive elsewhere; the Quintet makes something valedictory out of a variant of sonata form. But rondo and sonata-rondo tend to be favoured, usually with some elements modified.

Most of the references to Schumann's music in Pfitzner's writings concern songs, piano pieces, even *Genoveva*. It is Schrott who provides the information that Pfitzner particularly admired the D minor Piano Trio.[4] In the context of Pfitzner's earliest major chamber work, this is an interesting comment. The Cello Sonata, Opus 1, is usually thought of as Pfitzner's most Brahmsian work, and indeed its successor, the Piano Trio, might be considered the continuation of the Brahmsian vein in early Pfitzner. But it is at least imaginable that both were conceived under the aegis of the higher unity demanded by the *Sternenfreundschaft* of Wagner and Schumann. The example of the D minor Trio seems in particular to underlie one curious and attractive aspect of the first movement of the Sonata. At the beginning of the coda section of the first movement, Pfitzner wrote an episode which broke completely with the texture and style of the movement up to that point. The recurring conflict between 3/4 and the 6/8 of the time signature is clearly but temporarily resolved in favour of 3/4 (though not so notated). The minor mode of F♯ gives way to major, and the violently complex textures are replaced by a simple descending bass line for the piano's left hand and pizzicato cello; against this, the right hand provides off-beat chords. In due course this becomes the accompaniment for a step-wise melody in the cello that moves in a typically late-nineteenth-century fashion through B♭ and D, keys whose tonics stand with F♯ in a cycle of major thirds.

---

[4] Ludwig Schrott, *Die Persönlichkeit Hans Pfitzners* (Zurich and Freiburg, 1959), 111.

Pfitzner leads this material back to his first-subject theme (which has the last word in this coda) via a passage which has been described as a suggestion of *Der fliegende Holländer*.[5] In this moment, the influences of Schumann and Wagner seem to join, for if the specific echo is of Wagner, the more general procedure seems to recall Schumann, in particular the first movement of the D minor Trio, where a similar drastic change in texture and mood became the basis of a similarly luminous episode in a movement otherwise characterized by *Sturm und Drang*. Schumann marks his episode 'Tempo I. nur ruhiger', Pfitzner 'Etwas ruhiger', and the expressive intention seems to be the same in each case. By placing his episode in the development section, Schumann guarantees the possibility of returning to its material and securing its integration into the movement as a whole; with Pfitzner the effect is of a sudden intrusion of an alien voice which is neither subsequently integrated nor used in the later movements of the Sonata. Yet in spite of this, the parallel is a suggestive one, especially since such episodic handling of sonata form is not uncommon in Schumann; there is the unexpected quotation (hardly working-out) of an idea from the slow introduction in the development of the F sharp minor Piano Sonata's first movement, and the new melody for violins in the development of the first movement of the D minor Symphony; the 'Spring' Symphony resorts in its first movement to a new idea at the start of the coda. The point is of some importance in Pfitzner, since the Cello Sonata is not a particularly episodic work; apart from this episode, sonata form in the first movement is relatively orthodox. His Piano Trio in F on the other hand takes such episodic construction to extreme lengths.

The earliest reviews of Pfitzner's music were mostly if not uniformly encouraging. The Berlin concert of 1893, the first performances of *Der arme Heinrich* and *Das Fest auf Solhaug* were greeted by influential critics such as Wilhelm Tappert, Humperdinck, and Max Steinitzer with positive reviews that outshone anything received by Mahler in this period. With the first performance (in Berlin) of the Piano Trio this changed. In the list of reviews provided by Abendroth, the reproaches are many and varied. Adjectives such as 'scatter-brained' and 'bombastic' jostle the critics' traditional complaints of excessive length, excessive chromaticism, over-complex

[5] Kroll, *Hans Pfitzner*, 95.

working-out, and a tendency to the mystic teetering on the verge of hysteria.[6] In all of this, there is clear bewilderment over the working-out of Pfitzner's ideas. Although one critic in the time-honoured fashion complained of melodic nullity, others did notice (in the middle movements especially) the presence of attractive ideas. A more prevalent complaint was the lack of periodic articulation and of clarity of motivic construction; in other words, Pfitzner was not thinking organically, to use the dominant structural metaphor of the age. All of this is quite in accord with the fact that in the work, Pfitzner allowed full rein to the episodic manner tentatively broached at the end of the otherwise quite unexceptionable first movement of the Cello Sonata. In short, structural factors in the Trio (stemming probably from Schumann) were more of a problem than the idiom (which stemmed from Brahms, still regarded at that time as a difficult if not dangerous composer).[7] In the later chamber works the idiom grew more Schumannesque in details if not in the whole, but this liberation from the shadow of Brahms was accompanied by a withdrawal from the interesting formal position taken up in the Trio.

Whereas the Cello Sonata saved its episodic surprise for the coda, the Trio very quickly impresses the listener with a strong sense of discontinuity. A first subject in 9/8 is followed by a transition in 3/4 to a second subject in 4/4. What is striking is not so much the changes of time signature as the drastic loss of impetus. This is not simply to be regarded as a flaw; it is on one level the structural basis of the movement. Transition is almost the wrong word since Pfitzner on several occasions allows the rhythmic flow to collapse into irregular repetition of isolated chords and notes. The first page surges forward with a one-bar motive, whose syncopations establish a rhythmic strenuousness not entirely abolished by the regular flow which sets in from bar 10 (though even here the piano insists heavily on the upbeat against the imitative writing of the strings). The contrast with the opening of the Cello Sonata could not be more marked. There the cello presented a long-breathed melody, whose motivic constituents were firmly held in place by periodicity, a periodicity that was preserved into a less firmly defined second subject; in the Trio, the cello flings out a motive that only gradually exhibits

[6] Walter Abendroth, *Hans Pfitzner* (Munich, 1935), 423–4.
[7] Peter Gay, *Freud, Jews and Other Germans* (Oxford, 1979), 240–3.

signs of adapting to a periodic structure. What the two openings have in common is a certain rhythmic ingenuity, for the
syncopation of the Trio is equivalent in prominence to the
Brahmsian hemiola of the Sonata. But whereas the latter
gradually liquefies the periods into motivic extension for
the transition, the Trio simply collapses. As an indication of
the different approaches, the climax chords will suffice. The
Sonata reaches its first crux on a 6/5 chord, which points
unmistakably forward towards the dominant (Ex. 3.1*a*);

Ex. 3.1*a*

b **Kraftig und feurig, nicht zu schnell**

orthodox continuity is evident, Brahmsian ancestry is emphasized by the new rhythmic tug between triplets and duplets.
The Trio climaxes in the tonic, prompting the first of the
rhythmic collapses (Ex. 3.1*b*).

The most interesting aspect of the Trio now appears in the
form of a motive (*x*) which will recur in the slow movement
and finale. It represents a distinct character, even though
Pfitzner then starts to work at integrating it with the opening motive. The climax of such integration comes in a later
episode in D which corresponds to the retransition. Yet this
episode is in effect a paradox, illustrating the structural
limitations of motivic integration. Although the two motives
are played together, the episode is texturally and rhythmically so much at odds with the 9/8 surroundings as to cause a
new break in continuity; it is preceded by yet another collapse, this time on to the local tonic, D major. It is more
appropriate to speak of the subjugation of the first motive to
the character of the second, with the surge of the opening
replaced by a rhythmic augmentation and the direction *zart*.
As a result of this moment, the reprise bursts in with the
equivalent of bar 6, and with such variants as to make the
description 'recapitulation' seem inappropriate. Development engulfs the first subject's return rather as in several of
Brahms's first movements (of which those of the G minor and
C minor Piano Quartets will serve as examples). Variants tend
almost to the status of variations. Variation does not quite

correspond to Brahms's praxis in the C minor Piano Quartet, however, since there it tends to hold the structure together.[8] Pfitzner moulds his movement out of characters which seem irreconcilable for the moment. The coda reintroduces the motto theme and alludes to the retransition only as a fleeting apotheosis.

Pfitzner's motto theme is, on inspection, rather a plain affair. Perhaps that is why it is first presented after so portentous a silence. Its principal advantage is that in later movements it can be grafted on to other ideas with little sense of incongruity. Thus in the slow movement in C♯ minor, it appears in the theme of the second section, 'Sehr langsam', as a tail-piece (Ex. 3.2); its role throughout is to provide echoes

Ex. 3.2

of the first movement, in which it is assisted by some more of those curious transitions based on enigmatically repeated chords and octaves. The slow movement is in its own way as spasmodic as the first. Silence plays again a prominent part in the opening theme, a silence punctured by wisps of theme and a curious rhythmic shudder, 'sotto voce', that later marks the climax of the movement. The motto belongs with the flowing contrast material. It is again typical of Pfitzner that the appearance of an abbreviated sonata form is maintained, the contrast theme finally settling in G♯ minor, the key of the dominant. The return to the main theme, however, then sparks off a considerable extension that sustains a high dynamic level as it modulates away from the tonic. The relentlessly scalic motion of the melodic writing both in the theme and more particularly in this restatement-cum-

---

[8] For the use of variation procedures in Brahms's Piano Quartet in C minor, Opus 60, see in particular Jonathan Dunsby, *Structural Ambiguity in Brahms* (Ann Arbor, Mich., 1981), ch. 3, *passim*.

expansion suggests very strongly the opening of the finale, and here again the structural paradox of the work is underlined. For all the sense of discontinuity within the Trio, motivic integration is present, deriving from material in which scale segments are usually prominent. Thus the first movement's opening motive begins with a gap of a descending fourth which is filled by a chromatic scale segment. The slow movement begins with a descending melodic minor tetrachord. Decorated scale figures filling a descending fourth again are prominent at the start of the scherzo. In the finale, the scale ascends, with third segments as the motivic basis. Thus all the movements have at least some element in common, but at a fairly generalized level. Motives provide at best associations, but all other parameters tend to dissociation. In this may be seen a reflection of Pfitzner's strong opinions on the *Einfall*. Its function is not derived from some organic imperative. The context of the individual inspirations tends thus towards the dramatic juxtaposition of entities. In no other instrumental work does Pfitzner stand so close to the formal ideals that he adumbrated later in *Die neue Ästhetik*, nor so close to the music-drama. Whether at this time he had arrived at a clear picture of the *Sternenfreundschaft*, Wagner and Schumann, is open at least to a degree of doubt. But intuitively he seems to have felt the need to stretch abstract form to breaking-point, and the importance of dramatic elements in so doing becomes transparent in the finale.

Here form finally threatens to collapse. The inspiration for the opening might perhaps be sought in that long tradition of which the opening of the last movement of Beethoven's Ninth Symphony is the best-known exemplar. A headlong opening of five bars ('Rasch und wild') is most conspicuous for its tonal uncertainty. That it presents the main motive of the movement, three ascending steps of an F minor scale, is less immediately important than the underpinning Db, which eventually is combined with B to make an Italian sixth. The motto theme then appears, 'frei quasi recitat.', with a tail-piece that will later serve as a contrast theme. A slow fugue in F minor, with an irregular pattern of entries (F, F, Bb, C), then ensues (Ex. 3.3). It decorates the ascending step-motive (*x*), then incorporates it in stretto and augmentation, together with the motto theme as tailpiece. In effect, this is a long slow introduction which ends in another of Pfitzner's rather loose homages to sonata form, with the by now familiar Brahmsian

Ex. 3.3

device of concealing the point of recapitulation; instead of the rather blank first group, a further development of the fugue provides a climax. The fugue theme thus still exerts a fascination over Pfitzner, and the second subject, introduced within a recitative, never loses its original character; throughout it represents the music's attempt to break into a passionate rhetoric that is scarcely held within the bounds of instrumental music. The influence of late Beethoven in general hangs over this movement as a ghost which Pfitzner has no wish to exorcize. The formal combination of fugato, sonata, and recitative is clearly reminiscent of late Beethoven and such works as the Piano Sonata in A flat. Finally, in the coda the motto theme expands into its own musical paragraph, attaining a degree of continuity that recalls the contrast theme of the slow movement in tempo, texture, and mood. On either side of it stand violent workings-out of the main material of the finale, first as an unconvincing major-mode apotheosis, lastly as a violent affirmation of the minor, but the motto ignores these surroundings; its distinct character is sealed off in these bars from a movement that is quite unique in Pfitzner's output. The Trio is far from being a neglected masterpiece. It attempts to go beyond Brahms's conception of the genre in form, while paying lip-service to him in the thirds and sixths of the piano texture, much of the accompanying figuration, and the general harmonic style. It is Pfitzner's most radical formal experiment among these early chamber works, and for this reason it commands attention. But in the light of its brusque rejections of formal continuity, it is hardly surprising that sections are more memorable than the whole.

If the influence of Pfitzner's distinguished predecessors is everywhere apparent in the Cello Sonata and the Piano Trio, it remains to be asked in what matters his own style starts to become evident. The middle movements provide the best instances. Admittedly the scherzo of the Sonata is not the most thematically distinguished of Pfitzner's pieces, but it does reveal his liking at this stage for a style of fast middle movement which exhibits a unity of mood. There is no trio section, instead there is an orthodox exposition of material with themes in F♯ minor and its relative major, a development and recapitulation, all at the same headlong pace, all in an undertone. In effect the movement is a sketch for the much more attractive scherzo of the Piano Trio. The main thematic material is there much more distinctive, exhibiting that capriciousness of mood which Pfitzner favoured above outright humour. What stands out with particular clarity is the recurring call to attention of the main theme (Ex. 3.4), some-

Ex. 3.4

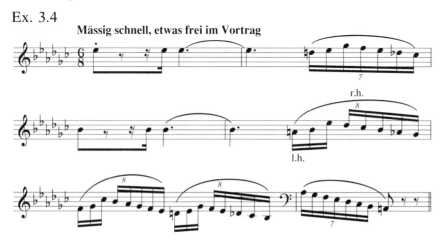

times in 6/8, sometimes in 2/4, against the more conventional
continuations. The dotted motive is the firm point from which
a variety of continuations proceed. Although sonata elements
are again present, the tonal scheme is unconventional, with
the moment of clarification coming when the continuation
heard in G♭ major at bar 54 finally returns in E♭ major, the
tonic major of the movement. Instead of a trio, Pfitzner prefers to write a development section with a much more complex tonal scheme than in the equivalent movement of the
Sonata. Stylistically, he shows himself capable of embracing
both unadorned diatonicism and chromatic development
within one structure, while providing traces of that fondness
for linear diatonic dissonance that characterizes his maturity.

In the slow movement of the Sonata, the main theme (Ex.
3.5) is a characteristic type which, in Hans Rectanus' words,

Ex. 3.5

'unfolds out of an opening motive as from a seed, expands
upwards in ever greater curves and waves, thus creating and
opening up musical space and pointing beyond itself'.[9] It was
with such themes from *Die Rose vom Liebesgarten*, *Palestrina*,
and the Cello Concerto, Opus 42, that Pfitzner illustrated his
book on musical inspiration. As Rectanus notes, such themes
first emerge in his music around the time of *Das Fest auf
Solhaug* and the Cello Sonata. Yet it is arguable that Pfitzner,
in choosing such themes for his thoughts on inspiration,
was not so much illustrating his style as inspiration in the
abstract. Thus if the influence of Brahms is strong in Example

---

[9] 'Pfitzners frühe Werke—Bestand und stilistische Anmerkungen', *SPB* 95.

3.5, this merely illustrates the common character that good melodic inspiration may have regardless of the composer. Its initial motive also returns to seal the close of the work as if in imitation of so classically Brahmsian a model as the slow movement of the G major Violin Sonata, whose principal motive (which opens and closes sections) is echoed in rhythm and fall. Knorr's legacy ran deep. But if the derivation is clear, there can be no doubt that Pfitzner adopted it as a valid model for his own style. By contrast, the thematic material in the slow movement of the Trio is initially somewhat un-promising. Neither the spasmodic opening idea nor the flow-ing cello melody of the 'Sehr langsam' really catches fire. Only when Pfitzner starts to develop them does the movement begin to fulfil the aspirations of the composer towards expres-sive intensity. The plain reiterations of tonics clash as inter-nal pedal effects against the leading-note in the first theme, and, more importantly, the contrast theme now expands to dimensions which suggest a real lyrical breadth. The periods which before tended to collapse bathetically on to severely plain cadences now lead to intenser chromatic incidents as antidotes to the placid rhythmic flow.

The predominant form in Pfitzner's early chamber works is sonata, albeit with variations in the manner in which mate-rial is recapitulated. Tonal procedures also tend to vary from work to work, without overstepping the limits of what would have been common practice in Brahms or Mahler. The polarity of tonic and dominant still persists, albeit in that weakened form contingent upon the late nineteenth century's interest in key relationships based on thirds. This is a less significant factor in a minor-mode movement like the first of the Cello Sonata, in which the second subject is orthodoxly in the relative major, and the dominant tends to be untonicized; it appears as a preparation for the exposition repeat and in the retransition as a preparation for the recapitulation, but C♯ is never used prominently as a local tonic. The dominant of F in the first movement of the Trio is reserved for the retransition, and D♭ becomes the key for the second sub-ject, yielding to D minor before the development; in the Schubertian tradition to which both Brahms and Bruckner sometimes subscribed, the second subject is less a theme with its own key than an evolving melodic fantasy that gradually establishes a key area for the close of the exposition, though neither Brahms nor Bruckner provide models for the tonal motion in an exposition from tonic to relative minor. In the recapitulation, this fantasy element in the second subject is chromatically intensified; in a fashion of which Pfitzner grew fond, tonality is obscured by holding A minor and C major in unstable equilibrium, neither attaining full tonicization; such deviation from the classical sonata scheme, however, can be found in Pfitzner's predecessors and contemporaries. Emphasis on the dominant in the coda helps to maintain the traditional polarity, however weakened. Thus far does Pfitzner remember common practice. A Schenkerian analysis would have no great difficulty in locating a structural bass arpeggiation between I and V.[10] The analyst in Pfitzner's earliest instrumental works experiences no greater difficulty with the harmonic and tonal language than in the first movement of Brahms's Third Symphony. Only a certain freedom with chromatic side-slips, contributing towards the intermittent tendency to the rhapsodic, suggests that Pfitzner had gone through a phase of intoxication with the language of *Tristan und Isolde* (*SS IV* 623) that had produced the sincerest form of flattery in the Prelude to *Der arme Heinrich*. Even the fugato in the finale does not stretch the bounds of coherence. Its appearance on the page suggests the 'linear ascetic' in Pfitzner, but this is more a product of the rests which break up the subject and the countersubjects than of the harmonic clashes (see Ex. 3.3). None the less, its idiom has something of that visionary quality encountered here and there in *Der arme Heinrich*. In particular, its use of seemingly abstract procedures, fugal devices such as augmentation and stretto in combination, remembers the reliance on close imitation within a chromatic context to depict the Alps in 'Dietrich's Narration'. For Pfitzner, counterpoint had always to be rendered latently expressive. Its presence in the finale of the Trio detracts from the sense of a sonata argument, but achieves an intensity within its own episodic confines.

When Pfitzner returned to chamber music after a gap of six years, the extremes of his style had been fixed. The critical experience was almost certainly the composition of the second act of *Die Rose vom Liebesgarten*, in which an orchestral counterpoint of extreme brittleness had evolved to a point comparable with Mahler in some of his *Wunderhorn*

[10] Schenker charged Pfitzner with being 'der grosse Störer der Urlinie', according to a story current in Vienna retold by Hans Rectanus; it was the sense of direction in the upper voices that he could not discern.

songs and later in the instrumental trilogy of symphonies. The slow movement of the Quartet in D represents the incorporation of that contrapuntal freedom and originality into the framework of abstract instrumental music. At the same time, it is an indication of the inadequacy of the description 'linear ascetic'; for if that can apply to the Quartet, it misses the mark by far in the 'Romantic Opera', where linear factors are part of an underground tableau of dwarfs and monsters. Pfitzner's counterpoint thus embraces a spectrum from the grotesque to the elegiac. The slow movement of the Quartet is contrapuntal in the sense that it employs devices which are

Ex. 3.6

traditionally appropriate to strict procedures such as fugue. Pfitzner wrote no more learned a page than that given in Example 3.6. This stretto uses a motive in augmentation, augmentation and inversion, and syncopated double augmentation. In a sense it is a preparation for *Palestrina*, and a warning that Pfitzner's sympathies are at least in part with the learned style in opposition to the more melodic principles espoused by Silla in the opera. The whole movement is fugal, without reproducing all of the familiar conventions. Thus the subject given out at the start by the first violin is answered in inversion by the second (Ex. 3.7*a*), but there is no statement of

Ex. 3.7*a*

either for viola, and a later statement of the subject in the
cello is delayed until long past the expected point for a third
entry in a fugal exposition; by this stage, Pfitzner is more
interested in the possibility of stretto than formal convention.
The same freedom with procedure, the same fascination with
stretto, is the hallmark of the second fugue which begins in
Eb just before *C*. The climax of the movement is the combination of the various subjects at the restoration of the initial
C minor. The combination of a radical approach to learned
counterpoint and a chromatically angular theme suggests at
least in part a homage to the opening of Beethoven's String
Quartet in C sharp minor such as Bartók attempted a few
years later in his Opus 7.

Nevertheless, it is not the learned aspects which appear
most striking in the work. In a copy of the score on which he
inscribed a somewhat fuller dedication to Alma Mahler than
appears on the title-page, Pfitzner also wrote over the opening
of the slow movement, 'die Harmonien gehören mir!', as if in
surprise at his own boldness.[11] These harmonies arise partly
from that same tendency to chromatic shifts which was noted
in the Piano Trio. Thus although the fugal answer seems
to point towards the traditional dominant, it is actually
part of a general movement from C minor towards B minor,
established in bar 8. The harmonic palette which Pfitzner
employs is familiar enough in his contemporaries. Augmented
triads and fragments of whole-tone scales were being used at
the same time with varying degrees of adventurousness by
Debussy, Schoenberg, and Berg. The use of pedals to control
wayward lines is reminiscent of Mahler, with whom one also

[11] *Katalog Nr. 288: Hans Pfitzner (1869–1949)*, 44. Wolfgang Osthoff has pointed out
to me, however, that the handwritten dedication might equally be addressed to
Pfitzner's later admirer Lilo Martin.

associates the idea of a freely dissonant counterpoint. Pfitzner, however, achieves in this quartet movement what Mahler was still moving towards. By 1903, Mahler had indeed achieved a striking degree of freedom in combining dissonant neighbouring notes with chord notes in parts of such songs as 'Das irdische Leben', 'Revelge', and 'Der Tamboursg'sell'; the remarkable chromatic episodes in the finale of the Sixth Symphony were still to come, however, and for a slow movement to parallel Pfitzner's Quartet, one must look ahead to the works of Mahler's last period. The whole-tone moments (Ex. 3.7*b*) are not in any sense Debussyan, since they tend to grow slowly out of the general chromatic web rather than carry that peculiar expressive charge which the whole-tone scale had possessed since Glinka; it is not a subtle overlay of tonal expectations but a harbinger of an organization totally chromatic. Such an organization Pfitzner never achieved, nor would he have wished to achieve it in the sense of the free atonality of the Second Viennese School. But that he hovered on the verge of it in this quartet and elsewhere is indicative of the folly of perceiving in Pfitzner only the 'last Romantic', a kind of embattled rearguard of a great tradition; equally it is a reminder that musical 'progress' cannot be measured solely by chromatic steps. The essence of Pfitzner's achievement in this movement resides in the fact that however many whole-tone segments, however many chromatic sideslips, the majority of Pfitzner's clashes arise from the extreme compression of contrapuntal phenomena, passing dissonances, suspensions, and neighbouring notes. To speak of line controlling harmony is a debatable musical concept which begs many questions, since the nature of that control may be located on many levels. But if a test of linear control is the degree to which tonics lose their gravitational force, then, for stretches of this movement, organization lies in contrapuntal means rather than harmony even as conventional as in *Tristan und Isolde* (where the pull of dominants is sufficient to compensate for the lack of firmly defined tonics).

The other movements of the work may be said to define the extent to which Conrad Wandrey's thesis is valid for all of Pfitzner's output. For if the slow movement may be said to be the clearest exposition yet of Pfitzner's linear manner, other movements reveal only limited adherence, if that, to this familiar image. The quartet as a whole divides into two categories. On the one hand, the first and third movements rep-

resent the linear, serious side of Pfitzner's nature, whereas the
scherzo and the finale reveal a markedly humorous approach.
In the score dedicated to Alma, Pfitzner again felt moved to
annotate at the outset of the scherzo, adding 'Die Bratsche ist
d. Hanswurscht in diesem Satz'.[12] Perhaps more accurately
he might have described the viola's particular motive as the
'buffoon' (Ex. 3.8). The source of the humour is the main

Ex. 3.8

theme's attempts to enter. Thus the cello almost at once
reintroduces it in the fourth bar of an eight-bar period, producing an imbalance or overlap in the symmetry of the
phrases. Other entries aim to restore the tonic, D major, with
the maximum of abruptness; thus both B major and B♭ are
supplanted in one way or another by the theme with the viola
constantly in the leading role until the coda provides it with a
whimsical cadenza. Throughout the movement, the humour
derives from musical process, from irregularities in modulation and phrasing. Although in this case a trio section can be
found (in B♭ major), it is stitched firmly into the musical
continuity, as if to suggest an element of through-composition;
here too the viola's motive plays a prominent role in securing

[12] Ibid.

the move from D into B♭. Such an approach to musical humour is broadly in agreement with the punning contextual side of Viennese Classicism. Indeed it is arguable that few composers after Schubert indulged to any extent in this kind of musical wit. The finale resembles that type of closing rondo that Beethoven created in the second finale of the String Quartet, Opus 130, and which Schubert imitated in the finale of his posthumous Sonata in B flat. The easy-going 2/4 time can also be found in Schubert's String Quartet in A minor. The tradition of completing an intense and dramatic work, full of juxtapositions of thematic types and moods, with a lighter movement lives again in Pfitzner's quartet. Not that it is in any sense neoclassical as that term came to be used in the 1920s. Rather it is a memory of a musical type that was already taking on a nostalgic character in Brahms's 'gipsy' rondos, or in the last movement of the Second Piano Concerto (yet again in B flat). When Alma showed the work to her husband, Mahler had not long finished his Fourth Symphony, in which classical conventions were similarly recollected and brought to new life. When Mahler declared Pfitzner's quartet 'the work of a master', it may have been in recognition of an achievement familiar to himself (though the Adagio was the movement that particularly impressed him).[13] It is not entirely chance that Mahler's Symphony ends with a child's view of heaven, while Pfitzner's Rondo uses a theme composed in his childhood that he later thought suited to an angelic chorus in *Das Christ-Elflein*, nor that both works delve into a vein of transfigured folk-melody in order to bring large-scale sonata-type structures to a tranquil conclusion.

The hardest movement of the Quartet to assimilate is the first, and here the problems are mainly rhythmical. That Pfitzner could manipulate rhythm adroitly enough is proven elsewhere in the work. In the opening sonata-form movement, however, the theme groups are based in effect on two rhythmic patterns, steady crotchets, maintained for whole pages, and similarly obsessional dotted crotchets with quavers; the relentless nature of the whole is further reflected in the deliberately 'severe' tempo direction, 'In mässig gehender Bewegung'. Pfitzner wrote few movements which look more intimidating on paper. Reactions may well be twofold: on the

---

[13] Alma Mahler, *Gustav Mahler: Memories and Letters*, trans. Basil Creighton, ed. Donald Mitchell and Knud Martner, 4th edn. (London, 1990), 60; Bruno Walter, *Briefe 1894–1962*, ed. Lotte Walter Lindt (Frankfurt am Main, 1969), 59.

one hand, to view the movement as an extreme example of the German musical tradition's indifference to foreground rhythmic variety in favour of balancing and variation of phrases and periods. In such a view, Schenker's belief that rhythm was the product of the contrapuntal interplay of levels may be taken as symptomatic, the theoretical reflection of a compositional reality.[14] The second, less tolerant, viewpoint is to look upon Mahler's estimate of the work as the kind of blind-spot which led him to perform such poor or indifferent works as Rubinstein's *The Demon*. That the movement's main interest is contrapuntal is almost self-evident from the opening, in which the violin's steady procession of crotchets is gradually incorporated into textures of increasing complexity, a procedure adopted later in the Bürger song, 'Trauerstille'. This gradual intensification leads to a more resolute figure in which the dynamic motion expected of the sonata is upheld by a more elliptical approach to phrasing, while being undermined by the oddly ambiguous harmonies from the motive's initial augmented triad onwards. Not a great deal of development comes from this transition theme, however, and Pfitzner prefers to work with his main subject groups and their persistent rhythms.

The whole movement has a more radical underlying structural feature, however, which the rhythmic stolidity helps to mask. Whereas earlier movements conformed to the standard monotonal picture of form which even Mahler used in the individual movement if not the whole work, Pfitzner here ends in B minor. This movement is an extreme case of that practice observed in passing in the Trio. Instead of employing an unequivocal tonic, the movement derives its tonal strategy from a complex embracing tonic and relative minor. This helps to explain a number of factors in the work's formal make-up. The second subject is in B major, to which the 'artificial leading-note' in the augmented triad of the transition theme (D–F♯–A♯) points at middleground level.[15] The most prominent key in the development is F♯ minor, in which a rather desolate melody combines rhythmic features of both subject groups; that it is perhaps the most memorable idea of the movement may be due to this summational quality

[14] See Heinrich Schenker, *Free Composition*, trans. and ed. Ernst Oster (New York and London, 1979), 118–27.

[15] For the 'artificial leading-note' in the augmented triad, see Arnold Schoenberg, *Theory of Harmony*, trans. Roy E. Carter (London, 1978), 191.

in the rhythms, or to the fact that it returns in the coda, now in B minor. The significance of this procedure may be read historically, in combination with famous instances in the 'Eroica' Symphony and the D minor Symphony of Schumann; a fresh, though derived theme is introduced in the development as an episode but comes to have an equal say in the movement. To the analyst, its importance may rather be that the polarity of tonic and dominant exists at any sort of background level only for B minor; there is no prominent role for A in the movement, with even the final cadencing taking place in a key other than the ostensible tonic, D major. If the movement is to be analysed as a prolongation, it is almost certainly not an illustration of the Schenkerian *Ursatz* with its directed downward linear motion from $\hat{5}$ or $\hat{3}$ to the tonic, but rather a continuous prolongation of F$\sharp$. To the theorist, the movement thus becomes an illustration of those 'alternatives to monotonality' which analysts increasingly have investigated in recent years.[16] Lastly, it should be noted that in a sense the opposition of D major and B minor contributes towards formal strategy in the whole work. Beginning as it does with two movements in D major, the Quartet allows the possibility of B minor as an important subsidiary area in the first movement by ending in it, and then roughly contradicts it by the renewal of D in the first bars of the scherzo through the simplest of cadence formulae (see Ex. 3.8). The tonal divergence of the first movement from the monotonal norm thus serves to strengthen it in the whole work, in which references to the keys of B and F$\sharp$ continue to be prominent. The tonal strategy thus creates a link forward to the scherzo, comparable to the more conventional harmonic link whereby a harmonically and contrapuntally intense slow movement yields to a mainly diatonic, good-humoured finale, a procedure accepted within the sonata since Haydn and his contemporaries appropriated features of the church sonata.

If the Quartet is rightly taken as typical of the mature Pfitzner, Wandrey's thesis holds to this extent, that the tempo of passionate intensity in Pfitzner is indeed andante or slower. If certain things may be said to be typical of Pfitzner's style, however, it is less easy to say that there is a typical Pfitzner chamber or instrumental work. He never again approached so

[16] Harold Krebs provided a start to such investigations with 'Alternatives to Monotonality in Early Nineteenth-Century Music', *Journal of Music Theory*, 25 (1981), 1–16.

rigorous an exploitation of limited rhythmic cells as in the first movement of the Quartet, nor did he resort to a structure that derived so single-mindedly from his interest in the 'extended diatonicism' of major and relative minor. This latter feature tended from now on to be an aspect linked to his linear manner, and neither of the chamber works which stand on either side of *Palestrina* takes this as the starting-point of a whole movement. Donald Henderson noted that towards the end of the first movement of the Piano Quintet C major and A minor start to overlap in a by now familiar manner.[17] Were it not for an emphatic coda which restores the main tonality, C major, the movement would almost have repeated the formal pattern of the Quartet's opening movement by sinking into the relative minor for the conclusion. This is particularly marked after *V*, where the main theme of the movement starts to disintegrate into fragments which are held together by precisely the contrapuntal devices favoured in the slow movement of the Quartet. The persistent use of stretto and augmentation comes ever closer to the style that is employed throughout much of Act I of *Palestrina*, particularly in the writing for strings; a polyphonic interlude saps the sonata form's will to integration, rather as the motto theme did in the Piano Trio. But this is not the dominant mode of the movement. As befits a sonata-form movement, this is a dynamic, thrusting structure, with a tonal strategy firmly based on the tonic–dominant polarity; the first subject is in C, the second moves through E minor to G. The recapitulation has the most conventional preparation and entry since the Cello Sonata, the development is relentlessly thematic and contrapuntal in a way that would have been familiar to Brahms, even if the harmonic idiom is in places more obscure than he would have tolerated. The movement thus forms a balance achieved in instrumental terms between the styles that characterize the 'two worlds' of *Palestrina*, in the key, if not the manner, of the Emperor Ferdinand. This is only surprising if it is assumed that Pfitzner's true voice is that of the first act of *Palestrina* alone. But the brittle contrapuntal entanglements of the second act form part of a stylistic continuum that stretches from Act II of *Die Rose vom Liebesgarten* forward to the quintet and into Pfitzner's third opera.

[17] Donald Gene Henderson, 'Hans Pfitzner: The Composer and his Instrumental Works', Ph.D. thesis (University of Michigan, 1963), 101.

If the Piano Quintet has never achieved popularity, it may be due to the difficulty of reconciling its different stylistic modes. The energy of the counterpoint generates tensions in the harmony which are worthy of the Schoenberg of the first two quartets. But Pfitzner struggles energetically to keep them within bounds; for all the assertion of C major in the climaxes, the mood does not partake of the triumphalism associated traditionally with that key. The tensions between harmony notes and passing and neighbouring dissonances caused by Pfitzner's polyphonic mode of thought are worthy of Mahler even if the style is in other respects quite different. As a result, the musical discourse is oddly unsensuous in spite of such injunctions as 'mit äusserster Kraft und Leidenschaft' and 'sehr ausdrucksvoll, mit aufgeregtem Ausdruck'. In this the work is characteristic of what might be termed Pfitzner's private manner, to which the first movement of the Violin Sonata forms a complete contrast. For here, the sonata structure is entirely given up to melodic fantasy against a variety of imaginative backgrounds. It is questionable indeed whether the movement may be thought of in terms of sonata structure at all, since what could be described as a false reprise of the first subject at the outset of the development is full enough to have caused one writer to describe the form as a rondo.[18] More interesting than this, however, is the character of the melodic lines themselves. In the opening theme, the generative nature of the individual cells subtly upsets the symmetry in something of the spirit that Rectanus noted in the slow movement of the Cello Sonata. This is far from being musical prose in Schoenberg's or Dahlhaus's sense, but the course of the movement makes much of such small irregularities. The development aspires through them to a more pronouncedly rhapsodic condition than Pfitzner had attempted outside of his slow movements, particularly after 6. It cannot be said, as Dahlhaus has of Schoenberg, that 'the neutral medium that held together the heterogeneous musical shapes in Mozart—the medium consisting of the regular "pulse" of beats and the uniformity of "harmonic rhythm"—has disappeared'.[19] Although the association of motives can conjure up pronounced echoes of individual motives from *Palestrina* in this development section, it never quite succeeds in dissolving the

[18] Ibid. 73.
[19] Carl Dahlhaus, *Schoenberg and the New Music*, trans. Derrick Puffett and Alfred Clayton (Cambridge, 1987), 119.

pulse and harmonic rhythm into a free asymmetry; Pfitzner's medium for this was usually more contrapuntal than lyrical. Difficult to grasp Pfitzner's music may be from time to time in the continuity of its periods, but his notion of form, however experimental in relation to the Brahmsian tradition, never quite succumbs to that condition found in the second of Schoenberg's Quartets in which a development section becomes unnecessary because all is development. Perhaps here Pfitzner's concept of the *Einfall* and its non-organic relation to form was an inhibiting factor. Yet when the variations apparent between presentations of themes are laid side by side in a movement such as the first of the Violin Sonata, Pfitzner's relationship to 'musical prose' is close enough to explain some of the directions his music took in the twenties.

One consequence of the fantasia-like character of the Sonata's first movement is that the slow movement possesses a more conventional melodic style in immediate comparison. Although its main theme subscribes no more exactly than that of the first movement to symmetrical phrases, its asymmetry is unthinkable save as a clearly traceable divergence from quadratic phrase-structure. The Sonata steps down from the intensity of the opening until the sonata-rondo of the finale provides the only example in Pfitzner's earlier instrumental music of a movement written to court popular appeal. The public aspect of the Sonata comes increasingly to dominate, as befits a work dedicated to the Royal Swedish Academy of Arts. This aspect of the work has correspondingly endeared itself less to Pfitzner's admirers than the much tougher Quintet, though Wilhelm Furtwängler thought the Sonata's finale Pfitzner's most striking (and misunderstood) attempt 'to write universally'.[20] Superficially the finales of the two works have much in common, being written in a clear major mode. But whereas the slightly superficial *élan* of the Sonata is in line with the traditional major conclusion to a work that begins in a contemplative minor mode, the Quintet seems to offer a less positive experience. As Adorno commented of the reprise in a Mahler movement, it 'dwindles to a hasty epilogue', with the rider that what seemed unusual in a symphonic first movement seems doubly surprising in the context of the whole work.[21] The Quintet's finale becomes an epilogue; its opening

---

[20] Wilhelm Furtwängler, *Notebooks 1924–1954*, trans. Shaun Whiteside, ed. Michael Tanner (London, 1989), 101.

[21] Theodor W. Adorno, *Mahler* (Frankfurt am Main, 1960), 13.

motive in the piano is scarcely to be thought of as a theme, but as part of a toccata-like motion that gradually subsides into a muted coda, in a manner that has become familiar from some of the finales of Shostakovich. If this is a sonata-form movement, as most commentators state or imply, it is the shadow of an old tradition that has been fractured by the weight accorded the slow movement. Equally, the notion that the Quintet as a whole is 'a work of classical greatness' overlooks the extent to which the classical model is under-mined by the relative balance of movements.[22] As a historical phenomenon this is not unfamiliar in such nineteenth-century composers as Bruckner, but seldom to the same degree as here.

The Quintet as a whole is, if not cyclic in the Lisztian sense, nor unified in the radical manner of Schoenberg's String Quartet in F sharp minor, held together by the strong focus thrown on the elegiac slow movement. Its intensity of mood is already foreshadowed in the contrapuntal episodes of the first movement's coda. Its immediate surroundings serve as mediating functions of that intensity, since their adherence to the traditional expectations of scherzo and finale is largely superficial. The scherzo is similar to that of the Piano Trio, inasmuch as the provision of a variety of continuations to a head-motive is of more importance than a firmly defined form. It is possible in this case to designate the section in E major as a trio of sorts, but here too the material is dependent on the head-motive of the main theme. The musical process, rather than form, evolves through the various transformations of the motive to a gesture marked 'sehr leidenschaftlich' that already seems to be part of the slow movement's ethos; this is the darker tone that underlies the Hoffmannesque scurrilities noted by Vogel.[23] Similarly, the coda of the finale reintro-duces an intensely chromatic question from the first move-ment's second theme-group, to which the final dwindling chords of C major provide a mere play-out. The surround-ings are levelled out in order to throw the Adagio into the strongest possible relief.

Harmonically, there are traces of *Palestrina* foreshadowed in this slow movement, though oddly enough they prefigure

[22] Joseph Müller-Blattau, *Hans Pfitzner: Lebensweg und Schaffensernte* (Frankfurt am Main, 1969), 70.

[23] Johann Peter Vogel, *Hans Pfitzner mit Selbstzeugnissen und Bilddokumenten* (Reinbek bei Hamburg, 1989), 64.

Silla rather than the hero.[24] The resemblance is further underlined by the viola solo of the Adagio, a restrained version of Silla's grotesquely shaped viola. Although this solo has been described as 'one of the most beautiful viola melodies of our German music',[25] it possesses a sufficiently loose structure to approximate more closely than anything else in Pfitzner's earlier music to musical prose. This is partly a result of its elevation of the motivic over the periodic, but even more of the supporting harmonies. The key of the movement in the long run is B minor, but the opening harmonies dwell on secondary dissonances braced by the linear motion of the bass line as it approaches a chord of F# major (bar 12), the first pointer to the main key. But the linear motion does not suffice to cancel the impression that the viola melody is actually the beginning of a remarkable collective cadenza for the strings that is made even more overt after *F* when the opening returns. The form in such a movement is particularly elusive, since the section after *F* has been described as a development; the section from *I* to the end then becomes a recapitulation with reversed subject groups.[26] But this is an unnecessarily clumsy way to describe that form which in Beethoven, Bruckner, and Mahler is often regarded as most fitted to the Adagio, rondo with variations. Admittedly the section after *F* does not form an exact variation in its underlying harmonic plan, but in this it resembles more than a few of its predecessors. The second statement of the main section aims to provide the climax, expressed in terms of freedom from the phrase and the bar-line at the movement's midpoint, and the third statement offers a compression to essentials in the closing bars.

The contrast to this is a funeral march in B minor, which is one of Pfitzner's most compelling pages (Ex. 3.9). This is not really comparable to Mahler's processionals, with their capacity for public rhetoric alongside private grief. Although the strings accompany the march with triplet shudders generated from the irregular pulsations of the main sections, although the piano's left hand marks the rhythm with Mahler's

[24] According to Wolfgang Osthoff, some of the earliest sketches for Silla's song overlap with sketches for the Quintet's slow movement ('Pfitzner—Goethe—Italien: Die Wurzeln des Silla-Liedchens im *Palestrina*', *Analecta Musicologica*, 17 (1976), 194–211).

[25] Müller-Blattau, *Hans Pfitzner*, 70.

[26] Henderson, 'Hans Pfitzner', 73.

Ex. 3.9

favourite fourths in an ostinato rhythm, the model for this march seems to go back to the slow movement of Schumann's Piano Quintet in the sobriety of its lamentation. Even if the intimately conceived march subsequently extends into a paragraph marked 'mit grossem Ausdruck', this does not efface the impression made by the reticent opening. To emphasize that this is the heart of the work, the return of the march is essentially unvaried, save for a change of key to D minor. The coda combines the beating triplets and the fantasia-like aspect of the main section into a cadence whose expressive shudder in the strings finally collapses on to two last reiterations of the fourth, F♯–B, in the cello. In this slow movement Pfitzner attempted something genuinely new in the chamber music tradition, in spite of the homage to Schumann contained in the march. The muted finale is a surprising but unexpectedly inevitable pendant that seems to discard all surplus expression. That it was not in any sense a farewell to that rhetoric of virtuosity and major-mode splendour was made clear later in the Violin Sonata. But in that intervening decade, the tone of the Quintet's slow movement found its consummation in the outer acts of *Palestrina*. The Violin Sonata in a sense was a paean to the release from that creative endeavour.

On several levels the Quintet and the Violin Sonata represent Pfitzner's maturity. If neither possesses the formal originality apparent in the chamber works being written at that time by Schoenberg and Webern, they none the less exhibit a coherence rooted in a fully formed musical style. Yet there is a double problem related to their reception. They have neither enjoyed the recognition of the connoisseur nor have they established a popular reputation; they have all the characteristics of untimeliness in their stubborn refusal to conform to this or that set of expectations. A possible clue to their difficulty in finding an audience resides in some comments of the American Pfitzner scholar, Donald Henderson, who accurately analysed the composer's tendency in the Violin Sonata to 'angular melodies, dissonant counterpoint, and frequent chromatic textures': 'These active elements are often juxtaposed to conventional and commonplace melodic and harmonic practices, a characteristic procedure of Pfitzner.'[27] Expressed in this rather crass manner, Pfitzner's

[27] Ibid. 66.

'characteristic' might seem a weakness to which any composer might succumb on an off-day. It must be established
now that what Henderson stigmatizes as commonplace
bears no relation to what was once labelled banal in Mahler;
Pfitzner is austere in this much, that he avoids any suggestion
of the urban popular music of his time. The conventional
and the commonplace, however, are not necessarily alien to
chamber music. Traditionally the genre was appropriate to
the exploration of techniques, styles, and indeed conventions;
even an instinctive melodist such as Schubert was capable of
writing an intentionally 'dry' piece on commonplace thematic
tags in the first movement of the Piano Trio in E♭. The lack of
thematic material with a wide appeal, of tunes, in short, need
not have been a barrier to the appreciation of Pfitzner's
chamber music as a kind of hermetic art. But the problem for
Pfitzner was a dialectic that also affected other composers.
Chamber music remained conceptually a species of *musica
reservata*, appealing to the connoisseur, but increasingly it
demanded the public concert hall in which specialist virtuosi
could provide the kind of performance which the music required. The technical demands of the Violin Sonata resemble
those made by other composers of Pfitzner's generation.
It belongs with the violin sonatas of Busoni, Strauss, and
Respighi, and like them it has received occasional rather than
frequent advocacy. Lacking the thrill of the controversial
which attracted heckler and connoisseur alike to Schoenberg's
chamber music, Pfitzner's Quintet and Sonata found themselves poised uneasily between the concept of arcane, intimate art and the kind of public statement that was best
provided then by the orchestral music of Strauss, and which
has since been found in the Mahler revival. Even as early as
the Quintet, Pfitzner's chamber music looks ahead to Opus
36 and Opus 44 when forms such as symphony and string
quartet, descriptions such as sinfonietta and sonatina, might
prove to be interchangeable. Whether this was in accord with
the higher stage demanded by the conjunction of Schumann
and Wagner, Pfitzner never disclosed.

4

In the Footsteps of Wagner

PFITZNER'S problem as a music-dramatist was that he was a
follower of Wagner who rejected Wagnerism. At first this may
seem a puzzling statement in the light of several obvious
parallels. Yet something like the shared admiration for
Schopenhauer is put into perspective when a distinction is
drawn between the erratic nature of Wagner's encounter with
the philosopher and Pfitzner's much more systematic attempt
to do him justice. The anti-Semitism common to both composers may appear a more general bond. Yet comparison
of their respective statements reveals little of Wagner's
apocalyptic tendencies in Pfitzner's relentlessly abstract discussions of the subject. The whole ideological baggage that
accompanied the Bayreuth entourage was an irrelevance to
Pfitzner from his first visit to the shrine; with this rejection of
Wagner's more questionable legacy went a rejection of Liszt
and the New German School, together with that illustrative
trend in modern music that tainted Strauss for Pfitzner, not
merely in his tone-poems, but also in *Salome* and *Elektra*.[1] To
offset this, he turned of necessity to the German Romantic
opera on which Wagner had built; there was no Brahmsian
opera, and in Schumann only the underrated but historically unfruitful *Genoveva*. Pfitzner's adherence to Weber,
Marschner, E. T. A. Hoffmann, and Max Bruch was a conscious effort to construct a German opera that would avoid
the worst consequences of following Wagner, an attempt to
provide it with an alternative history to the loudly proclaimed mainstream.

As a result of Pfitzner's ambivalent position in relation
to Wagner, his first work for the stage is perhaps his most
eclectic. In part this was also a legacy of its being a set of
incidental music rather than a fully independent music-
drama. In choosing to set *Das Fest auf Solhaug*, Pfitzner
opened one of the most adventurous chapters of his early

---

[1] See Pfitzner's essay of 1942, 'Die Oper' (*SS IV* 87–109).

career. The frustrating encounters with such luminaries as Ibsen, Ernst von Possart, and Hermann Levi were secondary to Pfitzner's consciousness that in the work he had achieved something worthwhile. Partly this was a product of an encounter with a genius to whom he particularly responded. But this is hardly the whole story, since *Das Fest auf Solhaug* is at once weak and uncharacteristic Ibsen but not untypical of the ethos of later Pfitzner.[2] Some of Ibsen's own comments place it, almost by accident, in a line of descent from such romantic drama as Kleist's *Das Käthchen von Heilbronn*, to which Pfitzner was later to turn.[3] The play was rich in romantic situations and complications conducive to a kind of poetry that Ibsen hardly brought himself to acknowledge in later years. Yet many musicians, Wolf, Delius, Stenhammar, and Strauss among them, were drawn to its mood and lyrical vein. The plot is a stock tale of two women who love the same man:

SYNOPSIS. Bengt Gauteson has married a young bride, Margit. She refuses the hand of her younger sister, Signe, to the king's sheriff, Knut Gjæsling, partly from pride, partly out of contempt for his character. He swears to have revenge. Three years of marriage have seemed an eternity to Margit, who compares herself in a ballad to the bride whom the Mountain King kept locked away from the sun and the valley. Gudmund, the sisters' cousin, arrives at Solhaug, a fugitive from the King of Norway. Signe already loves him, and her love is returned. Margit, stirred by his singing, also falls in love with him. At a feast in honour of her wedding anniversary, Margit, goaded by the obtuseness of her husband and a further song from Gudmund, collapses after recounting a tale which is an allegory of her own perceived fate, the bride of the Mountain King longing for rescue by a young and gallant minstrel. She poisons Bengt's drink, but he is prevented from drinking it when Knut attacks Solhaug. Bengt is killed in the battle, Gudmund is pardoned by the king and is free to marry Signe. Margit enters a convent to expiate her guilt.

The drama provided fairly obvious opportunities for music. The eight numbers that Pfitzner wrote included a prelude to each of the three acts, one chorus, and four that were either melodrama (No. 8) or else alternated between melodrama

[2] John Williamson, 'Pfitzner and Ibsen', *Music & Letters*, 67 (1986), 143–6.
[3] *The Oxford Ibsen*, trans. and ed. James Walter McFarlane *et al.*, 8 vols. (London, 1960–77), i. 371–3.

and song. The adoption of melodrama, a genre which was to climax in the first version of Humperdinck's *Königskinder*, was partly a reflection of Pfitzner's distrust of the musical competence of the average actor (something that Hugo Wolf disastrously forgot in his setting of the same text). This feeling for what was possible in the theatre may also explain why Pfitzner sacrificed no less than four choruses (though the Prelude to Act II was originally conceived as a chorus, and probably remained one until 1895, the year of the first performance in Mainz[4]). But if compromise was the order of the day in the demands Pfitzner placed on his executants, he had no intention of sparing his audience. In style, his music steered in a number of obvious ways towards the Wagnerian conception of music-drama.

As a gesture of solidarity with the moderns who were banned from the Hoch Conservatory, Pfitzner attempted to employ a system of motives reminiscent of Wagner (albeit lacking in real subtlety), which would unify the disparate demands of prelude, chorus, song, and melodrama. It is tempting to say that the influence of Wagner emerges here to complement that of Brahms in the Cello Sonata, but the truth is considerably more complex. The principal motive of the Prelude to Act I (Ex. 4.1) begins with a crib from the fourth

Ex. 4.1

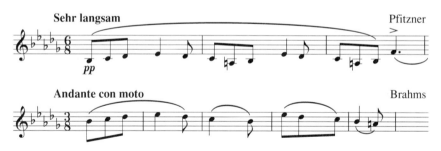

of the *Variations on a Theme of Haydn*, testimony to the hold that Brahms exercised as a model in the Conservatory. Whether this idea was conceived as dramatic music is doubtful, inasmuch as parts of the Preludes to Acts I and III may

---

[4] See *D-Mbs*, Tresor Mus. mss 9693: *Das Fest auf Solhaug*, sketches (numbering by Paul Winter [W]), SWI/2-12 to 2-13 and 2-17ʳ; also *A-Wn*, S.m. 30,401: *Musik zu 'Das Fest auf Solhaug'*, full score (autograph and one other hand), 62–99; also *A-Wn*, S.m. 30,402: *Musik zu 'Das Fest auf Solhaug'* (earlier version), full score (autograph and copyist), fols. 39–54.

have originated in a Scherzo (which has no connection with the published Scherzo in C minor).[5] As a result, there is a double aspect to the motive within the work, reflected in the variety of counterpoint which Example 4.1 generates. From the earliest sketches, it yielded canons and double canons, while the fast material with which it contrasted was combined with it in the Prelude to Act III, the kind of dramatic conjunction to which composers had resorted since Berlioz and his combinations of themes in his symphonies. As a result, the Prelude to Act I, in spite of the Brahmsian and 'learned' aspect of the canons, has a unity of mood and treatment that almost qualifies it as a Wagnerian 'elemental' prelude, while that to Act III is tone-painting of a more realistic kind. The two aspects tend to lie side by side in the incidental music, creating a tension with the dominant mood, which is indebted in its folk touches, as Franz Hirtler noted, to an earlier Romanticism, notably Schumann and Marschner (especially in the melodramas that recall Act III of *Hans Heiling*).[6] Hirtler claimed that the extent of Wagner's influence lay in sequence and suspension, overlooking perhaps the relationship between Example 4.1 and the opening of Margit's 'Ballade'. That both should be representation motives but also possess affinities with other material is a typically Wagnerian procedure. In a sense, Margit's 'Ballade' is the dramatic and musical centre of the whole work, on analogy with Senta's 'Ballade' in *Der fliegende Holländer*. Hirtler's emphasis on the Wagnerian harmonic legacy, however, is accurate where the opening of the Prelude to Act III is concerned.

The slow introduction to the Prelude to the third act is perhaps the most interesting page in the whole work from a historical point of view. In the vocal score (but not in the full score), it bears a title, 'Margit in Fieberträumen', and a programmatic description:

The 'Song of the Mountain King' comes into her thoughts—she imagines herself in the realm of the Mountain King; the revelling of the happy drunken guests at the feast seems a fantastic confusion to her, gloomy brooding alternates with intensified excitability.

Only as morning approaches do the visions of the night yield to a mild resignation.

[5] *D-Mbs*, Tresor Mus. mss 9693, SWI/2-35 to 2-43.

[6] Franz Hirtler, *Hans Pfitzners 'Armer Heinrich' in seiner Stellung zur Musik des ausgehenden Jahrhunderts* (Würzburg, 1940), 65–6.

This is reinforced in both full and vocal scores by the quotation of lines from the 'Ballade' below the instruments in parts of the introduction, suggesting that in the first thirty-five bars there is a depiction of Margit 'in the realm of the Mountain King' (which in the vocal score was also the title of the Prelude to Act I).[7] As befits a dream, this section has no clear form, but instead alternates elements in a seemingly random fashion. Among these is a sudden recollection of the guests' music at a faster tempo and in 4/4 as opposed to the predominant 3/4. As a mere decoration of a single major triad, this interruption recalls the punctuating festal music at the start of Act II of *Lohengrin*, though Pfitzner underpins his C major triad with a B♭ pedal. Elsewhere pedal notes break into stuttering timpani rhythms of a kind that inevitably recall Wagnerian procedures (particularly the punctuating timpani rhythms that are a marked feature of the 'Ring'). Such Wagnerian moments are intensified by the first sounds of the Prelude. An initially unaccompanied A in the lower strings becomes the foundation of a half-diminished seventh, against which the horn and violas introduce material from the 'Ballade'. This half-diminished seventh quickly falls to a diminished seventh, and from there to a 6/5/3 sonority, reducing the initial Wagnerian sonority to the status of a neighbouring note. More adventurously, Pfitzner refuses to permit his 6/5/3 chord to resolve orthodoxly, and keeps a tonic at bay by structuring the whole introduction on three pedals, A–B♭–C, of which the last is the dominant of the key first established in the Prelude, F minor. The pedal C is prolonged also by stretches of freer counterpoint which at one point settles for a moment in C minor. Margit's fever depends for its musical effect on a chromatic palette and an avoidance of the tonic that seems clearly indebted to the style Wagner evolved in his later works, and this introduction appears as a small-scale attempt to evolve the kind of structure that Pfitzner adopted in the Prelude to his first opera, *Der arme Heinrich*.

That a parallel exists between the Prelude to Act III of *Das Fest auf Solhaug* and the Prelude to *Der arme Heinrich* is implied by the presence of similar programmes. By com-

---

[7] The full score (Leipzig, 1896, then Stuttgart, 1903) used Emma Klingenfeld's translation, and the vocal score (Stuttgart, 1905) that of Christian Morgenstern; as a result, the lines quoted differ in form between the two scores. More surprisingly, they also differ in their placing from draft scores to vocal score and full score.

parison with the earlier work, the opera's Prelude merely
alludes to its subject by the motto 'Wilde Schmerzen und
wüster Traum', taken from one of Heinrich's monologues in
Act I. A musical idea, the principal motive of the opera, may
be said to correspond to the motto, and is presented by four
solo muted violas in the opening bars (Ex. 4.2*a*). This distinc-

Ex. 4.2*a*

tive sound is the symbol of the ailment of the hero (which is
spiritual in origin). The opening chord is an inverted French
sixth in C minor, but there is no attempt to resolve the chord
into that key. Instead, Pfitzner prolongs it by a variety of
devices that hold a tonal centre at bay. An expressive appog-
giatura, the neighbouring note B (N), turns the chord into a
half-diminished seventh. French sixth and half-diminished
seventh are the chromatic basis of the nineteenth century's
most imitated and discussed opening, that of *Tristan und*

Isolde: Pfitzner in a sense is here writing his own version of the Prelude to Wagner's masterpiece, but with a notable difference. The three famous 'Tristan chords' (all half-diminished sevenths, but with a subtle change of position in the third) resolve to dominant sevenths; the Prelude's sense of romantic *Sehnsucht* comes from the refusal of the dominants to resolve, particularly in the opening seventeen bars. For the first fifteen bars of *Der arme Heinrich*, Pfitzner delays a dominant. Such suggestions of dominant sevenths as there are come in the 6/4/3 and (enharmonic) 6/4/2 chords of bars 4 and 8–10; these are experienced as decorations of the basic French sixth, which occurs in two further forms, transposed in bar 8, and repositioned in bar 12. The other stressed chord, decorated like the main French sixth with the rising three-note figure of bar 2, is a half-diminished seventh (bar 5). The whole suggests a rather self-conscious attempt to go beyond Wagner. Although there is no tonic, it is hardly possible to speak of atonality, since the main chords do have traditional tonal associations, which are suspended in the sense of Schoenberg's *aufgehobene Tonalität*.[8] But the music is on the threshold of a more-than-tonal organization. All of the principal harmonies are closely related to one another in traditional function, or by neighbouring-note substitution, or by inversion. By comparison with Wagner, there is something a little forced about Pfitzner's opening. There are cases enough in *Tristan und Isolde* of adjacent half-diminished sevenths, notably in the music which accompanies Tristan's 'das Sehnen hin zur heil'gen Nacht' in Act II. Nothing quite corresponds, though, to the chromatic slither in bars 13–14 of Pfitzner's Prelude, whereby he restores the opening position of his French sixth, in readiness for its long-delayed resolution (Ex. 4.2*b*).

This takes place not into C but into A minor: the bass drops chromatically to E, and the dominant seventh of A minor is sounded. This is denied resolution, and here the Wagnerian parallel becomes irresistible. The recurring progression on which much of the central section of the Prelude is constructed is a deceptive cadence involving the half-diminished

---

[8] 'Suspended tonality' was used by Schoenberg in *Structural Functions of Harmony* (rev. edn., ed. Leonard Stein (London, 1969), 111) as an equivalent for the *schwebende Tonalität* of his *Theory of Harmony* (383–4). The phenomenon in the opening bars of *Der arme Heinrich* corresponds rather more to *aufgehobene Tonalität*, which Schoenberg preferred to call 'roving tonality' in the later treatise (*Structural Functions of Harmony*, 3 and 164–5).

seventh. A *locus classicus* for such a combination in Wagner is
the progression given in Example 4.3*a*, where the bass drops

Ex. 4.3*a*   *b*

a semitone from the dominant. In Pfitzner's case the bass
remains on the dominant, while the upper parts evade their
resolution to the tonic, moving to the flattened second and
leading-note (Ex. 4.3*b*). In both cases, the goal is the half-
diminished seventh. The progression in *Der arme Heinrich*
occurs over the dominants of A minor, B minor, and C♯
minor, and then, after some strenuous extension of all of the
material, over the dominants of E minor, F♯ minor, and G♯
minor; both groups exhibit the classically Wagnerian profile
of the rising sequence preparing a climax. It is no surprise
when the Prelude ends by restoring the initial French sixth as
the curtain goes up. As with the Prelude to *Tristan und Isolde*,
Pfitzner's variation ends on a questioning note; a climax has
been achieved, but only of dynamic. The achievement of a
stable tonic has been postponed; whereas Wagner ends on the
verge of C minor having started from the dominant of A
minor, Pfitzner remains with the same basic chord, which
serves as a structural centre for the prelude, though the structural framework for the whole first act is the same as in
Wagner, from the dominant of A to C (major in Wagner,
minor in Pfitzner). Unlike Wagner, Pfitzner maintains the
mood and style of his Prelude into the opening scene. In this
sense, the parallel is more convincingly with the Prelude
to Act III of *Tristan und Isolde*. Dramatic considerations
reinforce this: the curtain rises on a sick-bed (concealed in
Pfitzner's case) and a dialogue about the invalid. In a sense,
the resolution of the first French sixth in the direction of A
minor is a pointer to the eventual release of the dialogue into
the A minor of Agnes's 'Schön ist es, Mutter', in which the
heroine speaks of 'how much more refreshment my youthful
face provides him than fresh air and light'. Yet it is typical of
Pfitzner's procedures throughout that this A minor is initially

frustrated by a deceptive cadence into G♯ minor. With such side-slipping chromaticism, Pfitzner made his obeisance to the musical spirit of the age.

In Pfitzner's Prelude, and in much music of the half-century that followed *Tristan und Isolde*, the fluid chromaticism derived its tension from the implicit background of tonal resolutions which did ultimately arrive. Schoenberg's attempts to elucidate suspended or roving tonality relied principally on such phenomena as 'the classical development sections'. In the aftermath of Wagner, however, it is almost impossible to deny that words, drama, and programmes in no very particular sense became the stimulus for many of the most radical experiments with harmony, as in Wolf's 'Seufzer', Strauss's *Don Quixote*, and *Elektra*. The Prelude to *Der arme Heinrich* conforms to this pattern; the chromatic intensity of the music and the sickness of the hero are in dramatic collusion. Within Pfitzner's career, this Prelude becomes of particular interest in that it shows the composer escaping from an association of late-nineteenth-century chromaticism with a more particular aura that tends to be linked to a manifestation of an earlier Romanticism, the folk ballad. Margit's brooding on the Mountain King is only the central panel of a triptych of ballads that Pfitzner composed during or immediately after his time at the Hoch Conservatory. The others are *Der Blumen Rache* (1888), after Freiligrath, for alto, women's chorus, and small orchestra, and *Herr Oluf* (1891), after Herder, for baritone and large orchestra. Freiligrath's poem tells of the vengeance exacted on a sleeping maiden by the flowers in a vase by her bed. Its images offered Pfitzner ample opportunity to contrast the diatonic music of the flowers with the chromatic catastrophe which they precipitate. The tonic key of G♯ minor already represents the basic scene with traces of side-slipping chromaticism; the flowers stand in a facile B major that gives way to alternating diminished sevenths as they seem to come to life. From each group of flowers emerges an obviously symbolic form; the climax of each stanza reinforces the spectral action in a more or less conventional way, an augmented triad for the 'schlanke Frau' who rises from the roses, an alternation of seventh chords on B and F for the maiden who rises from the lilies ('Dünn wie Spinnweb' ist ihr Schleier'). Their chorus of vengeance is less interesting and the climax is again within the language of a faded Romanticism:

> Welch ein Rauschen, welch ein Raunen;
> Wie des Mädchens Wangen glüh'n!
> Wie die Geister es anhauchen!
> Wie die Düfte wallend zieh'n!

> What rustling and murmuring!
> How the maiden's cheeks glow!
> How the spirits breathe on them!
> How the scents simmer!

The predictable diminished seventh is used to clinch the musical climax on 'zieh'n'. Evidently the young Pfitzner's taste for the macabre was as dependent on this ancient prop as was that of his revered romantic masters. What is striking in Pfitzner's setting is a certain rhythmic fleetness and an undeniable charm, partly the result of the transparent, almost Mendelssohnian orchestration, which is allied to stronger melodic material than in the Scherzo in C minor of the previous year.[9]

The diction of Freiligrath's poem is rather too knowing and artful to be convincing as a ballad; it is a somewhat self-conscious evocation of the macabre. Ibsen's poem has more of the authentic ballad's *Sachlichkeit*. As a result, Pfitzner adopted a sparer musical language, with a climactic half-diminished seventh for the final word of the penultimate line with its striking disjunction of images: 'Im Berge ist Gold und ewige Nacht'. *Herr Oluf* approaches an authentic folk style in its text more closely still. The poem, properly entitled *Erlkönigs Tochter*, came from the second part of Herder's *Volkslieder* and was a translation from a Danish poem; from Herder's mistranslation of the Danish *Ellerkonge*, the Erlking made his epochal entrance into German poetry and ultimately music.[10] Certain features of the poem foreshadow Goethe's 'Erlkönig'. The father who rides with his child is suggested by Herder's hero:

> Herr Oluf reitet spät und weit,
> Zu bieten auf seine Hochzeitleut';

> Herr Oluf rode late and far,
> To summon his wedding folk;

---

[9] For a discussion of *Der Blumen Rache*, see Hans Rectanus, 'Pfitzners *Der Blumen Rache* und die Gattung der Chorballade', *PLZ*.

[10] *Herders sämmtliche Werke*, ed. Bernhard Suphan *et al.*, 33 vols. (Berlin, 1877–1913), xxv. 682.

like the child of the later poem, he is approached by a spirit, the Erlking's daughter. Oluf refuses to dance with her in spite of her blandishments. As in Goethe, the spirit finally turns to all too effective force:

> Und willt, Herr Oluf, nicht tanzen mit mir,
> Soll Seuch und Krankheit folgen dir.
>
> And if you will not dance with me,
> Plague and illness shall follow you.

Oluf reaches his mother's house 'blass und bleich', and when the bride arrives in the morning, he lies dead, leaving the enigmatic but, for the ballad style, typical explanation,

> Sagt ihr, ich sei im Wald zur Stund,
> Zu proben allda mein Pferd und Hund.
>
> Tell her, I am in the wood just now,
> Testing there my horse and hound.

Pfitzner's setting, unlike that of the Ibsen ballad, is deliberately diffuse. Despite the clear parallels with Goethe, Pfitzner refused to imitate the motivic and figural economy of Schubert's 'Erlkönig'. Rather, his model is the style of ballad linked with Loewe, which Schubert and others also used from time to time. The music for Oluf's ride is suitably turbulent, with the diminished seventh and the dominant minor ninth in the tonic key of B♭ minor much in evidence. The augmented triad accompanies the appearance of the dancing elves who attend the Erlking's daughter. The dialogue between Oluf and his temptress makes much play of repeated F♯s and As which belong to a D major that is constantly undermined by a C natural in the melody line. As her curse takes effect, Oluf's faltering heartbeat sounds on a naggingly reiterated dyad of B–C. All of this and the subsequent orchestral depiction of Oluf's stricken ride to his mother's home take place at the same headlong speed, in spite of many changes in texture. Now Pfitzner's true adherence to the ballad style becomes apparent as changes of tempo convey the dialogue between the dying hero and his mother, and a wedding march for his intended bride. Their styles are quite distinct, the diatonic style of the latter belonging to the world of the Dresden *Tannhäuser* or earlier, while the chromatic tensions of the former have a linear quality that reminds the listener that the work is a close contemporary of *Der arme Heinrich*. Diminished and half-diminished sevenths are more a product of the movement of parts, a suggestion of that linear polyphony that was to emerge most strikingly in the slow movement of the String Quartet in D. Both opera and ballad make the equation between chromaticism and sickness, though the shorter span of *Herr Oluf* does not in any sense condense the mood; rather, it emphasizes a lack of stylistic integration that points to Pfitzner's artistic aims. For the world of early Romanticism, that essence of Weber, Schumann, and Marschner which he prized, made a virtue of the knightliness which emerges in the diatonic march and which stands in unreconcilable contrast to the dying Oluf. That contrast is not immediately apparent in *Der arme Heinrich*, which bears the unequivocally Wagnerian description of *Musikdrama*, but it does emerge in the 'Romantic Opera', *Die Rose vom Liebesgarten*, and it is also present, albeit transmuted into something infinitely more personal, in *Palestrina*.

That Pfitzner should have been so attracted by the ballad casts an interesting light on his concept of musical drama, but raises more questions than it answers. The ballad, easy enough to define in literary terms, is a much more amorphous entity in music, expressive of an ethos as much as a form; and it was in terms of ethos and poetry that Pfitzner attempted to discuss his first two apparently unlike creations for the operatic stage. It cannot be said that the ballad had much influence on the saga tone of Wagner's music-dramas, apart from Senta's famous example. Nor did it have a statistically important place in the literature of Romantic opera in general, however striking individual examples might have been.[11] The period of Pfitzner's early attempts at musical drama might best be understood as an immersion in various genres characteristic of the Romantic tone to which he aspired. Thus *Herr Oluf* embraced the diffuse, macabre, and 'narrative' ballad, which had to wait until the much later *Das Herz* for an ampler treatment of some of its themes. *Der arme Heinrich* used aspects of Wagner's musical language in tackling the saga material which had dominated Wagner's output from *Tannhäuser* onwards. *Die Rose vom Liebesgarten* addressed the more general world of Romantic opera through a specific aspect, the fairy-tale. In neither stage work did Pfitzner attempt the all-encompassing kind of 'Romantic opera' which Carl Dahlhaus has discerned in *Lohengrin*, in which 'Mutually

[11] Siegfried Goslich, *Die deutsche romantische Oper* (Tutzing, 1975), 263–6.

exclusive opposites, myth and history, fairy tale and tragedy, are forced together without any of them suffering perceptible harm'.[12] Yet such descriptions of Pfitzner's two operas are not uncontroversial. His earliest admirers fought strenuously against describing *Der arme Heinrich* as Wagnerian, to such an extent that one can only assume Pfitzner's approval. In some measure this may have been to combat the inevitable charges of dependence, against which Strauss too had to fight. Pfitzner's critics on the other hand refused to accept that *Die Rose vom Liebesgarten* was a simple fairy-tale; the libretto of that work quickly acquired the reputation of an immensely difficult symbolic allegory, analogous to the aura of insuperable obscurity that later came to surround *Die Frau ohne Schatten*. It is easier to discern a stylistic pattern in Pfitzner's music, with *Die Rose vom Liebesgarten* following the chromatic *Der arme Heinrich* as *Die Meistersinger* follows *Tristan*, than to discern a clear dramaturgical consistency in the two works, in spite of their common librettist.

It would perhaps be a mistake to imagine that Grun wrote the two poems in an equally enthusiastic frame of mind. The idea of *Der arme Heinrich* had a relatively spontaneous genesis. Cossmann and Grun drew Pfitzner's attention to Hartmann von Aue's verse epic at the Hoch Conservatory, and Pfitzner began the work of realizing the project by writing the text of Heinrich's monologue in Act I, 'Duft! Duft! Herrlicher Duft!' While Grun took over the libretto, Pfitzner worked on the music with the opening theme and the Prelude, carrying on into the opening scene where he borrowed ideas from the rejected Cello Concerto (including Dietrich's distant horn). The composition took from 1891 to the end of 1893, and the only trouble which arose with Grun was over the drafting of a contract (*SS IV* 605–8). As Frances Grun has shown, the two collaborators were able to consult each other on a reasonably regular basis; they could also look upon each other as artistic equals, as Grun worked on the poems which were to be published with illustrations by Hans Thoma as *Glocken von Eisen und von Gold* in 1893. By contrast, *Die Rose vom Liebesgarten* was undertaken at a time when Grun had returned to England. Presumably he was on the verge of that transformation which saw him give up poetry and music and turn to social work

---

[12] Carl Dahlhaus, *Richard Wagner's Music Dramas*, trans. Mary Whittall (Cambridge, 1979), 35.

through the medium of the Salvation Army. Pfitzner persuaded him to leave London for work on the libretto, which took place in such settings as the Gruns' villa in Ostend during the spring of 1897. Abendroth leaves the impression that this was a less happy collaboration than the first. After finishing the libretto in May 1898, in some confusion in the face of Pfitzner's impatience (once again he had begun composing before the poem was complete), Grun returned to London and

... complained in a letter to Ernst Jedliczka (23 June 1898) about the 'difficult time in Berlin', which had 'set [him] back politically'. For all that, he let him know at the same time that he would 'seek to preserve the connection with art' and make a few studies 'for the eventuality of Pfitzner completing the "Love-garden" and wanting something new'.[13]

In spite of the final sentiments, their collaboration was now essentially finished, and their friendship in time came to the melancholy end recorded in a letter from Pfitzner to Grun's sister Ellinor on the occasion of the poet-reformer's death, a letter filled with pained inability to comprehend why Grun had turned against him (*SS IV* 770). Nevertheless, Pfitzner continued to defend Grun's contributions to *Die Rose vom Liebesgarten* in the face of its critics, none of whom could have been more intimidating than Mahler, who came straight out with the question, 'Where did you get this libretto?' (*SS IV* 689).

The two books which Grun provided differed in origins, in subject-matter, and in construction. The poem for *Der arme Heinrich* has always been less controversial, stemming as it does from one of the masterpieces of German medieval poetry by Hartmann von Aue. Grun's libretto follows the broad outlines and some of the verses of Hartmann's epic faithfully enough.

SYNOPSIS. *Act I* is set in the knight Heinrich's Swabian castle. Although he has been to all appearances a model of chivalry, he has been struck down by an illness that has defied all cures. In desperation, he has sent his retainer Dietrich to a monastery in Salerno to consult a famous doctor. As the curtain rises, Hilde and Agnes, Dietrich's wife and 14-year-old daughter, discuss the sleeping knight's ailment, with Agnes showing a particularly deep sense of grief. Horn calls announce

---

[13] Walter Abendroth, *Hans Pfitzner* (Munich, 1935), 103–4.

Dietrich's return, as Heinrich awakens in delirium. Dietrich relates his journey over the Alps to Salerno. The conclusion of his narration shatters Heinrich's hopes. He will only be cured 'when a pure and virtuous maiden offers here at the Lord's shrine her young blood with a cheerful heart'. The doctor is willing to carry out the sacrifice if such a maiden can be found. Heinrich bids farewell to his weapons, but collapses as he tries to wield his sword, and prays for death. As Dietrich leads Hilde and Agnes away, the latter tears herself free and rushes to Heinrich's side.

Act II. Dietrich and Hilde prepare for bed in an atmosphere of foreboding. Agnes enters to confirm Hilde's fears by announcing that she will be the sacrifice. Dietrich forbids her to think of it while Hilde pleads with her only child. Agnes replies that in return Hilde will have the redeemed knight as her child. Hilde is seized by divine inspiration and persuades Dietrich to accept Agnes's decision.

Act III. In Salerno, Hilde and Dietrich, once again a prey to human fears, listen to the monks intoning the 'Christe eleison'. Agnes bids them farewell and turns to the doctor who testifies before Heinrich to her fitness for the sacrifice as the monks sing the 'Dies irae'. Heinrich becomes aware of the shame into which his illness has brought him but Agnes will not be shaken from her purpose. She enters the monastery and the doctor closes the door. The full enormity of what is about to happen strikes Heinrich who first pleads with the doctor to open the door, then forces it open himself as his strength returns. Heinrich seizes the sacrificial knife from the doctor and raises Agnes to his breast. A miracle has taken place; Heinrich is now cured and sets forth, not as a knight but on foot, to proclaim what has happened, as the doctor kneels and kisses the hem of Agnes's garment.

Grun's aims in this adaptation have been discussed by Pfitzner in '*Der Arme Heinrich*, das Epos und das Drama', an essay appended to 'Zur Grundfrage der Operndichtung'. Perhaps wisely, he did not discuss its literary quality and its sentiments, in which too many high-minded people spend all too much time blessing and dedicating themselves to one another; although Grun did not subscribe to a Wagnerian verse scheme, the elevated diction of *Lohengrin* and *Parsifal* is all too apparent—how often does a line seem to begin with 'Gesegnet'! Grun's principal departures from Hartmann in

Pfitzner's view were to emphasize indirectly the possibility
that Heinrich's illness was 'the consequence of a sin' (*SS II*
78), to raise the parents' struggles to a prominent place, and
to eliminate the further happy end of a marriage between
Agnes and Heinrich. In more practical details, Grun also
changed the nameless peasant on Heinrich's estate into
Dietrich the retainer (and bestowed the names Hilde and
Agnes on his dependants). In Hartmann, Heinrich undertook
the first journey to Salerno himself; by sending Dietrich on
this mission, Grun provided Pfitzner with the most famous set
piece of the work, Dietrich's Narration, which was performed
in 1893 in the Berlin concert before the opera was finished.[14]
In Hartmann, the peasant couple had at least one other child,
but Grun sharpened the conflict for them by making Agnes
their only child. Finally and most importantly, the sudden cure in Hartmann came not when Heinrich rejected the
sacrifice in Salerno and accepted his illness with that patience
of Job which Hartmann held up as moral exemplar throughout, but on the journey back to Swabia, after Heinrich and
Agnes had spent a night of prayer at an inn. In Pfitzner's
account, all of Grun's changes were designed with two aims in
view. Of these, the less significant was to reconcile the distant values of the poem with modern taste, which could not
readily accept such details as Heinrich's marriage to a 14-
year-old girl and had to see in detail the mental suffering
which preceded the parents' acceptance of the sacrifice. The
more important was the need to emphasize the elements of
transformation in the plot. 'Grun saw this dramatic essence in
the complete spiritual transformation of the hero...who
is suddenly stricken by frightful unrelenting illness' (*SS II*
76–7). As Pfitzner explained the plot, the sacrifice was itself
the symbol of Heinrich's illness, the experience of another's
agony the moment of transformation. But the characters of
the doctor and Agnes revealed a theme which perhaps was
closer to Pfitzner than Grun realized, presaging as it does the
'sorrow of the world' of which Ighino sings in *Palestrina*.

[The doctor] is an ascetic by 'human will *quantum satis*'. The
medieval flagellant is significantly individualized in him. The look
into the nothingness of existence, into the sorrow of the world, into
the guilt of life, which Agnes had from birth onwards as a single

[14] As a consequence, Dietrich's Narration is numbered separately from the rest of
the full score (Leipzig: Max Brockhaus, n.d. [1901]).

direct feeling, which formed her entire existence, whose only possible consequence therefore is her 'Sterben will ich, Opfer bringen'—
this insight has come to the doctor above all through the intellect.
(*SS II* 85)

The twin Schopenhauerian ethos is thus present, not only
renunciation as transformation at the climax of Heinrich's
story, but also deep pessimism in the face of the world.

What this has in common with the libretto of *Die Rose vom
Liebesgarten* is far from clear. Pfitzner's second opera moves in
a world which owed its origin to an image, Thoma's painting
of an armoured figure standing as guardian before a paradise
in which humans and animals coexisted in a spring landscape. From this image of what Pfitzner persistently described
as a Germanic paradise, Grun extrapolated a basically simple
tale which nevertheless proved a stumbling block to the
opera's earliest critics. As befitted an opera which had its
origins in a painting, Pfitzner took great care over the details
of the scenery in later years, stressing to one producer that
'the stage picture and the scenic in general play a very important role in the "Rose", far more important than in all my
other operas' (*SS IV* 771). The love-garden itself, in which the
prologue and the close of the epilogue were set, required a
very detailed evocation with meadow, lake, island, sensation
of distance, marble balustrade, bridges, and temple. This
was to be the extremely matter-of-fact analogy to Thoma's
painting, in which the idealism of the subject was rendered
tangible with almost prosaic realism.

SYNOPSIS. In the *Prologue*, distant fanfares summon the inhabitants of the love-garden to celebrate the advent of spring;
maidens and boys arrive, then the singing master and the
weapons master, finally the noblemen and ladies. The guardian
of the winter door appears. He has done his task and now a
guardian for the spring door must be appointed. They set out
for the temple on a distant island in which are enthroned the
virgin of the stars and the sun-child, around whom lions
sleep. On the island, Siegnot brings a white lily to the deity
who gives him a rose from her breast. The cortège arrives
and in the Miracle of the Blossoming, a rain of flowers accompanies her blessing of the world. The rose reveals Siegnot as
the new guardian. He is crowned with a circlet to which the
rose is attached and sent forth to guard the spring door.

Act I. In the primeval forest before the garden Siegnot

takes his place. The Moormann, a dweller in the swamp, approaches the light from the open door of the garden. He aspires to enter, only to be told by Siegnot that it is not so easy. In response to Siegnot's challenge, 'weisst du, wo Minne leidlos wohnt?', the Moormann assumes that Siegnot refers to Minneleide who dances in the moonlight. Siegnot refuses him entry but allows him to stay with him on watch. The Moormann tells Siegnot of Minneleide, an elfin creature whom the dwellers in the swamp revere. In moonlight, she appears at the mouth of a cave and calls her servants. Two attendants bring her offerings. Siegnot, entranced, interrupts and offers to lead her into the love-garden. Minneleide knows little of the garden, having spoken to none of the inhabitants whom she has seen until Siegnot; now she knows that she belongs to him and not to the inhabitants of the wood. They embrace and sink on to the mossy rocks. She admires the rose and crown. He assures her that pearls and gold are to be found in the garden and crowns her with the rose. But as they ascend into the garden, Minneleide is blinded by the light and trembles before the animals of the garden. As she staggers back in fear, a storm arises in the wood and the door of the garden swings shut. Barbaric hordes led by the Nacht-Wunderer enter, strike down Siegnot, and carry Minneleide off into the wood. The Moormann revives Siegnot who resolves to follow the lost rose to death.

Act II. The Moormann leads Siegnot into the heart of a mountain where the Nacht-Wunderer dwells. When he dares to go no further, Siegnot bids him live freely and happily in the wood. In conflicting moods of resolution and despair, Siegnot presses on into the caverns. Surrounded by dwarfs, Minneleide prepares to sit by the Nacht-Wunderer's side at his triumphal feast. She breaks into bitter lamentations for Siegnot. As the inhabitants of the mountain appear, Siegnot enters to assure her that the rose protects her. The Nacht-Wunderer mocks Siegnot's efforts. Siegnot turns to Minneleide and tells her that he will bear her guilt. As she hesitates to follow Siegnot, he pulls down the pillars which support the Nacht-Wunderer's hall, killing everyone except Minneleide and her attendants. Dazed by the catastrophe, she realizes that she no longer fears the fiery light of the garden and the rose glows as a sign. But she collapses as she sees Siegnot's body beneath a rock.

Epilogue. The guardian sits motionless before the winter

gate in the moonlight. Minneleide leads a procession with
Siegnot's body towards him but with no response. She bids
farewell to the wood and beats with the rose on the door.
Distant voices curse and reject her. She calls on the virgin
who appears on her throne with the sun-child. Voices of
mercy call to Minneleide but as she steps towards them, the
winter guardian raises his sword. She sinks on Siegnot's
corpse and begs forgiveness. She will return the crown. As she
tries to enter by the door, the guardian makes to strike but
she collapses lifeless before the sword touches her. The walls
of the garden collapse, the guardian vanishes. In the garden,
Minneleide returns the rose to the virgin; Siegnot is awakened
by the sun-child.

It must be stressed that the plot itself is simple, almost
conventional. The appearance of complexity comes from the
dense layers of connotation provided by the setting. Pfitzner
was certainly right on one level to stress the Germanic qualities of the poem, and this does not exclusively apply to the
love-garden. The jovial sadism of the Nacht-Wunderer looks
back to such figures as Kaspar and Hagen in the literature of
nineteenth-century opera (but also forward to the *Oberförster*
of another, more chilling parable, Ernst Jünger's *Auf den
Marmorklippen*). Such parallels seem more pertinent than
the enchanters of Pfitzner's contemporaries, Humperdinck's
witch or Delius's Dark Fiddler. The Moormann, with his urge
towards the light, resembles Papageno in that he cannot enter
into the elect, but may live in peace in the wood; the first
act even features an offstage pipe, chromatically echoing
Papageno's, though it is given to the wordless character of
the Waldmann. The names themselves resonate with the
Wagnerian past, both in Siegnot and Minneleide (whose
vision of her spiritual solitude remembers the physical solitude in which Herzeleide dies in *Parsifal*), and in the two
attendants, Schwarzhilde and Rotelse, who might have stepped
from one of the Grimms' tales, but could also, one feels, have
ridden with the Valkyries. Alongside this, there are giants and
dwarfs in the Nacht-Wunderer's retinue who intensify the
atmosphere of a German fairy-tale. Into this, however, Grun
obviously wove biblical images; Siegnot's destruction of
the hall remembers Samson and the Old Testament, virgin
and child remember the New. The marble columns of the
temple and garden add a further dimension, that ceremonial

classicism of the Ringstrasse and Unter den Linden that hovered on the edge of the kitsch it undoubtedly later became in the aesthetics of the Third Reich.

Did Grun have a unified vision as he imposed this heterogeneous imagery on his tale of renunciation by Siegnot to effect Minneleide's redemption? So thought the first critics as they wrestled with the symbolism of the rose, the gates, the crown, Minneleide, and the virgin (who is Frau Minne, but not in any sense that Isolde would have recognized). In countering this, Pfitzner argued a little ingenuously that he had not realized 'a profound idea' had to lie behind his romantic opera; was not all art a game, 'the forming of an image of *life* in a sense that one can translate just as correctly by "reality" as "fantasy"'? (*SS II* 89) This latter sentiment was undoubtedly a true reflection of Pfitzner's aesthetics and of his dramaturgy in general, but the single 'profound idea' is not far removed from that governing conception which he wished to demonstrate in all valid opera poems. Whereas the essay on *Der arme Heinrich* goes out of its way to stress the central idea, the hero's sudden transformation, the essay 'Die "Symbolik" in der "Rose vom Liebesgarten"' seems to duck that very point. What was the governing idea that motivated Grun's poem? The closest that Pfitzner comes to defining it is in the 'atoning death' by which Siegnot 'wins a new soul for the kingdom' (*SS II* 93). But equally it might be the very idea of the love-garden itself. Instead of arguing to the point, Pfitzner took issue with his critics' failure to see that all difficulty resided in the fact that here was a freely invented fairy-tale; this merely begged the question of the idea that brought Thoma's painting to dramatic movement. What the opera stands for in Pfitzner's output is of enormous significance. On the one hand it gives expression to a vein of pantheism (Pfitzner's own word) such as is only encountered episodically in his other operas. It might almost be valid to see in this the central point of the work; such is the thought of Hermann von Waltershausen: 'Here above all resides the great significance of *Die Rose vom Liebesgarten*. The shapes of spring, winter, the moor landscape, the subterranean world of caverns, when all is said and done, are nothing other than the drama itself.'[15] On the other it projected a form of idealism into the most detailed of stage pictures, an expression of his

---

[15] 'Hans Pfitzners Naturgefühl', *FHP* 32.

conviction that dramatic art should be 'true and symbolic' (*SS II* 97). For such reasons, one might be justified in thinking that in calling *Die Rose vom Liebesgarten* a romantic opera, the emphasis was secretly placed on romantic rather than opera.

This raises the question of Pfitzner's conception of musical drama which superficially changed so much between his first two operas, from late Wagnerian music-drama to something rather older. This latter is not without controversy, when the historically finical Abendroth noted that *Die Rose vom Liebesgarten* was less a real romantic opera than a 'lyric variant of the music-dramatic form in the spirit of romantic opera'.[16] In other words, Grun and Pfitzner aimed for a romantic opera that took Wagner's later works into musical account. This is a significant, perhaps unwilling, modification of the view common to most of Pfitzner's earliest admirers who sought to distance the composer from Wagner as far as possible. This tendency is already apparent in one of the first substantial pieces on *Der arme Heinrich*, a pamphlet by the Munich critic Alexander Berrsche, published in 1913. The difficulties under which Pfitzner's champions laboured can be seen in Berrsche's need to concede that the libretto was, 'without being epigonal ... still the most Wagnerian' of the time.[17] But once the libretto was disposed of, Berrsche quickly got down to discriminating between such 'systematic' Wagnerians as Debussy in *Pelléas et Mélisande* (an opera whose music was structured only by the text, according to Berrsche) and an absolute musician such as Pfitzner. Nietzsche's vision of Wagner's 'overwhelming symphonic intelligence' which soared over the characters and their drama seemed to Berrsche more suited to Pfitzner; in one of the most extreme claims ever made for Pfitzner's music, he argued that Wagner stood as a special case to Pfitzner's higher concept.[18] What Berrsche was proposing was a view of Pfitzner that emphasized absolute musical construction in sophisticated periodic thinking, reduced leitmotifs to minimal proportions or raised them into larger 'symphonic' themes,

[16] Abendroth, *Hans Pfitzner*, 313.

[17] Alexander Berrsche, *Der arme Heinrich: Kurze Einführung* (Leipzig, n.d. [1913]), 3.

[18] Ibid. 5–6; Friedrich Nietzsche, *Untimely Meditations*, trans. R. J. Hollingdale (Cambridge, 1983), 242; Karl Halusa ('Hans Pfitzners musikdramatisches Schaffen', Dissertation, University of Vienna, 1929) presents a more substantial version of Berrsche's views (e.g. 119–21).

and countered the charge that Hermann Levi had made against *Der arme Heinrich* when Pfitzner first showed it to him, that the work was improvised (*RSB* 289). As a consequence, almost all of the musical examples selected by Berrsche from the opera were designed to illustrate Pfitzner's grasp of purely musical structure.

Twenty-seven years later, Hirtler in his study of the same opera was armed with the analyses of Alfred Lorenz when he rejected Berrsche's thesis with the words, 'The antithesis Wagner–Pfitzner is accordingly not possible in the form it has taken up to now'.[19] As Hirtler showed, however, attempts to construct a Lorenzian theory for Pfitzner would founder on the lack of overall tonal centres for acts; Lorenz's theories in any case are no longer uncontested among Wagnerians. What Hirtler did was to invert the comparison in effect, subscribing to a form- and period-building view of the Wagnerian leitmotif to which Pfitzner's small unities did not aspire. The principles to which the latter did give rise were song-like parts, sections unified by mood, and orchestral preludes and interludes, all of which led to the amorphous conclusion that form in Pfitzner's opera relied on romantic means, 'stylistic traits conscious of goal and purpose, standing apart from planned large-scale lay-out'.[20] Although the attempt at revision was welcome, it did not perhaps go very far. These characteristics of Pfitzner's dramatic style could be found just as easily in Wagner. Furthermore, the description of Pfitzner's *Einfall* and its consequences, far from being uniformly valid for his operas, could be a yardstick for a negative valuation. Although Hirtler used as illustration the spasmodic end of Act I (where his point is reasonable, given the fractured action with Heinrich's sword), the great weakness of Pfitzner's opera is the second act, where short-winded inspiration is a problem. Here Pfitzner put too much faith in simply following the text with parlando vocal writing and bare orchestral textures. The climax, Hilde's sudden inspiration, makes too little contrast with what has gone before (after some solemn brass calls against tremolando strings). Pfitzner's lyrical gift is not apparent (even in the final trio); in spite of an attractive cadence (Ex. 4.4) with clear dramatic point similar in its

---

[19] Hirtler, *Hans Pfitzners 'Armer Heinrich'*, 81.
[20] Ibid. 93; Pfitzner thought Hirtler's book a 'Machwerk' (Letter to Walter Abendroth, 3 Dec. 1939, *A-Wn*, Pfitzner Nachlass, 288/123).

Ex. 4.4

recurrence to an important idea in *Palestrina* (see below, Ex. 5.32, Cadence 3), Pfitzner lacked the dramatic skill to knit such pleasing moments into a more sustained unity. Although the act is developmental in the sense of a peripeteia, Pfitzner did not see that simple development of short motives was not enough for music-drama, a mistake that did not occur in Act I, nor in *Die Rose vom Liebesgarten*, let alone *Palestrina*; had Levi made his criticism of the second act, it would be hard to oppose. More recent writing on Pfitzner has tended also to dispute the justice of Berrsche's claim for the Wagnerian qualities of Grun's libretto. The central idea in Pfitzner's early dramaturgy, whether derived from Ibsen or Grun, was an idea of renunciation leading to redemption that obviously was not unique to Wagner. Standing behind it was Schopenhauer and a specifically Christian tradition that Reinhard Seebohm designated Gothic. His view, that Pfitzner and Grun opposed 'a more intimate Gothic to the Wagnerian monumental type', was a logical extension of Abendroth's claim that Grun and Pfitzner 'preserved a much stronger truly medieval spirit than Wagner'.[21]

The controversy over the degree to which Pfitzner followed or escaped from the influence of Wagner in retrospect seems sterile. It depended on a crude misinterpretation of Wagner which catalogued motives in guide-books, a mode of analysis from which Berrsche, Rudolf Louis, and others wished to shield Pfitzner. Hirtler had no difficulty finding leitmotifs when he came to analyse *Der arme Heinrich*, nor in finding

---

[21] Reinhard Seebohm, 'Die gotischen Wesenszüge in der Tonwelt Hans Pfitzners', *FHP* 48; Abendroth, *Hans Pfitzner*, 308. The above criticism of Act II of *Der arme Heinrich* substantially agrees with that of Carl Dahlhaus (*Nineteenth-Century Music*, trans. J. Bradford Robinson (Berkeley, Calif., 1989), 342); but that a quite different view is possible is shown by the reactions of Ernst Křenek and (surprisingly) Paul Bekker (Johann Peter Vogel, *Hans Pfitzner mit Selbstzeugnissen und Bilddokumenten* (Reinbek bei Hamburg, 1989), 51).

associated characters and dramatic concepts. This is hardly surprising in view of the music to *Das Fest auf Solhaug*. In that work Rectanus has detailed leitmotifs for Margit (see above, Ex. 4.1), Gudmund, Bengt, and the guests.[22] Pfitzner did not drop the practice in *Der arme Heinrich* or even in the later romantic opera. Rectanus again has catalogued the leitmotifs for *Der arme Heinrich* and *Die Rose vom Liebesgarten*, distinguishing them as to characters, situations, and structural function and coming to the conclusion that Pfitzner's approach to the leitmotif, particularly in *Der arme Heinrich*, was not intrinsically different from that of Wagner. This is not to imply that Pfitzner is simply the follower (as his admirers dreaded to hear) of Wagner, since there is more to Pfitzner (and Wagner) than guide-books of motives. The real distinction between Pfitzner and Wagner lies in stylistic rather than structural matters, though it is less apparent in the early operas than in *Palestrina*.

The criticism of Act II of *Der arme Heinrich* given above reflects a point which Pfitzner perhaps forgot and that critics have regularly forgotten: the difference between abstract form, even symphonic form in spite of Nietzsche, and the needs of musical drama. Dramatic structure is much more dependent on variation of pace and reflection of character. The clue to the dramatic style of *Der arme Heinrich* lies in the delineation and development of Heinrich's character, which may be another pointer to the problems of Act II, from which the knight is absent. The crucial aspects of the work lie in Act I as a whole and the climax of Act III in particular. In Act I, the claims of dramatic pace and character delineation are in harmony by and large, with one possible and significant exception. As Grun laid it out, it provided three scenes, to which the scrupulous analyst might append a coda. The first, between Hilde and Agnes, is a dialogue, though in that Wagnerian tradition which constantly threatens to expand into monologue; there is no suggestion of stichomythia, the characters do not really converse since they will not change. Agnes is already unconsciously destined to make sacrifice; Hilde does not grow, as her lapse from inspiration at the start of Act III makes clear. The second scene centres on Heinrich with the monologue whose text Pfitzner wrote himself at its

---

[22] Hans Rectanus, *Leitmotivik und Form in den musikdramatischen Werken Hans Pfitzners* (Würzburg, 1967), 20–2.

heart. Here the composer has the straightforward task of depicting the feverish knight (with appropriate recollections of large stretches of the Prelude). But throughout everything up to this point runs an undercurrent displaying what Heinrich had been, the knightly self which illness has tarnished. This theme joins the scene to the next which centres on Dietrich, since the relationship between Heinrich and his retainer is still unequivocally that of knight to vassal. The adventures which Dietrich recounts, the beauties of the landscape through which he passes, have their echoes in Heinrich's music, since they belong to an ethos to which Heinrich, as knight and minstrel, once belonged. Dietrich's monologue, the act's chief glory and problem, provides the climax to the whole, after which the structure tears itself apart in the episode with the sword, a coda which also points towards the second act in Agnes's final impulsive gesture.

From Heinrich's monologue onwards, there is a constant tension between the chromatic music of the Prelude and a diatonic vein which is most prominent in Dietrich's brass-dominated arrival; this is graphically illustrated by the manner in which that climax, with striding scalar bass and straightforward martial dotted rhythms, subsides into the cramped figures of Heinrich's awakening from his feverish sleep. The monologue proper opens with wide-spread drifting chords glinting with harp tone—chords which also begin Dietrich's monologue; the fresh air which Dietrich's arrival brings Heinrich corresponds to the mood of hope in which Dietrich begins his journey to Salerno. To underline the connection, Heinrich continues with a motive that will rise to importance later in the narration (see below, Ex. 4.5*b*), and which Pfitzner adapted from an early song, 'Nun, da so warm der Sonnenschein'. Only as Heinrich realizes that he can have no part in the human activity around him does major change to minor, and the music of the Prelude return, beginning with the agitated central developmental section and building to a climax that leaves Example 4.2*a*, now in woodwind, standing in isolation. Such a moment has its obvious parallels in *Tristan und Isolde*. That Hilde offers Heinrich a drink reminds the listener both of the potion in *Tristan* and of the suffering Amfortas. The monologue now fragments into a dialogue with Hilde in which the contrast between Dietrich's diatonic music and Heinrich's Example 4.2*a* is ever apparent. The principle of construction is thus through-composition with motivic cross-reference, in which contrasts of mode (major or minor), rhythm (regular or syncopated), and periodicity (paired phrases or sequences and pedals) define the opposition of knightliness and sickness. The monologue acts as an exposition of certain musical and dramatic themes to be taken up in the second monologue, Dietrich's Narration.

This latter section inevitably invites particularly close comparison with Wagner. The idea of a narration as the structural centre to an act occurs frequently in Wagner—the Dutchman, Wolfram, Tannhäuser, Telramund, Lohengrin, Loge, Siegmund, Wotan, Mime, Waltraute, Siegfried, Kundry, and Gurnemanz (repeatedly) further or recapitulate plot (and often music) in the time-honoured epic device of tale within a tale. Some of these narrations come close to the aria (notably Wolfram's 'Als du in kühnem Sange uns bestrittest'), others resemble more closely arioso or even recitative (as at the start of Wotan's monologue in Act II of *Die Walküre*), and it is in this greyer area that Dietrich's is to be found. Its theme, a journey across the Alps to Italy, makes comparison with Tannhäuser's 'Inbrunst im Herzen' irresistible. The parallel is underlined by the climaxes, in each case a pronouncement *ex cathedra* by the Pope or by the doctor that throws the hero into the deepest despair. Wagner structured his narration in three parts. The journey is dominated by a dotted motive that gradually turns into running quavers. Rome brings a more sustained theme in 6/4 with chorale-like textures and wind scoring. The Pope's verdict turns to declamation, with earlier figures prominent alongside minatory brass outbursts. Pfitzner to some extent followed the same pattern but spread himself more extensively. In particular, he followed Grun in dealing so spaciously with the journey as to risk dulling the dramatic impact of the scene in Salerno. The images of the two journeys are to some extent common: the sun, the ice and snow of the Alps, then the beauties of Italy. But Grun invented an episode in which Dietrich was despoiled by a knight's marauding followers and had to re-equip himself. The result was that Pfitzner structured his depiction of the journey itself in a tripartite form dependent on a small group of motives. The first (Ex. 4.5*a*) is the recurring motive of the journey; the second (Ex. 4.5*b*) is linked both to the spring in which the journey ends and to the beauty of Italy's landscape, and thus falls into the category of a nature motive (to which its horn tone adds confirmation). The third (Ex. 4.5*c*, a later and more

Ex. 4.5*a*

complete form) is the motive of the monastery in Salerno, with the repeated minims of the cloister bell (*x*). All three are stated or prefigured near the start of the narration and later transformed in a single burst of melody at the arrival in Italy (which is proof enough that Pfitzner's inspirations could give rise to convincing musical paragraphs). In between comes the more conventional conflict music of the altercation with the retinue, which turns by a move from minor to major into the knightly dotted rhythms of the renewed journey. This middle section also includes Dietrich's description of the Alps, a mysterious paragraph entirely in slow semibreves, founded on a three-note motive which threads its way through the full orchestra, playing quietly for most of the time. Although the image evoked, 'die Alpenriesen in Eis und Schnee', is far from anything in *Palestrina*, the abstract interweaving of patterns for an atmospheric purpose is a clear pointer towards aspects

c

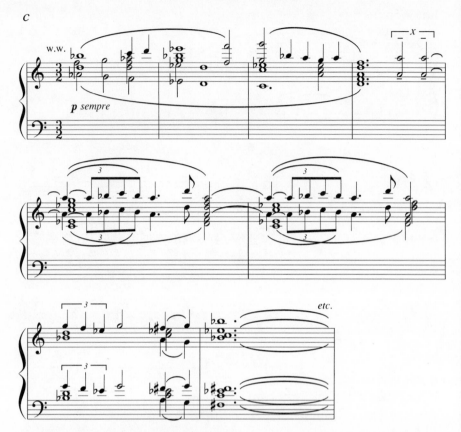

of the apparitions scene in the later opera and defines the type of tone-painting which interested Pfitzner; not for him the wind-machine of Strauss's *Alpensinfonie*, but rather evocation of mood by abstract means, a procedure which nineteenth-century composers such as Schumann would have appreciated as related to their own. The musical language of this most imaginatively conceived journey may seem superficially as Wagnerian as the structural model, but there are traits which suggest a growing independence. The horn music of Example 4.5*a* observes that general principle of Pfitzner's nature music noted by Waltershausen, the avoidance of the nineteenth century's favourite horns fifths.[23] The latter part of Example 4.5*c* has Pfitzner's fondness for melodic lines that circle around a nodal point. The music for the Alps

---

[23] Hermann Wolfgang von Waltershausen, 'Hans Pfitzners Naturgefühl', *FHP* 33.

(and of the progression which approaches it) shows a liking (especially prominent at the start) for chordal movement in root progressions, an archaic touch that crops up also in *Palestrina*. But however characteristic and convincing this section is as a whole, the fact remains that it delays the drama and overshadows the more declamatory music of the doctor. This is not to say that the latter is without interest. In the course of this section, the rising scalar part of Example 4.5*c* is gradually shaped towards the form of Agnes's Example 4.4. The climax, the shattering of Heinrich's hopes, is the occasion for a new transformation of Example 4.2*a* which brings it into a more threatening F minor form; the motive of sickness takes on the force of an anathema partly to counter the space which has been given to Dietrich's adventures, and to the various nature pictures. The problem is a purely dramatic one of an inexperienced composer allowing the musical beauties of a section to overshadow dramatic considerations; but it foreshadows the more serious weakness of the second act by revealing that Pfitzner tended not to equate the sustained musical climax with the dramatic high-point. For that he tended to fall back on more stock gestures.

That Pfitzner may have been conscious of the problem emerges in Act III. Heinrich's storming of the monastery gates is still over-dependent on a music of nervous reaction, but the situation is saved by the emergence of the arch of Example 4.5*c*, not so much a simple motive of the monastery and its inhabitants as a symbol of the grace which has fallen on Heinrich; as proof of this, the motive gathers Agnes's Example 4.4 into one continuous sweep of music. Just as this transfigures a potentially mundane climax, so a variant of it in triple time also marks the climax of the dialogue between Heinrich and Agnes as the ashamed knight attempts to dissuade her from going ahead with the sacrifice. This relatively conventional resort to the power of music contrasts with Pfitzner's surprising attempt to characterize Heinrich's earlier description of Agnes's youth and innocence by a single violin line that wanders for almost forty bars against the voice part, sometimes in unison, sometimes in an uncanny counterpoint which avoids an exact tonal centre and clear-cut cadences, while bringing suggestions of modal organization that are never developed systematically. This unsupported string line seems to belong with the violin line of Brunnhilde's mountain-top in *Siegfried* or the cello line in the 'Grail' scene in Act I of *Parsifal*, though those are far more definite in their harmonic implications. Its combination with the voice suggests the much more agonized dialogue between violins and male voice at the end of the second act of *Moses und Aron*. It is symptomatic of the historical position of *Der arme Heinrich* that this passage hovers between uncomfortable youthful experiment and a genuine and novel inspiration. There is nothing quite like it in later Pfitzner, not even in his famed 'linear' counterpoint (of which this in theory ought to be a good example). The contrapuntal style of the mature Pfitzner is more apparent in the Prelude to Act III, where the monks' singing is foreshadowed in music that points to *Palestrina*. Rhythmic fluidity (particularly in the growth of duplet against triplet motion) and swelling of melodic lines into chord streams, without regular cadential punctuation, goes alongside the deliberately modal touches to create the most distinctive sound in the opera. Act III may be a less convincing whole than Act I, but it contains the more daring moments which presage Pfitzner's later style.

Der arme Heinrich is an internal drama, dependent like *Tristan und Isolde* on growth of character rather than any sensational action; it is psychological in a limited sense (certainly in relation to Hauptmann's drama on the same subject), conditioned by the twin poles of *Ritterlichkeit* and renunciation, which by Pfitzner's time had come dangerously close to operatic cliché. In *Die Rose vom Liebesgarten*, these poles are still apparent, but the characters of a fairy-tale require little psychology, and Siegnot and Minneleide do the conventional things required of hero and heroine in both fairy-tale and opera. One would expect less through-composition in their drama, which would also be consistent with the generic expectations of romantic opera; even *Lohengrin*, the romantic opera closest to music-drama, has its arias and ensembles, choruses and marches—chunks which bleed less obviously than related things in later Wagner. In a limited degree, Pfitzner fulfils expectation. The choral tableaux of the Prologue and Epilogue go far beyond the choruses of the monks in *Der arme Heinrich*. Set pieces occur, most notably for the orchestra in the *Blütenwunder* of the Prologue, and the *Trauermarsch* which begins the Epilogue, both of which Pfitzner extracted for use in the concert hall without doing any real violence to their content. In the Prologue in particular, it is not difficult to see the outlines of a traditional beginning to a romantic opera. After the Introduction's echoing calls, a choral movement is developed in D major; this clearly has a ternary structure: full chorus (D)—semi-chorus (B♭) and soloists (the masters—G)—reprise (orchestra—D). Only the omission of the chorus in the reprise suggests that something historically later than romantic opera is being presented. The subsequent solo music for the masters begins as recitative and grows into more sustained arioso while retaining the motives of the choral movement. After an introduction in G, the procession to the island takes the form of a choral march in D, thus retaining a common tonality for the first scene. Only as the scene changes does the music assume the more motivically complex character of a post-Wagnerian 'symphonic' link. Siegnot's 'Die der Unberührbaren' is more or less a prayer, that favourite genre of nineteenth-century opera. Like a true number, it ends with a conventional perfect cadence (in B) though its opening is more equivocal; that it tends strongly towards the through-composed while being homophonic in texture is no less characteristic of the genre. B major is also the key in which the resumed procession closes. The music of the masters which leads to the *Blütenwunder* again savours at its outset of conventional recitative. Although the harmonic and melodic aura of post-Wagnerian opera is apparent throughout, the unmistakable skeleton of romantic tableau lies underneath: chorus, procession, recitative, set number, pantomime, and supporting it all the key of D major, to which most other tonalities relate by third: B♭, B, and the G♭ of the *Blütenwunder*. It is arguable that here at least Pfitzner comes close to something more 'abstract' than Abendroth's description allowed: for the opening tableau in many operas by Rossini, Weber, Schubert, Schumann, Marschner, and their contemporaries was to a remarkable extent an abstract pattern to which plot was tailored in a conventional way. That Pfitzner writes a variant (whether of music-drama or romantic opera) only becomes obvious in the central acts, though even here he finds opportunities for looking back.

Act I comes closest to opera rather than music-drama in the central section with Minneleide and her entourage, their games of hide-and-seek, and the D major duet for her attendants. Even the protracted duet for Siegnot and Minneleide falls into sections analogous to the large-scale duet of nineteenth-century opera with its contrasting fast and slow sections.

Though the two characters do not sing together, certain sections have the feel of self-contained solo songs, most notably
the F♯ minor strophes, 'Und sahst du die Sterne nicht tausend
Jahr', for Siegnot. In others, the dividing line between a
leitmotif and a section of a small form becomes blurred; ideas
such as Example 4.6 fulfil both functions, with their attrac-

Ex. 4.6

tively naïve periodicity recalling the ambience of Weber
and Marschner. Yet Pfitzner does not move into the much
more folk-like territory of *Hänsel und Gretel*; *Die Rose vom
Liebesgarten* remains a fairy-tale for adults on the same elevated themes as *Der arme Heinrich*, however distanced by its
conventions. As a result, it occupies a far more ambiguous
place in the history of opera after Wagner than many of its
contemporaries. The vein of *Ritterlichkeit* from the earlier
work, frozen into the monumental blocks of the Prologue,
comes closest to the self-contained sections of old-fashioned
opera. The two protagonists and some associates (such as
the Moormann) move in a more obviously Wagnerian world,
though attendant figures remember the traditions of Ännchen
and her kind. Further strands are provided by the role of
nature and the grotesque entourage of the Nacht-Wunderer.
   The nature music on the whole belongs to that long musical
tradition which, by following the view of nature as essentially
unchanging beneath her different manifestations, emphasized
pure stasis. This is most obvious in the very slow chordal drift
of the *Blütenwunder* (which was based on the trio section of
the early String Quartet in D minor), but is also apparent in
the introductory music to the two acts. The landscape on
which the curtain rises in Act I, rocky masses, caves, stream,
and swamp before the primeval wood, is conveyed by an
extended paragraph in F minor in which pedals control the
slow rate of chord change. The wind invades the texture in the

arpeggios which rustle against the chordal background with semitonal dissonance, while the birds and frogs of the stage directions enter into the melodic line; in Example 4.7, the

Ex. 4.7

scalar main theme of the nature music repeatedly breaks into an echoing call on a monotone. 'Waldesrauschen weit und wogend' begins Siegnot, whose awe in the face of nature is not the Oedipal sentimentality of Siegfried but owes rather more to Eichendorff; his conclusion, 'Ach wie schön ist doch die Welt, |'s ist Alles so heimlich, so wohlig bestellt', captures that *Waldeinsamkeit* hymned by Tieck and Eichendorff, with an echo of Lynceus in his tower. The introduction to Act II is more daring. Underground grottoes with their half-light and dripping water produce a remarkable piece of tone-painting in which the motive of the drops of water supplies a continuity in the absence of clearly defined tonality. Chord progressions are as directionless as in the Prelude to *Der arme Heinrich*; they function as sounds in the echoing void rather as do the tuba's chromatic fragments and the strokes of the tam-tam. Brittle combinations of harp and horns, flute and pizzicato strings intensify the atmosphere of this peculiar page.[24] True to his scorn for mere tone-painting, Pfitzner creates here an original and arresting contrapuntal and textural fragment that in addition to conveying a scene also prepares for the contrapuntal extravagances of the Nacht-Wunderer; for it is in this act that Pfitzner the writer of linear counterpoint comes of dramatic age, in a way that inevitably invites comparison with Mahler.

There can be little doubt that when Mahler became acquainted with *Die Rose vom Liebesgarten*, the brittle

---

[24] See Egon Wellesz, *Die neue Instrumentation*, 2 vols. (Berlin-Schöneberg, 1929), ii. 59–62.

orchestration and the sharp motivic fragments of the Nacht-Wunderer's kingdom must have chimed remarkably with his own musical experience. It was long the contention of Egon Wellesz that the thematic material of the Sixth Symphony was indelibly marked by acquaintance with Pfitzner's opera, down to individual motives (for instance, Ex. 4.8); that the

Ex. 4.8

Fifth Symphony's second movement has something of the same atmosphere has been further suggested by Wolfgang Osthoff, though this would require Mahler to have known the work in 1901/2, which is less likely on present evidence.[25] There is certainly something indisputably Mahlerian about the imitative treatment of the march figures in Pfitzner's second act (particularly in the manner in which the brass play a leading melodic role). The comparison also extends to the harsh timbres in which Pfitzner and Mahler set their contrapuntal combinations. The sharp harmonic clashes of the outer movements of the Sixth Symphony occur also in Pfitzner and spring from the sheer density of thematic working in which 'drop motive' and the Nacht-Wunderer's calls are combined to fantastical effect. Both composers provide momentary suggestions of bitonality which are usually found to arise from overlap of harmonic complexes, or from the expansion of line into chord streams in a manner analysed penetratingly by Ernst Kurth in Mahler;[26] Pfitzner's orig-

[25] Egon and Emmy Wellesz, *Egon Wellesz: Leben und Werk*, ed. Franz Endler (Vienna and Hamburg, 1981), 27–9; Wolfgang Osthoff, 'Hans Pfitzners "Rose vom Liebesgarten", Gustav Mahler und die Wiener Schule', *Festschrift Martin Ruhnke: zum 65. Geburtstag* (Neuhausen-Stuttgart, 1986), 265–93.

[26] Ernst Kurth, *Romantische Harmonik und ihre Krise in Wagners 'Tristan'*, 3rd edn. (Berlin, 1923), 368–9.

inality in arriving at such writing independently of Mahler (who was certainly the debtor in this case) has not been so widely appreciated. The Nacht-Wunderer's music approaches the same limits of orchestral virtuosity that Strauss was cultivating in the last decade of the century, and here and there surpasses it in the more functional clarity with which it is deployed. Not without reason has it been compared to the music which the Schoenberg school was to write in the years before the war. The comparison is apparent as early as the first bars of the work; the summons of nature is a rudimentary *Klangfarbenmelodie* as Wellesz and Osthoff have noted, certainly primitive by comparison with Schoenberg's much bolder experiments, but none the less a pointer to the twentieth century's preoccupation with timbre. In this field, Pfitzner was as much an innovator as he was a conservative in relation to the greater cultivation of rhythmic freedom that would climax in the orchestral pieces of the Second Viennese School, and in the ballets of Stravinsky and Bartók.

In the counterpoint of the Nacht-Wunderer scene, Pfitzner established a style which was to come to fruition in the central act of *Palestrina*. By then, a contrapuntal mode of organization would be more widespread in his music. It is not quite enough to equate the grotesques of *Die Rose vom Liebesgarten* with the world of affairs in *Palestrina*. None the less, the scene played an important part in his output in helping to dissolve that easy association of suffering and catastrophe with the chromatic language of late Wagner apparent in *Der arme Heinrich*. As a result, Pfitzner left the knightly ethos with its high-minded idealism and pious suffering behind with the nineties, as far as the operatic stage was concerned. Only much later in *Das Herz* did it reappear. In this Pfitzner followed a trend also apparent in the operas of his contemporaries. The knightly world of Wagnerian epic was attractive to others, too. D'Albert's *Gernot* (and to a lesser extent *Ghismonda*), Strauss's *Guntram*, and Schillings' *Ingewelde* all stood in this tradition as strongly as *Der arme Heinrich*. Although Pfitzner himself noted that 'the eclectic d'Albert' later 'went his own way' (*SS IV* 107), the residue of Wagnerism apparent even in the supposedly Byronic *Kain* shows how hard the path to verismo was for the latter.[27] The

---

[27] John Williamson, 'Eugen d'Albert: Wagner and *Verismo*', *Music Review*, 45 (1984), 30–3.

historical dilemma for these opera composers was twofold. In the technical sphere few had the nerve to revert unequivocally to a number opera, either in an old-fashioned sense or in the manner advocated by Busoni, for whom new forms were to take the place of those conditioned by pre-established moulds. More fundamentally, they still moved within that atmosphere of renunciation and redemption that Wagner had popularized and buttressed with selective interpretation of Schopenhauer. When Strauss moved decisively outside this in the third act of *Guntram*, following an ideology that has been traced (not without controversy) to the individualism of Nietzsche, Stirner, and John Henry Mackay, the result was a bitter quarrel with his hitherto revered master, Alexander Ritter.[28] Nietzsche's own prescription for the 'Mediterraneanization' of music had few outright followers in German opera; the example of Wolf's *Der Corregidor*, in which Wagnerian through-composition and the individual number sat in unhappy proximity, was unpropitious. Comic opera of a stylized kind was to be a salvation in the end for both d'Albert (*Die Abreise*) and Strauss (*Feuersnot*); Pfitzner, however, in *Palestrina* chose to fashion his own kind of Schopenhauerian drama, in a spirit arguably closer to the philosopher than Wagner, and in this the knightly ethos had no place (apart from the invisible character of the Holy Roman Emperor himself).

It is not too rash a simplification to maintain that the musical language of the outer acts of *Palestrina* grew out of the style of *Der arme Heinrich*, while that of the second reflected the contrapuntal style of the Nacht-Wunderer's kingdom. But the second act of *Palestrina* also has certain points of contact with 'romantic opera', in the music associated with Ferdinand and his son Maximilian. That the ethos of romantic opera continued to haunt Pfitzner's imagination emerges in his incidental music. Music for plays by Kleist and Ilse von Stach absorbed him between *Die Rose vom Liebesgarten* and *Palestrina*, though in relatively distinct ways. The knightly ethos predominated in the music for *Das Käthchen von Heilbronn*, which provided him with an opportunity to pay tribute to the world of romance unencumbered by the needs of opera.[29] In particular, the overture represents

---

[28] Willi Schuh, *Richard Strauss: A Chronicle of the Early Years 1864–1898*, trans. Mary Whittall (Cambridge, 1982), 269 and 293–7.

[29] See Reinhard Seebohm, 'Das Rittertum in der Musik von Weber bis Pfitzner', *MPG* 30 (Mar. 1973), 2–13.

a distillation of a type of chivalry that was at once old-fashioned among creative artists and yet contemporary through the growing interest in Kleist. His play, with its knightly hero and chaste heroine, witch-like villainess, secret courts, cherub, and somnambulism, is close enough to the world of romantic opera, closer perhaps than to the psychologically more modern dramas of *Penthesilea* and *Prinz Friedrich von Homburg*. The music which Pfitzner supplied for it is his most fitting tribute to the age of Weber and Marschner. The music for Ilse von Stach's *Das Christ-Elflein* may be seen as a complementary tribute to Lortzing. As a fairy-tale, it stands closer to Lortzing's generation than to *Hänsel und Gretel* or *Königskinder*. Yet in its first version, it is a fairy-tale with an element of tragedy; just as Humperdinck's royal children die in the snow, so Trautchen in *Das Christ-Elflein* dies in order that her brother Frieder may come to be saved. The whiff of Wagnerian redemption through woman's love, however, produces only passing hints of his style; in general Pfitzner's small orchestra, which is handled with great restraint, does not aspire to the rather involved counterpoint that here and there is a striking feature of Humperdinck's style.

The plot as Stach originally conceived it is not without echoes of *Die Rose vom Liebesgarten*, ending (if not beginning) in a paradise, though explicitly a Christian one; in Abendroth's account, it seems to have been Pfitzner who urged that he compose the music as early as 1901, the year of the first performance of *Die Rose vom Liebesgarten*.[30] When the work first appeared in 1906, dramatically it was the creation of Stach with Pfitzner content merely to supply punctuating melodramas and songs; the interest in melodrama, so pronounced in *Das Fest auf Solhaug*, had re-emerged in the last number of the Kleist incidental music. Stach's rather sticky parable, in which human characters are surrounded by a panoply of Christian and nature spirits, was a tableau of reconciliation. The human drama is slight, amounting to a parable of unbelief and conversion. Frieder and Trautchen, the children of Herr Gumpach, have been brought up to believe in Christmas. But Frieder has lost his faith and is converted only by Trautchen's illness and death. Around this situation, Stach set archangels and the Christ-child, but also more ancient pagan spirits such as the eponymous elf and the

---

[30] Abendroth, *Hans Pfitzner*, 118.

tutelary deity of the woods, an ancient fir tree who under-
standably shares none of the human delight in cutting down
trees for Christmas; mediating between the Christian and
nature deities is the seeming sorcerer, the traditional Knecht
Ruprecht with his sack full of presents. When Trautchen dies,
the elf follows her to heaven, where it receives an immortal
soul, becoming the Christ-elf (while Trautchen's parents are
comforted by a new baby daughter). The third tableau in
heaven in particular is a dramatic delaying action, with
archangels and elf in disputation about the soul, and Knecht
Ruprecht fulfilling his burlesque duty. Its only real relevance
to the human drama is in communicating the news that
Frieder has started to pray. It is hardly surprising that when
Pfitzner conceived the idea of revising the incidental music
into a *Spieloper* in the summer of 1917 (after the first performance of *Palestrina* in Munich), he jettisoned the third
scene and created a happy ending, which removed some of the
most pretentious verbiage in Stach's play and eliminated
several unnecessary characters. The elf receives a soul from
the Christ-child and ascends to heaven in order to provide
God with the soul which he expects (a most curious touch),
and Trautchen recovers from her illness. To make for a general happy ending, the elf is allowed to visit the ancient fir
tree (who includes elves among his entourage) each Christmas
Eve. With the music for Trautchen's death eliminated, the
motive of sickness becomes a less oppressive factor, and
results in a general lightening of the tone of the work.

Both *Das Christ-Elflein* and *Das Käthchen von Heilbronn*
represent, in the main, the diatonic pole of Pfitzner's art.
The qualification is necessary, since the most striking music
in both works is chromatic. The two overtures, which rank
amongst Pfitzner's most open and accessible works, serve
to illustrate the point, if only because Pfitzner followed the
practice of Weber and Marschner in relating the material of
his overtures to that of the later numbers. The Kleist Overture has the loosest relationship to sonata form: although
a tonal and thematic conflict is preserved (based on C and
E majors), the key areas are allowed to grow into distinct
sections with a programmatic purpose. In Pfitzner's elucida-
tion of the score, the opening section leads from 'a world full
of brutally healthy chivalry . . . [into] the "ruined ring of walls
where a twittering siskin built her nest in a sweet-smelling
elder bush"', the heroine's favourite place (*SS IV* 415). The

ensuing section in E, by virtue of its citation of Käthchen's 'mein hoher Herr' (with which she apostrophizes the hero, Wetter vom Strahl), is a portrayal of the heroine. There follows Strahl's feverish dream in which a cherub reveals that the heroine is a daughter of the Emperor, before the resumption of the opening material depicts Strahl 'returned to life in full vigour'. Even the poisoning temptress, Kunigunde, is present in the trombone fanfare, to the rhythm of Strahl's 'Giftmischerin!', which cuts across the final C major with an Ab. The diatonic ideas form the substance of much that follows in the incidental music. 'Mein hoher Herr' reappears in the Prelude to Act III and the 'Melodrama—Zwischenaktsmusik und Marsch'; the E major melody in the latter and in the 'Nach der Hollunderbuschscene'. The latter is a continuation, for much of its length, of the style of the hero's music in the Overture; even the fanfare for trumpets which in the Overture supplants Strahl's theme at the return of C major (a typical example of the traditional freedom with which the overture handled sonata form) appears in the final march. But the Overture also has moments when the external appearance of *Ritterlichkeit* dissolves into something more ambiguous. The idea of a transition section becomes a fantasy on mysterious brass fanfares. Even more episodic is what may be termed the exposition's closing section in E minor, the representation of Strahl's dream. The most remarkable music in the score, it moves beyond the feverish slumbers of Margit and Heinrich to create a momentary illusion of bitonality dependent on an E minor ostinato with prominent A♯ and D♯; the brass read these enharmonically to introduce in Eb major the fanfare from the march. Such 'paper bitonality' is not unknown in Mahler, but once again appears in its most extreme form in works like the Ninth Symphony, which was written rather later than Pfitzner's Overture.[31] The contrapuntal nature of the bitonality lends a distinct tone to this dream section; the depiction of spiritual sickness possesses greater concreteness than the post-Wagnerian chromaticism of earlier works, and

[31] The Overtures to *Das Käthchen von Heilbronn* and *Das Christ-Elflein* both featured in Mahler's concert programmes in New York in 1910 and 1911 (Knud Martner, *Gustav Mahler im Konzertsaal: Eine Dokumentation seiner Konzerttätigkeit 1870–1911* (Copenhagen, 1985), 131 and 145–7); accounts of the Kleist overture's reception as the 'ultra-modern' work of a 'would-be follower of Richard Strauss' may be found in Zoltan Roman, *Gustav Mahler's American Years 1907–1911: A Documentary History* (New York, 1988), 438.

suggests that Pfitzner, like Mahler and even his rival Busoni, was finding a style appropriate to what Wolfgang Osthoff has termed 'the historical state of the material' (a phrase borrowed with reservations from Adorno).[32]

With the Overture to *Das Christ-Elflein*, the potpourri elements are less marked. The various ideas recur with such persistence in the drama, particularly, but not exclusively, in the later version, that the impression is more of a symphonic web created out of motives appropriate to the various characters. Thus the introduction uses music associated with the Christ-child and Heaven in general; the main themes of the Allegro are the representation motives of the fir tree (in E minor) and the elf (in G major). The most episodic moment again provides the most serious music; Trautchen's themes are embedded in the development and provide in density of texture and chromatic coloration a foretaste of the Prelude to Act III of *Palestrina*; its heavy-dragging upbeat groups are also present. But just as the bitonality in the Kleist Overture is illusory since E minor is not seriously threatened, so this intrusion of brooding chromaticism dissolves into delicate flute and string textures which hint more clearly at the real nature of *Das Christ-Elflein*. It is in many ways the apotheosis of Pfitzner's interest in folk-like material. This recognition brings the traditional problem of categorizing German folk-song, which so persistently fails to exhibit the modal or rhythmic characteristics that render Magyar and Slav idioms eminently recognizable. The folk- and art-music of Germany lived in sufficiently close contact for the Classical era, in particular, to incorporate the former with little effort as a distinct strand, typified by Papageno, whose spiritual presence in *Die Rose vom Liebesgarten* takes on musical flesh and blood in Knecht Ruprecht's songs in *Das Christ-Elflein*. Diatonic melodies, four-square phrasing, and a certain primitiveness of rhythm trace a definite ancestry which also embraces much in Weber, as well as Hans Sachs's cobbling song in *Die Meistersinger*. From Brahms Pfitzner learned the further lesson of how such primitive material might be given a patina of sophistication. In the fir tree's 'invocation', in which he urges his fellow trees and the elves to disguise the humans' paths through the woods, the melody of 'O

---

[32] Wolfgang Osthoff, 'Pfitzner und der "historische Materialstand"', *SPB* 115–46; 132–46 contains an account of the episode in the overture.

Table 1   The Two Versions of *Das Christ-Elflein*

Opus 20 (1906)	Opus 54* (1917)
Weihnachtsmärchen	*Spieloper in zwei Akten*
Overture	unchanged
Erster Aufzug	*Erster Akt*
[No. 1]†	No. 1

This is initially unchanged, save for the replacement of melodrama by sung text; some expansion takes place in 1917; the voice part for the Tannengreis is new in 6/8, as is the section from 'Leicht, flott' (1917, p. 33).

[No. 2]	No. 2

A little expansion takes place in 1917; the accompaniment to the violins at *C* and the section in quadruple time are new in 1917; melodrama is replaced by sung text.

[No. 3]	No. 3 (unchanged)
[Nos. 4 and 5]	No. 4

A linking section (p. 50, bar 1 to p. 54, bar 16) is new in 1917, as is the section from *M* in 1917 (the latter replacing dialogue with two bars of music); from 'Mehr als das doppelte so langsam' considerable expansion takes place to cope with the change from melodrama to sung text.

[No. 6]	No. 5

Melodrama becomes song, with modifications to the text.

[No. 7]	No. 6

The Tannengreis speaks in 1906, sings in 1917; the elf speaks in both.

Zweiter Aufzug	*Zweiter Akt*
Einleitung	unchanged
Dialogue	This now incorporates Nos. 7 and 8.
[No. 8]	No. 9

Trautchen's words in 1917 are added.

[No. 9]

Table 1 *Continued*

Trautchen's death scene is omitted in 1917.

Nos. 10, 11 and 12. These are new, arising from the altered ending.

Dritter Aufzug

| [No. 10] | No. 13 |

The solo voice parts in 1917 are new.

| [No. 11] | No. 14 |

The words and characters are new until Trautchen's 'Ach!' (1917, p. 149).

* For reasons unclear to Pfitzner scholarship, the recent reissue of the revised version has been described as Opus 54 by the publisher; that of course is the opus number of *Krakauer Begrüssung* (see Worklist).
† The movements in Opus 20 are not numbered.

Tannenbaum' rings out without incongruity; Christmas is not such fun if you are a tree. The various choruses and dances are the clearest illustration of the developmental capacity of the folk-like; the rondo theme of the D major quartet becomes a chorus of cherubim and stands for the whole nexus of folk-like, 'neoclassicizing' diatonicism. Where the chromatic impinges, the manner recalls Strauss, particularly in the suggestion of archaizing. The very opening of the overture anticipates the style in which Strauss was to re-create the diatonic world after *Elektra*, particularly in the cadence with a rise to the third of the scale. There is nothing to suggest that Pfitzner took this peculiarly German brand of *Gemütlichkeit* with anything less than the seriousness that he bestowed on *Der arme Heinrich*. A letter of 27 April 1917 states most emphatically that he rated *Das Christ-Elflein* as highly as anything he had written, and wanted to revise it in order to save it from its 'Zwitterform'.[33] It is the bedrock of his style, the point at which he seemed to come in musical contact with the *Volk* that his prose works took as an ideal. That his musical individuality is to some extent swallowed by it is irrelevant; it is merely subsumed in an ideal community that was already in danger of seeming a myth.

[33] Bernhard Adamy, 'Pfitzner und der Verlag Adolph Fürstner', *MPG* 43 (Sept. 1981), 34–5.

Das Christ-Elflein is not simply a succession of diatonic songs, inasmuch as the revision of 1917 faced a fundamental problem with two possible answers. The melodramas could either be turned into pure spoken dialogue (legitimate enough in a *Spieloper*), or they could become musical conversation pieces and songs, with the implication of a measure of through-composition. By taking the second option (see Table 1), Pfitzner gave the whole a greater substance and disguised in a measure the simplicity of the original conception. But fundamentally the work remains a statement of basic themes that were only a residue in the much greater 'musical legend' that both followed and preceded it. In a sense, *Das Christ-Elflein* is the sport that made *Palestrina* possible.

5

Palestrina

FOR most musicians outside the German-speaking world, Pfitzner's name lives through his third music-drama, *Palestrina*. Deservedly this stands unchallenged as the peak of his art; *Palestrina* is not merely a music-drama (or musical legend, to use Pfitzner's description), but a reflection (not a representation) of the *Weltanschauung* expressed in the composer's prose works. It has been compared on dramatic grounds with the masterwork of his rival, Busoni's *Doktor Faust*, but whatever the general validity of such comparison, major qualifications have to be expressed.[1] *Doktor Faust* was in every sense the climax of Busoni's career, towards which the majority of his later compositions pointed and contributed as sketches and material. Appropriately it stands at the end of Busoni's life; in keeping with the speculative nature of Busoni's genius, it remained unfinished largely because of its hubristic attempt to evoke an unattainable ideal of beauty symbolized by Helen.[2] *Palestrina* in contrast stands in the middle of Pfitzner's career, inaugurating a further period of intense creativity which was to include the highly ambitious cantatas *Von deutscher Seele* and *Das dunkle Reich*, and the opera *Das Herz*. Both *Doktor Faust* and *Palestrina* were products of long periods of gestation, but whereas Busoni's opera fed cannibalistically on its composer's other works, *Palestrina* is quite self-sufficient, marked only by occasional references to Pfitzner's earlier works, the most significant of which is a clear quotation of the opening motive from *Der arme Heinrich* at Cardinal Borromeo's words to Palestrina, 'Ihr scheint mir krank in eurer Seele|Seit langem schon'; a continuity in the soul-states of Pfitzner's two most interesting operatic heroes is thus underlined.

[1] The comparison may be found, for instance, in the comments of Dietrich Fischer-Dieskau in the booklet accompanying the recording of *Palestrina*, DG Stereo 2711 013, [p. 10].
[2] Anthony Beaumont, *Busoni the Composer* (London, 1985), 347; 'Busoni's *Doktor Faust*: A Reconstruction and its problems', *Musical Times*, 127 (1986), 196–9.

The creation of *Palestrina* stretched over two decades. Initially it was a tentative business, dominated by the search for a librettist until the decisive moment when Pfitzner realized what had been implicit in his historical researches from the beginning and resolved to be his own poet. The subject came to his attention in Mainz, possibly in 1895 (the year of the first performances of *Der arme Heinrich* and *Das Fest auf Solhaug*) through reading Ambros's *Geschichte der Musik*.[3] The initial stimulus thus pre-dates *Die Rose vom Liebesgarten*, whose composition falls entirely within the period when *Palestrina* was little more than an idea. By 1897, Pfitzner must have accomplished much of the reading of accounts of the Council of Trent by Sarpi and Pallavicini which was his next declared stage in the process (*SS IV* 423). Negotiations then began with possible librettists. Initially he remained faithful to the tried and tested Grun; discussions probably took place in England in 1899 while Pfitzner was living at Herne Bay in order to satisfy residence requirements for his marriage to Mimi at Canterbury.[4] The focus of attention then shifted to Richard Voss, the Berlin novelist and essayist. By 1903, Pfitzner had almost decided on collaborating with Ilse von Stach. In a letter to Cossmann of 9 May, enthusiasm for the project vied with a sense of apprehension about his prospective colleague:

I have a poem, namely *Palestrina*. As was foreseen, it is not what I had in mind, but only I and no other could have done it as I imagined it, not even Grun. Why am I no poet? But I have read it with great emotion and am inflamed by it, and I shall compose it. Because Ilse is very amenable to reason and writes very fluently, it is also probable that the poem will come much closer to my ideal image; Ilse has already accepted a few important matters from my ideas and will carry them through; we shall still keep going in this fashion and get, I hope, a very good book. (*RSB* 293–4)

Pfitzner did not set Stach's poem, however, but collaborated with her on *Das Christ-Elflein*. In his essay on *Palestrina*, he dismissed her efforts by noting that she placed at the centre of the action a marriage between Palestrina's daughter and one of his pupils (*SS IV* 422). What emerges most clearly from the letter to Cossmann is less the contribution of Stach than the

---

[3] All references here are to August Wilhelm Ambros, *Geschichte der Musik*, 3rd edn., vol. 4, ed. Gustav Nottebohm, rev. Hugo Leichentritt (Leipzig, 1909), though obviously Pfitzner must have read an earlier edition.

[4] Bernhard Adamy, 'Das *Palestrina*-Textbuch als Dichtung', *SPB* 25.

notion of an *Idealbild* with which Pfitzner confronted his potential collaborators. What concerned him was not a historical incident that could be turned into tableau opera of the Meyerbeer type, which is not to say that elements of tableau are completely lacking in *Palestrina* (particularly in Act II), nor that Pfitzner failed to take the historical background to the opera seriously. The same letter continued: '...I must study the music (and the *history*) of this period and immerse myself in it so that it is in my blood, and from the mists of the conjuring-up of the period musical visions must appear to me'. Such study was to be subservient at all times to the ideal image which he had derived from reading Ambros. From Ambros to *Palestrina* was from history to ideal. The term 'musical legend' documented this shift. Legend did not imply fairy-tale, a term Pfitzner quoted from Ambros in dismissing Pope Marcellus II from the circumstances of the composition of the mass that bears his name; modern musical scholarship, admittedly, has been less confident in accepting this dismissal.[5] Legend implied an ideal poetic reworking of events that had some historical basis according to Pfitzner's sources. The central situation was to be the (greatly exaggerated) threat to polyphonic church music expressed at the Council of Trent. That Pfitzner followed the tradition which saw Palestrina as the instrument of saving church music was less a matter of history than a consequence of the 'particularly secret and peculiar light' which fell on the Roman master as the young Mainz conductor read Ambros (*SS IV* 421). It is thus legitimate to speak of a historical theme masking a particular vision of a genius that shaded into a general picture of what genius ought to be.

For Pfitzner, a principal attraction of Palestrina as hero was the relative indifference with which he was treated in his own time. Some popes, like Marcellus, treated him with favour. Others, like Paul IV, treated him badly, as when he was dismissed from the papal singers on account of his second marriage (*SS IV* 418–19). Palestrina thus became the type of the unrecognized genius devoted in obscurity to his art. That he lived in the shadows was almost a prerequisite of the ideal

---

[5] E.g. Hermann J. Busch (ed.), Preface to Giovanni Francesco Anerio and Francesco Soriano, *Two Settings of Palestrina's 'Missa Papae Marcelli'* (Madison, Wis., 1973), 5; see also Knud Jeppesen, 'Marcellus-Probleme: Einige Bemerkungen über die Missa Papae Marcelli des Giovanni Pierluigi da Palestrina', *Acta Musicologica*, 16/17 (1944/45), 28–9.

image, for the drama concentrated on the one moment when he stepped into the light of history (SS IV 421). But *Palestrina* was not simply to be a work about neglect and vindication. He stood alone in Pfitzner's eyes in a period of 'the degeneration of musical style, i.e. increase of voices, the growth of artificiality and mannerism, the obscuring of the text of the mass, etc.' (SS IV 420). That his music opposed this tide represented Palestrina's greatest importance; by opposing the decadence of a style, he triumphantly carried aloft a tradition sanctified by its past. It is almost too simple to say that Pfitzner identified with his hero. It would be more accurate to say that he represented a model for the operation of the 'pure intellectual spirit' that ought to justify art's innocence in the face of the Will-dominated chaos of history. Each of Pfitzner's operatic heroes to date had in some measure sacrificed himself in an act of renunciation that formed the climax of the work concerned. With Palestrina, a renunciatory bearing was part of Pfitzner's image from the start.

From Ambros, Pfitzner knew of supposed events in the life of Palestrina that post-dated the Council of Trent.[6] In the closing stages of that famous assembly, the issue of the reform of abuses in church music had played a part important enough to be mentioned in a letter from the Emperor Ferdinand I to the Council. It has been assumed (quite plausibly, but without firm evidence) that Palestrina entered the picture after the conclusion of the Council in 1563. Pope Pius IV placed the issue of the reform of church music in the hands of a group of Cardinals, prominent among whom were Vitellio Vitellozzo and Carlo Borromeo, the Pope's nephew. The task of writing test-pieces to prove the viability of polyphonic music for the ritual fell on Palestrina among others. He responded with three masses, of which one was the *Missa Papae Marcelli*. Ambros was quite clear that these masses were written for a specific purpose (much clearer than the actual evidence suggests), and that the *Missa Papae Marcelli* was performed before Pius. Whatever the validity of this as an accurate picture of history, it provided Pfitzner with the germ of his drama: Palestrina responded to a crisis of musical history and 'saved' the musical tradition of which he was part. Pfitzner's own description of the inspiring conjunction of ideas, written down after the work's completion, illustrates the salient points of the drama.

[6] Ambros, *Geschichte der Musik*, 17–20.

In the face of the world's threat to sweep away the polyphonic art of the past on account of the sins of the present, 'There went out to him, Palestrina, the cry, save music! It is as if the hands of his predecessors, who like him had lived, created, struggled, and worked, stretched out of the grave and called to him: you who are of our spirit, save our work' (*SS IV* 421). The implication is clear, the act of the present justifies (in the sense of saving) the tradition in which the artist worked. There can be no doubt that this was an essential part of Pfitzner's ideal image from the start, even though presented here as an 'as if'.

At the heart of this ideal image stands the twin symbol of the great artist and the great work; the work not only stood in a tradition, it renewed it (the *Missa Papae Marcelli* traditionally has been depicted as a clarification of Palestrina's style[7]). The essence of the drama lay in the interaction of this symbol with the world, which, for intensification, Pfitzner came to broaden from Pius IV and his cardinals to the Council of Trent itself.

That two worlds, so to speak, had to come into play against each other as factors in the action was clear to me from the beginning: the external one with its loud, wild commotion which unfolded in the temporal state, what we simply call 'the world', and the other still, inner one which seeks eternity in the heart of the creative human being. This one produces the work of genius, not at the command of the first world, but also not against its will, rather beyond and outside the first, in obedience to quite different laws from those that operate in 'the world'.

These two worlds thus must also be expressed in the form of the work. They formed the real action. So I saw then, before I knew it exactly, what had to happen in the individual acts, a kind of formal triptych: first and third acts for the authentic world of Palestrina, and in between, the image of the outer world's restless activity which is always at enmity with the still creativity of genius. This could only be the Council, the starting-point of the resolutions against art. (*SS IV* 422)

Pfitzner's ideal image implied an unresolvable contrast between Schopenhauer's life of the spirit and the blood-stained world, a contrast which became dramatic at the point where they touched, the Council's resolution (not now the Pope's) to have a trial work commissioned, and Palestrina's

---

[7] Busch, Preface, 5 and 9.

resulting composition of a mass (no longer three). The form proceeded from the fact that the mass operated in two different spheres, in one of which Palestrina was a mere subject, in the other a master.

The problem of the libretto was in large measure the problem of the mass. The composition of an opera about the creation of a piece of music was not without precedent. *Die Meistersinger* provided the most obvious encouragement in that it climaxed in the performance of a song whose composition had been witnessed step by step throughout the last act. The problem for Pfitzner was that the work in his case was an existing masterpiece in a style quite alien to his own. How Grun would have dealt with the problem emerges in a letter of Pfitzner to Richard Specht in which he noted that Grun wanted to deal with the mass in church. Frances Grun gives some indication of how her brother conceived the drama.

James's draft was conceived as a one-act drama and took place in church, where a mass by Palestrina should be performed before the Pope and the entire college of cardinals, so that a decision might be reached as to whether polyphonic music should henceforth be excluded from the service of God or not. Celestial powers intervened in the performance of Palestrina's mass and helped the music to victory. From all parts of the church, the great angelic figures joined in the praise of God with song and trombones. The columns shook, and from the heights and from the crypts there came wonderful song and sound.—The sketch made a great impression on me. I particularly loved the moment when the great angels put their silver trombones to their lips in the *Sanctus*, all the icons and figures around the tabernacle seemed to come to life, and even the saints carved in stone raised their voices out of the gate and the tower.[8]

Voss's part in formulating Pfitzner's solution is described by Pfitzner himself. 'Voss declared the idea dramatically impractical because he simply took the *performance* of the mass as the only possible climax of the drama. It is possible that I came to solve the problem of the mass in my own way because of his decided opinion.'[9] According to the experienced man of the theatre,

[8] Walter Kreuzberg (ed.), *Hans Thoma und Frances Grun* (Frankfurt am Main, 1957), 26–7.
[9] Adamy, 'Das *Palestrina*-Textbuch als Dichtung', 25.

...this material may actually not be susceptible to drama. For either I must take the entire *Missa Papae Marcelli* by the historical Palestrina as it stands into the opera, or I must recompose it, because the performance of the mass on stage must represent the climax and close of the work; and both might be impossible. Naturally I don't know any longer, but it might have been precisely this opinion, which the professional dramatist expounded with such certainty, that led me to the idea that it must be exactly not the performance of the mass that represented the closing-point of the work, nor the climax either; instead this climax must be the *conception* of the work. (*SS IV* 422–3)

So surely does this chime with Pfitzner's emphasis elsewhere on the primacy of inspiration that it is slightly surprising that it should have taken him so long to sense the dramatic point of the close of Act I.

According to Pfitzner's most substantial essay on *Palestrina*, the fourth possible collaborator was another typical lady who put the composer's wife at the centre of the action (*SS IV* 422). This does some injustice, however, to the writer who helped to turn the 'as if' of Palestrina's forerunners in the great tradition into a dramatic idea. Therese Rie was a Viennese novelist and journalist (who contributed to Richard Specht's *Der Merker*), known to the public by her pseudonym, L. Andro. Of late she has enjoyed some attention in La Grange's biography of Mahler, in Adamy's important essay on the libretto of *Palestrina*, and in Elisabeth Wamlek-Junk's documentary volume on Pfitzner's Viennese circle.[10] This circle formed around the performances of *Die Rose vom Liebesgarten* under Mahler's direction in 1905, and centred on Victor Junk, who combined the careers of literary scholar and musician. A close friend of Junk, Rie raised the possibility of collaborating with Pfitzner by sending him a libretto, *Sonnenwende*, in the months following the Viennese performances.[11] Pfitzner declined the libretto, not unkindly, and Rie was drawn into the propaganda on the composer's behalf carried on by Junk and others. In 1909, Pfitzner began seriously to prepare for the

---

[10] Henry-Louis de La Grange, *Gustav Mahler*, 3 vols. (Paris, 1979–84), ii. 1034–5, iii. 120, 126, 329, 505; for Adamy, see above, n. 4; Elisabeth Wamlek-Junk, *Hans Pfitzner und Wien: Sein Briefwechsel mit Victor Junk und andere Dokumente* (Tutzing, 1986).

[11] All references to Rie's essay on her relations with Pfitzner are taken from Wamlek-Junk, *Hans Pfitzner und Wien*, 153–81; Wamlek-Junk also publishes substantially more extracts from Rie's *Palestrina* libretto than Adamy. References to Victor Junk's letter of 9 Oct. 1924 are given as in *Hans Pfitzner und Wien*, 33–6.

writing of *Palestrina*. This was the time at which he made his own annotated copy of the *Missa Papae Marcelli*.[12] On 30 May, he wrote to Rie complaining that 'the image will not concentrate into a "conception"', and appealed for her help as a poet. A further letter of 4 June asked not for details 'but the necessary starting-point for everything'. What Pfitzner proposed was exactly the same kind of collaboration that he had envisaged with Stach, beginning with a personal meeting in Munich in mid-July.

We were together then only for a few days and he elaborated on his plans to me while walking in the English Garden. I now come to the most important and at the same time the subtlest point of my statement. At that time, Pfitzner still had no other idea of his *Palestrina* than the facts that stood in that textbook of music history: the Tridentine Council's ban and Palestrina's resolve to save music; behind these he still felt something deeper which had not yet been shaped for him, not even in the draft texts which Georg Hirschfeld and Richard Voss had already attempted for him.[13] Palestrina fully realized that he would have to accomplish his task for the sake of the masters of the past, *but that the masters would appear in person and demand it of him had not yet occurred to Pfitzner!* This, however, immediately struck me as the dramatic and spiritual starting-point of the whole business. Still in the same night, like a vision, this and only this scene formed in me: how his wife returned from the grave to bring him the masters of the past, how the angels sang for him, and even a suggestion of the conclusion, how the pupils doubted the value of the aged master's creation, leading to 'day'. I sent the scene to P[fitzner] at Gossensass and received the following telegram: 'Am entranced, more, more, please your address'.

Subsequent correspondence shows that Pfitzner was not so entranced as to have lost his critical faculties: 'Only Palestrina at the centre, no counterpart of equal rank'. That this concerns the role of Palestrina's wife Lukrezia is clear from comparison of Rie's draft with the final libretto. Whereas Lukrezia appears in the latter at the height of the angels' scene and leads to a momentary drop in tension (*Tb* 23), Rie's Lukrezia led the apparition scene and acted as muse in the following scene with the angels. Thus far, Pfitzner's later complaint

---

[12] Wolfgang Osthoff, 'Eine neue Quelle zu Palestrinazitat und Palestrinasatz in Pfitzners musikalischer Legende', *Renaissance-Studien: Helmuth Osthoff zum 80. Geburtstag*, ed. Ludwig Finscher (Tutzing, 1979), 187–9.

[13] The role of Hirschfeld is a minor puzzle which the references in Wamlek-Junk do not clarify (*Hans Pfitzner in Wien*, 157–8, 233).

about Rie's libretto is consistent with her story. Rie, however, had a bigger claim that struck Junk at the time as just. After comparing the differences between Rie's draft and Pfitzner's libretto ('the construction of the entire apparition scene, the more vividly shaped Borromeo, the individualization of the masters, the human and artistic deepening of all characters, especially Palestrina himself; and then the sphere of the other-worldly, your dawning and growing pale, the note of resignation, the world-weariness, and lastly beauties of language like the wonderful comparison of the Creator with a goldsmith'), he noted the similarities: 'the setting with the pupils' scenes coiled round the apparition scenes, then the apparition scene itself as a dramatic image, the role of the angels, the figure of Lukrezia, etc.' Junk was driven to conclude that Rie had 'shaped for the first time the idea—your idea—to a living dramatic image'. But Junk was writing in 1924, after the relationship between Pfitzner and Rie had degenerated into rumours and charges of plagiarism.

Of Rie's lines Pfitzner used only one, turning 'Ich bin ein todesmüder, alter Mann' into 'Ich bin ein alter, todesmüder Mann' (*Tb* 19). Of the sketches Rie made for Act II Pfitzner made no use, complaining that Rie's scheme with Palestrina confronted by a group of cardinals (including Borromeo and Vitellozzo) left nothing for the last act. Obviously Pfitzner was too committed to the form inherent in the 'two worlds' to accept any compromise; the form was of a piece with the ideal image. By 4 August, when Pfitzner rejected the sketches for Act II in a considerate fashion, Rie had clearly been consigned in his mind to the same category as Voss and Stach. A monologue for the hero which Rie sent Pfitzner in 1911 made no difference since Pfitzner had already written his libretto. Rie's conception must have struck him anew as at odds with his own, her monologue being full of nature imagery worthy of Dietrich's Narration, whereas the monologue of Palestrina in Act I was to be built around an image of human desolation derived from Dante's dark wood.[14] Pfitzner, Rie claimed, promised her (and this seems scarcely credible) that her monologue would be printed at the front the score. When

[14] Ludwig Schrott, '*Divina Commedia* im *Palestrina*', MPG 32 (1974), 36–9; Wolfgang Osthoff, 'Pfitzner—Goethe—Italien: Die Wurzeln des Silla-Liedchens im *Palestrina*', *Analecta Musicologica*, 17 (1976), 195–6; see also Wolfgang Osthoff, 'Palestrina e la leggenda musicale di Pfitzner', Proceedings of *Palestrina e l'Europa*, (Rome, 1991), 529–68.

the libretto was published in a limited edition for Pfitzner's friends, Rie was astonished to discover not only no monologue but that 'my closing scene for Act I was used here, admittedly with altered words, but complete enough in construction, mood, and curtain'. Here was the origin of the breach between Pfitzner and Rie, publicized not by Rie herself, but by Elsa Bienenfeld, who tactlessly wrote in the *Wiener Journal* that 'the most dramatically effective scene did not exactly derive from him' (which was, however, a fair reflection of Rie's opinion).

Rie's apparition scene was a three-sided affair between the soul-weary Palestrina, the inspiring shade of Lukrezia, and the supplicating masters of the past. Their pleas were dominated by contrasts between their condition ('Verloren in der ungeheuern Leere') and his ('du lebst in Licht'); music was 'Das wunderbare Märchenreich der Seele', a formula that might well have made an initial impression on Pfitzner; the masters' claim on Palestrina is twofold: that he lives, and, 'What would you be without music?'. What was missing was an adequate image of the prime cause, the origin of creativity itself and the source of the apparitions. For this *creator spiritus* Pfitzner eventually shaped the image of 'the nameless old master of the world who is also subject to the age-old word on the edge of infinity'. This is hardly a conventional picture of a Christian deity, and Pfitzner clarified his image in the metaphor of the goldsmith which so appealed to Junk. There is no equivalent in Rie to the lines:

> Er schafft sein Werk, wie du das deine,
> Er schmiedet Ringe sich, Figuren, Steine
> Zu der schimmernden Kette der Zeiten
>   Der Weltbegebenheiten. (*Tb* 20)

> He does his work, as you do yours,
> He forges rings, images, and stones
> For the shimmering chain of the ages
>   Of the events of the world.

In the opera this image is quickly linked to that of Palestrina's earthly task, to add 'den Schlussstein zum Gebäue', and thus bring the great tradition to an end; the image of the stone thus figures in two metaphors, that of the great edifice and as the 'last stone' of the chain. But it was the latter which came first in the writing of the libretto: late in 1909 Pfitzner began the libretto with the opera's last quatrain.

Nun schmiede mich, den letzten Stein
An einem deiner tausend Ringe,
Du Gott—und ich will guter Dinge
    Und friedvoll sein. (*Tb* 56)

Now fashion me the final stone
On one of your thousand rings,
Oh God! And I shall be of good heart
    And live in peace.

Until this central image came into being, an image which is
encapsulated in the motive to which Thomas Mann could not
quite give a name (see below, Ex. 5.32, Cadence 3), Pfitzner
could not create his apparition scene, which was then written as the first complete scene in March and April of 1910.
Undoubtedly Rie felt that she gave him the basic dramatic
conception which turned the 'as if' into a reality. She failed
to see that the animating factor, the central image of creativity, remained unspoken in her draft. As a postscript to this
curious squabble over the libretto, it should be noted that
Junk later had access to Stach's draft, and discovered that
'the idea of the appearance of the dead masters of music was
first mentioned in this sketch...even if she did not let the
masters themselves set foot on the stage as Pfitzner then did
himself'.

The libretto was still not completed easily after this breakthrough. Like several of his contemporaries, Pfitzner was
forced to do much of his creative work in the summer months
while the theatres and concert halls were closed. The libretto
for Act I was finished by 28 July 1910, as a letter to Willy
Levin shows.[15] But by November he was plunged into defensiveness and doubt. Already he had justified 'forging Nothung
myself' to Levin on the grounds of extreme need (*RSB* 302). In
a letter to Arthur Eloesser, he expanded upon this theme in an
effort to distinguish himself from other nameless composers
who wrote their own libretti and thought themselves poets
with no justification. Both Mimi and Cossmann had praised
one scene, but now he was stuck on Act II, whose mood he
knew, but whose contents evaded him (*RSB* 302–3). Pfitzner's
later reminiscences do not quite tally with his correspondence. A letter to Cossmann of 28 July 1911 begins with

---

[15] The significant dates in the composition of *Palestrina* have been compiled by
Walter Abendroth (*Hans Pfitzner* (Munich, 1935), 159, 162, 165–8, 176, 185–8, 197–
202); some of the letters used have been published in *RSB*.

a half-serious suggestion of a visit to Trent, which is then dismissed on the grounds of pressing work (*RSB* 303–4). Speaking of the second act, he noted that although he hadn't written a word in ten months, he should finish it in six or seven weeks. According to the *Palestrina* essay, he began work on Act II in the spring; this is partially clarified in the letter (though certainly not explained as far as the ten months are concerned) by the admission that a few scenes were sketched and one made ready (*RSB* 304, *SS IV* 425). Pfitzner eventually did journey, to visit the Cossmanns in Munich. Here Act II was finished on 1 August before he travelled on as far as Partenkirchen, where ill-health forced him to enter a sanatorium. In the world of *The Magic Mountain* Act III was dictated by 7 August, and the whole poem was read to his Munich friends on 13 August. The reading was repeated for Strasbourg's benefit on 19 October, and by the beginning of 1912, the libretto stood in print in Levin's sponsored edition.

By any standards this was a remarkable achievement. Although Pfitzner later turned occasionally to verse (as in the six sonnets), it is rare for a composer to produce a libretto that is as varied in versification as *Palestrina*, as interesting in form ('sui generis' as a friend described it to Pfitzner's gratification), and as consistent in imagery. Adamy has noted that the metre in its variations reflects the importance of the characters from Pius IV downwards. 'The Pope sings hexameters—a singularly grand idea,' noted Thomas Mann (though, as Adamy points out in his invaluable analysis of Pfitzner's use of rhyme and metre, he might more accurately have said elegiac couplets, the alternation of the classical dactylic hexameter and pentameter).[16] Four- and five-foot iambics and blank verse form basic structures on to which other metres and rhyme schemes are grafted for Borromeo, who tends at times towards the *Knittelvers* elevated for all time in Goethe (and to a lesser extent in *Die Meistersinger*); Ighino has a ballad-like style; the masters move at solemn moments from iambics to anapaests; over all there is a skilful use of enjambment, especially for Palestrina's monologue in Act I.

Although the spectacle of a versifying composer might suggest a Wagnerian epigone, *Palestrina* as a libretto easily

---

[16] Thomas Mann, *Reflections of a Nonpolitical Man*, trans. Walter D. Morris (New York, 1983), 302; Adamy, 'Das *Palestrina*-Textbuch als Dichtung', 46–7.

outstrips Wagner's 'poems' in the strength and skill of its language. But Wagner's libretti undoubtedly work in the theatre, and this is not simply a product of his skill as a composer; rather it also reflects his ability to shape an argument or, as Pfitzner might have said, a conception towards appropriate high-points and through moments of repose. *Palestrina*, wedded to the image of the two worlds, is a drama whose eponymous hero plays no part, other than by report, in the central act. Furthermore its most grandiose character (to judge by musical depiction), the Emperor Ferdinand I, does not appear at all. In this may perhaps be seen the influence of the writers Pfitzner had discussed in *Bühnen-Tradition* in 1905. The question of indirect characterization, brought on by some thoughts on Melot in *Tristan und Isolde*, provoked considerable discussion.

In poetry it is immaterial how much of the characterization takes place behind the scene, what is pressed on us from the mouth of another, or in whatever other way the poet effects it; what matters is that it's *there*, in the piece. We know of figures who don't appear even for a part of the time but actually vanish entirely behind the scene and yet can be drawn as clearly as many a hero who discourses on stage for five acts. I think of Gretchen's mother in *Faust*. We know this 'over-meticulous' middle-class wife in her bigotry and hard respectability as well as we know Gretchen, who has inherited her vigorous scolding of poor erring maidens, just as Valentin has inherited her pitiless moral rectitude. The great master at depicting such invisible stage figures is Ibsen. How Beate lives in *Rosmersholm*! He juggles formally with this type of presentation in *Ghosts*. The poet leads us by the nose and shows us Captain Alving in various images, each of which later corrects the previous; first Alving as the generality sees him and also as the young Oswald holds him in his heart. Frau Alving, who knows her husband more accurately, presents a better image, that is, a worse one, and paints a terrible picture. But even this is significantly altered, precisely through the mouth of the heroine herself whose inner developments and reminiscences teach her and us to see this character otherwise ... (*SS I* 23–4)

How Pfitzner attempted to employ such techniques within the more cramped confines of a music-drama is at least as much a question of musical motive and characterization as libretto. But the striking technical feature remains that the dramatic catastrophe latent within Pfitzner's concept, the overturning of Palestrina's world by imprisonment and threats

of torture, is conveyed to the audience entirely by dialogue
and report. Admittedly the dialogue of Cardinals Novagerio
and Borromeo culminates in the most intimately sustained and
correspondingly agonized climax on the Torture motive, but
then 'the indigestible' (Palestrina's tragedy) is 'spat out' with
Novagerio's grape-seed into the world of chaos and the Will.
Traditional dramatic structure came close to being stood on
its head in *Palestrina*, to the bafflement of many critics.

Synopsis. *Act I* begins towards evening in Palestrina's dark
and simple room, which is dominated by a desk with blank
music paper, a portative organ, and a portrait of the dead
Lukrezia. Palestrina's pupil Silla sings over his newly composed song in the latest style while accompanying himself on
a large violin 'in one of the random forms of the time'. He
dreams of going to Florence and escaping from the conservative polyphony taught by Palestrina in the militant Rome of
the Counter-Reformation. Palestrina's son Ighino enters and a
dialogue ensues that leads gradually into a monologue for
Ighino. Palestrina has fallen into a profound torpor in which
even his fame hangs on him like a shroud. Envied by his
colleagues, driven from the papal service, he still worked on
until Lukrezia died. Since then he has been an empty vessel,
possessed of the knowledge of 'the sorrow of the world of
which the poets speak . . . One lives and weeps because one is
born', an idea that is too much for Silla.
   The latter's remedy for Ighino's depression is to perform the
new song. This is interrupted by the entry of Palestrina and
Cardinal Borromeo. The latter's disapproval is expressed
in his 'intelligent countenance and passionate eyes'. The
latent tension between Palestrina and Borromeo emerges as
the latter asks, 'Is this the art you teach, Praeneste?', using the
ancient name of Palestrina's birthplace with a humanistic
precision that borders on contempt. Palestrina can see the
sinful sounds for what they are, the happiness of youth revelling in fashionable dilettantism. But he is also aware of the
threat it implies to him and to the 'art which masters of many
centuries, in secret alliance throughout the ages, have built
steadily to a wond'rous dome'. His calm contemplation of the
threat moves Borromeo to speak of the Church, 'the rock your
own art is built on'. By not practising this art, Palestrina
reveals a sickness of soul which Borromeo has the means to
heal: 'The angels hold watch and desire songs of praise'. In

the most extended section of the act, Borromeo reveals the true threat. The Council of Trent, as it comes to its turbulent end, is debating the singing of the mass. Corrupt modern practices have led Pius IV to contemplate consigning the entire corpus of polyphonic music to the flames and reverting to Gregorian chant. Against this Borromeo has fought hard until an unexpected long letter from the Emperor Ferdinand came to his aid with its request for the exemption of 'the well-invented old works from the time of the great masters, because they awaken and sustain the spirit of piety'. With this ammunition, Borromeo proposed the composition of a test-piece whose style and bearing would be a model for reformed church music. Palestrina will write this mass in his pure style, thereby winning eternal fame and crowning 'music's wond'rous dome'. To Borromeo's astonishment, Palestrina refuses; he is not the right man and will not be budged by Borromeo's vision of the dead masters' reaching out to him. So appalled is Borromeo at the extent of Palestrina's dereliction that he detects heresy in an unguarded reference to the thoughts of the dead; uttering threats, he leaves Palestrina's sulphurous presence for Trent.

In deepening gloom, Palestrina says a farewell to his last friend and laments the deep and dark wood in which he finds himself. Before Lukrezia's portrait he asks why his love was not strong enough to keep her. Even Ighino has no meaning for him. Before the empty music paper, he turns over Borromeo's idea as much in resignation as despair.

The apparitions now begin. Nine masters, from the thirteenth century to the verge of Palestrina's own time, appear in the dress of their respective epochs and nations. In response to Palestrina's baffled search for reason, they offer an at first unheard answer, 'For Him, it is His will, He must, so must you'. Palestrina becomes conscious of the apparitions and greets Josquin and Isaac by name. The masters explain that Palestrina has been chosen to complete the circle. Palestrina still refuses, at first on grounds of age, then on the grounds of the age; artistic vigour has ebbed with the rise of consciousness. But the masters invoke the master of the world and demand the final note, the last stone, 'the meaning of the age'. They disappear, reminding Palestrina of his task as he begs not to be left in the darkness.

The despair which reigned before has now given way to a true spiritual terror. But this 'dark night' is the prelude to enlightenment. An angel sings the 'Kyrie eleison', and Palestrina begins to compose. More angels appear, illuminating the stage with an unnatural brightness which pales as Lukrezia appears to inspire her husband. As Palestrina works on, the scene darkens to the pale light of early morning. As he finishes, daylight increases and the fading angelic voices blend into the tolling of church bells whose clangour grows until they fill the whole room. Palestrina falls asleep. Silla and Ighino enter and discover the mass, composed in one night. With a connoisseur's eye, Silla notes some lightening in the old style. But the effort cannot mean that the mass will do the master much credit. In response to this dilettantish judgement, the bells swell up again with an echo of the angelic song ringing between the beats.

Act II is set in the hall of the Prince-Bishop of Trent, Cardinal Madruscht; it is open to a small garden at the front and to the streets of Trent at the rear, and is lined with tiers of benches for the Council, arranged according to eminence and nationality. In preparation for the last General Congregation before the closing ceremony, the Pope's second Cardinal-Legate, Novagerio, is supervising the laying-out of the hall (and the placing of an unofficial chair for the head of the Spanish delegation) with the Master of Ceremonies, Bishop Ercole Severolus. The Pope's command is for speedy resolution of business, but Severolus remembers when Lainez the Jesuit spoke for two hours; he receives confirmation from Novagerio to cut such eloquence short. The Italian, French, and German servants are warned not to repeat their recent riots in the streets, or else the formidable Madruscht will deliver them to the 'cradle' in the green tower. Madruscht now enters, suggesting in bearing more the warrior and nobleman than the cleric whose robes he wears. He knows that the first Legate, Cardinal Morone, has been visiting the Emperor in Innsbruck, and that the duration of the visit has been too long for mere courtesy. A political deal is obviously being worked out, but Novagerio steers the conversation towards the Pope's preference for Bologna (where the Council had previously resided), the discomfort of German Trent, and even the weather. The arrival of Borromeo exceeds Madruscht's capacity to tolerate Italians, and he leaves after ordering fruit and red wine for Borromeo.

The conversation between the two Italians which ensues deals with the character of Ferdinand, and of Maximilian, the

Emperor's son and heir. Ferdinand desires the Spanish throne and with it the domination of the world. Maximilian, however, favours heretics, and the unity of Ferdinand's policy is further undermined by the heretical German clergy who, with one exception, have absented themselves from the Council. Morone's task is to keep Ferdinand from Trent by promising Maximilian the kingship of Rome (thereby guaranteeing the imperial succession for the Habsburgs), and by granting certain church reforms that will leave the matter of final interpretation firmly in the Pope's hands. The question of the reform of church music is an attractive sop to the Emperor. Novagerio assumes that the composition of the test-piece by a composer whose name he has forgotten is under way, only to hear of Palestrina's refusal. This confirms him in his view that 'all art comes from the devil', and that force must be applied. Borromeo replies that Palestrina has indeed been imprisoned, but doubts if force can break his resistance. In such cases, Novagerio recommends 'the old institute of Paul IV' (Pius's immediate predecessor and a notorious believer in rope and stake), and when Borromeo shrinks from 'the most extreme measure', tells him that 'the indigestible must be spat out', like the seeds of the grape he has just eaten.

Madruscht re-enters with the Cardinal of Lorraine. Both resent the speed of the Council's conclusion, but are divided by national outlook from combining to frustrate it. On the news of Morone's arrival, the Italians depart and the Archbishop of Prague, Anton Brus von Muglitz, enters to join the others in complaint. The stage fills and the Spanish contingent, led by Philip II's orator, Count Luna, mock the Italians, 'creatures of Pius', whose messengers bring 'the Holy Ghost in their baggage to make their decisions for them'. The Italians are no better than described. The garrulous Bishop of Budoja is the buffoon of the Council and dominates his fellows, not least in discussing financial compensation. The others are timorous and credulous where heresy is concerned, and geographically ignorant of anything beyond the Alps. An oddity is Abdisu, the ancient Patriarch of Assyria, a figure from a somewhat older conciliar age, who imagines that he is witnessing 'the rebirth of all Christendom'. Novagerio warns Morone to expect trouble, and the Council takes its place on the summons of Severolus.

Morone urges the fathers to follow the Pope's advice and become 'angels of peace', though his subsequent unChristian remarks about heresy produce the first interruption from Budoja. Having counselled the fathers against 'the rising winds of erudition', Morone proceeds to business by assuring the assembly that the Emperor has been satisfied. A reservation concerning the papal position strikes Luna as significant. The Council now falls out over procedural questions even before reaching the contents of the Emperor's propositions. To general cries of 'placet', Avosmediano of Cadiz repeatedly opposes 'non placet', insisting on full discussion of every point. Lorraine (who has been 'squared' by the offer of a legateship) suggests that non-controversial matters be taken first. But the least controversial, the question of church music, leads the Bishop of Cadiz to enquire how the test-piece is proceeding. Borromeo replies calmly that the mass will be written, seconded by Novagerio who by now remembers Palestrina's name (though others clearly do not). Brus raises the Utraquist question, the subject dearest to the Emperor, only to be told by a Spaniard that he should really say 'dearest to the Bohemians'. The ensuing imbroglio leads Luna to repeat Avosmediano's request for the fullest discussion of every point. This in turn develops into a squabble between Luna and the reluctant papalist, Lorraine, who wonders how Luna has acquired a chair to which he is not entitled. Insults are traded and matters exacerbated by Budoja's conduct, first by a grotesque sermon on the evils of discord, then by awakening the aged Patriarch and prompting him to address the Council on the subject of 'Trinaspales' long after that subject had been exhausted. When Lorraine claims that only Spain wants the Council prolonged, Luna makes the hubristic mistake of stating, 'If Spain wants it, so does the world'; he is promptly told by Budoja and the Italians to read Ptolemy. Enraged, Luna threatens to invite the Protestants to the closing ceremony. As the clock strikes noon, the Council degenerates into pandemonium, and Morone is forced to adjourn with a plea for wisdom to prevail in the afternoon. The Council floods out, a gesticulating rabble, but behind them the principals continue to argue. After their departure for lunch, the quarrel is taken over by the servants, Spaniards against Italians and Germans. A full-scale riot in the streets breaks out, terminated by the arrival of Madruscht and his troops. A volley into the crowd restores 'order' and the survivors are dragged off to the rack, as Madruscht asks if this is the meaning of the Holy Council.

Act III returns to Palestrina's room in Rome. The bells that ring now are those of evening. Aged by prison, Palestrina sits silent, surrounded by Ighino and his choristers. The mass is being performed before the Pope. Silla and the singers had gathered the pages together after the soldiers had arrested Palestrina, and given them to the Pope's men. Palestrina doesn't even recognize his own choristers. Approaching cries of 'Evviva Palestrina' are heard in the street. The Pope has described Palestrina as the greatest man in Rome and Pius himself enters with Borromeo to deliver his verdict on the mass and bless Palestrina. After his departure, Borromeo wordlessly dismisses the singers, save for Ighino who cowers in a corner. Borromeo throws himself at Palestrina's feet in remorse, but Palestrina raises him in reconciliation, describing them both as vessels of the glory of God. Unable to express his feelings, Borromeo rushes off. Ighino observes that his father remains very quiet. Silla has been absent from the scene, and Palestrina realizes that he has left for Florence. He asks Ighino to stay with him. His son agrees and then feels the impulse to join the crowds still rejoicing in the streets. As he leaves, Palestrina contemplates the portrait of Lukrezia. He sits at the organ and asks God to 'fashion me the final stone on one of your thousand rings, and I shall be of good heart and live in peace'. As he improvises, distant cries of 'Evviva Palestrina' can still be heard. 'Palestrina appears not to hear them.'

The synopsis reveals that before Pfitzner had seriously begun to consider the music, a number of symbols and images, some verbal, some visual, were being used to further the drama. The method of symbolic use of stage props analysed by John Northam in Ibsen was present at a simpler level in *Palestrina*.[17] The blank music paper, the portrait, and the silent organ all reflect Palestrina's soul-state as the drama begins. The arbitrary shape of Silla's violin is a comment on the wilful dilettantism of his music. Of course such features are found in the operas of Strauss and Berg. What Perle identifies as 'verbal *Leitmotive*, that are not associated with specific recurrent musical figures' are to be observed in *Palestrina*, such as the notion of a *Wunderdom*, which blends with a whole family of musical figures without ever attaching

---

[17] John Northam, *Ibsen's Dramatic Method* (London, 1953), *passim*.

itself firmly to any one of them.[18] The recurring theme of heresy never acquires a musical face. Such images may in time harmonize with the music, such as the visual symbol of the silent organ of Act I which comes to life under Palestrina's fingers at the close (in itself a suggestion that the interpretation of Peter Franklin may perhaps lean too much towards despair in the concluding bars[19]). Such confident handling of dramatic detail is only to be expected in Hofmannsthal or in Berg's operas with their basis in stage plays. Pfitzner's achievement is to be mentioned alongside them.

From the start, Pfitzner realized that the predominantly male cast would require some doubling of parts, but, unlike similar devices in other operas (notably *Lulu*), this is merely a matter of convenience. On a sketch page for Act I, opposite Palestrina's despairing 'alles, alles, alles!', the likely requirements were noted.[20] The three tenors among the masters would take Abdisu, Novagerio, and Budoja; the three baritones would take Luna, Severolus, and Lorraine, the last a miscalculation crossed out and replaced by Morone; and the basses would take Lorraine, Imola, and Madruscht. Pfitzner stressed in the full score that these doublings were for convenience and need not be followed absolutely. Subsequently other economies crept in, notably that of giving the part of the Pope in Act III to one of the basses (usually Madruscht). The doublings in no sense imply a symbolic equation of the masters and the squabbling fathers of Act II, since the sense of tradition which unites the former is disastrously missing among the leaders of the Council.

Although *Palestrina* is a legend, Pfitzner made as much use of historical events and words as possible to enhance the authenticity of his drama. The Emperor's long letter in Pfitzner's version uses a translation of the recorded Latin text at:

> Er will darin vor völliger Verbannung
> Die Figuralmusik gerettet sehn;
> Weil doch, schrieb er,

---

[18] George Perle, *The Operas of Alban Berg*, vol. 1, *Wozzeck* (Berkeley and Los Angeles, 1980), 94.

[19] Peter Franklin, *The Idea of Music* (London, 1985), 123.

[20] *D-Mbs*, Mus. mss 9709, *Palestrina*, Skizzen und Fragmente, SW23C; the sketch pages were numbered by Paul Winter (the W of the page reference), whose method of numbering each side of a bifolio, the standard 'unit' in his pagination, with a capital letter has been followed here.

'aus grosser Meister Zeit
das wohlerfund'ne Alte
so oft den Geist der Frömmigkeit
erwecke und erhalte'. (*Tb* 41)

He hopes with this to see polyphony saved from complete proscription because, he wrote, 'Well-made music of the past from the time of the old masters so often awakes and sustains the spirit of piety.'

'Quo quidem si id agitur, ut cantus figuratus protinus ex ecclesia in universum tollatur: nos id probaturi non sumus, quia censemus, tam divinum Musices donum, quo etiam animi hominum, maxime eius artis peritorum vel studiosorum, non raro ad maiorem devotionem accenduntur, ex ecclesia nequaquam explodendum esse.'[21]

The Pope's couplets render words that Pfitzner found in Ambros into verse:

Wie einst im himmlischen Zion Johannes der Heilige hörte
Singen die Engel der Höhe, also lieblich und hehr
Tönte im Ohre die Messe mir eines andern Giovanni. (*Tb* 54)

As once in celestial Zion St John the Divine heard the voices of angels singing on high, just so was my ear ravished by the sublime beauties of a Mass by another John [i.e. *Giovanni* Pierluigi da Palestrina].

'Das sind die Harmonien des neuen Gesangs, welchen der Apostel Johannes aus dem himmlischen Jerusalem tönen hörte, und welchen uns ein irdischer Johannes im irdischen Jerusalem hören lässt.'[22]

   In the Trent Act, Pfitzner again used words from his reading, notably for the Patriarch's first solo (though the words were part of a letter to the Council; the aged Abdisu did not travel to Trent), for Morone's speech, for the peculiar image of the Holy Ghost in the baggage of the Pope's messengers, and for the confrontation between Luna and the mocking Italians.[23] This example suffices to illustrate Pfitzner's use of existing material, since the sentence identifying Spain and the world was spoken in Rome by a Spanish ambassador to Pius IV, who responded by urging him to read Ptolemy. The incident over the chair and much of the historical detail surrounding Morone and Ferdinand has its basis in fact, as does the young

---

[21] Rudolf Kriss, *Die Darstellung des Konzils von Trient in Hans Pfitzners musikalischer Legende 'Palestrina'*, publication by author (1962), 6–7.
[22] Ambros, *Geschichte der Musik*, iv. 24.
[23] *SS IV* 423; Kriss, *Die Darstellung des Konzils von Trient*, 11, 13–14, 17–18, 22–3.

Max's heretical leanings and Luna's threat to invite Protestants to the closing ceremony. From time to time, Pfitzner
adjusted a name or a detail. Why the historical Navagero
became Novagerio is not clear. To enrol Budoja among the
Italians, Pfitzner changed his see from Budua (Budva) on the
coast of Montenegro. In general, the characters of Pfitzner's
fathers do not stray far from the mark, and Morone's animad-
versions against heretics come all the more convincingly from
one who had been imprisoned for suspected heresy under Paul
IV.[24] Even minor details like the reference to Lainez are
taken from the historical record; it is understandable that
the ignorant Italians should confuse Brus with Drakowitz
(Draskovics), since both 'defended the Habsburg conciliatory
line in sharp opposition to the prevailing ultramontane rigid-
ness which eventually won the day'.[25] Brus's concern over
communion in both kinds was historically founded. Only
Ercole Severolus is depicted as something he was not, since
he was neither a bishop nor master of ceremonies, but pro-
curator and layman. Whatever Pfitzner's divergences from
history, they were in general carried out with an eye to
dramatic effect; the only members of the Council who make
an ambiguous impression are Borromeo, who operates in both
worlds, and the warrior-priest Madruscht.

Pfitzner began to compose his opera on 1 January 1912,
beginning with the Prelude to Act I.[26] For the composition of
Silla's song, he was able to use a sketch dated 5 May 1909,
originally intended for a setting of Goethe's 'Nachtgesang', an
appropriate source for his 'Italian' opera, since Goethe's poem
was in part a free translation from an anonymous Italian
text.[27] Act I, begun on 6 June 1912, was half-finished by 8
August. Most of the rest was composed next year in two
summer months, but there was still much to be done in the
summer of 1914; on 19 June came the comment quoted by
Abendroth, 'richtiger Anfang der Arbeit am P.'. According to
the first fair copy of Act I which is in the possession of the
Bayerische Staatsbibliothek, the act was completed on 27
July 1914.[28] By an irony of history, as Pfitzner ended his

---

[24] Ludwig, Freiherr von Pastor, *The History of the Popes from the Close of the Middle Ages*, ed. Ralph Francis Kerr, vol. 14 (London, 1924), 289–307.
[25] R. J. W. Evans, *Rudolf II and his World*, rev. edn. (Oxford, 1984), 106.
[26] See above, n. 15.
[27] Osthoff, 'Palestrina—Goethe—Italien', *passim*.
[28] *D-Mbs*, Mus. mss 6572, *Palestrina*, Akt I, erste Niederschrift (*EN*).

vision of inspiration and angelic hosts, Germany was blundering into a war that Pfitzner, like many artists of his generation, accepted as necessary. By 28 August, the Prelude to Act II was sketched (it survives with each bar numbered in the Bayerische Staatsbibliothek[29]), as was the first scene and the songs for the Spaniards and the Italians. The complete sketch for the act was finished on Christmas Day, and the orchestration begun next day. Finally the war forced itself into the composition process; Pfitzner broke off to compose 'Klage' in February 1915. On its completion on the 25th of the month, he worked at the second act, finishing it in Munich on 12 April. Strasbourg saw the composition of Act III from 26 April to 19 May, and its orchestration from 31 May to 17 June. The whole work was finished after some tidying up on 24 June at 5.55 p.m. *Palestrina* was thus the work of four summers, though some composition was done during the winter seasons, principally in 1914/15.

Since the opera is a parable of inspiration, it is of some interest to observe the flow of Pfitzner's own inspiration. He sketched in a variety of formats, from two-stave systems to pages of full score, though it is safe to assume that the latter belonged to the phase of orchestration rather than composition. The short scores confirm, however, that Pfitzner heard much of *Palestrina*'s unique sound-world with spontaneity and in orchestral terms. In *Über musikalische Inspiration*, he emphasizes the difference between cases where inspiration 'flowed autonomously' and those where motives had to be worked out (*SS IV* 296–9). There are many cases of the latter in *Palestrina*, a legacy of the type of symphonic motivic writing transferred to music-drama by Wagner. Pfitzner's method in such cases was often to write a short variant of a motive or combination of motives and then elaborate this into something more continuous. A typical instance is the combination at bar 30/9 (Ex. 5.1), where he brought together the chords which symbolize Palestrina's fame and the main theme of the Prelude to Act I (see below, Ex. 5.31).[30] Having envisaged the combination, Pfitzner then elaborated it in such a way as to replace the lame chord at x with the more characteristic and interesting chord at y, the beginning of a further statement of the Fame motive.

[29] *D-Mbs*, Mus. mss 9709, SW37.
[30] Ibid. SW3D.

Ex. 5.1

Occasionally, such a process could founder on over-elaboration. When the main theme of the Prelude to Act I strikes imaginatively into Ighino's music at the image of the rebirth of past times through ecstasy induced by music (an image which suggests that Ighino, however ill at ease with his father's genius, intuits correctly the meaning of the great tradition of the ages), Pfitzner drafted a statement of it as from bar 14/2, though in values of half the final length.[31] Having then established the time values to his satisfaction, he added a florid counterpoint for clarinet. Dissatisfied with this, he sketched ways of using the theme of Florence (a dramatically inappropriate choice) in the piccolo (an inappropriate instrument). This solution was taken into the fair copy of the full score of Act I (*EN*), but was then scored out and the clarinet idea restored.[32] Where combinations of inspirations were concerned, Pfitzner could be as fallible as anyone.

The same was true of variants of motives. The setting of 'Zum Gregorianischen Choral | Soll alles wiederkehren' in Act I posed a double problem (*Tb* 13). In both sketch (Ex. 5.2) and *EN*, Pfitzner tried out a version of the vocal line that began in bar 67/2, and in each case he crossed it out and introduced the voice in bar 67/4.[33] The peculiar motivic character of this passage also contained a rhythmic problem resulting from the presentation of a cantus firmus as 'Gregorian chant', which is also a foretaste in skeleton of the Emperor's motive. How the latter will appear is completed by the pizzicato interpolations

[31] Ibid. SW7C–D.
[32] *D-Mbs*, Mus. mss 6572, 27.
[33] *D-Mbs*, Mus. mss 9709, SW16B; Mus. mss 6572, 147.

Ex. 5.2

of the strings on weak beats and off-beats. As first conceived, the quintuplet and combination in bar 67/9 has a slightly different form, and there is no sign of the minim triplet in bar 67/7; indeed it is difficult to say from the sketch what Pfitzner's precise intentions were at this stage since the sketch seems to offer two possible forms of bars 67/6–7 that may or may not represent the interplay of wind and strings (Ex. 5.2).

The Emperor's motive was also one of the few that caused Pfitzner problems with that 'autonomous stream' which he so passionately invoked. The first of the Munich sketch pages includes a continuity draft headed 'Kaiser Ferdinand', which carries the music in a memorable burst from bar 72/9 to bar 75/7 and (more tentatively) beyond.[34] In this sketch of an advanced stage, there is a surprising slip or variant in bar 73/6 that was not present in earlier drafts, which approximate more closely to the final version. But the real surprise on an earlier page is that on concluding the Emperor's motive as at bar 73/7, the lines,

> In einem langen Schreiben
> Wünscht er: es möchte bleiben
>> Aus grosser Meister Zeit
>> Das wohlerfund'ne Alte,
>> Weil es den Geist der Frömmigkeit
>> Erwecke und erhalte, (Tb 13)

are set to a development of a motive from bar 75/7.[35] There is no trace of the complex diatonic dissonance of the final version which describes the 'long letter', nor of the intense motive of the Masterpieces of the Past (see below, Ex. 5.36). This important 'inspiration' was almost certainly an after-thought. With certain exceptions of this kind noted, and the special case of the Missa Papae Marcelli reserved, it has to be granted that Palestrina for long stretches flowed as autonomously as could be expected, given Pfitzner's enforced activities as conductor in Strasbourg. There was little conscious forcing of inspiration, which is remarkable if only because the composition was in some measure affected by research into a specific epoch in history. Only at the greeting to Josquin did Pfitzner produce a tenuous draft lacking in clear harmonic and motivic profile.[36]

---

[34] D-Mbs, Mus. mss 9709, SW1D.
[35] Ibid. SW17D.
[36] Ibid. SW23D.

Discussion of the musical language of *Palestrina* is necessarily complex. Certain of its aspects seem to demand assessment in the light of Wagner's handling of motive and orchestra. To place it in its own time, however, demands something more than consideration of the musical language as Wagner's German successors had developed it. Features which recall Pfitzner's contemporaries, notably his highly fluid polyphony, are crossed with deliberate pastiche, raising the question of how important his 'research' was, a matter that blends into dramatic and aesthetic issues.

The role of the musical motive in Pfitzner's operas has not been uncontroversial, mainly as a result of the need to distinguish his practice from that of Wagner. In the writings of Pfitzner's early champions like Walter Riezler, the matter was confused by the tendency to play down the leitmotif in Pfitzner in order to focus on closed sections in contrast to the more open-ended procedures of Wagner. This was first seriously questioned by Hans Rectanus, who presented a far more complex picture, in which 'the intellectual range of the work entailed a many-layered use of the leitmotivic principle'.[37] Since *Palestrina* is Pfitzner's most ambitious and fully achieved stage-work, it is legitimate to regard it as his most considered attempt to combine dramatic motivic working with the need for some form of structuring. Superficially his practice recalls Wagner's fondness for basing scenes on central monologues; this is particularly marked in Act I with its set pieces for Ighino, Borromeo, and Palestrina, less so in Act II in spite of Morone's long address, while Act III features brief solos for Ighino and the Pope rather than monologues. Other aspects of Wagner's praxis are recalled in the incorporation of self-contained songs into dialogue sequences (as in parts of *Die Meistersinger*); this is seen in Act I with Silla's song, and more extensively in Act II with the episodes for the Spaniards, the Italians, and Abdisu. Fittingly Act I presents the most complex case. As for the building-bricks of the sections, the motives may be classified according to many criteria. In their relationship to the drama, motives may be denotatory, connotatory, or conceptually evolving; in relation to the music, they may be relatively discrete or part of a

---

[37] Walter Riezler, *Hans Pfitzner und die deutsche Bühne* (Munich, 1917), 60–1; Hans Rectanus, *Leitmotivik und Form in den musikdramatischen Werken Hans Pfitzners* (Würzburg, 1967), 179.

metamorphic chain. Attempts at correlating the dramatic and
musical aspects of the motives are as helpful as in Wagner.
The denotatory motive may be part of a metamorphic chain;
in *Das Rheingold* the relationship between the motives of
the Rhine, earth, and the Downfall of the Gods is musically
unmistakable, but the differences are clear enough to cause
little uncertainty as to Wagner's dramatic intention. That
there may also be conceptual evolution involved in such a
chain of thematic transformations can be seen in Donington's
interpretation of the Downfall of the Gods as return to nature,
which in turn divides into earth and water on the musical
axes of mode and metre.[38] On the other hand, terms such as
'evolution' may be unhelpful if the parts of a proposed chain
of variants stand for fixed things or properties which have
little substantial in common. If this seems a plea for the
treatment of each motive on its own merits (and potentially
an abjuration of all attempts at a taxonomy of Pfitzner's use
of the music-dramatic motive), it is initially necessary in the
face of such statements as the following:

In matters of form Pfitzner, like Wagner, made use for the characterization of individual figures, dramatic events or symbols, of
certain leitmotifs, but he employed them far more sparingly than
Wagner. Pfitzner's music seems to depict, beyond the words and
action, unseen elements, the 'spirit' of what occurs on stage.[39]

In this a core of truth is mystified by the idea of spirit (*Seele*)
and the result is to miss a crucial point. There is no doubt
that certain motives in the opera stand simply for a character;
the motives of Lukrezia, Silla, and Ighino given in Example
5.3 are obvious instances. Each of these motives retains its
meaning over the entire span of the opera. The same is true of
other motives though they may require more gradual clarification. Example 5.4 is introduced in Act I to accompany the
Pope's command that the Council be speedily wound up, and
is the main motive for some eleven lines of text that range
widely over the business of the Council. In Act II it appears at
Novagerio's mention of 'the question of church music' (bar
60/5). Since this too rests on the Pope's word, the combination
of contexts provides a clear definition of its meaning. It is thus

[38] Robert Donington, *Wagner's 'Ring' and its Symbols* (London, 1963), 278.
[39] Helmut Grohe, 'The Miraculous a Possibility: An Account of the Origins of Hans
Pfitzner's *Palestrina* from the Historical and Artistic Viewpoints', Booklet of
Palestrina, DG Stereo 2711 013, [p. 9].

Ex. 5.3

Ex. 5.4

a representation motive but is also used to organize a section of Borromeo's monologue. Where a motive is used only in the latter fashion, its meaning becomes harder to specify. Example 5.5 seems to carry the association of sorrow, but

Ex. 5.5

only in the context of the scene between Silla and Ighino; the lack of other contexts imparts a vagueness to its operation that encourages talk of 'spirit' rather than meaning. Certain motives are indeed difficult to label crisply with a single word or concept, but it is precisely here that evolving complexes of ideas may cast light. Rather than speaking of motive and spirit, constellations of ideas, both dramatic and musical, should perhaps be the ruling concept. However complex this question, and it is certainly not beyond analysis, Grohe's statement also mystifies in that it overlooks those motives which do firmly denote, and which are not used sparingly but as occasion and inspiration demand.

Motive implies repetition. Such a statement of first principles is necessary if only to disqualify certain attractive figures from detailed consideration. *Palestrina* is noted for its elegant evocation of locale, in particular cities. Rome, Florence, Bologna, and Trent all have their figures. Rome receives the most complex treatment inasmuch as it belongs to both worlds and cannot be considered outside the constellation of ideas surrounding the hero. Florence as the goal of Silla (who is something more than a subsidiary figure without quite standing on the main plane of the drama) attaches itself to his music (Ex. 5.6). Bologna and Trent are

Ex. 5.6

the cities of the Council, but whereas Trent has a repeated if secondary motive, Bologna, fleetingly mentioned as the Pope's 'beloved city', is charmingly characterized by a non-recurring figure (Ex. 5.7). The hierarchy thus established serves as a model for other motives. To place such emphasis on the representation motive, however, takes insufficient account of the fertility of Pfitzner's imagination, which proves capable of handling without musical repetition such key concepts as heresy (albeit with a suggestion of 'Ein feste Burg' at Act II, bar 51/9 for the 'Lutherpest'), or such ideas of secondary importance as 'communion in both kinds', a phrase with pardonable overtones of Bach and *Parsifal* that is given to Brus von Muglitz.[40]

A large category of motives belongs to the individual characters; some of these can be simply described. The least significant is given to Theophilus of Imola, who trembles at the mention of heretics and becomes a mere subsidiary in the

---

[40] Rectanus believes quite plausibly that the setting of 'das Abendmahl in beiderlei Gestalt' (Act II, bars 145/10–146/1) is a minor-mode variant of 'Nehmet, esset, das ist mein Leib' from the 'St Matthew' Passion (*Leitmotivik und Form*, 141; see also Hans Rectanus, 'Die musikalischen Zitate in Hans Pfitzners *Palestrina*', *FHP* 23–5).

Ex. 5.7*a*

Ex. 5.8

scherzo of Budoja's music (Ex. 5.8). Budoja's histrionic talent emerges in his arresting initial chords and then dissolves into the rapid patter of quavers that eventually becomes a mere part of the general commotion in the Council (Ex. 5.9). His music's claim to be self-sufficient is thus true to a point, but it lacks clear conclusions and is easily swept away by Morone or Severolus. Morone himself is curiously bland, with music that alternates between the tritonally pivoting progression from D minor to A♭ major, and the suave injunctions that come from the Angels of Peace motive, material that shows a greater tendency to grow in Wagnerian sequential extension than anything else in the opera (Ex. 5.10). According to Kriss, Pfitzner accurately caught Morone's sense of his own worth and the

Ex. 5.9

Ex. 5.10*a*

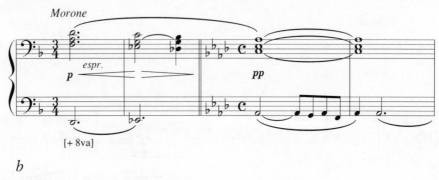

b

importance of his mission.[41] The first Cardinal-Legate comes close to being the central figure of Act II, but in a curiously decorative and extrinsic manner that shows how emphatically Pfitzner loaded the dice against the 'world': Borromeo's cold-blooded lie and Novagerio's readiness to go to extremes combine with Morone's rhetoric to sap the vitality of the Council's proceedings in order that the frank violence of the Prelude to Act II may break into the deliberations and spill over into the streets of Trent.

The treatment of the two rivals in dignity, Lorraine and Luna, provides an interesting contrast in method. The motive to which Lorraine and Madruscht enter at the start of Act II, scene 4 (Ex. 5.11) may be regarded as Lorraine's, if only

Ex. 5.11

because Madruscht already has his own figure. Yet this is one of the least interesting motives in the score and might with

---

[41] Kriss, *Die Darstellung des Konzils von Trient*, 18.

equal plausibility be seen as a suitably 'blank' figure to build up the polite dialogue which is the substance of the scene. Lorraine's personality emerges more from the libretto than the music, particularly in his exchanges with Madruscht:

LORRAINE [*delicately*]. So let us—act out this play.
MADRUSCHT [*coarsely*]. Or, to put it another way, since we cannot reach a Christian agreement, let us, since we must, bring it to a decent end.

The course of the act reveals that if Madruscht is consistent in his brutal frankness, Lorraine's refinement can lead to perceived loss of dignity which, in this context, is tantamount to brutality in language and, for his servants, in deed as well.

Luna sings his little verse about the Roman messengers with the Holy Ghost on their backs to a motive which is related in style to that of the Spanish contingent (Ex. 5.12).

Ex. 5.12*a*

Together these motives provide relief along with those of Budoja and his hangers-on. But Example 5.12*b*, which varies in meaning between Luna and Spain in general, undergoes a rhythmic broadening and harmonic intensification when the subject is the Spanish throne as key to universal dominion over the Catholic world, the perceived goal of Ferdinand and Maximilian. In such a context, Example 5.12*b* draws the Emperor's own motive into polyphonic combinations; it is not too fanciful to see Ferdinand's motive losing something of its pristine C major as the tawdry Spanish scherzo acquires dignity.

Other characters in the world of affairs have more substance. Pius IV has a motive that remains essentially unchanging until he appears in person to pronounce his blessing on

Ex. 5.13*a*

Pius IV (Act II)

b

Sehr langsam. ($\downarrow$ = $\downarrow$ vorher)

33/1

Pope Pius IV
(Act III)

Wie einst im himm - li - schen Zi - on

Palestrina (Ex. 5.13*a*). Then it changes in melodic contour and acquires a modal dignity from the antique parallel fifths and octaves and the Lydian F♯ (Ex. 5.13*b*). Pfitzner paints the office, not the man, a procedure that Berlioz employed in devising a suitable motive for the Pope in *Benvenuto Cellini* (though Clement VII gives much more of his real character away in that opera). Something of the same is true of Ferdinand I, whose noble C major, perhaps the most immediately recognizable theme in the work, is not above being sullied in the forum of the Council (Ex. 5.14). But even in the Council, certain priorities must be preserved, and Morone's invocation of the Emperor in his address sparks off a loud statement of the motive that sets the producer a minor problem: how to reflect this grandiose outburst (with its regrettable trumpet *ossia*) in stage business? The Munich production of recent years resorted to Novagerio's orchestration of a standing ovation at Ferdinand's name, a cynical gesture hardly reflected in the music though it suits the Legate's style. Ferdinand's motive is only gradually revealed. A suggestion of it is first heard in Act I at Borromeo's rebuke to Palestrina, 'Es drohet nicht von eitlen Dilettanten' (bar 57/7), corresponding so precisely to 'Dilettanten' as to suggest that this is an apt descrip-

Ex. 5.14

The Emperor Ferdinand (I)

tion of the Emperor's musical stature (though the talk is not of Ferdinand, but rather of Silla and the Florentines). It then recurs at 'Wir fürchten uns da nicht so sehr', the object of Borromeo's contempt being cheeky pupils like Silla; if this is an intentional foreshadowing, then its presence is slightly puzzling. With the much more obvious use of the imperial theme for the cantus firmus of Gregorian chant (Ex. 5.15), Pfitzner informs the hearer in advance of the Emperor's love of music, but only by interpolating the missing notes of the motive between the long values of the wind; Ferdinand's love of 'figural music' resides in the 'little notes'.

Abdisu, a figure out of time and place, presents two brief cameos on material that is unlike anything else in the work. His first and more extended solo uses an exotic harmonic and melodic palette with modal shifts and modal scale degrees in one motive (Ex. 5.16*a*), then antique fourths and fifths in an unexpected key in the second (Ex. 5.16*b*). Melismas and more conventional chromaticism involving augmented triads help to depict the exotic figure in European surroundings, and further intensify the problem of what in *Palestrina* is stylistically consistent and what dramatically motivated.

The most puzzling motive from a dramatic point of view

Ex. 5.15

Ex. 5.16*a*

belongs to Brus von Muglitz. As noted, he is concerned with ecclesiastical matters of great spiritual weight and raises the historic question associated with Bohemia since the time of the Hussites, Utraquism (communion in both kinds). It is a reflection of the seriousness of his position that Pfitzner states his long theme in its virtual entirety three times in the course of Act II (effectively every time Brus speaks or is mentioned) and also elevates it to a position of structural importance in the Prelude (Ex. 5.17). This may reflect the fact that (as a stage direction notes at bar 113/1) Brus is the only German cleric present. Kriss felt that Pfitzner's musical portrait was accurate in its 'somewhat stepmotherly' and 'slightly boring' depiction of 'a weaker infusion of the strongly profiled

Ex. 5.17

Madruscht',[42] but this hardly explains why Pfitzner should have laboured in such detail and provided so extended a theme for Brus when the Prince-Bishop's musical treatment is so perfunctory.

Madruscht presents a problem of perspective, the more so since Peter Franklin put in a claim for him as Pfitzner's 'own representative' at the Council. 'There can be little question that Madruscht, an idealistic, romantic German knight beneath his Cardinal's robes, represents what in the nationalistic Pfitzner was dangerously in accord with that element in his society that would shortly replace democratic inoperancy with Fascist intolerance.'[43] This over-ambitious interpretation rests on the libretto. Loyalty and trustworthiness are qualities that Novagerio and Borromeo allow Madruscht, but also suspicion and bad temper. He is as ready to be as brutal in telling the truth as Pfitzner could be. Perhaps a valid reac-

---

[42] Ibid. 23.
[43] Franklin, *The Idea of Music*, 132.

tion to the character is to admire Pfitzner's ability to hit off a combination of qualities that figured so prominently in his own personality. Pfitzner too was fully capable of finding allies in 'idealistic' knights with a fondness for extreme measures such as Tirpitz. Madruscht's music fails, however, to deepen the character. The theme which accompanies Novagerio's warning to the servants about Madruscht's unwillingness to tolerate their brawling emphasizes only his brutal side, and it is this motive which most persistently portrays him throughout the act (Ex. 5.18). The music of his

Ex. 5.18

dialogue with Novagerio uses a motive which, like Lorraine's, could be regarded as a blank backdrop rather than character depiction (Act II, bar 35/3). It is ideally suited to reflect Madruscht's attempts to pry and Novagerio's slippery evasions, but it does not properly belong to either. There is something demeaning about Pfitzner's musical treatment of Madruscht that suggests a certain contempt for his sadistic forthrightness. It is not so far removed from that accorded Novagerio, Madruscht's most skilful antagonist, who opposes the Prince-Bishop's brutal seriousness with a diplomatic evasiveness that can also contemplate a more subtle and cold-blooded brutality in remedying Palestrina's recalcitrance. If Madruscht's music is perfunctory, Novagerio's is almost non-existent. His word is the Pope's 'Schnell zum Schluss', which in addition to inverting into the increasingly ill-suppressed motive of violence, acquires a new head-figure that might stand for Novagerio himself, but might equally refer (as at bar 151/8) to the chair in which Luna sits against all protocol, or to the servants who are directed by Novagerio and Severolus to

Ex. 5.19*a*

place the chair, as Rectanus thinks (Ex. 5.19).[44] If there is a
dramatic connection between these ideas, it would seem to be
that the chair which Novagerio cedes Luna out of diplomatic
convenience later becomes the trivial cause over which the
session founders. But such details belong more properly in
discussion of the wider significance which Pfitzner saw in
the Council, or more accurately in the 'world' which knew
nothing of the intellectual life.

   Alongside the material relating to the individual characters
of the second world, there are motives appropriate to the
proceedings of the Council (bar 130/3), the cries of 'placet' and
'non placet', and the music of violence which starts to build
up momentum in the latter stages of the act from its quiet
intrusion at the beginning of the discussion of the inoffensive
thirtieth proposition on church music. Such strokes of irony
are an often unobtrusive feature of Pfitzner's depiction of the
Council; of related kind is the counterpoint of the violent
material and 'placet' in the Prelude to Act II (bar 4/6). The
climax of this escalation of discord is the outburst following Luna's threat to invite the Protestants to the closing
ceremony. The bells which toll the hour of midday oscillate
between F♯ and C (initially in support of a half-diminished

---

[44] Rectanus, *Leitmotivik und Form*, 132; he also connects this ambiguous motive
with Severolus.

seventh), a dramatic symbol against which a furious dissonant counterpoint of motives creates a counter-image to
the vision of harmony which climaxes Act I. Even Pfitzner's
intentions seem to slip out of focus, the stage direction which
notes the Spaniards' refusal to join in the uproar being
apparently contradicted by the six horns' braying of their
motive. How far this image of discord is Pfitzner's idea of the
inevitable outcome of human legislative assemblies is difficult
to say. In Schopenhauer he may well have encountered the
preference for autocracy governing by consent that could
have envisaged a useful function for some limited form of
parliament.[45] But as Adamy has pointed out, Pfitzner's mon-
archism was of an idealistic cast;[46] for Wilhelm II he had
little but contempt. In Pfitzner's eyes politics was always a
matter subject to ideals and to the notion of nationalism in an
almost mystical sense. There is something limited about the
interpretation that would see Act II as a kind of commentary
on parliamentary and democratic assemblies;[47] there is
little that is democratic about this Council in any case, controlled as it is by the Pope through his legates and cardinals.
The Council fails because it is contaminated by the world in
the widest sense. What it might have been is reserved for
Borromeo to articulate. But a more ambiguous picture is
presented by a motive which at times refers to the Council
and at others to the Master of Ceremonies, Ercole Severolus
(Ex. 5.20). Severolus is the Council's figure-head, and possibly
the motive denotes the Council's public face; the idea of the
Council demanded separate treatment. Severolus himself is

Ex. 5.20

[45] Bryan Magee, *The Philosophy of Schopenhauer* (Oxford, 1983), 205.
[46] Bernhard Adamy, *Hans Pfitzner* (Tutzing, 1980), 285.
[47] Jon Newsom, 'Hans Pfitzner, Thomas Mann and *The Magic Mountain*', *Music & Letters*, 55 (1974), 142; Franklin, *The Idea of Music*, 131.

regularly characterized by music derived from individual
bars of Example 5.20. The relationship is best summed up
from Act II, bar 104/8, where the Bishop makes his Kothner-
like summons to the Council, thus launching the processional
review of themes relating to the assembly, its members, and
proceedings. This section is the longest orchestral interlude in
an opera that makes little use of the device apart from the
Bell crescendo in Act I and the subtle gathering of motives in
the closing pages of the whole work. The summons is based
on motives resembling Example 5.20, at first in unison and
then in counterpoint. Ideas from the main Council theme (see
below, Ex. 5.28: Motive 3) are interwoven to lend dignity
to the catalogue of delegates. The procession begins with
Example 5.20 in the woodwind, accompanied by melodic
counterpoints in the brass which include reference to the
Spanish Example 5.12*b*. An increase in chromatic complexity
leads to a surprising climax on the motive of Torture (see
below, Ex. 5.48), a reminder of the ultimate law on which the
Council rests, before the procession subsides into the main
Council theme (Ex. 5.28: Motive 3). This interlude serves to
present a composite image of the Council that highlights both
ceremonial and actual aspects of its proceedings. How these
relate to the ideal of the Council (to which Motive 3 partly
refers) is best considered along with the figure of Cardinal
Borromeo.

Borromeo is the one figure who links the two worlds.
Appropriately he is treated with greater amplitude than his
fellow priests and bishops. On his entry he is accorded a
motive that is intensely expressive in its spasmodic rhythm of
the fiery Cardinal's irritability, superficially in the face of
Silla's 'sinful' song, more deeply at Palestrina's sickness
of soul (Ex. 5.21). It is thus appropriate to his 'silent but

Ex. 5.21

somewhat vehement' gestures to the singers in Act III, as
he attempts to dismiss them before making his atonement
to Palestrina. When he wears his public face in Act II, this

Ex. 5.22

figure is all but imperceptible, appearing inconspicuously at bar 43/9. In the scene with Novagerio, the thread on which denotatory ideas hang is a motive which applies to the scene rather than to a specific character (Ex. 5.22). It catches up one of Borromeo's other motives from Act I (Ex. 5.23), and also the

Ex. 5.23

Ex. 5.24

motive of Fruit and Red Wine, provided by Madruscht for Borromeo's refreshment (Ex. 5.24). In Act I, Example 5.23 stood for Borromeo's hope of saving church music, but in Act II it seems to lose particular meaning and acts as a mere pointer towards the Cardinal. Quite apart from its grotesque prolongation at Novagerio's little demonstration of spitting out the indigestible, Example 5.24 forms an at all times ironic counterpoint to the Cardinals' dialogue as it ranges over affairs of Church and State.

In Act I, Borromeo also launches several motives which either express personal qualities, such as his consternation at Palestrina's refusal (Ex. 5.25), or else arise from the content of his monologues, the first of which is the principal expository

Ex. 5.25

section of the opera. As a result, figures not specifically associated with his personality none the less cling to him on
occasions. The same is true of Ighino, whose monologue also
exposes certain basic themes (in both literary and musical
senses). Since it is this feature which stresses the self-contained
nature of the monologues and builds a musical profile of the
two living characters who stand closest to Palestrina, the
opera's hero may best be approached by considering aspects
of these sections and their relationship to their surroundings.

Both monologues arise out of their context in a relatively
seamless manner. The ease of transition from dialogue to
monologue is most marked in the case of Ighino. Silla's question, 'He [Palestrina] is famous, what more does he want?'
introduces the motive of Fame (Ex. 5.1, top stave). Ighino
prefaces the core of his monologue with a few remarks as to
Silla's likely response (to the motive of silent suffering, Ex.
5.5). The monologue proper then begins dominated by Fame,
which hangs on Palestrina like a ceremonial robe (*Feierkleid*)
(Ex. 5.26). This has earned him only the envy of his col-

Ex. 5.26

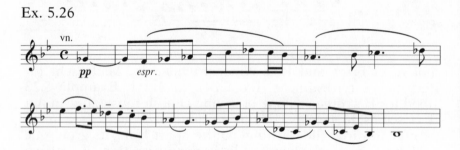

leagues. Apart from the motives of Lukrezia and Ighino,
together with material relating to Palestrina himself, Example
5.26 and Fame dominate the monologue.

Fame is of concern to Borromeo also. Palestrina's task will
ensure his fame throughout the ages, but the music makes no
reference to the motive from Ighino's monologue. The reason
is simple: Borromeo and Ighino do not share the same notion
of fame. Ighino sees reputation as something which should
bestow temporal happiness. When this finally arrives in Act
III, the recapitulation of Ighino's music brings back both
Fame and its ceremonial robe, his perception of the glory that
Palestrina has won; only his observance of Palestrina's silence
informs him that there is something in his father to which

reputation is not adequate. This much Borromeo realizes, and he stands correspondingly nearer to Palestrina. At the climax of his monologue, he offers Palestrina 'eternal fame' to music that blends motives from many different sources, none significantly linked to himself. There are several ideas in his music which do reveal the cast of his thought, of which the most musically eloquent is the motive of the Great Masters of Rome, a noble idea which Borromeo bears as a reproach through each act, first against Palestrina, then against himself (Ex. 5.27). Inasmuch as this seemingly general idea comes to

Ex. 5.27

be seen through Borromeo's eyes but is never sung by, nor accompanies, Palestrina, a grain of limitation appears in Borromeo's character which finds reflection in other features. Motive 3 (Ex. 5.28) from the Prelude to Act I, the motive of the Council of Trent, is given him at the outset of his monologue. If Example 5.20 represents the Council's public face, Borromeo sees a deeper meaning in Motive 3; to him (as to Madruscht in his violent way), it is the *holy* Council of Trent. It has an ideal dignity in Borromeo's eyes that reminds the listener of Palestrina's recognition of Borromeo's 'noble soul'. Given such dignity, the motive of the Council no longer appears as in the Prelude to Act I as a mere counter to Palestrina's world and its music. It is an idea of comparable worth, before it is drawn into the hurly-burly of Act II. Yet for all Borromeo's nobility, it is too liable to be confined to 'beautiful words', as Palestrina describes his great idea. There is little sign in this future saint of that gentler sanctity which Manzoni described in another Borromeo.[48] As a devotee of Goethe, Pfitzner was doubtless aware that this restless Faustian cardinal also had a

---

[48] Cardinal Federigo Borromeo, the cousin of Pfitzner's Cardinal, succeeded him as Archbishop of Milan and plays a particularly saintly role in *I Promessi Sposi*.

Ex. 5.28. Motive 3

touch of Mephistopheles in his capacity to achieve good by
the wrong methods.[49] He clearly would have few scruples
about burning heretics, whatever his regret over proceeding
to extremes against Palestrina. Appropriately it is in his
music that the Torture motive (which Mann particularly
associated with Novagerio[50]) is first adumbrated in a pre-
liminary version (Ex. 5.29).

Ex. 5.29

If the figure of Ighino represents the limitations of family
ties in appreciating genius (which may have had its later
reflection within Pfitzner's own family in much sharper form),
Borromeo defines the limitation of the *Kenner und Liebhaber*
(did Pfitzner see anything of the restlessly autocratic Cossmann
in Borromeo?). Inasmuch as he can appreciate Palestrina's
'pure style', Borromeo is more a connoisseur than a mere
music-lover. It is given to him to present ideas which have
a considerable bearing on Palestrina, notably the figuration
which seems to stand for his genius and which revealingly
turns into the diatonic music of the angels at bar 55/4 (Ex.
5.30). He is aware that there is a mysterious source for that

Ex. 5.30

genius but fails to realize that it cannot be forced. His diagnosis of Palestrina's soul is close to the truth by the com-

---

[49] If Mephistopheles is 'a part of that power which always wills evil but
accomplishes good' (*Faust*, Part I, 1335–6), Borromeo shows a not dissimilar
confusion over ends and means in handling Palestrina.
[50] Mann, *Reflections of a Nonpolitical Man*, 302.

poser's own admission. His cure, to write the mass, is the correct one, but he fails to see the need for Palestrina to find it for himself. Borromeo's monologue is the corner-stone of the opera in that it represents the world's demand on inspiration to be at its beck and call.

Grohe's comment quoted above rests principally on the music which grows out of the two main motives of the Prelude to Act I to become the most important in the work. These ideas, given here as Examples 5.31 and 5.32, are rather more than motives in the musical sense; periods would be a more accurate analytical term insofar as there are balancing phrases and cadences; but even the latter acquire a significance beyond the purely musical (Ex. 5.31: Motive 1). Motive 1 divides into a number of cells. Cell 1 is the rising fifth which expands to seventh and octave in the opening bars. Cell 2 descends from d^3 (8) through a fourth, another figure with a capacity for extension as happens at *A*, where a full octave descent becomes a countermelody to Cell 1 and its expansion. A motive for Palestrina's own name (Pierluigi) is also presented and extended. Two cadential figures complete the motivic potential of this material. The first is the deceptive shift from chord V to chord IV in bars 7–8 (Cadence 1); considerable play is made with this figure later. The second ends the whole period and is labelled here Cadence 2. If the decorative triplet is overlooked, this is a simple enough figure with a long history. The simultaneous suspension of seventh and fourth is an obvious archaism, the more marked for not being, as Jeppesen points out, a common feature of Palestrina's style.[51] It is of earlier currency. Since pastiche elements have a part in the opera, this cadence is a reminder that Motive 1 is not simply an evocation of Palestrina achieved by grafting elements of his music on to Pfitzner's own style. This is confirmed by the presence of the same progression in Motive 2 (Ex. 5.32).

Motive 2 follows immediately in the Prelude, retaining the tonality of D minor but changing to triple time. Again there is clear periodic articulation and cellular use of motives, of which Cell 3 is the head motive of the whole. The organum-like movement of parallel fifths and octaves again has no part in Palestrina's own style. Yet although there is a case for

[51] Knud Jeppesen, *The Style of Palestrina and the Dissonance*, trans. Margaret Hamerik, 2nd edn. (Oxford, 1946; repr. New York, 1970), 253–5.

Ex. 5.31. Motive 1

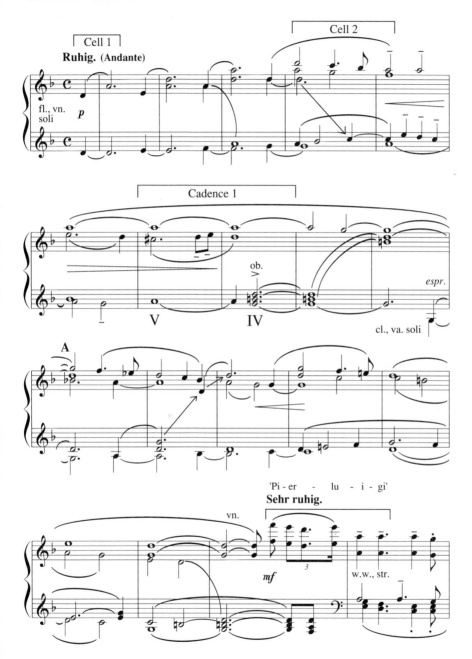

saying that Motive 1 belongs broadly to Palestrina and Motive 2 to the masters of the past, they have much in common. The second statement of Cell 3 after *C* is counterpointed (as in the corresponding moment of Motive 1) by the full octave extension of Cell 2. Cadence 2 ends the first phrase; then offers a more independent use of the harmony comprising augmented fourth and major seventh (B♭−E−A). 'Pierluigi' is also incorporated. But the most distinctive feature of Motive 2 is fabricated from Cell 3; Cadence 3 is perhaps the most striking feature of the opera and received close comment from Thomas Mann in *Betrachtungen eines Unpolitischen*.[52] Initially it should be noted that like Cadence 2 it tends to move freely beyond the context of its specific motive. It quickly reappears in Motive 3 before *F*, and not by chance; Cadence 3 is the opera's enigma, of which only close reading of context permits solution.

In both the scene between Silla and Ighino and that between Palestrina and Borromeo, the introduction of Motive 1 is a crucial step, form-building in a dramatic if not an architectonic sense. Throughout much of Act I, verbal imagery and musical motives proceed in a fascinatingly disjunct manner. Palestrina is initially characterized verbally rather than musically. To Silla, he is an 'old master' in two senses. The notion of constricting polyphony (from which Florence provides an escape) leads to a pastiche based on a passage from Palestrina's *Missa Aspice Domine*, which Pfitzner prob-

---

[52] Mann, *Reflections of a Nonpolitical Man*, 310−11.

Ex. 5.32. Motive 2

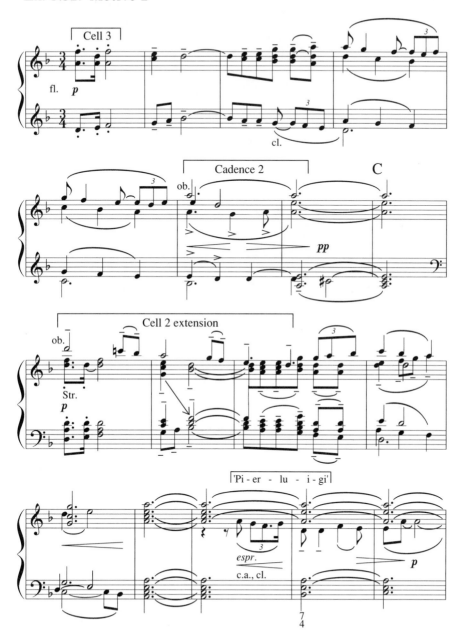

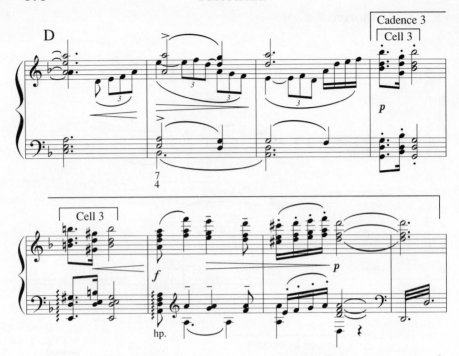

ably knew from the same volume as the *Missa Papae Marcelli*[53] (Ex. 5.33). Palestrina is also the representative of Rome as guardian of the old; Silla makes an equation between the Rome motive (Ex. 5.34), the bell figure which follows it (Ex. 5.35), and the composer. The connection is reinforced by the use of Cadence 2 at Palestrina's name (bar 7/10). The first image is extended in Silla's comparison of learned polyphony to donkeys in the same yoke (again with reference to the *Missa Aspice Domine*). Later in the act, the second image is incorporated more fully into Palestrina's world when the Rome theme and the bell motive become the transfigured aftermath of the composition of the mass. What seems forced to Silla fills Ighino with the ecstasy of universal wholeness, and it is this image which evokes the first recall of Motive 1 (bar 14/2). Particularly relevant at this point is the fact that Ighino senses the rebirth of old times in the act of re-creating polyphony, thus linking Motive 1 to the concept of remem-

[53] *Pierluigi da Palestrina's Werke*, vol. 11, *Zweites Buch der Messen von Pierluigi da Palestrina*, ed. Franz Xaver Haberl (Leipzig, 1881).

Ex. 5.33

brance that Pfitzner later extolled in *Die neue Ästhetik der musikalischen Impotenz*.[54] Divorced from Cadence 2, the 7/4 sonority (in its most distinctive form with augmented fourth and major seventh) reappears at the notion of Palestrina's grief (bar 18/8). This is the central idea of the scene between Ighino and Silla, and it is in the increasingly depressed context of Ighino's monologue that Motive 1 next occurs. Significantly it is associated with Cadence 3 in the presentation of Palestrina's creative fortitude in the face of all blows until the death of Lukrezia. With that event, however, everything in him became 'still and empty', which provides the first significant context for Cadence 3 since the Prelude. Ighino thus equates the material of the Prelude both with Palestrina's fortitude in creation and with the drying-up of that creativity

---

[54] See above, 34.

Ex. 5.34

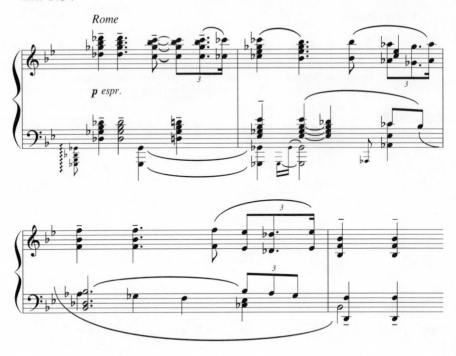

Ex. 5.35

under the blow of bereavement; the Prelude's motives remain relatively constant points in the exposition of the dramatic situation. The only solution that occurs to Ighino is that poetic 'sorrow of the world' which is significantly shaped from a minor-mode version of his own motive.

In the scene between Palestrina and Borromeo, Cadence 3 is the first of the Prelude's motives to recur, as Palestrina meditates on the possibility that Silla's outlook might be the correct one, and on the difficulty of accepting the transience of 'what we thought eternal'. Characteristically Borromeo takes the motive over, bending it first towards the C major of the Church, and then, by virtue of the link between its four rising semiquavers and the four rising quavers of the opening of *Der arme Heinrich* (see Ex. 4.2*a*), into the sickness of Palestrina's soul. The semiquaver figure threatens for a time to develop an identity of its own, fluctuating in mood between the characters. Finally, it is reincorporated in Cadence 3 as image of the threat to art which the Council represents. At the outset of Borromeo's monologue, the presence of Cadence 3 in the Council theme (Ex. 5.28*x*) seems easier to grasp than in the Prelude; from now on, the rising semiquavers will also be assimilated to the Council theme in an inner part (Ex. 5.28*y*).

It is Borromeo who links Motive 1 to the masters of the past by introducing the motive of the Masterpieces of the Past (Ex. 5.36), which takes Cell 2 (though no longer starting from $\hat{8}$) as its head-motive, and the Emperor as its cadence. From there it is a short step to the introduction of Motive 1 for 'the sense of devotion which raises our spirits to the heights, delighting in the miracle of interweaving sounds'. In Borromeo's grand peroration, as his words cluster into rhyming stanzas, Motive 1 carries the connotations of 'Meisterwerk', reconciliation, and praise; Cadence 3 now accompanies 'Rettung und Reform'. It is an indication of the way in which ideas (or even the two worlds) interweave in Borromeo's exaltation that Palestrina's mission is proclaimed to the Council theme (Motive 3) at the moment when Pfitzner directs the Cardinal to spring to his feet (as though addressing the Council). A peak seems to be achieved as Motive 1 leads to the Rome theme in connection with Palestrina's future fame as 'saviour of music in Rome', but Borromeo has still one further metaphor to cap this, as the rising intervals of Cell 1 thrust towards 'der höchsten Spitze Kreuzensblume' while a perfect cadence, replacing the deceptive shift, V–IV, concludes the image

Ex. 5.36

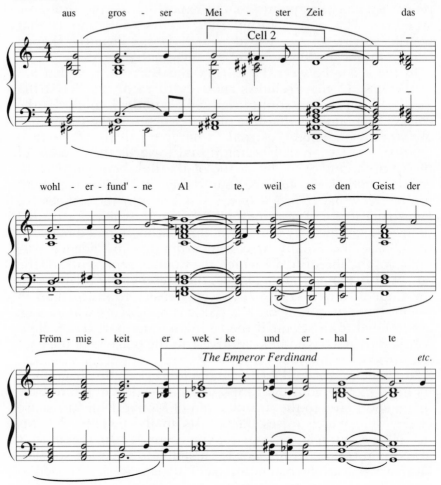

of the 'wond'rous dome'. It is in such contexts that the inadequacy of labelling Motive 1 and its associates appears. Far
from standing for a clear concept, Motive 1 is swept along by
a stream of verbal images which create new contexts. But this
is only in Borromeo's perception.

Motive 1, then, connotes a variety of states and ideas, representing an ideal substance lurking behind them: ecstasy,
inspiration, music, and creation. To see these in operation, the
passive figure of Palestrina has to pass through a prolonged
crisis which is made up of figures from which Motive 1 is
conspicuously absent. The material of his monologue conveys
a sense of apartness by its unique tone-colouring, but even

Ex. 5.37

more by its intense concentration from its midpoint on
Example 5.37. This gains added resonance by being linked to
the Dantean image of the dark wood. Comparison with Dante
could be pursued further since it is hard not to see a shrunken
Beatrice in the figure of Lukrezia. It is only as the thought of
writing the mass (a thought dismissed as senseless) passes
through Palestrina's mind that Motive 1 starts to stir against
the motive of the Masters of the Past (Ex. 5.38), to which the

Ex. 5.38

Masterpieces of the Past is added at bar 123/4. It is through
the masters that illumination comes to Palestrina. Here
Pfitzner's powers of musical suggestion and construction
reach their most intense and, paradoxically for a dramatic
crux, their most abstract. The symbol of pointlessness, the 7/4
sonority, becomes a referential collection at the pitch-level
Bb–E–A, which is symmetrically completed by the Eb with
which the brass introduce the masters. The same sonority
dominates and closes the whole scene, usually in association
with Example 5.39x, whose modal colouring adds to the

Ex. 5.39

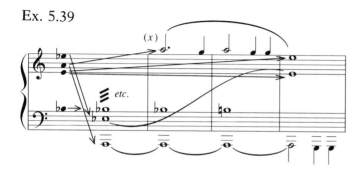

Ex. 5.40

unearthly atmosphere. The tendency towards symmetrical
construction is intensified by simultaneous presentation of
Example 5.38 and its inversion, the esoteric symbol of the
creator spiritus (Ex. 5.40). The initial sonority is a transposition of the referential collection.

The confrontation of Palestrina and the masters brings
previously heard motives to full fruition. The vision of the
transience of creation which Palestrina offered the enraged
Borromeo (Ex. 5.41) is set against the masters' material. It
gains added point from Palestrina's awareness that he is the
child of a decadent (because over-conscious) age. As the return
of this motive in Act III at Palestrina's moment of triumph
suggests, this vision is never permanently overcome. But it is
transcended in Act I by the masters' revelation of the nature
of inspiration, to the music of Motive 1; it is not a matter of
commission but of imperative. At this crux, Motive 2 returns
for the images of the last sound and 'the crown of the structure', with Cadence 3 reserved for 'the last stone'. Although it
seems to dominate the whole opera, this is the last statement
of Cadence 3 apart from the final bars of the opera, where
the sense is the same. It does continue to haunt the Council
theme in shrunken form, with a sense that is contained in the
Schopenhauerian motto of the whole work. There it is maintained that both worlds draw their ultimate essence from the
Will. It is hardly too extravagant to say that in Cadence 3,
something of that essence and Will is symbolized in the compulsion of the perfect cadence. This is not entirely to discount
Mann's interpretation, that 'it belongs to Palestrina's personality', merely to note that it has a more general aspect
than 'the look of melancholy, the look backwards'.[55] When
Mann added, 'It is, all in all, the magically melodious sound-

[55] Mann, *Reflections of a Nonpolitical Man*, 310–11.

Ex. 5.41

zeit - lich trü - ben   un - ter - tan?

ing formula for his special type of productivity, a productivity of pessimism, of resignation and of longing, a romantic productivity', he particularized a symbol which Pfitzner believed as general as the constraints of time would permit.

As Junk noticed, the masters are also particularized, both Josquin and Isaac being addressed by name. The formula, 'Tedēsc' Enrīco', by which Isaac is identified could have come from Ambros's 'Ārrhigo Tedēsco', with the alteration motivated by metrical considerations. Both figures, like the anonymous first master in the monastic garb, provoke sections which, if not motives, seem to confirm the characters' identity. These moments of pastiche are too short, however, to estimate how accurately Pfitzner reproduced their styles. The Josquin 'parody' includes a reference to 'Pierluigi' which further obscures any possible model. What is noticeable is the use of specific cadences with 4–3 suspension for Josquin and under-third for Isaac. This in a sense confirms the limited extent to which Pfitzner was interested in authenticity, since either cadence could be found in Josquin or Isaac, though the under-third would be a stylistic solecism in Palestrina. Both cadences are used elsewhere. The 4–3 is decorated at 'Erwählter du!' (bar 138/1), while the under-third occurs at bar 129/10 in the orchestra. Such cadences contribute to a general sense of the archaic that is reinforced by the organum-like parallel intervals in the first master's music and in Motive 2. But there is no sense in which Pfitzner's pastiche was intended as accurate reflection of the real thing; what he sought was an impression of antiquity captured within his own idiom with the additional bonus of a number of interest-

ing sonorities. Thus Motive 1 begins with the rising fifth of so
many points of imitation in sixteenth-century counterpoint,
but the chord of fourths in bar 2 breaks the norm of dissonance treatment in Palestrina's time, while the melodic rise of
a seventh would also be contrary to the historical Palestrina's
practice. Similar holes could be picked in Borromeo's description of Palestrina's pure style, where dissonant fourths and
irregular suspensions (both from rhythmic and harmonic
points of view) belie the superficial appearance of 'antique'
polyphony. When a catalogue is made of the harmonic features which arise from Pfitzner's archaizing, avoidance of
leading-notes, parallel fifths, modality, and pentatonicism, it
is hardly surprising that Albert Fleury raised the spectre
of Debussy and *Pelléas et Mélisande*.[56] The comparison is a
superficial one, though, in that the features they have in
common are bent to quite different use.

In the first place, Pfitzner's use of the archaic has a markedly
'learned' flavour. This is not to say that a motive like that of
the Masters of the Past may not be used to create dramatic
effect, as when Borromeo pictures the masters stretching
forth their hands to Palestrina. Indeed the combination of
motive and inversion for 'Der alte Weltenmeister' illustrates
the convergence of learning and dramatic impression. It
resembles some arcane first-species contrapuntal exercise in
three parts that proceeds from point of maximum tension
to resolution, while preserving an uncanny quality derived
partly from its anti-tonal beginnings, partly from its tone-
colour. The earlier ensemble, 'Aus weiter Ferne', is reducible
to bar-long harmonies moving away from and back to F
major, but having uncovered its enigmatic progression, one
has to concede that the life of the passage resides less in the
prolongation of F over a twenty-four-bar span than in the pattern of imitative entries in the voices combined with the
pentatonic Example 5.39x. Strong progressions of fifths in
the bass support at times 6/4 chords, at times sevenths, thus
turning a staple of Pfitzner's harmonic world into something
more random that might sustain Fleury's invocation of the *ars
antiqua*,[57] were it not for the intricacies of the imitation
scheme that remind us that Ambros and other sources could

---

[56] Albert Fleury, 'Historische und stilgeschichtliche Probleme in Pfitzners
Palestrina', *Helmuth Osthoff zu seinem siebzigsten Geburtstag*, ed. Ursula Aarburg and
Peter Cahn (Tutzing, 1969), 237–8.
[57] Ibid. 237.

have provided Pfitzner with numerous examples of the inter-weaving of melodic and rhythmic 'puzzles'. The most sur-prising feature of the passage in many ways is the sudden clarification on to the 4–3 cadence, for which there is little preparation in the previous bars. What Pfitzner has achieved is less a re-creation of a style than a submerging of style within a purely dramatic image.

Pfitzner's own thoughts go to the heart of the matter:

About the style of the music, only so much: the material of the work had this consequence, that in order to bring the sixteenth century closer to the listener the music had to adopt a somewhat archaic, i.e. stylistically antique, character. Likewise the hero must have, particularly at the beginning of the work, a still, resigned bearing, indeed must seem to strive from all his spiritual and intellectual, human and superhuman experiences of asceticism to be clothed in tones from this sphere. That is why in evaluating the work they coined such expressions as 'archaic', 'ascetic', etc., and the linear counterpoint already discovered in me was observed anew. But since these expressions were put into circulation, they count as valid among the vast majority of those who write about me for my entire work before and after *Palestrina*, no matter if the compositions to which these ideas are applied prove exactly the opposite in all details to them. I am latterly branded as the linear ascetic. If I open a journal or paper in which I am mentioned, the first thing that meets my eye is that my musical style is purely and simply ascetic. (*SS IV* 426–7)

Far from being uniformly ascetic, the counterpoint of the masters is designed to open up mysterious vistas, the esoteric realm of the initiate. As such it could hardly form a greater contrast with the more open and harmonically conventional contrapuntal bustle that prevails for long stretches of Act II (which is itself far from uniformly 'cantankerous', as Ernst Bloch described it[58]). Nor is there any sense of asceticism in the predominantly contrapuntal setting of the writing of the *Missa Papae Marcelli*.

What Pfitzner presented in the scene which follows the masters' appearance is less the writing of the mass than, as he pointed out, its conception. It is pertinent here to remem-ber his fondness for the Skald's words to King Skule in *The Pretenders*: 'No song is born in daylight. It may be written

[58] Ernst Bloch, *Essays on the Philosophy of Music*, trans. Peter Palmer (Cambridge, 1985), 79.

down in sunshine; but it is composed in the still hours of the night.'[59] In Pfitzner's legend, the mass is indeed written down to the angels' dictation in one night, but this too is only a symbol. Composition here means the origin and growth of the conception. Thus the problem raised by Voss was solved since the conception could be depicted by a fantasy wrought out of the skin and bones of the *Missa Papae Marcelli* and, as Osthoff has shown, out of fragments of the *Missa Aspice Domine*. The motives that Pfitzner used are set out in Example 5.42. Several of these were bracketed in advance in Pfitzner's own copy of the mass, and even in the sketches for the opera there were places where Pfitzner wrote down a bar or two from the mass though these were not always put to use; unused references to 'Patrem omnipotentem' from the *Missa Inviolata*,[60] and from 'Et in unum Dominum' in the *Missa Papae Marcelli*, were written down on one stave as if signalling to some musical intention never to be fulfilled; these figures are obviously similar to other ideas that Pfitzner did use, an inevitable product of Palestrina's highly controlled and limited style.

Most of the derivations given in Example 5.42 are the result of considerable scholarly enquiry, most notably by Wolfgang Osthoff, who established numerous doubtful cases and cleared up a number of misconceptions from study of Pfitzner's sketch material.[61] The divergences between Palestrina and some of Pfitzner's versions suggests that style and mood were of more significance than the exact relationship of words and music. Only in the case of Example 5.42*d* does Osthoff produce a solution that looks artificial; the alternative given here, in spite of the intrusive *cambiata* figure, has the merit of establishing the two components of Pfitzner's motive in succession. A particular feature of Pfitzner's treatment is the cavalier way in which ideas associated with certain words in Palestrina are transferred to others in the opera. The opening clauses of both *Gloria* and *Credo* in the *Missa Papae Marcelli* were left as intonations, but Pfitzner provided them with 'polyphonic' motives. One sketch suggests that he was undecided whether to set Example 5.42*i* as 'Gloria in excelsis Deo' or 'Gratias

[59] For Pfitzner's liking for this extract (*The Oxford Ibsen*, ii. 299), see *SS IV* 286, and Ludwig Schrott, *Die Persönlichkeit Hans Pfitzners* (Zurich and Freiburg, 1959), 169.

[60] The *Missa Inviolata* is contained in the same volume as the *Missae Papae Marcelli* and *Aspice Domine* (see above, n. 53; it will be remembered that Ambros spoke of three masses: see above, 129); see Osthoff, 'Eine neue Quelle', 199–200.

[61] Osthoff, 'Eine neue Quelle', 189–200.

Ex. 5.42*a–i*

tibi' (scored out); the latter wording is preferred in both sketches and full score to 'Gratias agimus tibi'. Pfitzner thus paid little attention to liturgical proprieties in creating his fantasy on Palestrina's mass. He remained true to a notion of religious music that is defined most clearly in the reply which he wrote to a questionnaire on the subject, 'Was ist geistliche Musik?'; there he described this section of *Palestrina* as his 'light mass' as opposed to the 'dark mass' or requiem which he had created in *Das dunkle Reich*, in total defiance, as

d *Pfitzner*
c.a.

(Both segments are in
Palestrina's *Christe*, but not
in immediate succession)

Palestrina

Bass 1: Mi - se - re - re

e *Pfitzner*

Chorus: Cre - do in u - num De - um,

Palestrina [*Aspice Domine*]

Cantus: Pa - trem om - ni - po - ten - tem,

f *Pfitzner*

Chorus: pa - trem om - ni - po - ten - tem,

Palestrina [*Aspice Domine*]

Cantus fac - to - rem coe - li et ter - rae,

g *Pfitzner*
vn. 2

Palestrina

Cantus: su - sci - pe

Abendroth noted, of the ritual significance of such terms as 'mass' or 'requiem' (*RSB* 45–6 & 329; *SS IV* 64–5). Religious music in this context is merely a metaphor for the highest grade of the power of inspiration. The music of Palestrina's masses is as much motive in the opera as the Emperor or Florence. This is borne out by the process of metamorphosis to which the material is subjected. Examples 5.42*g* and *h* form links in a chain which culminates in the related motive of Lukrezia (bars 165/7–166/8). Other figures have similar contexts, notably the numerous ascending scale segments which Osthoff traces to 'Patrem omnipotentem' in the *Missa Papae Marcelli*. These eventually climax in Example 5.43*a*, a figure with extensive ancestry in music of the sixteenth century which does not belong in Pfitzner's form in the *Missa Papae Marcelli*.[62] Like Example 5.43*b*, its presence in the

---

[62] Hans Rectanus, '"Ich kenne dich, Josquin, du Herrlicher . . .": Bemerkungen zu thematischen Verwandtschaften zwischen Josquin, Palestrina, und Pfitzner', *Renaissance-Studien*, 215–18.

Ex. 5.43*a*

b

opera points to the thin dividing-line between quotation, pastiche, and invention throughout the later stages of Act I.

The material taken from Palestrina functions as an *objet trouvé*, a metaphorical cantus firmus (rather as Ighino's theme is literally treated as a cantus firmus within the motivic combination which accompanies the references to psalm-singing throughout Act I; there is a certain appropriateness in this combination on its recurrence at bar 178/7 being followed by another complex, comprising Ighino, the psalm-motive of *Aspice Domine*, and Example 5.42*a*, as Silla scans the new mass with a critical eye). The counterpoint towards which it contributes remains dramatic and blends easily both with parallel imagery in the text and with the complex demands of Pfitzner's *mise-en-scène*, as when the bracketed segment of Example 5.43*a* blends into the tolling of Example 5.35 thanks to the melodic movement 5̂–6̂ common to both.

The composition of the mass has a wide modulatory scheme, beginning in A major, moving through D and G to C major, before an excursion to the flat keys for the Lukrezia episode. The second bout of composition after bar 170/3 moves from B♭ back to C, the key of the Church as 'the rock on which [Palestrina's] art is built' (*Tb* 11). Within each tonal area the style is no more chromatic than much of *Die Meistersinger*, which is to say that Pfitzner's vision of inspiration is predominantly diatonic. The diatonicism is quite complex, however, and demands some consideration of how far this represents a personal synthesis of linear counterpoint and traditional tonality. It is not to be explained in simple terms of invertible chord functions as Skouenborg tends to suggest in his analyses of Pfitzner.[63] From Hugo Riemann Pfitzner would almost certainly have acquired sophisticated knowledge of harmonic

[63] Ulrik Skouenborg, *Von Wagner zu Pfitzner* (Tutzing, 1983), *passim*.

theory adequate to explain most of his diatonic dissonances.
There is no doubt, for example, that the 6/4 is treated in such
a way as to suggest that for much of the time Pfitzner viewed
it as an inversion of the tonic rather than as contrapuntally-
derived dissonant prolongation of a 5/3. But cadential harmony
in general in *Palestrina* is at the mercy of Pfitzner's treatment
of the leading-note. Even where he consciously uses a formula as at bars 162/1–2, he goes his own way as a result
of linear factors (Ex. 5.44). That Pfitzner writes 6/5/4 in-

Ex. 5.44

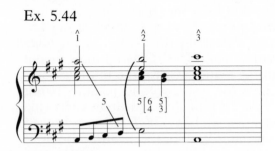

stead of the more conventional 6/4 is a product of the linear
motion $\hat{1}$–$\hat{2}$–$\hat{3}$; the resulting parallel fifths with the bass (in
Palestrina's and many other styles) constitute the sort of
howler that counterpoint teachers traditionally expect from
the beginner. So much for Pfitzner's research, would be a
forgivable reaction. But parallel movement in fourths, fifths,
and octaves is a specific feature of Pfitzner's creation of an
archaic tone. The movement of complete seventh chords in
parallel accompanies the description of the Emperor's long
letter (Act I, bars 73/10–74/1). Parallel movement of various
kinds is present in the composing of the mass, though not
as object of interest in itself in Debussy's manner. Rather,
the use of such traditional forms of dissonance treatment as
accented and unaccented passing notes and suspensions, often
in combination, generates diatonic dissonance and parallel
movement, particularly where neighbouring-note movement
and tension is extended to the combination of neighbouring chords (as, for example, in Example 5.1*y*). The parallel
with Debussy is less suggestive in reality than others taken
from Pfitzner's more immediate surroundings. Modality,
pentatony, parallel movement, and diatonic dissonance
created by linear means sound as much like a description of
Mahler's late style as Pfitzner's; indeed the parallel between

the angels' scene and the predominantly diatonic polyphonic complexities of Mahler's setting of *Veni creator spiritus* in the Eighth Symphony has been drawn.[64] The terms such as heterophony in which Mahler's work has been discussed would be valid for some of Pfitzner's contrapuntal complexes of motives. It is a Mahlerian style, however, without reference to the contours of folksong and dance, without the sharply profiled rhetoric of Mahler's aggressively brilliant orchestration, and without that element of gigantism that also separates Pfitzner from another revelatory climax, the final chorus of Schoenberg's *Gurrelieder*. In spite of the angels, the scene remains individual vision rather than pantheistic rhapsody; the cosmos does not sing with Palestrina, the visionary is solitary.

The forms of dissonance created in the scene are less remarkable than the diatonic atmosphere in which they are generated. There is ample evidence that they are fundamental to Pfitzner's style whether the context be diatonic or chromatic. Thus there is little sense of incongruity when the mass passes over into the tolling of bells which builds up into the greatest point of chromatic tension in Act I. The join is effected by the lulling pentatonic complex from bar 174/2. By using and repeating only the bracketed segments of Example 5.43, passing and neighbouring-note tensions, D ($\hat{2}$) and A ($\hat{6}$), are added, producing the overlapping and sounding together of all degrees of C major save for the two leading notes with their semitonal tension. When this turns into the bell figuration proper (Ex. 5.35), C gradually yields to E minor, in which key harmonic tension is increased by the movement of inner parts until a peak is reached in the decoration of a diminished seventh by neighbouring chords. Since the neighbouring motion takes place at two different rates (crotchet and minim), the decorative chords achieve considerable complexity (Ex. 5.45). The first chord is simply the diminished seventh, but the others are worthy of more comment, and can be viewed as derivatives of the octatonic scale (which contains the pitches of two adjacent diminished sevenths).[65] But however complex the individual sonorities, however frequently they appear in Bartók and Stravinsky, the function of the dissonances in the

[64] Franklin, *The Idea of Music*, 134.
[65] The chords formed in Example 5.42 also can be related to the family of α chords in Ernö Lendvai, *The Workshop of Bartók and Kodály* (Budapest, 1983), 353–6.

Ex. 5.45

bell crescendo derives from the diminished seventh's ancient
capacity to cope with virtually any modulatory requirement,
in this case the large-scale pivot between the C major of the
mass and the G♭ major of the expansive, almost Puccinian
Rome theme (or is it merely that the morning bells of Rome
create a memory of *Tosca*?).

Dissonance treatment is no more complex in Act II, whether
in the 'neoclassical' sonorities of Budoja (which again hinge
on neighbouring-note motion as in Example 5.9, bars 1–3), or
in the more chromatic flurry of the Prelude. Although the
latter suggests Shostakovich to Franklin, he analyses this
impression in rhythmic and instrumental rather than harmonic and contrapuntal terms.[66] At the climax (after bar
9/6), the repeated dissonances derive again from traditional
formulae of sustained tension such as the augmented sixth
and diminished seventh with added neighbouring notes,
which might have come from the climax of Wagner's Paris
Bacchanale. That such music can evoke such different impressions as Wagner and Shostakovich illustrates how convincingly Pfitzner created a polyphonic idiom out of the material
of his time without regard to the more extreme chromaticism
practised by the Schoenberg circle. Without implying a
qualitative judgement, it could be maintained that in some
ways his style in *Palestrina* is less retrospective than many
elements in Strauss. The feeling of a re-created diatonicism in
the *Rosenkavalier* manner is less strong in *Palestrina*, partly
because the model of archaic polyphony was so far removed
from the norms of the time. Hence the comparisons which
are sometimes made with Hindemith's 'noble' manner, as in
the *Künstleroper*, *Mathis der Maler*, are not so misguided;

[66] Franklin, *The Idea of Music*, 132.

granted the prominence of motor rhythms in Hindemith's style, it might seem appropriate to substitute his name for Shostakovich in Franklin's comparison.[67] Such thoughts must be qualified by the realization that what in Hindemith is all of a piece, controlled by a unified system, may at times in Pfitzner fly apart (though it is naïve to explain the difference between the acts of Pfitzner's opera in terms of stylistic canons, as Ernst Bloch does[68]). The clearest case of a retrospective idiom in Pfitzner is as likely to come in a look back to nineteenth-century chromaticism as in his handling of diatonic dissonance.

In the account of Palestrina's arrest given Novagerio by Borromeo, a highly imaginative example of the substitution of a narrative for a dramatic catastrophe, the most acute tension is provided by a sonority that (if viewed enharmonically) derives from a favourite practice of Mahler, the minor triad on the Phrygian second superimposed on the tonic, though the chromatic flux permits few keys to establish more than a very temporary hold (Ex. 5.46). (The same motive is approached in

Ex. 5.46

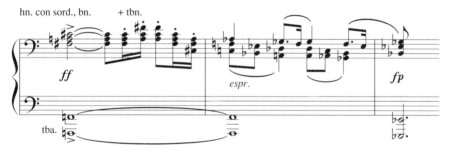

a different manner in the Prelude to Act III.) The climax of the section provides a new context for the sonority. Novagerio's advocacy of force achieves great power in a statement of the ceremonial Example 5.20 as the Council is invoked to justify his suggestion. The tonic pedal which supports this subsequently controls the Mahlerian chord, now the expression of Borromeo's regret, as a neighbouring chord (Ex. 5.47).

[67] For one aspect of the relationship between *Palestrina* and *Mathis der Maler*, see Max See, 'Berührung der Sphären: Gedanken zu einer musikalischen Reminiszenz', *Melos*, 4 (1978), 312–17; see also Adamy, 'Das *Palestrina*-Textbuch als Dichtung', 57–9.

[68] Bloch, *Essays*, 79.

Ex. 5.47*a*

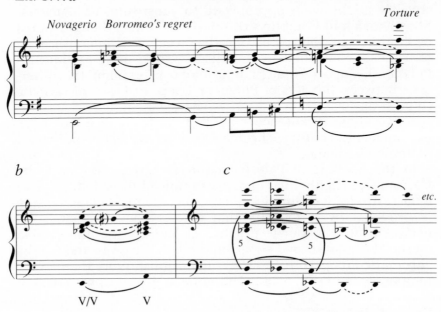

Novagerio's oath ('Bei Christi Marterholz!') carries the dialogue into D minor, but in this key the pedal E is quickly
restored for a full statement of the Torture motive as
Novagerio had already adumbrated it to the erring servants
(Ex. 5.48). The initial chord of the motive is capable of resolution in D minor as a secondary dominant. Pfitzner avoids such
a norm (Ex. 5.47*b*) in favour of a sideways slip to E♭ in the
bass, resulting in the suspension of D in a high register (d^3);
the D does not resolve until the bass itself has moved on to D
as the foundation for a half-diminished seventh (Ex. 5.47*c*).
Such harmonic treatment of a dramatic climax is related to
Wagnerian practice and remains as retrospective as anything
in the more diatonic pages of Act I. Counterpoint in Pfitzner
bridges stylistic rifts arising from harmonic developments, a
verdict not without relevance to Mahler and Strauss. This is a
way of saying that the style of *Palestrina* gains its integrity
and tension (particularly in Act I) from linear factors also to
be found among the music of his contemporaries to varying
degrees, while the rhetorical elements especially prevalent in
Act II exhibit models from the harmonic vocabulary of the
Wagnerian past more clearly. Even in Act II, however, there
are examples that depart from the kind of harmonic charm

Ex. 5.48

exhibited by Abdisu, the Spaniards, and the Italians with their closed songs and sections: notably Severolus and his heterophony of short-winded motives.

Motives and contrapuntal combinations are the most obvious means whereby Pfitzner generates musical drama in *Palestrina*. Occasionally such combinations go beyond specific textual moments and reach out to make larger summaries. The Council's procession in Act II is one such example. The closing pages of the whole work provide an opportunity to restate music associated with the drama of Act I, seen through Palestrina's experience of prison and subsequent elevation. The motive of the Masterpieces of the Past blends into Motive 1 in D minor counterpointed by the Rome theme, until Cadence 1 leads not to G but G♯ in the bass. Lukrezia's theme appears with its characteristic harmonic colour; the G♯ feels like a supertonic pedal in F♯ minor until it rises to A to presage the return of D minor. This is not achieved without a further chromatic digression to the theme of the *creator spiritus*, as in Example 5.40. There is time for a brief resumption of the music to which the masters sang of the compulsion to which both the master of the world and Palestrina were subject, before Motive 1 resumes its interrupted course in D minor. The last sounds heard against the distant rejoicing in the streets are of Motive 2, between the drifting improvisations of Palestrina at the organ, and Cadence 3, which brings the work to a close with 'the last stone'. Like the mature music-dramas of Wagner, *Palestrina* ends by gathering its main motives about it; even D minor, the key of the Act I Prelude, of Borromeo's *Wunderdom* and of the last stone is restored. The opera comes full circle from its initial tonic (d^1) to conclude on the same pitch. But the mood is far from a Wagnerian apotheosis; triumph resounds outside Palestrina's study but is muted in his own world. That has its inner triumph; the silent organ now sounds. But the impression is one of great fragility.

It is difficult to talk of Act III in conventional musical and dramatic terms. Apart from the Prelude, little new material is introduced, and the themes of the Prelude are deliberately repressed, an echo of Palestrina's mood in the opening stages of Act I deepened by the shadows of prison. In this the Prelude comes to stand for a whole dimension of Pfitzner's music that moves at an almost subliminal level. The monologues and songs of earlier acts are replaced by brief explanations, the

Pope's blessing, and the short exchanges between Palestrina, Borromeo, and Ighino. Thematic recollections of the mass, of the absent Silla, and of the motive of imprisonment create no synthesis. Franklin's reading, with its insistence on its valedictory nature, an epilogue 'heavy with sleep and sunset solemnity', comes as close as any description to catching the elusive tone of the act.[69] Yet Act III in its final moment does bring a curious sense of formal completion both in thematic and tonal terms. Tonality is used throughout to suggest the spheres of the world (the E♭ in which Act II begins and ends), Church and angels as the rock of Palestrina's art (C major), Rome (G♭), and the mysterious power of the Will to shape inspiration (D minor). But this is not a rigid system of key characteristics; analysis of this kind, all too tempting with music-drama, would have to be very flexible to deal with so subtle a text for music as *Palestrina*. The quotation from Schopenhauer at the outset, if it says anything beyond the vaguest idea at the heart of the work, speaks of the governing power of the Will in all spheres of human activity. Hence if D minor is the key of the Will, it is appropriate that the monologue of Borromeo (in whom the Will is strong) should stand bound by the tonal unity of that key. Palestrina comes in contact with it solely through the masters. His own monologue in Act I stands outside it in a state of tonal flux that tends to clarify towards C♯ minor, notably for the image of the dark wood. In Act III, the prevalent music, that of the Prelude, is in B♭ minor, the key of Ighino's 'sorrow of the world', rising to a climax in C♯ minor. It is not by accident that Ighino's motive drifts through the slowly paced Prelude, nor that the motive of Palestrina's earlier despair (Ex. 5.37) returns as he remembers the music of the mass, written in a single night. Unlike any other character in the work, Palestrina is an illusionless man, strange though that may seem of one visited by so many phantoms. The music which describes his compulsion is also that of 'No comfort in heaven, no comfort on earth' save in oneself (bar 148/4); there is no reason to suppose that Pfitzner any more than Schopenhauer drew consolation from thought of a conventional afterlife and established religion. Act III seems to draw a line not under the real drama, but between Palestrina as man (renunciatory, Will-less) and as composer (through whom the Will still

[69] Franklin, *The Idea of Music*, 133.

works, but 'guiltless and unstained by blood'). As he re-enters, if only retrospectively, the second sphere in the final pages, the music once more conjures up the noumenal essence of that part of his self which does not belong to the world. In this sense, the element of Wagnerian *Verklärung* is appropriate. The tone is thus rather different from the attitude of Mathis in the final scene of Hindemith's opera, who departs exhausted to die 'like a beast in the forest', or indeed of Busoni's Faust. In his last moment Faust affirms though Mephistopheles questions, whereas Palestrina knows. Perhaps this is why Pfitzner's D minor seems so much more positive in its finality than the C major which Beaumont convincingly places at the end of Busoni's opera. Palestrina's reference to the last stone in the final quatrain hardly seems to refer to his death at all; Pfitzner's hero would be aware of the Schopenhauerian truth that death was merely 'falling out of the phenomenal world'.[70]

A paradox remains in *Palestrina*, in that this opera which has little to do with Christian views of death and afterlife takes place in an ambience derived entirely from the Christian Church in its ancient Roman form. If consideration is taken of *Der arme Heinrich* or *Das Herz*, it becomes almost impossible to envisage Pfitzner's music-dramatic practice without some reference to the religiose, as Werner Schwarz has demonstrated. His description of Pfitzner's operas, 'a form of musical service to God outside the bounds of church music, religious play of a particularly sublime kind', shoots well over the mark, however, in assessing quite why Pfitzner found this particular aura so congenial.[71] In part it is a matter of longing for 'the great community which at all times has its deepest essence in accordance with music in transcendental, metaphysical, and otherworldly things' (*SS IV* 64), which in Pfitzner's view explained why composers continued to write religious music after the dissolution of mankind's ties to the Church. In this sense, the Church is merely another symbol for that sense of community in which Pfitzner believed. Yet it is hardly accidental that some of the finest music of the work speaks of the spirit of piety invoked by the Emperor (Ex. 5.36). In addition to community, reverence is a religious

---

[70] Magee, *Philosophy of Schopenhauer*, 215–16.

[71] Werner Schwarz, 'Die Bedeutung des Religiösen im musikdramatischen Schaffen Hans Pfitzners', *Festgabe für Joseph Müller-Blattau*, ed. Christoph-Hellmut Mahling (Kassel, 1966), 117.

concept that Pfitzner carried over into the music-drama, which may explain why *Parsifal* is so often invoked in discussing *Palestrina*. Yet there is a measurable distance between *Palestrina* and the religiosity of the *fin de siècle* to which its symbols might seem to point.

In part this is a reflection of orchestral language, if this rather loose term may be permitted to cover tone-colour and the idioms which this conveys. Such a quality is close to the concept of *tinta* in a sense raised by Frits Noske, though it is not quite synonymous with his *tinta musicale* 'found in the characters rather than in certain dramatic situations'; orchestral colour as a conveyer of a special tone may both differentiate and unite the characters in a drama.[72] If linear factors have a prominent place in discussing *Palestrina* precisely because of the needs of the subject, as Pfitzner suggested, then the nature of the medium becomes of central importance. This is reinforced by Pfitzner's fondness for launching an opera with a tone colour of special distinctiveness: the four solo muted violas of *Der arme Heinrich*, the *Klangfarbenmelodie* of *Die Rose vom Liebesgarten*, and here the reticent sound of four flutes and solo violins. In general, the timbre of the flutes points towards the organ tone with which it blends in the final pages. The liking for reduced groups taken from a very large orchestra is familiar practice among Pfitzner's contemporaries from Mahler onwards. To speak in such terms, however, does tend to drift towards that asceticism that Pfitzner explicitly rejected as an encompassing metaphor, and rightly so in the light of the orchestral exuberance of Act II.

Certain tone colours go beyond linear considerations, however, to provide *Palestrina* with its distinctive timbral world. The differentiation between the gongs and bells of Rome in the outer acts, and of these from the tritonal bell of Trent, is a striking feature of the score. The weighty sonority of lower strings and brass seems to be highlighted once in each act in connection with the Masterpieces of the Past, particularly when that idea launches the final review of motives. Another aspect of heavy brass timbre, the mysterious muted effects of the apparition scene, contributes to the uncanny sound of that whole section. Nowhere is tone colour more penetratingly used than when the clarinet 'mit

[72] Frits Noske, *The Signifier and the Signified* (The Hague, 1977), 294, 308.

erhobenem Schalltrichter' cuts through the close of the scene with Example 5.39x, the embodiment at once of the masters' urgent warning and Palestrina's despair, a passage which, if the clarinettist takes his courage in his hands, has an almost physical pain. But when these factors are considered and catalogued, there remains the persistent role in Act I of the viola as launcher of themes. The four solo violas of *Der arme Heinrich* return as early as bar 10 of the Prelude to Act I. Two solo violas characterize Silla's extravagant violin. A single viola is prominent in the Rome theme and has Ighino's motive to itself. Later, viola tone is the basis of the 'sorrow of the world' with which Ighino concludes his monologue. The viola d'amore has a privileged part in the music to which Borromeo describes the watching angels. The violas, first the section, then a soloist, dominate the tone colour of Palestrina's monologue; the section leader has an obbligato role here. As an echo to this, the Prelude to Act III is launched by the viola section. Such a preponderance of tone colour goes beyond the identification of the viola with a specific character or mood. It bathes the score in a colour that is far removed from the textures of *Parsifal*, of Mahler's setting of *Faust*, or of the Jochanaan scenes in *Salome*. It is perhaps responsible for establishing the atmosphere, intimate rather than ascetic, esoteric rather than religiose.

That much of *Palestrina*, particularly the outer acts, should raise talk of instrumentation based upon the solo instrument or group perhaps encourages the belief, most clearly articulated by Skouenborg, that Pfitzner's achievement in general was to make the musical language of the nineteenth century a vehicle for modern trends of pessimism, renunciation, and disillusionment.[73] Such an interpretation has the merit of acknowledging the work's status as a classic of twentieth-century opera, rather than merely portraying it in the standard interpretation of Thomas Mann as the last breath of the Romantic spirit. As it becomes part of the modern age, so it seems less polemical than sometimes depicted. It is no bad thing to view it apart from the later *Futuristengefahr* as a work of art with its own internal logic, to which polemics are properly subordinated. That the opera is about inspiration is undeniable; that it is anti-modern is debatable. If there is an identifiable antagonist in *Palestrina*,

---

[73] Skouenborg, *Von Wagner zu Pfitzner*, 34–8.

it is the world, and even that is less clear-cut than might appear, given the ambiguities present in both Borromeo and Madruscht. The other threat, the Florentine *Camerata* so anachronistically present in the opera, is indulged by Palestrina albeit with some scorn as dilettantism; but he does recognize that the world can go that way. In any case, Silla's little song is not so alarming. It partakes of the same diatonic dissonance as much else in Act I. It shares certain traits with the *Missa Papae Marcelli*, as Fleury noted.[74] It features the all-pervasive viola, if distorted, and it brings the work, albeit indirectly, within the orbit of the Italian theme analysed by Osthoff, which appears at its deepest in the Dantean symbol of the dark wood, followed by the spiritual journey to the 'underworld' and out to the angels. In this sense *Palestrina* is an Italian opera, Mediterranean in a deeper and more ancient sense perhaps than the Spanish opera *Parsifal*. Pfitzner's hero follows a symbolic journey through an underworld of classical epic (as did Goethe's Faust, another Germanic hero with antique classical aspirations). Yet as with *Der arme Heinrich*, this is not the polemical musical Mediterranean of Nietzsche, with whom Pfitzner exhibited so little affinity. It is an Italy of tradition and continuity, and humanism too, within certain definably pessimistic limits. There would seem to be a germ of this even in Silla, who perhaps has learned the master's lesson better than he knows. Whether this be so, the final message of *Palestrina* would seem to be that the future of music is not so dark and that inspiration in the blackest hour may bring not merely restatement but renewal, 'the old style, but not so heavy'; there is the promise of a spiritual serenity in Palestrina's last lines such as his creator seldom knew.

[74] Fleury, 'Historische und stilgeschichtliche Probleme', 236.

6

Pfitzner and the Lied

THE two genres which Pfitzner most persistently cultivated were chamber music and song, but whereas his quartets and sonatas have established their reputations mostly among connoisseurs, his songs have been the subject of wider acclaim and are more regularly performed. Song-writing was not a lifelong preoccupation for Pfitzner. His interest in the Lied broke off in 1931 with a group of sonnets after Bürger and Eichendorff that have an unmistakably valedictory character, not least through a quotation in the last ('Das Alter', Op. 41 No. 3) from *Die Rose vom Liebesgarten* in association with farewell followed by 'the spring that never ends'. Even in earlier years his songs cluster into groups with 'points of concentration', as Hans Rectanus has noted, in 1888–9 and in 1922–4.[1] Neither Rectanus nor any other writer on Pfitzner has been able to clarify all the chronological details of Pfitzner's song-writing between 1889 and 1901, though it is probably safe to say that the period in Koblenz was the first substantial gap. From 1901 onwards, however, there is a fairly consistent production of songs that breaks off in 1909 on the verge of *Palestrina*. After the completion of the opera, there was a single opus in 1916 consisting of five songs, and then silence until 1921 when a new period of song-writing began. This lasted until the orchestral song *Lethe* (a memorial to Mimi) in 1926, and then there was silence until the last nine songs in 1931. The significant gaps are all associated with times of great stress: the indigent years as he struggled with *Der arme Heinrich*, the composition of *Palestrina*, the period when he was forced to leave Strasbourg and take up residence amid the Munich political upheavals at the end of the war, and the years of depression which followed Mimi's death in 1926 (after which Pfitzner avoided all composition for a substantial time).

[1] Hans Rectanus, Foreword to Hans Pfitzner, *Sämtliche Lieder*, 2 vols. (Mainz, 1979–83), 8.

These divisions also help to clarify the style periods of Pfitzner's Lieder. The earliest attempts are to a large extent under the shadow of Schumann and Brahms. But more striking is that Pfitzner never quite abandoned the types of accompaniment figuration to be seen in these deeply traditional examples of the genre. Thus the Schumannesque syncopations of 'Warum sind deine Augen denn so nass?' (Op. 3 No. 1) crop up again in such late songs as 'Lass scharren deiner Rosse Huf' (Op. 32 No. 4) and 'Leuchtende Tage' (Op. 40 No. 1). The Brahmsian folk style of 'Kuriose Geschichte' (*Jl*. No. 6) recurs in virtually all periods. In spite of numerous attractive songs in the early period, the Eichendorff settings of Opus 9 mark an increase in intensity which leads to the mature songs of 1901 and after, in which Pfitzner creates some highly characteristic pieces without, on the whole, the more hermetic features of the 1920s. The variety of this period before and immediately after *Palestrina* is considerable, embracing chromatically rich love songs such as 'Venus mater' (Op. 11 No. 4), narrative songs such as 'Leierkastenmann' (Op. 15 No. 1), songs with melodies ranging from folksong to the more complex evocation of popular tone in 'Schön Suschen' (Op. 22 No. 3), songs of a polyphonic character such as the Petrarch sonnet (Op. 24 No. 3) and the outstanding 'An die Mark' (Op. 15 No. 3), and mood pieces of which the most evocative is 'In Danzig' (Op. 22 No. 1). The songs of the twenties are less immediately attractive in many cases, representing an extension of the more advanced features of Pfitzner's style into a language that is often startling in its abruptness and angularity for a composer widely regarded as a conservative; yet alongside such introspective masterpieces as 'Abbitte' (Op. 29 No. 1) and 'Hussens Kerker' (Op. 32 No. 1), there are more extrovert and accessible songs such as 'Willkommen und Abschied' (Op. 29 No. 3). The distance of these songs from Pfitzner's starting-point is easily measured by comparing the early Brahmsian version of 'Das verlassene Mägdlein' (written probably in 1887 but not published as *Jl*. No. 5 until 1933) with the delicate setting of the same text (Op. 30 No. 2) from 1922 which may be compared with the famous Wolf setting without detriment.[2] Finally the songs of 1931 retreat from

[2] Werner Diez, *Hans Pfitzners Lieder: Versuch einer Stilbetrachtung* (Regensburg, 1968), 17–26.

this advanced position towards the style of the early years of the century.

It is scarcely possible to point to one single poet to whom Pfitzner the song-writer was attached at all periods. If one makes an exception for Eichendorff, it is because the one significant period in which Pfitzner wrote no Lieder to his poetry was 1921–6, in the aftermath of the large-scale cantata, *Von deutscher Seele*, which uses poems by Eichendorff exclusively. Eichendorff at any rate was set some nineteen times by Pfitzner, over twice as much as any other single poet. What this says about the type of poetry to which Pfitzner was attracted is best dealt with under the theme of Pfitzner the Romantic. What is worth observing now is the way in which Pfitzner avoided challenging Schumann and Wolf on their own ground, apart from an early attempt at 'Waldesgespräch' which was never finished. With other poets he was not so shy about attempting to rival his predecessors and contemporaries. Of his eight settings of Gottfried Keller, five had been set earlier by Wolf, two by Brahms. Keller and Ricarda Huch were relatively late enthusiasms who mainly contributed to groups devoted exclusively to a single poet. Their cases are not dissimilar to that of Heinrich Heine, who was set eight times in Pfitzner's youth but never thereafter. If the special cases of Walther von der Vogelweide and Petrarch are overlooked, Pfitzner set no composer who was born earlier than Bürger in 1747, and he somewhat surprisingly was the poet of five mature songs which include 'Schön Suschen', perhaps the most sensuously appealing song which Pfitzner wrote, and 'Trauerstille' (Op. 26 No. 4), a particularly complex masterpiece of a kind comparable to Wolf. Surprisingly there are only four settings of Goethe, all famous poems set by other composers and none earlier than 1906. In the early period, there are four settings of Grun and two of Cossmann, which speak for Pfitzner's loyalty, if not literary taste, and it is in this period that we also find isolated attempts at setting the epigonal talents of the Munich *Dichterkreis* which included the muses of Wolf's 'Spanish' and 'Italian' Songbooks, Heyse and Geibel. After the turn of the century, however, they were replaced by such as Hebbel and Pfitzner's contemporaries, including Dehmel, Liliencron, and the less renowned Carl Busse. Later than this Pfitzner never went, apart from Ricarda Huch, and the confrontation of the Second Viennese School with George, Rilke, and Trakl left him completely unaffected. This was less because of conservative taste than because of pronounced opinions on the kind of poetry which was suitable to music. Thus he hardly ever turned to Hölderlin, for similar reasons, one suspects (though when he did, the result was the remarkable 'Abbitte', perhaps his most progressive piece from a purely harmonic point of view). Among the poets that Pfitzner set in his maturity there are certainly some negligible talents, in whose poems he saw perhaps just once an image that sparked off a song. His best songs tend to be to the better poets, including Conrad Ferdinand Meyer, who has seldom figured much in the history of the Lied, though 'An die Mark' provides a notable example of a minor poet (Ilse von Stach) who also happened to be a personal friend providing the text that generated a fine song. A curious special case is his attitude to Mörike, of whose poems he set only two, one of which, 'Denk es, o Seele' (Op. 30 No. 3), had been rendered immortal by Wolf; the other, the twice-set 'Das verlassene Mägdlein', was one of German lyric poetry's most used texts. Since the second setting and 'Denk es, o Seele' were both mature songs from 1922, this can hardly be ascribed to youthful pretensions; Pfitzner clearly felt that he had something to say about them, as also in the case of such Goethe poems as 'Willkommen und Abschied' and 'Der du von dem Himmel bist' (Op. 40 No. 5), or the settings of Dehmel and Liliencron which had also appealed to Strauss.

Pfitzner consistently chose to present his songs in small groups of anything between two and eight. There are no grand collections as in Wolf. Where unity exists between the songs of a group, it is usually of poet. Thus the Opus 4 collection is entirely to poems by Heine, Opus 9 entirely to Eichendorff, and Opus 19 consists of two very contrasted settings of Carl Busse. In the twenties, there are three such cycles, to poems by Conrad Ferdinand Meyer (Op. 32), Gottfried Keller (Op. 33), and Ricarda Huch (Op. 35). But there is seldom a specific literary theme, outside of the Huch love songs, to create a deeper impression of the cyclic. Even the Meyer group was likened less to a traditional song-cycle than to a four-movement symphony, a claim which is less transparent than would appear.[3]

As in much early writing on Pfitzner, a combative element

---

[3] According to the theory of Peter Wackernagel, quoted in Walter Abendroth, *Hans Pfitzner* (Munich, 1935), 363.

is present in appreciation of his songs. In Abendroth's brief survey, the need to place them in relation to the Schubertian succession is accompanied by a denigration of Strauss, whose songs 'approximated with the most refined window-dressing to the taste of the pre-war bourgeois salon'; this frankly partisan viewpoint hardly seems pertinent, save to a debatable thesis.[4] Pfitzner, for Abendroth, was the heir both to Schumann's Romanticism and Brahms's Classicism, and above all an exponent of purely musical values who avoided 'the psychological or illustrative interpretation of the individual word'.[5] The whole literature on Pfitzner's songs, as Volker Freund has shown, has in large measure been plagued by the need to demonstrate, as with the operas, that they are 'absolute music'.[6] Undoubtedly this claim was raised for a number of reasons, and some of these had a real significance in Pfitzner's own writings. Pfitzner's songs possess an unquestioned formal clarity, which is bound closely to the poetic strophe. Simple varieties of strophic form are present in all phases of his output, though particularly so in his conservatory days. Most of his strophic songs involve some element of variation, either in melodic line, accompaniment, or tonal direction. Thus 'Die Nachtigallen' (Op. 21 No. 2) varies both melodic line and figuration in the second strophe, while 'Nun, da so warm der Sonnenschein' (*Jl.* No. 4) has a first strophe that ends on the dominant, a second that ends in the tonic; the last of the group of early songs without opus number, 'Kuriose Geschichte', carries this a stage further in that each of the three strophes has a different harmonic goal. Such practices are the simple forerunners of the much more sophisticated procedures of 'Herbstbild' (Op. 21 No. 1) and 'Die stille Stadt' (Op. 29 No. 4), in which it would be more correct to speak of each poetic stanza beginning with the same motive which then goes on to a different continuation. To suggest that this is a general trend would not be entirely accurate, however, since each period boasts at least one almost pure strophic song: 'Abschied' (Op. 9 No. 5), 'Ich fürcht' nit Gespenster' (Op. 33 No. 2), and 'Wenn sich Liebes von dir lösen will' (Op. 40 No. 2). One of these, 'Ich fürcht' nit Gespenster', admittedly is a sophisticated imitation of a folk-

[4] Abendroth, *Hans Pfitzner*, 349.
[5] Ibid. 350.
[6] Volker Freund, *Hans Pfitzners Eichendorff-Lieder* (Hamburg, 1986), 9–15.

song, but this is not a precondition for strophic form in Pfitzner, and the Lienhard setting, 'Abendrot' (Op. 24 No. 4), is a striking combination of the most intense chromatic melody and harmonies with a fairly transparent strophic design.

Most of the other standard forms employed are in some measure also dependent on strophic divisions. Ternary form is always prominent in Pfitzner's song output, and gradually acquires a preponderance over other forms to the point where three out of the Meyer cycle are in ternary form of some kind. The setting of Goethe's 'Mailied' (Op. 26 No. 5) may serve as an example of a balanced three-part design in which each section contains three of the poem's strophes, but this is perhaps less common than variants in which the central, modulatory, or developmental section contains the majority of the strophes, all clearly delineated; examples in this category include early songs such as 'Herbstlied' (Op. 3 No. 2), but also the Eichendorff setting, 'Der Gärtner' (Op. 9 No. 1), one of Pfitzner's most inward treatments of his favourite poet. The first setting of 'Das verlassene Mägdlein' spreads the stanzas differently, with two in the final section, which is further reworked in some details to give an impression of through-composition rather more skilful than the song's early date would suggest. Where the song sections do not correspond to strophic divisions, Pfitzner is often to be found indulging in a delayed or abbreviated reprise of the main material, most notably in 'Michaelskirchplatz' (Op. 19 No. 2), where the return of the opening idea is held back until it has little more function than a coda. A special case where a ternary design is created from a two-strophe poem is 'Abbitte'.

Less commonly encountered are *Bar* and rondo forms. The former is usually associated with folk poetry, either of a deliberately naïve kind as in 'Gretel' (Op. 11 No. 5), or of a much more artistically polished variety (as in the second setting of 'Das verlassene Mägdlein'). These *Bar* forms are of the kind that Lorenz defines as *Reprisenbar* (*AABA*), and Pfitzner usually varies one or both of the later *A* sections.[7] In the case of rondo form, this tends to lead, with the exception of 'Untreu und Trost' (1903), to rondo variations, of which the finest

---

[7] Alfred Lorenz, *Das Geheimnis der Form bei Richard Wagner*, 4 vols., 2nd edn. (Tutzing, 1966), i. 107–8.

example is 'Hussens Kerker', the only song in this group
which is not folk-inspired; the other notable example of a
rondo with variations is the Keller setting, 'Singt mein Schatz
wie ein Fink' (Op. 33 No. 5). Once again, sections depend upon
the poetic strophes, as they also do in sonnet settings, where
divisions are marked by the octave and the sestet, but also by
subdivisions into two groups of four lines, then two groups of
three; the most conspicuous exception here is the Petrarch
sonnet, where the poetic enjambment results in a sectional
division in the middle of the fifth line of the octave. Even
through-composed songs, which grow steadily more frequent
throughout Pfitzner's career, exhibit strong control derived
from the poem's natural structure. Strophes may define tonal
strategy as in 'Wasserfahrt' (Op. 6 No. 6), 'Sehnsucht' (Op. 10
No. 1), or the narrative ballad after Busse, 'Leierkastenmann'.
In these, thematic and motivic continuity is so bound to the
poem's structure as to make the distinction between through-
composed and strophic virtually disappear, as is also the case
in the march song, 'Der Arbeitsmann' (Op. 30 No. 4). Consistency of figuration rather than motive dictated by the
poetic stanza is the hallmark of 'Ich und Du' (Op. 11 No. 1).
Only in occasional special cases, such as 'Nachtwanderer'
(Op. 7 No. 2), does the content of the song, in this instance
a typical reworking by Eichendorff of the necrophiliac
Romanticism associated with Bürger's 'Lenore', provide
the music's principal subdivision, though as often as not
poetic structure and content will proceed in tandem, as in
'Willkommen und Abschied', where the drastic change of
texture after two strophes corresponds to a change of mood.

To view Pfitzner as an absolute musician, then, at least
acknowledged the formal nature of his response to the text
in many cases. But the campaign for the song-writer as
'absolute' musician may also be seen as part of the distancing
of Pfitzner from any suggestion of the New German School
and its supposedly 'illustrative' tendencies. Equally, it was
meant to distance Pfitzner from the idea of a predominantly
text-orientated approach. In its simplest form this was a
rejection of facile word-painting, on a more complex level a
rejection of the declamatory style supposedly practised by
Wolf, about whom Pfitzner's own writings are remarkably
silent. What remains puzzling is how these easily understandable goals became warped to the point that Valentin could
maintain that Pfitzner's songs were 'absolute music like . . . a

sonata, a quartet, or a symphony of Beethoven'.[8] Inasmuch as the text must make at least a degree of difference, Valentin's point is absurd, but few writers on Pfitzner before the present day altogether managed to avoid it. Freund falls into the obverse trap of trying to relate Pfitzner's songs to an old-fashioned aesthetic of 'Romanticism', as persistent in music history as it is one-sided, in which the poetic idea (a concept which Pfitzner scorned) is restored to the kind of prominence craved for it in late nineteenth-century music by Constantin Floros.

Pfitzner himself as usual laid the foundations for a possible appraisal of his song output. The relevant passage of *Die neue Ästhetik* proceeds from 'the entire problem of vocal music' (*SS II* 211). In it is to be found no outright condemnation of poetic ideas as such; rather, Pfitzner acknowledges the possibility of poetic ideas stimulating the musical imagination, but only where there are already musical powers. He grants similarly that a poem may provide 'the strong sensuous element of the inspiring rhythm which is often already half melody', but only to a real musical talent. This seems unexceptionable, but then Pfitzner begins his part-historical survey of 'das Wort-Ton-Verhältnis':

On the whole the relationship of tone to word can be divided into three large areas, which naturally cannot always be cleanly separated from one another. The first is that which Schopenhauer envisaged, and actually the only one he knew. Here the composer writes himself out of melodies, and those of near instrumental character, leaving the text, which is then certainly as absurd or as general as Schopenhauer assumed it, more or less to sort itself out. That was the old Italian opera, that was and is much church music, that was the bulk of vocal music in the past. The majority of vocal music in later and present years occupies the second area. There the composition proceeds from the word. In this principle lie the dangers and the unmusicality of the procedure; the earlier method was more musical. The more the composer devotes himself to the word, the more he must cling to the word as a consequence of lack of musicality, so much more is the virtue of the song endangered: naturalness becomes 'good declamation', characterization becomes word-painting, atmosphere [*Stimmung*] becomes manipulation of the audience [*Stimmungsmache*]; driven from the summit, as happens today, the musical organism, which the literary composer forgets on account of the syllables of the poem, is nullified and the

---

[8] Quoted in Freund, *Hans Pfitzners Eichendorff-Lieder*, 12.

musical residue is meaningless. But the third area embraces the idea of vocal music which has a deep justification and represents the ideal of the same. There are the cases in the art where two different sources of the same spirit run and flow together to an entity in which word and tone become one, where the mood accords as in a pure consonance. But it must flow from deep springs, especially the music; this is not born wearily from the spirit of the poem; it must come from its own domain and in its own way independently conjure up the same atmosphere which the poem expresses; this can happen *entirely* independently, *before* knowledge of the poem, or gently touched by it, as with a divining rod. In this way come into existence songs like 'Mondnacht' or 'Frühlingsglaube', the pride of their genre, sparks produced by the contact of two opposite poles. (*SS II* 211–12)

The idea that the composition of a song may proceed in some measure independently of the text and yet be appropriate to it no longer seems surprising since Schoenberg's account of his working methods.[9] Even Schoenberg did grant that he might have begun by looking at the text; he might have shared Eckart Busse's surprise that Pfitzner could be stimulated to a song before the text lay to hand. 'Is it thinkable that the composer compiles an immense number of poems *after* the musical inspiration until he has found ... the one adequate to the musical invention?'[10] But this is to take a naïvely literal view of Pfitzner's argument.

Too much writing on Pfitzner has depended on the assumption that a coherent system could be extracted from his aesthetics. The impossibility of always pinning down the *Einfall* to some firm musical conceptual shape should be sufficient warning that it is necessary to evaluate Pfitzner's words very carefully. Even if a piece of music acquired a text retrospectively, factors such as mood and musical imagery might already hint at the possible verbal partner; thus the music for Italy in 'Dietrich's Narration' was conceived before the text, in connection with a quite different poem, 'Nun, da so warm der Sonnenschein', but this was close enough in literary images to the Italian sun for the music to survive the transplant without doing violence to the narration. Whether Pfitzner ever added words to a pre-existent piece of music or not, it is hardly possible to doubt that musical motives may have preceded and come to the aid of many a setting. That

[9] Arnold Schoenberg, 'The Relationship to the Text', *Style and Idea*, trans. Leo Black, ed. Leonard Stein (London, 1975), 141–5.
[10] Eckart Busse, *Die Eichendorff-Rezeption im Kunstlied* (Würzburg, 1975), 106.

Pfitzner at some point worked out the strictly musical consequences of a melody, theme, motive, rhythm, or chord sequence as the basis for a song is scarcely surprising. In this limited sense, there can be no doubt that his songs are indeed 'absolute', if only because of the insufficiency of the approach that would claim them for an opposite point of view. This is the drastic weakness of Freund's thesis, since his enthusiastic tracing of word-painting in Pfitzner only occasionally finds a case that is not derived by musical means from the motivic substance of the song.

Perhaps the two most prominent categories of tone-painting in Pfitzner's songs concern bells and bird-song. The former have already been seen to play prominent parts in *Der arme Heinrich* (the cloister bell in Salerno) and *Palestrina*. At least seven of the songs use bell effects, beginning as Abendroth noted with 'Über ein Stündlein' (Op. 7 No. 3), a setting of Paul Heyse dating probably from 1888/9 which is one of the most motivically consistent of Pfitzner's many Conservatory songs.[11] Most of the thematic material derives from the piano's introductory figure (Ex. 6.1a) and the setting of the

Ex. 6.1a

b

Dul - de, ge - dul - de dich   fein!

c

---

[11] Abendroth, *Hans Pfitzner*, 356.

first line, 'Dulde, gedulde dich fein!' (Ex. 6.1*b*); neighbouring notes and the intervals of third and fourth thus are the very substance of the setting. It is from the third that the bell motive is developed for 'Über den First, wo die Glocken hangen'. Motive becomes ostinato which swells to the 'storm of the bells' (Ex. 6.1*c*). A similar procedure is adopted in 1906 for 'Michaelskirchplatz', a song which may initially seem discouraging through its plain procession of heavy chordal quavers reminiscent of Schumann. But in characteristic style, Pfitzner diversifies his accompaniment by neighbouring-note figuration which eventually settles on an oscillation of seconds for the bells of St Michael's church. The particular figure and the supporting seventh chords in regular quavers look forward with particular clarity to the climax of Act I of *Palestrina*. Sometimes, as in the Eichendorff setting, 'Der verspätete Wanderer' (Op. 41 No. 2), the last but one of Pfitzner's songs, it merely requires a transfer of the main accompaniment figure to a deeper register to convey the suggestion of evening bells, while the similarly deep figuration of another Eichendorff song, 'Nachts' (Op. 26 No. 2), seems to be created with bell sounds partly in mind from the start. Where Pfitzner does not prepare his bell effects in advance, they are usually integrated in retrospect. Thus 'Im Herbst' (Op. 9 No. 3) departs from its semiquaver arpeggiated texture for a repeated octave in an inner part at 'und Abendglocken schallen | fern von des Waldes Saum'. The musical significance of the moment lies less in the specific echo of a regularly tolling bell than in the motive it accompanies, which dominates the rest of the song. In a less sophisticated context such as the folk-like 'Gretel', bell-effects and other pieces of word-painting provide the opportunity for small variations within the individual strophes. Pfitzner seldom permits his response to an image to disturb either the logic of the composition or the predominant mood.

Pfitzner's use of bird-song is much less open to classification, an inevitable consequence of the different manifestations stemming from such traditional symbols as the cock or the crow. Pfitzner, in common with all other composers of Lieder, was continually called upon to respond to such a wide variety of bird evocations that uniformity is obviously not to be expected. There are clear cases where bird-song in Pfitzner is so general as to suggest that word-painting was indeed far from his thoughts, as in the repeated semiquavers at 'In der

Vögel Morgenlieder' in the early 'Naturfreiheit' (*Jl.* No. 3), which may or may not evoke the chatter of a dawn chorus. Elsewhere, as in 'In der Früh', wenn die Sonne kommen will' (Op. 2 No. 1), the mention of larks at the start is simply ignored, as are the birds in the Cossmann setting, 'Die Bäume wurden gelb' (Op. 6 No. 5); Pfitzner responds not to them but to the quality of their singing ('leise') with a sudden drop in dynamic. In some of Pfitzner's chosen poems there are examples of birds which fail to stand out from a stream of natural images which combine to illustrate an emotional state; thus 'Mailied', one of his most spontaneous and attractive pieces, uses a famous Goethe text in which the song of the lark is simply part of the general benevolence of nature. No break in the ceaseless figuration is required, though it does momentarily soar into the lark's normally high musical register. The Keller setting, 'Singt mein Schatz wie ein Fink', by contrast seems to stake everything on word-painting, but the final songs take the same reserved attitude towards bird-song as before: it is mildly decorative in 'Sehnsucht' (Op. 40 No. 3), almost ignored in the two Eichendorff songs which conclude Opus 41.

The most revealing case is the song of the nightingale, since here Pfitzner does seem to follow in a specific tradition, based on the equation of nightingale song and the trill, that is present at both ends of the nineteenth century in the 'Pastoral' Symphony of Beethoven and the 'Resurrection' Symphony of Mahler. Yet Pfitzner is surprisingly reticent in places, often favouring a limited slow oscillation through a second, first encountered as an evocation of the nightingale in 'Herbstlied'.[12] This slow oscillation is particularly attractive when shared between voice and piano, as in 'Die Einsame' (Op. 9 No. 2), another setting of Eichendorff (Ex. 6.2). The same type of figuration is employed, less evocatively, in 'Nun, da so warm der Sonnenschein', though there the poet simply speaks of 'das Vögelein'. It is noticeable that Pfitzner seldom uses this musical symbol for more than a few bars at a time; the Eichendorff setting 'Die Nachtigallen' makes no overt use of it, nor of bird-song in general. There is at least one case where Pfitzner departs from the tradition, but the choice of 'Unter den Linden' (Op. 24 No. 1) is rather unusual, the poem being

[12] For the same motive in Strauss's 'Ständchen', see Barbara A. Petersen, *'Ton und Wort': The Lieder of Richard Strauss* (Ann Arbor, Mich., 1980), 73.

Ex. 6.2

by Walther von der Vogelweide; it belongs with that archaizing group of songs which can be seen as preparatory for the musical language of *Palestrina* and which includes one other setting of Walther and a sonnet by Petrarch.[13] In 'Unter den Linden' the nightingale song is onomatopoeically conveyed by the poem, 'tandaradei', and Pfitzner sets this and extends it in the piano with the kind of baroque flourish that would not seem out of place in a song by Britten. Only two songs use the full exuberant trill motive, and of these one is, not surprisingly, the unashamedly illustrative 'Singt mein Schatz wie ein Fink'.

The final instance is perhaps the most revealing of all in considering Pfitzner's use of word-painting, since its resonance goes far beyond local contexts. Bürger's sonnet, 'Trauerstille', belongs with the group of songs that Pfitzner composed in the aftermath of *Palestrina*.

> O wie öde, sonder Freudenschall,
> Schweigen nun Paläste mir wie Hütten,
> Flur und Hain, so munter einst durchschritten,
> Und der Wonnesitz am Wasserfall!
>
> Todeshauch verwehte deinen Hall,
> Melodie der Liebesred' und Bitten,
> Welche mir in Ohr und Seele glitten,
> Wie der Flötenton der Nachtigall.
>
> Leere Hoffnung! nach der Abendröte
> Meines Lebens einst im Ulmenhain
> Süss in Schlaf von dir gelullt zu sein!
>
> Aber nun, o milde Liebesflöte,
> Wecke mich beim letzten Morgenschein
> Lieblich, statt der schmetternden Trompete!

Oh how emptily and joylessly silent now are palaces and hovels, meadow and grove, which I once cheerfully strode through, and the place of joy by the waterfall! The breath of death has blown away your echo, melody of love's conversation and pleading, which slipped into my ear and soul like the fluting of the nightingale.

Empty hope! At the end of the evening of my life to be lulled sweetly in sleep by you once in the elm trees' grove! But now, oh gentle flute of love, wake me on the last dawn sweetly instead of with the blaring trumpet!

---

[13] Pfitzner himself described the Petrarch sonnet Op. 24 No. 3 as 'Vorstudie z. *Palestrina*' (*Katalog Nr. 28: Hans Pfitzner (1869–1949)*, 58).

The opportunities for word-painting here are obvious: flute, nightingale, and trumpet, but more important is the overall possibility of *Stimmung*, which in the Lied is usually central in a way that *Tonmalerei* is not. Pfitzner holds the text together by a gradual increase in speed and density of figuration. The desolate A minor quavers of the main motive (Ex. 6.3*a*) grow from unaccompanied line to two and three parts through the first three lines of the octave, the very image of 'linear asceticism'. The main motive turns to B minor in

Ex. 6.3*a*

the bass at the waterfall, as the figuration above turns to semiquavers and the texture swells at first intermittently and then consistently to four parts (the 'breath of death' being captured by the Wagnerian half-diminished seventh). The climax of this gradual process of intensification is the nightingale's song in B major, first in the slower, measured oscillation, then swelling into real trills. This ecstatic moment fades, and B major turns desolately to G minor at 'Leere Hoffnung!' (Ex. 6.3*b*). It is one of the strengths of the song that Pfitzner does not attempt to prolong this most intense moment, but swiftly returns to the main motive now in F major with a rich mixture of homophonic texture and imitative elements for the consoling image of sleep. Trills return as the music drifts back towards A minor for the 'flute of love', and the final lines take place entirely over a drone of A and E. The music at this point is a minor version of the previous nightingale song which gradually drifts into the major for 'lieblich', resolving all tensions save for the 'blaring of the trumpet': this stands as a

Ex. 6.3*c*

tiny bitonal enclave of C major in the final A, the original
motive now supported by the horn fifth idiom, the 'blaring'
suggested rather than stated in the piano's finger staccato,
which resonates in the haze of pedal (Ex. 6.3*c*). The song
travels a vast distance from initial monotone through polyphony and homophony to a final impressionistic haze of
sound. Each figural change seems to be suggested by the text,
and yet one motive seems to have generated everything. If this
song is set beside a comparable one by Wolf, 'Karwoche', it
can readily be seen that both composers share a remarkably
similar approach, generating bird-like trills out of a sustained
process of development from an initial motive or figuration.
Both rely on drone pedals in places, and there is the same

skilfully contrived fading-away of the bird-song into a transition to the original figuration. But surprisingly Wolf is more 'architectonic' in his approach, returing eventually to a literal restatement of the opening material; in the field of song-writing the ability to blend word-painting with organic development of material is hardly the prerogative of any one composer, nor can one be claimed to be more of an 'absolute' musician than the other. Such comparisons stress the extent to which the supposedly Wagnerian and declamatory Wolf and the absolute Pfitzner belong to the same tradition.

In the case of another group of songs, the question of word-painting and illustration is less pressing. These are the songs in which persistent rapid, often arpeggiated figuration conveys the essence of a natural scene. In such songs, the figuration is the counterpart of waves, rivers, wind, rustling tree-tops, vague natural sounds, everything that floats and rustles. Such songs are to be found from the earliest period onwards, beginning with 'Naturfreiheit', Pfitzner's only setting of Uhland as a solo song. They raise that other question of Pfitzner studies, the nature and extent of his relationship to German Romanticism. The question is intimately bound up with his choice of poetry. If the label is to be employed scrupulously, the majority of the poets set by Pfitzner can hardly be considered romantic. The exact relationship of Goethe or Heine to Romanticism is hardly something that can be argued here; what is more important is the spirit in which Pfitzner set them. In the case of composers who were chronologically closer to Pfitzner's age, the question grows even more relevant, since in general Meyer and Liliencron did not subscribe to particular doctrines of Romanticism, however much they may have been aware of a certain residue which Romanticism bequeathed to the lyric poetry of the later nineteenth century. In some of the texts that Pfitzner set, this residue is tantamount to the entire content of the verse: into this category come some of the poems of Grun and Cossmann, and of obscure figures such as Richard Leander and Alexander Kaufmann. When Pfitzner turned to writers such as Rückert and Heyse, he tended to disregard the formal, antiquarian aspect of their writings, preferring lyrics in which the images of nature and folk were prominent. This is particularly true of the early songs; of the two Leander settings, Abendroth noted, 'The specific "Pfitznerian note" . . . is nevertheless given in the unerring folksiness of the invention', a statement which surely limits the real 'Pfitznerian note' to a quite absurd degree.[14] It would be better to point to the folk qualities of these songs as more truly the feature which indicates the limitations of their historical situation; Mahler's early settings of Leander show far more of his own personality, while the folk-like 'Hans und Grete' is stamped with its composer's later style to a much greater degree than in Pfitzner's rather conventional settings. But the folk dimension is something of a red herring in considering Pfitzner's relationship to Romanticism save in the most general of terms.

Much more central is the romantic language of nature. Pfitzner repeatedly turned to texts in which the loneliness of nature figures prominently. Central to this category are the settings of Eichendorff. As early as the first Eichendorff song, 'Der Bote' (Op. 5 No. 3), the images touch lightly on stars and distance, on wind, mountain, and wood, and on nocturnal music. With 'Lockung' (Op. 7 No. 4), Pfitzner succumbs wholeheartedly to 'the yearning for the transcendent and the search for natural origins' that marks the familiar picture of Eichendorff.[15] In the group devoted entirely to Eichendorff (Op. 9), this mood engulfs most of the songs and is encapsulated in 'Abschied', with its forest rustlings in the evening 'aus den tiefen Gründen'. The poem is an adumbration of the side of the poet encapsulated later in the nocturnal sequences of *Von deutscher Seele*. The presence of the 'Lord who kindles the stars' does not overcome the vague sense of terror in the chasms of the forest. In Pfitzner's setting, the constant arpeggios drift in and out of focus in a blend of complex rhythms, semiquavers in 6/8 underpinned by quavers grouped in eights and sevens, symbols of the intangibility of the verse. The simple modified strophic form serves to hold a single mood in suspension.

In 'Nachts', the case is more complex.

> Ich stehe in Waldesschatten
> Wie an des Lebens Rand,
> Die Länder wie dämmernde Matten,
> Der Strom wie ein silbern Band.
>
> Von fern nur schlagen die Glocken
> Über die Wälder herein,

---

[14] Abendroth, *Hans Pfitzner*, 352.
[15] Brigitte Peucker, *Lyric Descent in the German Romantic Tradition* (New Haven, Conn., and London, 1987), 1.

Ein Reh hebt den Kopf erschrocken
Und schlummert gleich wieder ein.

Der Wald aber rühret die Wipfel
Im Traum von der Felsenwand,
Denn der Herr geht über die Gipfel
Und segnet das stille Land.

I stand in the forest's shadows, as at the edge of life, the lands like darkening meadows, the stream like a silver band.

From afar only the bells toll hither over the forest, a deer raises its head in fright, and returns again to sleep.

But the wood stirs the tree-tops as they dream of the rock-face, for the Lord passes over the summits and blesses the silent land.

Pfitzner's deep arpeggios, fluctuating in mode in a manner that reaches far back into the rhetoric of the nineteenth century, serve not only for the bells but for the shadow which lies over everything; only for the stream does the voice rise momentarily. Although the divisions of Pfitzner's song again mirror the strophes, a more complex design is required as the quaver movement quickens first to triplets for the final stanza, then to semiquavers for the last two lines, only to sink back by degrees to quavers, now in unalloyed major, for a repetition of 'das stille Land'. In such a song, the figuration is as intrinsic to the overall shape as the melody, a point which bears some consideration. For it was in relation to this song that Berg attempted to hoist Pfitzner with his own petard: Pfitzner's 'Wie schön!', an inadequate reaction to 'Träumerei', was an adequate comment on the implicitly inadequate melodic inspiration of his own song.[16] But Berg's argument is just as easy to turn inside out; if Pfitzner's point was that 'Träumerei' was somehow beyond analysis, it hardly needs to be pointed out that analysis can uncover something more than Berg was prepared to concede to 'Nachts'.[17] This much can be granted even if one feels that in picking on this song, Berg hit indeed upon a case where the melodic 'inspiration' of the voice part was perhaps not of the subtlety which Schumann might have lavished on the text. Simply by itself, the melody is too immediate a response to the elevated tone of

---

[16] Alban Berg, 'The Musical Impotence of Hans Pfitzner's "New Aesthetic"', in Willi Reich, *The Life and Work of Alban Berg*, trans. Cornelius Cardew (London, 1965), 205–18.

[17] See Johann Peter Vogel, 'Das Lied *Nachts* von Hans Pfitzner: Ein Nachwort zur Kritik Alban Bergs an der *Neuen Ästhetik*', *SPB* 217–31.

the poem, a counterpart of the high-flown sentiments that pall in *Der arme Heinrich*. But there is more than that to 'Nachts', and it is pertinent to be reminded by Eckart Busse that a sequence of chords can be of more importance as *Einfall* than a melody.[18]

Songs such as 'Abschied' and 'Nachts' speak directly out of a tradition that is rooted in early nineteenth-century Romanticism, and the musical style that is cultivated there is adaptable enough to cover not only 'Zum Abschied meiner Tochter' (Op. 10 No. 3), in which the perceiving subject is more strongly objectified, but also episodes in the extrovert 'Studentenfahrt' (Op. 11 No. 3). That this romantic tradition extends far beyond Eichendorff to embrace aspects of other poets is self-evident. If the 'Grund' in Eichendorff is 'a meta-phor for the inner self', then the moon in Goethe's 'An den Mond' (Op. 18) may be the agent of 'an intermingling of self and world . . . a dissolving of boundaries'; 'the yearning for the transcendent and the search for natural origins' may produce uneasy tensions, but it is amid such tensions that Pfitzner finds one aspect of his mature musical voice.[19] If Romanticism locates itself in such a context, then Pfitzner is its unabashed heir. Yet even within the world of Pfitzner's Eichendorff set-tings there are other themes. 'Zorn' (Op. 15 No. 2) reveals an aspect of the poet absent from Schumann and not well rep-resented even in Wolf. 'Sonst' (Op. 15 No. 4) is an elaborate pastiche, which draws Pfitzner into a more humorous (and, in the depiction of the flight of Cupid's arrow, illustrative) parody of the eighteenth century than the scherzo and finale of the Quartet in D. As Pfitzner developed, so he came to grasp aspects of Eichendorff that lay outside the Lied to this date. For a song such as 'In Danzig' the rustling of tree-tops had no meaning. It is not that the poem bears no relation to earlier choices; the images are as consistent as ever, but the geography has changed; a 'fairy-tale world' or 'ein uraltes Lied' may also be perceived in a silent city by night. The musical language adapts to meet the challenge, arguably to a point where Pfitzner's relationship to Eichendorff enters a different dimension from that of Schumann or Wolf. For Busse, this had an aspect that was reflected in choice of text, Schumann (and partly the early Pfitzner) aiming for

[18] Busse, *Die Eichendorff-Rezeption im Kunstlied*, 141.
[19] Peucker, *Lyric Descent*, 1, 5, 28.

Stimmung, Wolf achieving a formal relationship to texts characterized by 'one-line semantic coherence', and Pfitzner seeking gradual intensification in which the ending usually clarified the content; in this sense, both 'Nachts' and 'In Danzig' are typical of Pfitzner's approach.[20] This seems a more valid differentiation than the related classification in which Schumann seeks 'hermeneutic intensification' of the text and Wolf's form arises from the poem, while Pfitzner worked out the 'architectonics of the primal inspiration'.[21] In the latter, commentary again bows to the 'absolute music' thesis. Busse none the less draws attention to the degree to which Pfitzner had gone beyond the relatively simple-minded Romanticism that had sufficed to set Grun or Cossmann. The technical correlative to this progression in the reception of the text lay in the contrapuntal qualities that achieved full stature in 'An die Mark'.

In the songs from the Frankfurt period counterpoint tends to be an inconspicuous feature, an enrichment of a style dominated by harmony and keyboard figuration: 'Verrat' (Op. 2 No. 7) is a good illustration of the way in which contrapuntal detail is caught up in Schumann's manner into a constant rush of figuration which decorates traditional harmonic progressions. During this period, the most conspicuous departure from such a norm tends to be the use of (the ineptly entitled) 'progressive tonality'. In Pfitzner's career as a song-writer some fourteen songs out of over a hundred end 'out' of the key of the beginning (this excludes both those that merely change mode, from major to minor or, very rarely, as in 'Schön Suschen', the reverse, and also cases like 'Abbitte' or the Huch setting, 'Eine Melodie singt mein Herz', Op. 35 No. 5, where the opening is deliberately obscure in regard to tonality). Of these, four are to texts by Heine. Ambivalence of key is almost a counterpart to Heine's technique of irony. This is clearest in the setting of 'Sie haben heut' Abend Gesellschaft' (Op. 4 No. 2). Pfitzner paints the contrast between the company of the first line and the suffering poet in terms of diatonic dance music and chromatic distortions. The main motive of the opening is first dragged into chromatic obscurities after 'Dort oben am hellen Fenster/ Bewegt sich ein Schattenbild' and then rhythmically ex-

---

[20] Busse, *Die Eichendorff-Rezeption im Kunstlied*, 109.
[21] Ibid. 139–40.

tended. From this C♯ minor emerges as a new key centre, and although the dance music whirls to a new climax in A, the fact that the beloved still fails to see the poet's heartbreak is enough to drag the postlude back into C♯ minor. (In Wolf's relatively early setting, the unchanging dance music frames the whole.) It is more usual in the Heine settings to end, not with so ineluctable a loss of key, but poised on the dominant, a question mark rather than a definite statement of heart-break. In this 'Ich will mich im grünen Wald ergehn' (Op. 6 No. 2) is typical; the tonal plan is contingent upon the revela-tion of the text, which begins and ends with the green wood, flowers, and bird-song, but in the central section the poet remembers that the grave will shut up eye and ear, and the final resolution into the tonic falters.

Such weakening of monotonality, which is to be felt also in the songs of Wolf and Mahler, is one strand in the harmonic development of Pfitzner's songs. But in others, notably the Jacobowski setting, 'Ich aber weiss' (Op. 11 No. 2), an imagin-ative use of chromatic harmony goes alongside a contrapuntal style which is reminiscent of Brahms, particularly in the way that a single short motive controls much of the development. 'An die Mark' is a development from this, but with a greater emphasis on the dissonant element which arises from linear polyphony; its text, by virtue of its stoical resignation, helps to make this the first clear example in Pfitzner's Lieder (as late as 1904) of the composer as 'linear ascetic':

> Bereifte Kiefern, atemlose Seen,
> Die träumen, einem dunklen Auge gleich,
> In ew'ger Sehnsucht von des Frühlings Reich;
> Und drüber hin ein schwarzer Zug von Kräh'n.
>
> Viel junges Leben will die Sonne sehn.
> Da sitzt die Schwermut schon am Waldesrand
> Und schreibt geheime Zeichen in den Sand,
> Kein Frühlingssturm wird ihre Schrift verweh'n.
>
> Und eines Tages kommt der junge Mai;
> Und dennoch, unter glückverlor'nen Küssen
> Lebt ein Bewusstsein, dass wir sterben müssen,
> Dass alles nur ein Traum und schmerzlich sei.
>
> Dies Land, da Wunsch und Hoffnung selig sind,
> Und doch in ihrem rätselvollen Wesen
> Von stiller Trauer niemals zu erlösen,
> Dies Land ist meine Heimat und ich bin sein Kind.

Frosted pines, breathless lakes, which dream, like a dark eye, in eternal longing for the realm of spring; and above it a black procession of crows.

Much new life will the sun see. There sits melancholy already at the wood's edge and writes secret signs in the sand, no spring storm will blow away its writing.

And one day comes young May; and yet, under kisses lost in happiness lives a knowledge that we must die, that everything is only a dream and sorrowful.

This land, where wish and hope are blessed, and yet in its enigmatic being never to be redeemed from silent grief, this land is my home and I am its child.

This song has always seemed to be central to Pfitzner's ethos. 'Sehnsucht, Klage und Einsamkeit' were the particular qualities which Lindlar, author of the first systematic study of the songs, perceived as essential qualities in Pfitzner, and they are personified in 'An die Mark'.[22] Equally it has always been recognized as a stylistic landmark for its radical polyphonic character,[23] even if this has been interpreted at times as also traditional:

... in Pfitzner the principle of song construction is often not bipolar (from vocal 'melody' and chordal-harmonic supporting accompaniment), but more homogenous, resembling chamber music, in which the piano part is not treated chordally but controlled in 'voices' of which the vocal part is then also one. Something can also be found to correspond to this even in Schumann.[24]

The examples chosen by Diez, which include Schumann's 'Auf einer Burg' and 'An die Mark', a not inapposite pairing, illustrate his other main point, that such polyphony arises out of a single motivic entity. None the less, 'An die Mark' is not to be regarded as simply epigonal. Its enharmonic shifts are the legacy of nineteenth-century chromaticism, but the persistent decay of full textures to bare octaves is a feature which stamps the song with its own personality; this is the symbol of reality, the crows which intervene on the longing for spring, 'melancholy sitting at the wood's edge', downward turns which blast the recurring reminders of 'wish and hope'. These chromatic slips help to disguise the fact that many of

[22] Heinrich Lindlar, *Hans Pfitzners Klavierlied* (Würzburg-Aumühle, 1940), 26.
[23] Abendroth, *Hans Pfitzner*, 358–9.
[24] Diez, *Hans Pfitzners Lieder*, 86–7.

the most unexpected dissonances generated by the polyphony are diatonic, creating fleeting moments of quartal tension through the prolongation of passing notes; most of the motives are scale segments, as also are many of the underlying bass movements. The opening motive (Ex. 6.4*a*) falls by step through a fifth (*x*), while the voice part takes over from the piano an ascending motion through the minor third (*y*), which is part of a longer-term attempt to balance that opening motive; characteristically that balancing ascent finds its fullest form in a middle part. But this ascent, which covers the first line and part of the second (*z*), is itself counterpointed with the same motives, the descending fifth and the rising minor third, to produce a complex tapestry over an extremely slow-moving ascent in the bass. The effect is of polyphonic activity against a virtually unchanging background. The coming of May brings greater activity and a figure which struggles out of the predominant step-wise motion, but this too collapses back into the music of the opening for the last verse; the inner and outer landscapes, desolate in their 'breathlessness', are still home, and the last bars return to A minor from

Ex. 6.4*a*

Langsam und schwermütig, mit unbelebtem Ausdruck

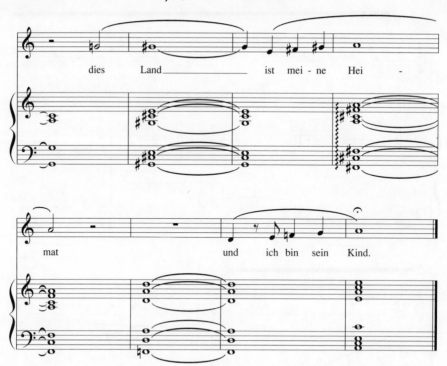

the edge of C♯ minor on which the music had faltered at
'Trauer' (Ex. 6.4*b*); Pfitzner thus conjures a curious sense
of muted affirmation out of this seemingly featureless material. This is music which already looks forward strongly to
Palestrina and helps to define not merely the polyphonic mode
of writing characteristic of its hero, but also his moods, the
meaninglessness of life in Act I, the stoic serenity of the ending. As befits a song, it concentrates these to a distillation
which almost outranks the music-drama, particularly in
the final bars where the verses emphasize the irredeemable
quality of the grief which is still human life. As a tribute
to the landscape of the Mark of Brandenburg, this song is
unmatched, but it is at the same time close to a self-portrait,
one of its composer's most personal achievements.

Pfitzner's counterpoint in 'An die Mark' is hardly strict in
the traditional sense. Only in a certain visual resemblance to
the *stile antico*, as Peter Cahn has observed, does it approximate to traditional concepts of contrapuntal skill; its dense
network of motives, at least at foreground level, does not

aspire to the complex of strettos, augmentations, and diminutions to be found in the somewhat later 'Tragische Geschichte' (Op. 22 No. 2), which belongs to a rather different idea of comic, parodistic counterpoint with roots deep in the nineteenth century.[25] Nor is it as complex from chromatic and contrapuntal standpoints as the slightly earlier slow movement of the D major Quartet. The Petrarch sonnet of five years later, 'Voll jener Süsse' (Op. 24 No. 3), represents a refining of the same free counterpoint towards that chamber-music texture described by Lindlar. The piano maintains an unbroken three-part texture until the end, into which the voice threads itself, now in counterpoint, now partly in unison with one or other contrapuntal strand. The sonnet is a love poem (set also by Schoenberg in his Opus 8), depicting the emotional turmoil into which the glance of 'a beautiful face' throws the poet; such a situation is uncommon in Pfitzner's operas before *Das Herz* (with the exception of the fairy-tale love affair in *Die Rose vom Liebesgarten*). *Palestrina* enters such an emotional territory only in connection with the dead Lukrezia. The sonnet is no preparation for Silla's little song either, but instead aims to create a seamless continuity, in which keys arise from sideslips of an often enharmonic character; the polyphony of 'An die Mark' is thus shaped towards the love songs of the Ricarda Huch cycle, in which such linear chromaticism is also encountered. Some of the figuration suggests the main motives from Act I of *Palestrina* in diminution, others, particularly in the sestet, recall the hero's monologue from 'Man fühlt es nicht im frohen Rausch der Jugend' onwards. Cadences on occasion have a 'modal tinge, substituting a fall through flattened seventh and sixth for the traditional leading-note.

The 'linear ascetic' in Pfitzner is the aspect which seems most strikingly to move in historical tandem with such contemporaries as Mahler and even Schoenberg. Yet there is a more purely harmonic dimension to Pfitzner's 'progressive' idiom, if so it may be called, that has its reflection in the styles of his contemporaries. As early as 'Venus mater', a vein of pronouncedly chromatic writing in a post-*Tristan* idiom is apparent, so much so that commentators rushed to draw comparisons with Strauss (who set the same text in the famous 'Wiegenlied'). This may have been a reflection of

[25] Peter Cahn, 'Kontrapunktische Züge im Liedschaffen Pfitzners', *PLZ*.

the 'erotic' dimension of the poem to which Lindlar draws attention.[26] Whether this be the case or not, Erwin Kroll established a trend by suggesting that in this harmonically 'luxurious' song Pfitzner drew close to Strauss's own style, abandoning to some extent his usual 'linear' approach.[27] This theory, like many others in the earlier Pfitzner literature, seems strained almost to breaking point, in that much of 'Venus mater' is dependent, chromatic or not, on contrary-motion step-wise progressions in the outer parts (Ex. 6.5), whereas Strauss's song is woven almost entirely out of melody and accompanying arpeggiation; in any case, Pfitzner's linear style was only just coming to fruition in 1901. None the less, later songs revealed harmonic dimensions to Pfitzner's songs which brought in train much more surprising comparisons.

In the single song of Opus 18, 'An den Mond', Pfitzner appeared to his commentators to challenge Debussy on his home ground by extensively using the whole-tone scale; that they did not consider to any extent the presence of the scale in Berg and Schoenberg brings out the latently nationalist flavour of the comparison. Again Kroll in 1924 provides the basic stance which remains unchanged in Lindlar, who wrote in times when crude national judgements were almost mandatory. Broadly speaking, Pfitzner is seen to use the scale as living formal entity, while the Frenchman thought in terms of atmosphere, impressions, and the picturesque.[28] Few analysts of Debussy nowadays would accept so facile a comparison.[29] Equally, it might be noted that the scale is at least partly employed as evocation of the moon and the 'Nebelglanz' which it casts over landscape and the poet's soul. But that is not to gainsay the difficulty of categorizing the whole-tone scale in relation to traditional tonality. Several techniques are apparent in Pfitzner's treatment of it. One is simply to view it as a linear decoration of an augmented triad, in this case G–B–D♯.[30] Since the whole-tone scale

[26] Lindlar, *Hans Pfitzners Klavierlied*, 27.
[27] Erwin Kroll, *Hans Pfitzner* (Munich, 1924), 144; he is followed by Abendroth (*Hans Pfitzner*, 357); see also Werner Heller, 'Pfitzners Dehmel- und Liliencron-Vertonungen und die textgleichen Lieder von Strauss und Reger', *PLZ*.
[28] Kroll, *Hans Pfitzner*, 149–50; Lindlar, *Hans Pfitzners Klavierlied*, 35.
[29] For an example of a whole-tone segment underpinning a structural progression, see James Hepokoski, 'Formulaic Openings in Debussy', *19th Century Music*, 8 (1984/5), 55.
[30] For Pfitzner's linear use of the whole-tone scale, see Wolfgang Osthoff, 'Pfitzner und der "historische Materialstand"', *SPB* 120.

Ex. 6.5

eliminates the traditional prop of the dominant, this augmented triad does duty for a dominant in various local progressions, the D♯ acting as leading-note to the tonic, E
minor. G is used as bass, moving down to the tonic eventually
through F♯; the vocal line defines the triad with D♯ and G
as the limits of the initial descending line, B the point to
which it returns (Ex. 6.6*a*). By reading the whole-tone scale

Ex. 6.6*a*

b

bars   90   93   94   97   98

c

bars   102   103   105

enharmonically, Pfitzner then retains the possibility of side-slipping from E minor (in which D♯ is leading note) to E♭ minor.[31] A further structural factor is provided by the use of the two different transpositions of the scale, a property which Arnold Whittall has termed both 'a strategic use' and an 'enhancement' in Debussy.[32] This is clearest in the final

[31] Osthoff (ibid. 122) has pointed out that the relationship between E♭ and E minor is also involved in the bitonal passage from the Overture to *Das Käthchen von Heilbronn*.

[32] Arnold Whittall, 'Tonality and the Whole-Tone Scale in the Music of Debussy', *Music Review*, 36 (1975), 271.

stanza; a descending segment of the leading-note's scale is immediately balanced by a rise through a segment of the other transposition (Ex. 6.6*b*). Since it is this 'tonic' scale which continues to the end of the piece, a new cadence must be found which employs a flattened, but rising, seventh scale degree (Ex. 6.6*c*). Only at bar 69 is the dominant fully elaborated for a few bars, a reminder that this is not so consistent a whole-tone piece as the outer sections of 'Voiles' (though the B in the bass escapes towards the tonic through a whole-tone segment ($B-A-G-F-E$)). Pfitzner regularly employs segments of the scale as motives, or even more potently as long-note cantus firmi in the piano, but surrounds them with figuration that mixes augmented triads with other chromatic chords or passing notes.[33] His approach, then, resembles Debussy's in that features of the scale are employed as enhancement of basic tonality, and that properties both of the scale and of its limited transposition are used for strategic purposes, albeit locally. But it is also compatible with his own fondness for creating linear structures out of scale segments; in this sense, 'An die Mark' and 'An den Mond' complement one another.

If 'An den Mond' sustains the comparison with Debussy remarkably well while remaining close enough to Pfitzner's own style, 'Abbitte', his only setting of Hölderlin, represents the extreme limit of his harmonic experimentation. As with many of Pfitzner's chosen texts, images of nature are prominent, especially in its second stanza:

> Heilig Wesen! gestört hab'ich die goldne
>   Götterruhe dir oft, und der geheimen,
>   Tieferen Schmerzen des Lebens
>   Hast du manche gelernt von mir.
>
> O vergiss es, vergib! gleich dem Gewölke dort
>   Vor dem friedlichen Mond, geh'ich dahin, und du
>   Ruhst und glänzest in deiner
>   Schöne wieder, du süsses Licht!
>
> Holy being, I know, often I've troubled your
>   Golden, god-like repose, so that you learned from me
>   Much that might have been spared you,
>   Life's more hidden, obscurer griefs.

---

[33] For the use of the whole-tone scale as cantus firmus see Osthoff, 'Pfitzner und der "historische Materialstand"', *SPB* 124.

O forgive me, forget! Look, as the clouds up there
  Veil with black the slow moon, I drift away, while you
    Stay and shine in your beauty,
      Gentle light, as you shone before.[34]

In spite of this, the poem sounds a new note in Pfitzner's output. That the poem has its origin in the veneration of Diotima (Hölderlin's Grecian idealization of Susette Gontard) may have been secondary to Pfitzner's appreciation of it, though it is one of only two songs that he dedicated to Mimi. (In general, as Bernhard Adamy has suggested, Pfitzner cannot be counted amongst Hölderlin's warmest admirers.[35]) In addition to the moon and clouds of the second stanza, Pfitzner may have responded to the unexplained suggestion of grief contained in the second and third lines of the first stanza. But the key image from which the music starts out is none of these, but rather the contrast between the 'Holy being' and the disturbance which the poet has caused. This discordance is reflected in the extraordinary chromatic chords of the opening, which resolve unexpectedly on to a C major triad in the third bar. The progression is repeated from 'gestört', but without so decisive a resolution; in place of C comes A♭ major in its first inversion at 'Götterruhe' (Ex. 6.7*a*). Later it returns and is extended for the final couplet, with the most unexpected resolution of all into D major at 'Licht!'. Few commentators on Pfitzner have failed to draw attention to these striking bars, though their full significance has seldom been analysed in detail.

The first three chords have related structures when considered simply as unordered collections of pitches without regard to roots or voice-leading. They are all based on a whole-tone scale segment with one extra semitone (*). Chord 1 is transpositionally equivalent to Chord 2 save for the omission of one pitch necessary to complete the collection. Chord 3 is slightly different, though based on the same principle (Ex. 6.7*b*). It is contained like Chord 2 in the parent collection of all these sets, the whole-tone scale plus one semitone. The persistent relevance of the whole-tone scale is intensified when the bass's D♭ in the third bar produces a pure whole-tone chord before the resolution into C. These

---

[34] Translation by Michael Hamburger as in Friedrich Hölderlin, *Poems and Fragments*, rev. edn. (Cambridge, 1980), 39.
[35] Bernhard Adamy, *Hans Pfitzner* (Tutzing, 1980), 179.

Ex. 6.7*a*

Sehr langsam und feierlich

b

c

particular pitch class sets are familiar enough. In George
Perle's analysis of Berg's *Wozzeck*, they occur frequently as the
basis of motifs.[36] It was left to Allen Forte, however, to spot
that the collection of Chord 2 was in fact one form of the so-
called 'mystic chord' familiar in late Scriabin.[37] Pfitzner's
collection is the tritonal antipode to the most frequently cited
transposition of the 'mystic chord' (Ex. 6.7c). But the structural basis of Pfitzner's opening is not so much the interesting chord formations themselves as the contrary-motion
chromatic scale segments in the outer parts which not only
lead towards C but also convert the whole-tone segments from
one transposition to another. Only one other event in the song
causes one to think of Scriabin or other composers of the era,
and that is the superimposition of two diminished triads at
the words '(gleich dem Ge)wölke dort | Vor dem (friedlichen
Mond)'. This combination produces the collection often referred to as the octatonic scale. Its importance in Rimsky-
Korsakov and Messiaen, in Bartók and Stravinsky, quite apart
from Scriabin, is well known. In the bell sequence in Act I of
Palestrina, the combination of diminished sevenths with
neighbouring notes frequently generated chords which belong
in the octatonic scale. The latter instance, however, may
easily be explained without reference to the scale, and in
'Abbitte' the chord is only sounded for two and a half bars
before it changes by step-wise motion; it is sufficiently cloudy
for the image and then clarifies to a major triad in first inversion at 'Mond'. It is not of deep structural import save as a
point of extreme chromatic tension. As his admirers have
always sensed, Pfitzner's chromatic language was as capable
of extension into extreme fields as those of his contemporaries.
What distinguishes him most clearly from them, however, is
his need to resolve extreme chromatic tensions into the pure
light of the unsullied triad. To this extent, his response to
Hölderlin's troubled Hellenic muse was instinctively correct.

Songs like 'An den Mond' and 'Abbitte' are rare in Pfitzner's
output in placing so much emphasis on harmonic innovation.
It is more usual to find a dense chromatic idiom combined in
some way with the linear style of the Petrarch sonnet. Even
then, both linear polyphony and chromaticism are liable

[36] The most recent statement of Perle's analysis is in *The Operas of Alban Berg*,
vol. i (Berkeley and Los Angeles, 1980), 155–7.

[37] Allen Forte, *The Structure of Atonal Music* (New Haven, Conn., and London,
1973), 28.

to be episodic, as in the middle section of the harmonically more conventional Hebbel setting, 'Gebet' (Op. 26 No. 1). The full force of Pfitzner's original handling of line and harmony is usually reserved for one song in each opus, such as 'Herbstbild', 'In Danzig', and 'Hussens Kerker'. The latter two in a sense make a pair to the extent that the Meyer setting is almost a variation in all but themes on the earlier Eichendorff song. The constituent elements are a complex harmonic idiom, use of ostinato both for contrast and cohesion, and the pervasive sense of chorale textures. The latter were apparent in earlier Pfitzner, in the often hymnal harmonies of 'Der Gärtner' and its more concentrated minor-mode parallel to a poem by Hebbel, 'Ich und Du'. But the chorale becomes the very fabric of the imprisoned Hus's meditation on approaching death and forms the impressively sustained climax of 'In Danzig'. High claims have been made for the latter, notably by Smeed, who felt that it could 'in its beauty and atmospheric power, stand comparison with any song by Wolf'.[38] As in many of Wolf's most intense religious songs, the voice part is in places an inspired fusion of melody and declamation, distinguishable as Pfitzner's principally through a certain rhythmic stolidity, particularly where the chorale influence is strongest:

> Dunkle Giebel, hohe Fenster,
> Türme, tief aus Nebeln sehn,
> Bleiche Statuen wie Gespenster
> Lautlos an den Türen stehn.
>
> Träumerisch der Mond drauf scheinet,
> Dem die Stadt gar wohl gefällt,
> Als läg' zauberhaft versteinet
> Drunten eine Märchenwelt.
>
> Ringsher durch das tiefe Lauschen,
> Über alle Häuser weit,
> Nur des Meeres fernes Rauschen—
> Wunderbare Einsamkeit!
>
> Und der Türmer wie vor Jahren
> Singet ein uraltes Lied:
> Wolle Gott den Schiffer wahren,
> Der bei Nacht vorüberzieht!

Dark gables, lofty windows, towers gaze out of dense mist, pale statues like ghosts stand noiselessly at the gates.

[38] J. W. Smeed, *German Song and its Poetry, 1740–1900* (Beckenham, 1987), 207.

Dreamily the moon shines down on the town of which it is so fond, as if petrified by magic lay down there a fairy-tale world.

All around, as I listen intently, far beyond all the houses, only the sea's distant roar—miraculous solitude!

And the watchman, as for years past, sings an age-old song: may God protect the sailor who passes by in the night.[39]

The song exemplifies Pfitzner's treatment of ternary form, the outer stanzas being based on the same material, with the two central strophes presenting an elaboration that still falls into two clearly defined sections. The text's key images are not neglected: the brooding chords of the first section are as petrified as houses, towers, and statues (Ex. 6.8*a*), but are extended in the final section into the chorale apotheosis. In the central strophes, the moon rises in the music to a new texture which gradually liquefies into the roar of the sea. The linking motive is given out here in the left hand's first two bars. Although it is then abandoned, overall it is of more significance than the debatable reference to the 'Dies irae' in the right hand of bar 4 which recurs later.[40] The dissonant chord on which the voice enters is again a reflection of the movement of parts, particularly the bass's chromatic ascent. The tension thus indicated between E♭ and E is extended into the elaboration. As the main motive returns at bar 10, the E on which it is dependent supports C major, but gradually takes on the force of a tonic in an ostinato. The steady harmonies gradually turn into two interlacing lines in the right hand in which a D♯ minor triad gradually becomes prominent at 'Märchenwelt'. The pull between this and the insistent E in the bass is the pivot round which the return to E♭ minor takes place, the E being interpreted enharmonically as the flattened second scale degree (Ex. 6.8*b*). Once this return has been achieved, the interweaving lines in the right hand gradually dissolve into a single quaver strand from which isolated pitches stand out; with the left hand ostinato now in E♭, the music dissolves into the distant roar of the sea. In the impressive invocation of the watchman's song which concludes, the ostinato punctuates phrases and underpins the close.

---

[39] Translation by William Mann, Booklet accompanying the recording by Dietrich Fischer-Dieskau, *Live in Salzburg: Recitals 1962, 1963 and 1964*, EMI CMS 7 63167 2, p. 21.

[40] Freund, *Hans Pfitzners Eichendorff-Lieder*, 170–1.

Ex. 6.8*a*

Blei-che Sta - tuen wie Ge - spen - ster laut - los an den

Tü - ren stehn.

Träu - me - risch der Mond drauf schei - net,

Ex. 6.8*b*

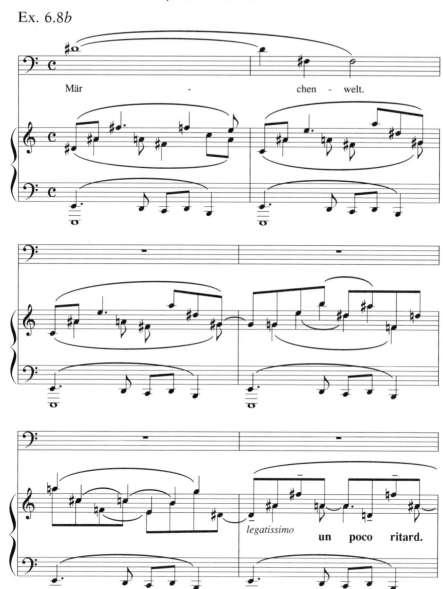

The link between this outstanding song and 'Hussens Kerker' arises partly because both are in some measure water pieces. But whereas Eichendorff's poem is a nocturne, Hus's meditation, in spite of the dungeon in which it is set, is of the daylight, however heavily filtered. Meyer's epic cycle *Huttens letzte Tage* was one of Pfitzner's favourite books, whose note he strove hard to interpret in the essay 'Pantragismus und Pessimismus':

There sits Hutten late one evening with his friendly landlord under the starry night sky before the house; they discuss the new teaching of Copernicus, according to which the stars up there are worlds like our earth, which all rotate around the sun, and are inhabited by beings like us, and that perhaps we will be reborn after death on one of these stars; they make other similar reflections, and Hutten sums up:

'All right, if one distributes new fiefs on the stars, I propose to stand my ground!'[41] (*SS IV* 52–3)

There may seem little real connection between the careers of Ulrich von Hutten, the sixteenth-century humanist, and the martyred Hus, though one writer has somewhat mysteriously referred to 'Hussens Kerker' as 'the definitive Hutten poem', in the sense, presumably, that it establishes the style of the future epic.[42] The only real point of contact resides in that they are both, on their quite different time-scales, preparations for death.

---

[41] 'Verteilt man auf den Sternen neue Lehn— | Wohlan! ich denke meinen Mann zu stehn.'

[42] Heinrich Henel, *The Poetry of Conrad Ferdinand Meyer* (Madison, Wis., 1954), 215.

Es geht mit mir zu Ende,
Mein' Sach' und Spruch ist schon
Hoch über Menschenhände
Gerückt vor Gottes Thron,
Schon schwebt auf einer Wolke,
Umringt von seinem Volke,
Entgegen mir des Menschen Sohn.

Den Kerker will ich preisen,
Der Kerker der ist gut!
Das Fensterkreuz von Eisen
Blickt auf die frische Flut,
Und zwischen seinen Stäben
Seh ich ein Segel schweben,
Darob im Blau die Firne ruht.

Wie nah die Flut ich fühle,
Als läg' ich drein versenkt,
Mit wundersamer Kühle
Wird mir der Leib getränkt—
Auch seh ich eine Traube
Mit einem roten Laube,
Die tief herab ins Fenster hängt.

Es ist die Zeit zu feiern!
Es kommt die grosse Ruh!
Dort lenkt ein Zug von Reihern
Dem ewgen Lenze zu,
Sie wissen Pfad und Stege,
Sie kennen ihre Wege—
Was, meine Seele, fürchtest du?

For me it is nearly over, my case and sentence are already removed high over the hands of men to God's throne. Already the son of man floats towards me on a cloud, surrounded by his people.

I wish to praise the dungeon, the dungeon is good! The crossbar of iron looks on the fresh waves. And between its bars I see a sail floating, over it last year's snows rest in the blue.

How near I feel to the waves, as if I lay sunk in them, with wonderful coolness my body is drenched. I see too a bunch of grapes with red foliage which hangs down deep into the window.

It is the time to celebrate! The great rest comes! There a flight of herons steers to the eternal spring. They know the paths and tracks, they know their way—what, my soul, frightens you?

Here the seven-line strophes are less in accord with the song's sections, since Pfitzner regularly divides each strophe into groups of four and three lines by changes of key and texture. The tonal strategy hinges on F minor in the main sections, and D major in the contrasting sections, which typically catch the 'floating' of the son of man and the waves of the central strophes. The use of a floating right-hand line in the first contrast section is close again to ostinato as it counterpoints the steady chorale textures; in the second, a true ostinato starts up in the same deep register as the roar of the sea in 'In Danzig'. It is here that the two settings are at their closest, and in each case the chorale breaks in with increased solemnity for the final section. The close is a positive counterpart to the much bleaker ending of 'An die Mark' where a halt on the edge of C♯ minor was redeemed by the return to the normality of A minor; in 'Hussens Kerker', D major returns with fervour for the herons' knowledge of the way; the voice part, hitherto inhibited by the marking, 'Das ganze Lied leise', is encouraged with 'vollere Tongebung'. The return to F (now major) which follows has the force of a deep reality after the moment of insight (Ex. 6.9). Elsewhere Pfitzner alternates long pedal points with solemn chord changes, none more weighty than those with roots an augmented fourth apart, such as accompany 'Der Kerker will ich preisen'. A fine touch is the expansion of a counterpoint to the main theme's first return into the floating line for the herons in the second return. The undifferentiated brooding Nature of Eichendorff, in which all is enshrouded in 'miraculous solitude', is humanized in Hus's dungeon; of Pfitzner's four fine Meyer settings, it is the one which seems most completely matched to the resonances of the text.

To insist on 'An die Mark', 'An den Mond', 'Abbitte', 'In Danzig', and 'Hussens Kerker' as the peaks of Pfitzner's Lieder, is perhaps to do him an injustice. It is not so much a matter of reinforcing the 'linear ascetic' stereotype as lending weight to the somewhat crasser formulation, that 'his songs of a solemn nature are far more effective than those supposed to be jolly'.[43] 'Mailied' and 'Sonst' are obvious contradictions of this in their different ways. But if the judgement were glossed to suggest that the solemn songs more clearly reveal the range of Pfitzner's stylistic development, then it would contain more than a grain of truth. The traditionalist in Pfitzner, the problem in historicist music criticism, is closer to the surface

---

[43] Hans A. Neunzig, 'Hans Pfitzner, der streitbare Erbe', booklet accompanying Hans Pfitzner, *Lieder in dokumentarischen Aufnahmen*, Michael Raucheisen Lied Edition, Acanta 40.23 532, [p. 7].

Ex. 6.9

amongst the Meyer songs when he resorts to march themes in 'Säerspruch' (Op. 32 No. 2) without Mahler's transfiguring irony, to Brahmsian melody and accompaniment in 'Eingelegte Ruder' (No. 3), and to nineteenth-century rhetoric in 'Lass scharren deiner Rosse Huf'. Alongside the sizeable number of outstanding songs in Pfitzner's output, there are others which seem epigonal, tailpieces to a great tradition. These are perhaps most numerous among those which are closest to a folk style, such as 'Gretel' or 'Untreu und Trost'. Even here, however, Pfitzner should not be written off as an imitator. 'Schön Suschen' confirms that as a melodist in a popular idiom he did not need to fear the more consistently fluent Strauss. The voice's opening melody is a perfect exemplar of the art of quadratic phrasing. The first motive (Ex. 6.10*a*) is a melodic curve that remembers a

Ex. 6.10*a*

b

Gregorian motive (used extensively by Liszt in *Die Legende von der heiligen Elisabeth*). When the piano introduces the contrasting melody, the bass line supports the tune's lingering descent with a balancing ascent in model contrary motion (Ex. 6.10*b*). 'Schön Suschen' is clear proof that Pfitzner's style could successfully embrace a conventional diatonic melody as well as declamation and counterpoint; it is the most immediately attractive of the songs, analogous in tone to the finale of the Violin Sonata in the instrumental works.

This is not the only direction in which the folk elements in Pfitzner's style developed, since the second setting of 'Das verlassene Mägdlein' is arguably closer to the folk spirit than the more famous setting by Wolf. The sophistication of Wolf's chromatic melody and elliptical augmented harmonies is replaced in Pfitzner by a melodic line naggingly enclosed within the diapente of the minor mode, save for occasional isolated climaxes. The whining repetitiveness of the accompaniment and the conclusion on a second inversion of the tonic chord brings this folk re-creation almost to the verge of the kind of setting associated with Bartók, in which an ancient style is revitalized with modern means. 'Das verlassene Mägdlein' points to the surprising developments of folk style that take place in the cycle derived from Gottfried Keller's *Alte Weisen*. Whereas the earlier 'An die Bienen' (Op. 22 No. 5) is a typical example of a kind of faded charm that presupposes a soubrette style of singing no longer much in fashion,[44] 'Mir glänzen die Augen' (Op. 33 No. 1) has a new extravagance of vocal flourish that leads to an almost manic evocation of the ridiculous lover's prancing on his charger; in this and the bird-song extravaganza, 'Singt mein Schatz wie ein Fink', the comparison with Wolf is almost inverted. Whereas the text of the latter song prompts Pfitzner to discard continuity in favour of mosaic construction that emphasizes the poem's fluctuating moods, Wolf provides a traditional well-made song that organically grows out of one piano figuration and relegates bird-song to an incident. How little conservative Pfitzner appears in these folk sketches is again illustrated by the accompaniment to the mock folk tune of 'Röschen biss den Apfel an' (No. 6), worthy in its comical abruptness of dissonance treatment to be compared with Bartók. The mosaic principle incorporates linear counterpoint, as two glacial chord streams in 'Wie glänzt der helle Mond' (No. 8); the discrete sections into which it falls separate images of moon, distant youth, and a whimsical paradise as if they reflected three mutually exclusive realms of experience, whereas Wolf in the older Lied tradition unites the images into one awe-struck vision; a similar comparison arises in the case of 'Wandl' ich in dem Morgentau' (No. 4). Only in 'Tretet ein, hoher Krieger' (No. 7) do both composers adhere to the same kind of scheme, a march in which Wolf's unexpected harmonies under a plain surface makes the more interesting impression. To appreciate the Keller cycle requires a certain

---

[44] The art of singing Pfitzner's more folk-like settings is perhaps best exemplified by Erna Berger in the Raucheisen Lied Edition.

detachment from the traditional image of the German art-song; Keller's vein of realism prompted Pfitzner to develop his folk-style beyond its Brahmsian origins towards something that chimed more aptly with the *Sachlichkeit* of the 1920s. But it was followed almost at once by the more conventional lyricism of the Huch cycle. Even here, the freely wandering pentuplets of 'Ich werde nicht an deinem Herzen satt' (Op. 35 No. 2) speak of the distance which Pfitzner has travelled since his first Schumannesque songs, as do the disembodied lines of 'Eine Melodie singt mein Herz' (Ex. 6.11). The bounds of tradition, however, are not broken even here; the outlines of

Ex. 6.11

C♯ minor in the uncertain opening finally crystallize on to a tonic chord of that key.

That Pfitzner's songs of the 1920s should have eventually climaxed in a cycle of love-poems is not the least striking aspect of his career. The love of which Ricarda Huch writes is no love recollected in tranquillity, but a real passion which flares into a species of *Liebestod*. Love is a flame snatched from strange powers, desire is divine, and the soul's flood will cease only when absorbed into the beloved. Yet the experience recounted in Huch's *Neue Gedichte* of 1907, from which Pfitzner took all but one of his texts, is not merely personal but also the outcome of an act of contemplation which resulted in her famous study, *Die Romantik: Ausbreitung, Blütezeit und Verfall*, first published in two parts in 1899 and 1902. 'Over all these poems, however, increasingly extends the shadow of transitoriness.'[45] In Pfitzner's settings, it is not so much transitoriness as the legacy of the past. Several of the Huch songs, most notably 'Bestimmung' (No. 1) and 'Wo hast du all die Schönheit hergenommen' (No. 3), already have an elegiac tone which turns memories of Wagnerian chromaticism inwards:

> Weil du die Jugend hast, wird alles alt,
> Weil du das Leben hast, muss alles sterben ...

The composer offers a Romanticism that has become reflection; the experience of the 'linear ascetic' tends towards that re-creative spirit which he had avoided in the Munich *Dichterkreis* of Heyse and Geibel. 'Pfitzner sets the astonishingly sensual lyrics in brittle, transparent two- to four-part writing, but at the same time with an extreme scale of expression from harsh reserve over individual loss to the most passionate daemonism.'[46] Further distilled, this is the mood of the close of 'Der verspätete Wanderer' and 'Das Alter'. On a grander scale it is also the key to Pfitzner's last opera, *Das Herz*.

[45] Gunter H. Hertling, *Wandlung der Werte im dichterischen Werke der Ricarda Huch* (Bonn, 1966), 174.
[46] Johann Peter Vogel, *Hans Pfitzner mit Selbstzeugnissen und Bilddokumenten* (Reinbek bei Hamburg, 1989), 96.

7

Nationalism and Modernism

THE first performance of *Palestrina* on 12 June 1917 in Munich under Bruno Walter was the most visible sign of a climax to Pfitzner's career. In reasonably close succession followed his adoption as a member by the Royal Swedish Academy and the foundation of a Hans-Pfitzner-Verein für deutsche Tonkunst. His music of this period was possessed of a resultant self-confidence, as evidenced in the finale of the Violin Sonata (written for Stockholm), while *Das Christ-Elflein* in its new version as a *Spieloper* represented the most complete working-out of the folk-like vein which always resided in his style. But then came the military disasters of late 1918 which led to his departure from Strasbourg. His chosen place of refuge, Munich, became the scene of a revolution best described as a comedy which turned into a tragedy. For a whole generation of Bavarian conservatives, the rule of Kurt Eisner became a by-word for anarchy, giving way through his assassination to a government of poets and the *Räterepublik*, which planted the fear of Bolshevism deeply in the psyche of all men of the right (though the blood shed by the *Freikorps* which brought the *Räterepublik* to an end surpassed anything carried out by the revolutionaries; in this, the whole episode provided a less violent echo of the Paris Commune). The diary of Josef Hofmiller is a vivid account of the fears in Cossmann's circle. Yet a musical life, in which Pfitzner played his part, was maintained even during the revolution. Glimpses are caught of him playing *Davidsbündlertänze* to a private audience which included Cossmann and Alexander Berrsche.

Pfitzner said that he played because he wanted to appear in public again, to accompany his songs and also to play his Piano Trio. I had the impression that he needed the purely technical claims of piano-playing to stifle a monstrous grief: the grief for lost Strasbourg. For that reason he wants to play in public. Each time he appears still more sorrowful. Moreover I am convinced that even he and his family are starving.[1]

Hofmiller wrote this in September 1918, when the Allied blockade was still in effect, before armistice and Versailles made Strasbourg a national rather than a personal loss. Starving or not, Pfitzner was still so absorbed in his art that his conversation in these momentous months circled relentlessly around music. He criticizes Mendelssohn and his influence for the continuing tendency to take Schumann's music too fast, and compares Schumann with Wagner in terms that point ahead to the later essay on their *Sternenfreundschaft*; Zelter and Liszt are excoriated, while Loewe is praised for his 'extraordinarily *pictorial* piano writing'.[2]

In December, amidst the growing political turbulence, the revised *Christ-Elflein* received its first performances in Munich under Bruno Walter. That the work was a success in its new guise was one sign that Pfitzner's musical star was still favourable. When he moved with his family in March 1919 to a house at Schondorf on the Ammersee, he also moved out of the immediate danger in Munich, as the revolution drifted to its violent climax. None the less, these months for Pfitzner were of momentous significance. Much subsequent Bavarian anti-Semitism can be seen as reaction against Eisner and Bolshevism, while the disaster of Versailles in June was to warp German political and cultural life for the following decades; to none of this was Pfitzner immune. The extent of the coarsening of his outlook may be gauged by comparing *Futuristengefahr* with the polemical sections of *Die neue Ästhetik*. When Pfitzner explained the title of his next major work, *Von deutscher Seele*, as 'no better nor more comprehensive expression' for the 'contemplative, high-spirited, grave, sweet, vigorous, and heroic in the German soul' (*SS IV* 448), it may seem as though a note of defiance was intended.

The background to this 'romantic cantata to texts and poems by Eichendorff' in reality was much more complicated. The projected title, *Eichendorffiana*, originally carried no potential political charge, being appropriate to a 'cantata after verses by Eichendorff composed in the romantic style'.[3]

---

[1] Josef Hofmiller, *Revolutionstagebuch 1918/19*, 2nd edn. (Leipzig, 1937), 22.
[2] Ibid. 49–50, 92, 94.
[3] Bernhard Adamy, 'Pfitzner und der Verlag Adolph Fürstner', *MPG* 43 (Sept. 1981), 36–7.

It seems to have been Pfitzner's friends who persuaded him that the title was 'sloppy', and he took refuge in a formula, *Aus deutscher Seele*, that had once been used for an anthology of verses by his Berlin acquaintance, Ludwig Jacobowski, though he hesitated over 'Aus' or 'Von'. This revision is documented as late as 2 June 1921, when the composition's close was already in sight.[4] The final title was settled by 16 June, and used in a letter to Hermann Suter seven days later; in other correspondence of the period, Pfitzner and Mimi had simply used the description 'cantata' for the new work.[5] When Fürstner objected to the damaging dimensions of the title, Pfitzner strongly denied that it had any political intention. Whatever the disasters that had assailed Pfitzner (and to these was added family tragedy in the shape of the encephalitis which affected his son Paul), *Von deutscher Seele* is proof that neither his combative nature nor his musical genius had been affected. The cantata indicated clearly that *Palestrina* was far from being the lonely peak of his career. It was merely the mid-point; from *Von deutscher Seele* was to unravel a series of works that have not perhaps met with much appreciation, but which, with one conspicuous exception, contain fine music.

A curious feature of the 1920s is Pfitzner's avoidance of opera and music-drama. Instead two genres come to the fore with little precedent in his output. Since his student days, Pfitzner had largely avoided works for chorus with vocal soloists. The chorus had been used in incidental music, such as the 'Gesang der Barden' from Kleist's *Die Hermannsschlacht*, and, a cappella, in *Columbus*. Chorus and bass soloist had been combined with keyboard accompaniment in the *Rundgesang zum Neujahrsfest 1901*, an occasional piece, while a male chorus was an optional addition to the *Zwei deutsche Gesänge*. This was a scanty background to the sudden interest in large-scale choral music which grew into *Von deutscher Seele*. Whether this would have led in turn to *Das dunkle Reich* (composed in Schondorf, Munich, and Berlin in the winter of 1929–30) without the shock of Mimi's death in 1926 is open to question. 'A dog lies on a grave and dies from longing, the human writes a choral fantasia in the same state. I would

[4] Letter to Oswald Kühn (copy), *A-Wn*, Pfitzner Nachlass, 140/132.
[5] Adamy, 'Pfitzner und der Verlag Adolph Fürstner', 39; a copy of the letter to Suter is in *A-Wn*, Pfitzner Nachlass, 140/226; earlier letters which avoid a title and speak only of a cantata may be found in the Nachlass under the numbers 140/196 and 140/220.

not have thought it!'[6] Whatever the impulse to compose, these two related works, a 'romantic cantata' and 'a choral fantasia', stand at opposite ends of the decade as perhaps Pfitzner's most substantial achievements after *Palestrina*. In spite of his dislike of the concept *Weltanschauungsmusik* (*SS IV* 449–51), that is how they have often been described.[7] The title, *Von deutscher Seele*, was always liable, as Fürstner may have feared, to produce the sort of acclaim that saw Pfitzner developing from 'the witness of his soul to the herald of the nation'.[8] But in a deeper sense, the work does seem to define an outlook. As for *Das dunkle Reich*, Pfitzner himself related it to the musician's desire to make a statement about the circumstances of life in the spirit, if not the form, of religious music:

I too have written my 'mass', and of course here I went a step further than Brahms. When he rendered the requiem in his beloved German, he still took the words from the Bible. By contrast, in *Das dunkle Reich* I gathered from the whole of world literature words which dealt in poetic form with death, sorrow, and, in short, the nature of this life and its overcoming. (*SS IV* 65)

The relevance of the comparison with the 'German Requiem' is increased by the similarity of forces, with soprano and baritone soloists joining chorus and orchestra.

At first sight there is no clear connection between these large-scale choral works and the other genre which sprang to prominence in the 1920s, the concerto. But if both genres are viewed as indirect overtures to the writing of a symphony, then their coexistence at this mature period of Pfitzner's output has a surprising measure of aptness. This view has received its strongest support from Rudolf Stephan in perhaps the best essay written on *Von deutscher Seele* since Pfitzner's time. Stephan's thesis is that Pfitzner proceeded from opera to symphony through the *Palestrina* preludes, which he joined into a concert work, rather as Hindemith developed as a symphonist from *Mathis der Maler;*[9] suggestions of a symphonic dimension to *Von deutscher Seele* were encouraged by Pfitzner's creation of a *Sinfonische Trilogie*

---

[6] Walter Abendroth, *Hans Pfitzner* (Munich, 1935), 282.

[7] E.g. Rudolf Stephan, 'Hans Pfitzners Eichendorff-Kantate *Von deutscher Seele*', *MPG* 50 (June 1989), 18.

[8] Erwin Kroll, *Hans Pfitzner* (Munich, 1924), 178.

[9] Stephan, 'Hans Pfitzners Eichendorff-Kantate', 19.

from its interludes. This interpretation may seem wilful when
Stephan discerns symphonic movements in some of the songs
which comprise *Von deutscher Seele*. It would be sad if Pfitzner
scholarship were to tumble into the pit from which Mahler
scholarship is only just emerging, in which the second part
of the Eighth Symphony is arbitrarily and unconvincingly
partitioned into Adagio, Scherzo, and Finale.[10] When Pfitzner
himself compared the cantata to a Mahler symphony, it was
only as a measure of its dimensions and its demands on the
orchestra.[11] But Pfitzner's cantata is a very complex hybrid,
and the symphonic interpretation is only one strand in its
make-up, as Stephan himself clearly points out. Certainly the
indirectness of Pfitzner's approach is adequately conveyed by
the curious fact that in the end he 'wrote' a symphony by
transcribing a string quartet.

Broadly speaking, the choral works of the 1920s were the
product of a deeper need than the concertos, and the success of the latter, in particular of the Piano Concerto, is less
sure. There is an element of hubris in Pfitzner's music of this
period. Who but he would have written a Piano Concerto in
E♭ and a String Quartet in C♯ minor, when Beethoven had
left an imprint of such weight on those genres and keys? But
the Quartet at least is one of his finest works, though the
Piano Concerto is as close to an outright failure as anything
between *Palestrina* and *Das Herz*, and for quite different reasons than those that make his later works initially somewhat
puzzling. Fortunately the Violin Concerto is a more substantial piece, which illustrates that Pfitzner could write for a
specific performer without loss of the more personal aspects
of his style. None the less, the two choral cantatas and the
Quartet do tend to dominate in any discussion of the period,
not least because of the complexity of their writing. 'From the
purely stylistic point of view, in none of Pfitzner's works is the
co-existence of linear and harmonic methods of expression, of
symphonic and song-like construction so clearly recognizable,
so organically linked as in this one.'[12] So wrote Kroll of the
first cantata; of the second Abendroth could write of a vein of
experimentation that places *Das dunkle Reich*, with the String

[10] That this ancient misconception is convincingly refuted is one of the principal
points of Donald Mitchell, *Gustav Mahler: Songs and Symphonies of Life and Death*
(London, 1985), 533.
[11] Letter to Otto Klemperer (copy), 1 July 1921, *A-Wn*, Pfitzner Nachlass, 140/135.
[12] Kroll, *Hans Pfitzner*, 179.

Quartet, at an extreme point of dissonance and angularity for Pfitzner's output: 'The opponent of the aharmonic principle pushes harmony and linear writing to the extreme limits of the possible, writes chords like C–B–b♭–a^1–g♯^{2}–g^3 and others not less unbelievable, without the feeling of arbitrariness arising anywhere, indeed without harmonic logic being negated anywhere or even the mere style of sound being experienced as essentially dissonant.'[13] The music of the 1920s shows quite clearly that Pfitzner kept abreast with the more radical vein of twentieth-century music in harmony and counterpoint, if not in rhythm; at a time when the music of the Schoenberg school had yet to be taken seriously outside a fairly narrow circle, Pfitzner's music could not simply be written off as an epilogue to a great tradition which had in the meantime spawned a far more radical modernist branch. In some ways, the strengths of his music in this decade are parallel to those of the contemporary works of Schoenberg, being founded on a linear approach to the regulation of musical tension, which was all the keener in Pfitzner's case for still remaining in touch with tonality in an overt fashion. Even the weaknesses of the two composers are not dissimilar, bound up with a rather staid approach to rhythm and phrase structure that appears all the more drastic in Schoenberg's 'neoclassical' suites and serenades on account of the thematic weight that rhythms are expected to bear. Such parallels should not be pushed too far, for they merely serve to recall Alma Mahler's image of the two composers as the stylites on either side of Strauss. It is another interesting parallel that the latter was also drawn to the concerto in his later years, but whereas his works for oboe and horn are essentially works of re-creation, Pfitzner tended in the 1920s to use the concerto, like the cantata, as a vehicle for experimentation.

Pfitzner himself gave an account of the genesis of *Von deutscher Seele* which all subsequent writers have drawn upon, including Abendroth, who further ascertained some of the principal dates.[14] The first ideas for settings of Eichendorff's 'Sprüche' and 'Wandersprüche' were jotted down in Strasbourg, but the real composition began in Schondorf

---

[13] Abendroth, *Hans Pfitzner*, 346.

[14] *SS IV* 443; Abendroth, *Hans Pfitzner*, 240–1 and 244; the dates of completion of the two parts, 'Unterschondorf d. 9 Januar 1921' and 'Unterschondorf d. 8 August 1921', are indicated at the end of each volume of the autograph full score (*A-Wn*, S.m. 30,423).

at the start of June 1920. Perhaps it was now that Pfitzner annotated the first volume of his copy of Eichendorff's complete works, which survives in the Österreichische Nationalbibliothek.[15] Not all of these annotations refer to *Von deutscher Seele*; those marks on the contents page in red pencil always refer to poems included by Schumann in his *Liederkreis*, Opus 39, while annotations in pencil refer to songs by Pfitzner himself. The texts for *Von deutscher Seele*, however, are clearly singled out by crosses in pencil, and on the pages themselves further annotations give clues to his intentions. Usually these were altered as work progressed (see Table 2 for the disposition of forces in movements); thus of the 'Wandersprüche', 'Herz, in deinen sonnenhellen Tagen' is simply marked 'Tenor', 'Die Lerche grüsst den ersten Strahl' merely 'Sopr.', as if these were to be songs for one voice. Similarly 'Ewig muntres Spiel der Wogen!' and 'Der Sturm geht lärmend um das Haus' are designated for alto and bass respectively by all-embracing brackets. That a choral work is in prospect, however, is clearly shown by 'Chor' written against 'Der Wandrer, von der Heimat weit' and 'Wenn der Hahn kräht'. More extensive markings suggest that 'Was willst auf dieser Station' is to be shared by tenor and chorus, though the exact division is slightly unclear. Most extensively annotated is the first text of the cantata, 'Es geht wohl anders, als du meinst'; its first line is specified 'Chor', the next three 'Bass', and the next two 'Sopr.', a specification which bears only partial resemblance to the completed musical section (in which the chorus does not sing). At this stage, 'Wohl vor lauter Sinnen, Singen' is already envisaged as 'Canon', while among the 'Sprüche' the closing words of 'Von allen guten Schwingen' ('Leid') and of 'Gleich wie auf dunklem Grunde' ('Lied') are suggestively underlined.[16] By now Pfitzner had been appointed successor to Richard Strauss as teacher of a masterclass at the Hochschule in Berlin (where, by a neat coincidence, his rival Busoni also taught). Composition was thus discontinued in the winter months, and he did not resume work on the cantata until 22 March 1921, finishing it on 8 August. In the essay which he wrote to introduce the work at its first performance in 1922, he spent some

[15] *A-Wn*, Pfitzner Nachlass, 472/1, *Joseph Freiherrn von Eichendorffs Werke*, vols. i–ii of 4 (Leipzig: Gustav Fock, n.d.).
[16] Ibid. i. 56 and 83–4.

Table 2 *Von deutscher Seele*: Movements and Forces

PART I. 'MENSCH UND NATUR'

1. 'Es geht wohl anders, als du meinst'   'Wandersprüche', No.
   soloists   1,—'Wanderlieder'
2. 'Was willst auf dieser Station'   'Wandersprüche', No. 3
   T soloist
3. Interlude: 'Tod als Postillon'
   orchestra, later SAB soloists and
   chorus
4. 'Herz, in deinen sonnenhellen Tagen'   'Wandersprüche', No. 2
   soloists and chorus
5. 'Der Sturm geht lärmend um das   'Wandersprüche', No. 5
   Haus'
   soloists
6. Interlude: 'Abend—Nacht'
   orchestra
7. 'Die Lerche grüsst den ersten Strahl'   'Wandersprüche', No. 4
   soloists
8. 'Wenn der Hahn kräht'   'Wanderlieder'
   soloists and chorus
9. 'Ewig muntres Spiel der Wogen'   'Wandersprüche', No. 6
   soloists
10. 'Der Wandrer, von der Heimat weit'   'Wandersprüche', No. 7
    TB soloists
11. 'Nachtgruss'   'Geistliche Gedichte'
    soloists and chorus

PART II. 'LEBEN UND SINGEN'

1. 'Werktag'   'Geistliche Gedichte'
   chorus
2. 'Was ich wollte, liegt zerschlagen'   'Der Umkehrende', No.
   T soloist   3, 'Geistliche
      Gedichte'
3. Interlude: 'Ergebung'
   orchestra
4. 'Der jagt dahin'   'Geistliche Gedichte'
   chorus
5. 'Gleich wie auf dunklem Grunde'   'Sprüche', [No. 2],
   B soloist   'Sängerleben'

'Liederteil'

6. 'Der alte Garten'   'Romanzen'
   S soloist

Table 2 *Continued*

7. 'Von allen guten Schwingen' chorus, a cappella	'Sprüche', [No. 1], 'Sängerleben'
8. 'Die Nonne und der Ritter' AT soloists and chorus	'Romanzen'
9. 'Intermezzo' ['Wohl vor lauter Singen, Singen'] chorus	'Sängerleben'
10. 'Hast du doch Flügel eben' S soloist	'Sprüche', [No. 3], 'Sängerleben'
11. 'Der Friedensbote' B soloist	'Zeitlieder'
12. 'Schifferspruch' soloists and chorus	'Geistliche Gedichte'

time explaining why the work was a cantata as opposed to a *Singstück*. The subtitle referred not to any sacred or ceremonial aspects of the work, simply to the large part for the orchestra which seemed to be a characteristic of the genre to Pfitzner; as Stephan has suggested, one of the work's roots is more accurately the choral ballad of the nineteenth century (as in *Die erste Walpurgisnacht* of Mendelssohn).[17] But more interesting is Pfitzner's acknowledgement of its other source in the song-cycle. It was a curious feature of his music-making (even in public) that he would sometimes improvise stylistically appropriate links between songs from Schumann's *Dichterliebe* and the Eichendorff *Liederkreis*; an offshoot of this practice was the orchestration of *Acht Frauenchöre* by Schumann in 1910, for which he also supplied links between choruses. Pfitzner thus avowed the model of the Schumann-esque song-cycle, though he predictably made no mention of the hybrid works of Mahler like *Das Lied von der Erde* which Stephan adduces as a parallel.[18] It is clear from the surviving sketches for the cantata, however, that Pfitzner did not compose the vocal sections first and then the interludes as the Schumann parallel might suggest. The indications are that 'Es geht wohl anders, als du meinst' was sketched with its final 7/4 chord in mind.[19] Some interludes took time to reach their final shape. The organ link into 'Herz, in deinen

[17] Stephan, 'Hans Pfitzners Eichendorff-Kantate', 5.
[18] Ibid. 6–7.
[19] E.g., *A-Wn*, S.m. 30,424, Hans Pfitzner, Op. 28, Skizzen zu den Eichendorff-Sprüchen, fol. 2[r].

sonnenhellen Tagen' is present in the sketches with somewhat different harmonies.[20] The harp cadenza which connects 'Gleich wie auf dunklem Grunde' to 'Der alte Garten' was written for that instrument alone in the appropriate part of a short score; Pfitzner then wondered 'Horn dazu *Es?*', and added it at the appropriate place.[21] Random sketch pages and more extended short scores all tend to confirm that Pfitzner composed *Von deutscher Seele* with most of the structural details clearly envisaged from an early stage.

The texts which Pfitzner chose are conspicuously short, with some notable exceptions. The aphoristic verses entitled collectively 'Wandersprüche' and 'Sprüche', from which the cantata grew, were placed by Eichendorff amongst his 'Wanderlieder' and 'Sängerleben' when he came to publish his collected verse. In his cantata Pfitzner set in an order of his own choosing all but one of these poems, each containing one or two stanzas: the 'Wandersprüche' in the first part, entitled 'Mensch und Natur'; the 'Sprüche' in Part II, divided into 'Leben und Singen' and 'Liederteil' (see Table 7.2). The single omission is surprising, the most famous of these 'maxims', perhaps the most famous of all Eichendorff's verses, 'Schläft ein Lied in allen Dingen', which was initially marked for inclusion in Pfitzner's copy of Eichendorff;[22] perhaps he felt that the cantata as a whole was an exemplification of that 'Zauberwort' needed to awaken the universal song. Apart from these 'maxims', he selected poems which blended with their themes. The four lines of 'Wenn der Hahn kräht' are as short as any of the 'maxims', and only 'Nachtgruss' in Part I is of any great length at three four-line stanzas. The poems of Part II are initially scarcely any longer, and it is only with 'Der alte Garten' and 'Die Nonne und der Ritter' that Pfitzner expands to poems of more than three stanzas. One consequence of this is that he frequently resorts to extensive repetition of text in what Stephan regards as a fashion typical of the cantata.[23] These repetitions are often of some structural significance. Thus the interlude, 'Tod als Postillon', picks up the significance of the tenor's 'Wie bald nicht bläst der Postillon, | Du musst doch alles lassen'; when it has run its course, the other soloists and the chorus repeat the text as

[20] Ibid., fol. 16[r].
[21] Ibid., fol. 72[r].
[22] *A-Wn*, Pfitzner Nachlass, 472/1, i. 84.
[23] Stephan, 'Hans Pfitzners Eichendorff-Kantate', 9.

recollection. But equally Pfitzner often set his small texts as links themselves, as is conspicuous in Part II, which contains fewer significant orchestral interludes. The only a cappella setting, 'Von allen guten Schwingen', treated almost as a chorale, is experienced as such a link between the two longest Lieder, while the last of the 'Sprüche' is given to the soprano soloist as a declamatory recitative before 'Der Friedensbote'. Orchestral interludes and vocal sections may have equal weight, as is clearly indicated by Pfitzner's giving of titles to the most significant links. The titles of the second of these, first 'Abend' then 'Nacht', are also titles of poems by Eichendorff, but it was not Pfitzner's intention to evoke these specifically in his orchestral interlude.

Broadly speaking, Pfitzner followed a similar plan in *Das dunkle Reich*, combining vocal sections with instrumental interludes into a whole. But whereas *Von deutscher Seele* ends up as a 'portrait of Eichendorff', *Das dunkle Reich* is a meditation on death, to which Goethe's words from *Iphigenia* provide both invitation and warning:

> Und lass dir raten, habe
> Die Sonne nicht zu lieb und nicht die Sterne;
> Komm, folge mir ins dunkle Reich hinab!

> And take advice, hold not
> The sun too dear, neither the stars;
> Come, follow me into the dark kingdom.

Once again the orchestra plays an important linking part, with its interludes spilling over into one full-sized section, a dance of life which is later balanced by the organ's *Fugato* (see Table 3). The parallel between the works extends to the Dehmel setting, 'Chorspruch', entitled thus in a manner which clearly recalls the 'maxims' of the Eichendorff cantata (whereas Dehmel's title was 'Gleichnis'). The setting also recalls the a cappella chorus in the earlier work in its sober chorale-like syllabic setting; the lines of the poem are threaded into the texture like a chorale cantus firmus in Bach. Something of the same is true of the later Michelangelo chorus, which uses the same translation as Wolf's song. The latter is of course one of the supreme masterpieces of the nineteenth-century Lied; here is seen, as in the cases of 'Das verlassene Mägdlein' and 'Denk' es, o Seele', Pfitzner's occasional compulsion to measure himself against Wolf at his very best (though in this case the two approaches are so unlike as

Table 3 *Das dunkle Reich*: Movements and Forces

1. 'Chor der Toten' chorus	C. F. Meyer, 'Genie'
2. 'Schnitterlied' 'Chor der Lebenden' chorus	C. F. Meyer, 'Stunde'
3. 'Tanz des Lebens' orchestra	
4. 'Chorspruch' chorus	Richard Dehmel, 'Gleichnis', *Weib und Welt*
5. 'Gretchen vor der Mater dolorosa' S soloist	Goethe, *Faust*, I
6. *Fugato* und Chor ('Alles endet, was entstehet') organ, then chorus	Michelangelo, *Rime*, No. 136, trans. Walter Robert-Tornow
7. 'Scheiden im Licht' B soloist	C. F. Meyer, *Huttens letzte Tage*, lxx
8. 'Chor der Toten'	C. F. Meyer

to make comparison redundant). What principally distinguishes Pfitzner's 'Requiem' from *Von deutscher Seele* is a certain element of tableau in the later work. This is symbolized in the physical partition of the chorus into two, one group representing the dead, the other the living, a separation which Pfitzner's note in the score asks to be as clear as possible (even to the extent of perhaps using two platforms); in a sense the organ is the instrument of the dead, the orchestra of the living, though Pfitzner's writing for the two is never quite so schematic. That there is also a 'plot' is apparent in that whereas the opening choruses are sung only by the appropriate choral group, dead or living, the reprise of the 'Chorus of the Dead' is sung by all. Furthermore, the central moment of the work marks a turning-point if not a dramatic catastrophe; the intrusion of Dehmel's verses about the fountain of woe is the mirror image—'Er sieht im tiefen Wasserschacht | Sein lichtes Bild umrahmt von Nacht'[24]—which converts the 'Dance of Life' into the mourning of the second half. Even the ensuing setting of Goethe is dramatic tableau, in the sense that it is a complete scene from *Faust* (which in Part I of Goethe's drama follows on from another 'fountain scene'). The symmetry of the structure round the central movements is

---

[24] 'He sees in the deep well his luminous image framed by night.'

further suggested by the presence of two settings of Conrad Ferdinand Meyer at the beginning and the end. Pfitzner's interest in Meyer was particularly strong in the 1920s (the song-cycle to his poems preceded *Das dunkle Reich* by six years in 1923), and 'Scheiden im Licht' reinforces the dramatic aspect of the cantata in that it is the penultimate 'scene' of Meyer's curiously sectional but magnificent epic, *Huttens letzte Tage*, the humanist hero's invocation of a death in the early morning on the sun's 'golden wings'. Fundamentally both cantatas are meditative works, in which texts follow one another as different facets of some common experience, but the later cantata has the simpler, less allusive structure by virtue of its theatrical externals.

The structure of *Von deutscher Seele* is in large measure an exemplification of the different natures of poetic and musical inspiration as defined in 'Zur Grundfrage der Operndichtung': the 'poetic conception' is the 'universal' idea realized by the particular musical ideas (*SS II* 7–28, *passim*). But in the cantata's case, the 'poetic conception' was Pfitzner's reading of Eichendorff, which yielded him certain broad and not uncommon insights; this is most clearly illustrated by the first part, in which the title, 'Mensch und Natur', is the unifying conception rather than any more extensive coherence. Pfitzner contented himself in his elucidations with noting the suitability of the title, almost as an afterthought (*SS IV* 446). Ostensibly the individual poems are special cases of that broad theme. Over and above this primary relationship, Pfitzner incorporated a secondary grouping by making Nos. 7 to 11 a cycle: morning, day, evening, and night; the interlude of No. 6 is thus a prelude to this cycle within the whole part. Whether it was also a postlude to a previous cycle is less clear from Pfitzner's remarks. The storm of No. 5 may have been a daylight storm, but Pfitzner's remarks are ambiguous, even coy, on this subject (*SS IV* 445). Whereas the later sections of Part I are cohesive and cyclic in literary theme, the earlier numbers exhibit a more processive relationship. 'It may turn out differently from what you imagine' offers hope of the sun shining again, but for the wanderer there can be no rest as the posthorn blows in the second 'Wanderspruch'. Yet the eruption of death's 'Totentanz',[25] an unlooked-for qualification of

---

[25] The image of the Dance of Death is regularly encountered in connection with 'Tod als Postillon' (e.g. Kroll, *Hans Pfitzner*, 181).

the posthorn, is itself qualified by the later reprise of the text; there will be no lingering at death in Pfitzner's cantata, though it is a recurring theme. The next 'Wanderspruch' urges no holding back, but to build on God, a hopeful sentiment that is ironically qualified in the final section before 'Abend'; the wise man stays at home in the storm, but deals with it bravely if caught in it. Collectively the first sections of 'Mensch und Natur' reflect on the wandering and transient nature of life, a theme which never quite vanishes, and re-emerges prominently at the start of Part II. The remainder of Part I is a kind of variation on the same collection of ideas: the inspiring yet terrifying powers of nature (Nos. 7 and 10), particularly at night; but also the religious (or to Pfitzner quasi-religious) consolation which the same night may bring (No. 11); the courage which may be illusory (No. 9). The imagery in which these sentiments are couched is universal in Eichendorff, from 'die tiefen Gründe', those peculiar chasms of mystery and unexplained foreboding, to the battlements of the king 'im stillen Reich'; from the eternal light which para-doxically shines in the night, to the stars which keep watch, and to the natural creatures like birds and waves which may inspire or threaten.

The two titles of Part II divide it much as the onset of evening divided the first. Again the second section is part response to, but more exemplification of, the first. The texts of the opening circle again around wandering but with the added distillation of disillusionment, the shattering of hopes which finds its only answer in resignation, here the subject of an interlude; since night catches all, regardless of how one travels, the only consolation is in song. The 'Liederteil' is thus a demonstration of the role singing (or more precisely music) has in human life, as is made clear in 'Der alte Garten' by the 'wonderful sound' given out in the night by the sleeping woman and her lute (represented by harp and guitar). For Pfitzner, these songs were the 'arias' of the traditional cantata (*SS IV* 447), gathered together into one section. Not all is properly song or aria, since the a cappella chorus intrudes to comment on the power of suffering to break the power of time. Since this is precisely the subject of the next song, it stands beside the ensuing narration like a chorale in a Bach Passion: the nun's ceaseless nocturnal longings for her past take the form of an illusory visit from a dead knight. The emotions expressed are profoundly ambiguous: does the

knight wander astray, or does the mention of Christ's grave
suggest that for him there is a release? Does the nun welcome the visitation which dissolves the tyranny of time? Her
meditations speak of longing, the rushing waves, oppression,
melancholy, and confusion. If there is consolation, it seems to
lie in final renunciation, but once again the nocturnal world's
salvation floats over the abyss 'of long sunken times', the
obverse of that still melancholy 'happy old time' in 'Der alte
Garten'. The relationship of recitative to aria was explicitly
acknowledged in the bass solo of No. 6 when Pfitzner compared it to 'O Freunde, nicht diese Töne' (though the sounds
are hardly as joyful as his further quotation of Beethoven's
words seems to imply).[26] Each 'aria' has its recitative, solo as
here, or choral in the case of the a cappella introduction
to 'Die Nonne und der Ritter'. The one true chorus in this
'Liederteil' (No. 9) points to a paradox, that without music life
might not be worth living, although it may seem that singing
interferes with living. Then the alternation of recitative and
aria is resumed once more, the soprano extolling the 'wings'
and the enabling word which raise humanity over the trials of
life. It provides the introduction for the cantata's rather sticky
belated lurch towards patriotism in 'Der Friedensbote',
which seems to break the pattern, inasmuch as the vision of
the land's freedom (the only feature of the text to which
Pfitzner drew attention) seems an inadequate illustration of
'das gewalt'ge Wort'; the power of invocation for a moment
counts as a reality, and inevitably conditions the listener's
response to the concluding 'Schifferspruch'. For the latter
finally urges daring in the face of the storm; the happy ending
which the work's opening merely suggested is couched by
Eichendorff in inevitably religious terms: God has provided
the waves on which to travel, the stars to guide. But the
doubt persists about the storm Pfitzner had in mind. The
scars which the war had inflicted on the European mind are
all too readily reflected in that triumphalism at whose edge
Pfitzner's music stands. It perhaps needs to be stressed that
the problems of 'Der Friedensbote' are not simply ideological;
the sudden surge of C major seems to run counter to the
overall sense of the poem, and also to the scale of Pfitzner's

---

[26] Pfitzner's citation of the recitative from the Ninth Symphony is an obvious
source for Stephan's view of the work as a symphony ('Hans Pfitzners Eichendorff-
Kantate', 17).

setting. In this may be detected the greatest possible contrast with 'Scheiden im Licht', the penultimate song of *Das dunkle Reich*. Its climactic outburst in C major makes a completely different impression. The combination of a counterpoint derived with great economy from a scale and a neighbouring-note figure, and a dotted (sometimes double-dotted) motive at a steady tempo there adds up to an almost Brucknerian intensity, appropriate to Meyer's meditation on the final peace brought by daylight's 'first arrow'. The climax is contained within the aesthetic vision, whereas 'Der Friedensbote' simply slips out of focus.

As a consequence of the pattern suggested to Pfitzner by his chosen text, the musical structure of *Von deutscher Seele* is of considerable complexity. Neither cantata, symphony, nor song-cycle suffices as description. Neither part possesses the monotonality of the traditional symphony, 'Mensch und Natur' moving from D minor to Bb major, Part II from E minor to D major. Monotonality exists in the individual setting on the whole, though there are exceptions. Even monotonal sections do not necessarily close on the tonic. Thus 'Es geht wohl anders' moves from a chromatically unstable D minor through A minor to F major; that the text to some extent guides the tonal strategy is indicated by the release into D major when 'the sun shines'. Although this subsequently pales to D minor, the orchestral postlude carries this to the dominant of F minor (the 7/4 chord), which is the key of the tenor's posthorn. The first section may thus be understood as song with single strophe, whose principal deviation from the monotonal norm is motivated by the need for a link to the next section. But it may equally be understood as slow introduction, since the complex of the tenor solo and 'Tod als Postillon' approximates perhaps to exposition and development, though the exposition lacks modulation and thematic contrast; the wide-ranging modulations begin with the clearly developmental orchestral interlude. The thematic material of the interlude mostly derives from the tenor's strophe, and the return of the voices brings a choral reprise of the tenor's material, heralded by the return of the 7/4 chord after *T*. The question of tonal closure in relation to both tenor strophe and the whole complex is rather similar to that in the case of 'Es geht wohl anders', since the tenor strophe is closed in F minor, while the whole complex would also exhibit tonal closure were it not for the organ's intrusion to provide a link to the next text; the strophe will bear consideration both as song and as exposition. The remainder of 'Mensch und Natur' exhibits generic traits of symphonic movements, rather than complete symphonic structures. 'Herz, in deinen sonnenhellen Tagen' comes close to being a scherzo (in an A major without modulation that recalls Budoja's music in *Palestrina*), with a trio in the tonic minor; the text's turn to exhortation in the second stanza is reflected in the modality of the music. But the storm of the next text is in a quite unrelated, brusque B♭ minor. Both sections are tonally self-contained, and their link is the first of the cadenza-like sections that are true links rather than developments.

With the onset of 'Abend', Pfitzner's music, already vivid in its response to the text and daring in its deployment of the orchestra, touches real greatness. While 'Abend' develops the polyphonic aspect of his style in directions not fully realized in *Palestrina*, 'Nacht' resorts to the chorale for the first time in the cantata; his sketches show him persistently trying to find the precise form and key for his newly composed but traditionally structured chorale.[27] But the structural many-sidedness of the interlude is still marked; in symphonic terms it would be easy to regard this interlude as an Adagio of true Brucknerian depth. But since this is also part of a new structure based on the cycle of the day, it relates more strongly to what follows than what went before. The interlude is a statement, on which 'Der Wandrer, von der Heimat weit' and 'Nachtgruss' constitute a free variation. A sketch page entitled 'Nachtstück' (which is not a title of any one section in the completed work) contains a mixture of motives and jottings that seem intended for the entire complex of interlude and songs covered by the themes, evening and night.[28] Thus the words 'fröhlicher Tag' coupled with an injunction, 'Dur Akkord im Bass', point to 'Der Wandrer, von der Heimat weit'. But a list of motives could equally well refer to 'Abend' from such descriptions as 'Triolen-Motive', 'Motiv d', 's. oben b-moll Stelle bringen', 'Fantasie', and 'Nachtigallruf'. It is not easy to identify these labels, which recur on related pages, though another page identifies the harp figure of Figure C^1 as 'Motiv a', while its chords of ten bars after C^1 are clearly 'Motiv c'.[29] Six motives in all are listed here and seem to

[27] *A-Wn*, S.m. 30,424, fol. 10ᵛ.
[28] Ibid., fol. 38ʳ.
[29] Ibid., fol. 39ᵛ.

refer to 'Abend', but the words 'die ew'gen Zinnen' recall
'Nachtgruss' and are associated with 'Motiv b', the motive
found in the second to last bar of Part I (Ex. 7.1). 'Abend' and

Ex. 7.1

the more compact 'Wandrer' have in common the initial harp
figure (which resembles the viola solo in the slow movement
of the Piano Quintet in beginning as decoration and growing
into a theme), the horn calls, and the violin melody at E^1 (Ex.
7.2); 'Nachtgruss' adds words to the chorale, which becomes

Ex. 7.2

the solemn climax of the whole part. The interlude is tonally
open-ended, the songs closed, though both may be said to be
in B♭, moving over the whole span from minor to major. The
symphonic Adagio thus grows to engulf the whole of the part's
final stages, gathering in the more song-like sections with lark
and cock-crow as a middle section which takes A minor as a
central tonality.

A similar refusal to fall into one definite structure marks
Part II. Here the increasing dominance of the orchestra does
make the symphonic analogy, up to the start of the 'Liederteil',
increasingly plausible. For long stretches of *Von deutscher
Seele*, the impression arises of an orchestral work into which
chorus and soloists are intermittently invited. Of no section
is this truer than the opening of 'Leben und Singen'. 'Wir
wandern nun schon viel' hundert Jahr'' begins with an orches-

Ex. 7.3*a*

tral prelude of over eighty bars of moderately paced movement, carrying two thematic ideas (Ex. 7.3) from E minor in
wide modulatory sweeps to the C minor in which the voices
enter. Since the section is quite firmly closed in the original E
minor, the impression is of a musical process (vividly illustrating the wandering of the text) that incorporates a text
almost as an afterthought, rather than an orchestral introduction to a choral song. Since the next major section is the
orchestra's 'Ergebung' (in scope another symphonic Adagio),
only with the scherzo-like 'Der jagt dahin' do the vocal forces
take over, and even here a motoric orchestral postlude (almost
suggesting Prokofiev in its manic energy) sweeps the chorus
aside. With the bass recitative, however, the work reverts to
its vocal origins, and tonally enclosed songs dominate until
the 'Schlussgesang'. With the closing section, the question of
overall cohesion is raised in a slightly different form. In
Dichterliebe and *Frauenliebe und -leben*, Schumann provided
Pfitzner with examples of song-cycles that had cyclic musical
elements as well as narrative cohesion. If *Von deutscher Seele*
is an expanded song-cycle with links, its literary cohesion
is not a matter of narrative but of *Stimmung*, as in the
Eichendorff *Liederkreis*,[30] and it is affinity of mood that dictates the recollections in the 'Schlussgesang': from 'Es geht
wohl anders', in recognition that however predictable the

---

[30] For *Stimmung* and the Eichendorff *Liederkreis*, see Patrick McCreless, 'Song
Order in the Song Cycle: Schumann's *Liederkreis*, Op. 39', *Music Analysis*, 5 (1986),
11–12.

goal, the act of journeying and wandering is an imperative to be faced with courage (Ex. 7.4*a*); from 'Wenn der Hahn kräht', in recognition of the image of the watching stars, which it holds in common with 'Schifferspruch' (Ex. 7.4*b*); and from

Ex. 7.4*a*

the wave figuration of 'Ewig muntres Spiel der Wogen'. This type of gathering together would be no less plausible in a symphonic peroration, however, though it is not on the whole characteristic of Pfitzner's approach throughout the cantata. While 'Die Nonne und der Ritter' borrows a specific motive from 'Abend' in acknowledgement of their common nocturnal atmosphere (Ex. 7.4c), and more generalized figures from 'Ewig muntres Spiel der Wogen' (they are both seascapes), thematic cross-references tend only to occur between adjacent sections or in the deeper relationship of the diurnal cycle in Part I. In the 'Schlussgesang', the sudden accretion of references back has the advantage that the triumphant major-mode surge comes to seem a valid climax for the whole, rather than an extension of the C major outburst in 'Der Friedensbote'.

Where individual sections most clearly resemble songs, they tend to exhibit formal divisions closely based on the poetic strophe. In this they are consistent on the whole with Pfitzner's songs with piano. This is not to say that Pfitzner may not repeat a strophe for musical purposes. Thus 'Herz, in deinen sonnenhellen Tagen' fits the ternary structure only by repetition of the first of its two stanzas. But this is an extreme case of the manipulation of the text. The 'arias' are much more typical of the style of Pfitzner's Lieder. This is particularly true of 'Die Nonne und der Ritter', which allots each stanza to alto and tenor in alternation (with the chorus reserved for one line, 'Geht ein Schiff, ein Mann stand drinne'). The alternation extends also to motives and textures, since the knight's music is quite distinct from that of the nun. The impression created is of two different musical processes threaded through each other but with little interaction. A similar mode of musical thought underlies the link to the next section, since material suggesting 'Wohl vor lauter Singen, Singen' (no longer 'Sinnen, Singen' as in Eichendorff) in the organ is introduced as overlay to the playing-out of the nun's music in the orchestra, a layer construction that is not apparent in any other link.

Layering of texture is often to be found in the orchestra, however, even to the extent of bitonality and polyrhythms. This is most apparent in the violent disruptions of 'Tod als Postillon', which required far more extensive sketching than any other section of the work. At the equivalent of eleven bars after *F* in an isolated leaf of short score, Pfitzner noted that one part seemed to be in E minor, while everything else adhered to Eb minor (a similar bitonality to that in *Das Käthchen von Heilbronn*).[31] Polyrhythms are even more strik-

---

[31] *A-Wn*, S.m. 30,424, fol. 26ʳ.

Ex. 7.5*a*

b

ing. Thus duple and triple metres are blended after *L*, in a double ostinato of considerable energy (Ex. 7.5*a*); later an even more interesting polyrhythm starts up but is not sustained (Ex. 7.5*b*). Such passages suggest that Pfitzner was aware of the rhythmic developments occurring in the music of his contemporaries, even if he chose only to make limited use of them. Frequently a polyrhythm required the most careful sketching (as in the case of the passage beginning in the fifth bar after *O*).[32] Layer construction elsewhere is more a matter of what has been termed in Wagner, Mahler, and Zemlinsky studies *Klangflächenkomposition*—composition with sound levels or planes. In the writings of Lichtenfeld and Gruber, criteria for such a technique include extended passages of stasis with the suspension of a sense of musical progression, and with choric differentiation of instruments or instrumental

[32] Ibid., fol. 16ᵛ.

groups.[33] 'Abend' most clearly exhibits such a tendency in its differentiation of harp motive, horn calls, and string melody; what earlier writers on Pfitzner were perhaps content to refer to as 'linear' is in fact more complex, since the sum total of the many lines is less directional than a dense saturation of a musical space. In Mahler, such passages ultimately thinned out to the angular combinations of lines in the outer movements of the Ninth Symphony, and a similar development may be seen in *Von deutscher Seele*; if 'Abend' is Pfitzner's equivalent to the many moments of nature depiction in Mahler (the posthorn in the Third Symphony, the bell episodes in the Sixth), then 'Ergebung' moves closer to the 'cadenza' in the first movement of the Ninth Symphony, with the resemblance extending to the intimate, chamber-music scoring. Such scoring is not without precedent in Pfitzner; the first bars of the cantata with their solo string textures recall the opening of *Der arme Heinrich* and much in *Palestrina*. For that matter, the dissonant brass-dominated counterpoint of 'Tod als Postillon' recalls the Nacht-Wunderer (even down to motivic reminiscences in the use of the melodic cell, $\hat{1}-\hat{2}-\hat{3}$, in the minor mode). But 'Ergebung' is more an extension of the mood of the slow movement of the Quintet, expressed in woodwind timbres. Although the solo flute launches the interlude with a diatonic melody in E♭ major, the fundamentally homophonic structure quickly 'liquefies' to solo arabesque figures, which alternate with chromatic sequences in the strings. The subsequent developments do not lose contact with tonality, though several passages of intertwining arabesques in the woodwind seem to focus on augmented triads and diminished sevenths as tonal landmarks grow more attenuated. The peak of harmonic tension occurs with a reference to the tenor's earlier 'Was ich wollte, liegt zerschlagen' in the flute (whose role here borders on the concertante). After that the diatonic melody re-enters softly in the horns and strings, and as the orchestral texture fills out, the effect is of colour slowly seeping into a pale canvas. Not even in *Palestrina* did Pfitzner surpass his achievements in these

---

[33] Monika Lichtenfeld, 'Zur Technik der Klangflächenkomposition bei Wagner', *Das Drama Richard Wagners als musikalisches Kunstwerk*, ed. Carl Dahlhaus (Regensburg, 1970), 161–7, and 'Zur Klangflächentechnik bei Mahler', *Mahler: Eine Herausforderung*, ed. Peter Ruzicka (Wiesbaden, 1977), 121–34; Gernot Gruber, 'Klangkomposition in den Opern Zemlinskys', *Alexander Zemlinsky: Tradition im Umkreis der Wiener Schule*, ed. Otto Kolleritsch (Graz, 1976), 93–100.

moments of evocative orchestral polyphony. That the chromatic language of the cantata on the whole does not move much beyond the usual diminished and half-diminished sevenths, augmented sixths, and the augmented triad, illustrates that the originality of Pfitzner's writing (as with Mahler) is heavily dependent upon the layering of the orchestra. The long-drawn-out transition from 'Nachts' to 'Die Lerche grüsst den ersten Strahl' is less remarkable for the control of chromatic tension than for the way in which the texture is lightened and gradually spread until the arrival of A is given added depth by the underpinning of the texture with the subdominant.

This is less true of *Das dunkle Reich*, however, where the chromatic language comes close to complete tonal disruption from the Dehmel setting onwards. In many sections, cohesion is provided by methods which recall the experiments of Schoenberg and his pupils in the period of 'free' atonality. Pfitzner depends on response to the text, motives, reference chords, and contrapuntal devices, rather than conventional forms of tonal prolongation. The organ *fugato* which precedes the Michelangelo setting is the clearest instance of a contrapuntal process providing a shaping force for dense chromaticism (though pedal points intermittently help to maintain a sense of control). The impression is not dissimilar to that produced in some of Liszt's chromatic organ music, particularly when Liszt is echoing Bach, though the comparison would doubtless have displeased Pfitzner. In the Dehmel and Goethe settings, however, counterpoint is less traditionally structured. All sense of tonality here is not lost, though the use of flattened leading-notes in such places as the phrase first sung to 'Es ist ein Brunnen, der heisst Leid' renders it amorphous. In Gretchen's 'Ach neige, du Schmerzensreiche' tonalities are suggested, and sometimes fully tonicized. But the connecting voice-leading depends more on fusion of dominant chords with tonic pedals than on triads. Thus modulations are enharmonically occasioned by correspondences between diminished and dominant sevenths, to the point that these become controlling sonorities in their own right. In his analysis of 'Der alte Garten' Skouenborg makes a case for considering harmonic procedures in Pfitzner's music as dissonance integrated in the lines, unintegrated in the chords.[34] But this distinction is less valuable in the later

---

[34] Ulrik Skouenborg, *Von Wagner zu Pfitzner* (Tutzing, 1983), 127–32.

cantata by virtue of the near-structural status achieved by dissonant harmonies. They act as the focus for short chromatic decorating figures that take on the aspect of neo-Baroque affects, wordless ciphers of grief.

Both the Dehmel setting and Gretchen's scene make referential use of a chord composed of superimposed fourths (G–A–D in its initial form), which proliferates both by transposition to other cycles of fourths and by addition of chromatic neighbouring notes (which in turn spawn new neighbouring notes). In 'Chorspruch', most of the latter are only neighbouring notes in their adjacency as pitch classes, since the defining interval is a seventh rather than a second. Thus the orchestral accompaniment on one level is elaborated by extending the chord of fourths to include E; both A and E acquire neighbouring notes, F and Bb (Ex. 7.6a), which subsequently

Ex. 7.6a

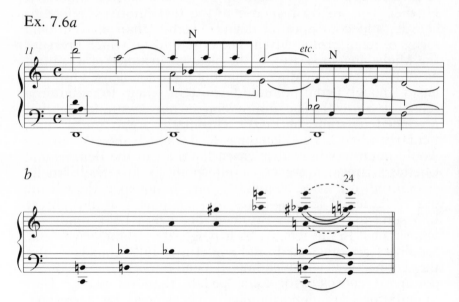

expand by the addition of Eb. In a sense the passage derives as much of its tension from interpenetration of two cycles of fourths as from stretto or voice-leading, though it is easy enough to spot slow chromatic linear motions in various parts, most obviously the bass. The presence of the sevenths helps also to clarify the climax chord which so impressed Abendroth. Although this 'resolves' back on to, and may be seen as structurally dependent upon, the chord of fourths, it also derives from the superimposition of various major sevenths, thus turning a partly melodic phenomenon into a simultaneity (Ex. 7.6*b*). In Gretchen's scene, the fourths acquire an additional pitch, at first a melodic neighbouring note, E♭ (Ex. 7.7*a*). This tends to recur with greater regu-

Ex. 7.7*a*

Ach nei - ge, du Schmer - zen - rei - che, dein

b

das Herz zer - bricht in mir

c

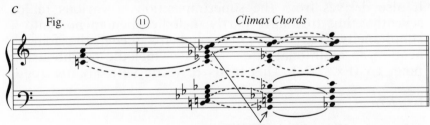

Fig. ⑪   *Climax Chords*

larity than a specific key centre, using also the pitch level
Ab–D–G–C at the reprise between *7* and *8*. This transposition reflects the move of the reprise towards the subdominant, the C♯ minor of the opening yielding to F♯ minor.
Here the music takes a different course, leading to another
semitonal dissonance (Ex. 7.7*b*). At its first appearance,
graphically illustrating Gretchen's heartbreak, it is simply
thinned out to reveal an Eb minor triad at its core, and this
becomes the point of departure for a more diatonic section. If
this savours of evasion, however, Pfitzner restores it at the
climax and resolves it largely by step on to the transposed
collection. What was chord with melodic neighbouring note
briefly becomes harmonic event, before reverting to the
original (Ex. 7.7*c*); the parallel with the symmetrical pitch
collection in the 'Apparitions' Scene' in *Palestrina* is close.
Ultimately C♯ minor is restored, a diffident reminder that
tonality in *Das dunkle Reich* bends in sympathy with developments in Pfitzner's contemporaries, but does not break.

    In Gretchen's music and in 'Scheiden im Licht', the solo
vocal writing takes on bolder, more theatrical dimensions
than in *Von deutscher Seele*, and the choral writing becomes
bolder as well. Admittedly in both works the choral writing is
heavily dependent upon traditional types, chorale, cantus
firmus, and imitative counterpoint. But in *Das dunkle Reich*
the voices are less engulfed in the near-symphonic web than is
the case in the earlier work. As a result, Pfitzner's 'requiem' is
the closer approximation to the well-made choral work, with
its vocal protagonists. Only the complexity of its harmonic
and contrapuntal web places it beyond the abilities of the
average choral society. A certain dourness in the choral movements also makes it in some ways a difficult work to pen-
etrate. Like the Quartet in C sharp minor, it is a very personal
work and lacks the moments of sensuous evocation in *Von
deutscher Seele*. The choral fantasy has had less active support
from Pfitzner's admirers than *Von deutscher Seele*, but that

may reflect the conviction that the latter's title and its subsequent resonance have obscured the fact that the cantata is the finest choral work by a German-speaking composer between *Gurrelieder* and *Carmina Burana*.

For neither of the concertos composed between the cantatas can such large claims be made. The exact motive for Pfitzner's rediscovery of the concerto as a genre has never been fully explained by his biographers, though doubtless it provided for the possibility of a more permanent breakthrough to the concert hall than *Von deutscher Seele*, which would always be a work for special occasions; in this Pfitzner had a degree of success, since the early soloists for the concertos included Walter Gieseking, though, as ever, misfortune also dogged him in the shape of irresponsible conductors and soloists (*SS III* 183). Most of the comments on the concertos in the old Pfitzner literature are of a fairly perfunctory kind; only in the introduction to the recently published study score of the Piano Concerto has Johann Peter Vogel made out any sort of case for that work.[35] Whether the case is convincing is another matter. Pfitzner's general approach to the formal side of the concerto remained surprisingly consistent throughout his life. The early Cello Concerto set an interesting precedent. If its musical language is conventional in a mid-nineteenth-century idiom, its form is decidedly unusual. Formal experimentation in the nineteenth-century concerto took many shapes, and it would be surprising to see Pfitzner adhering to the kind of one-movement form found in Liszt's A major Piano Concerto. What he created, however, was a two-movement work which resembles a traditional concerto but omits the finale. The first movement is in a sonata-form lacking all traces of the orchestral ritornello, but with a slow introduction. The second movement 'combines a binary song-form with developmental features',[36] some of which erupt into an allegro climax to an adagio movement; the impetus for this transformation comes from the motive that subsequently became Dietrich's horn-call in *Der arme Heinrich*. The climax also restates the main theme of the first movement. By thus injecting an element of drama into a song-form, Pfitzner seemed to think that he had balanced his concerto formally,

[35] Johann Peter Vogel, Preface to Hans Pfitzner, *Concerto for Piano and Orchestra [in] E flat major*, Op. 31 (London and Mainz: Eulenburg, 1987).

[36] Wolfgang Osthoff, Preface to Hans Pfitzner, *Concerto for Violoncello and Orchestra [in] A minor*, Op. posth. (1888) (London and Mainz: Eulenburg, 1989), p. vi.

since the work ends with a slow coda based on the first movement, prompting its editor, Wolfgang Osthoff, to speak of
the mirror-like aspect of the whole.[37] The tendency to link
the final movements of the concerto in Beethoven, which
Mendelssohn and Schumann had carried on, is here carried to
the point where the traditional finale dwindles to an episode.
This was an experiment that Pfitzner never repeated exactly,
but the tendency to go beyond the traditional concerto form
resurfaced in the 1920s. Here his treatment is as radical
at times as in Berg's later Violin Concerto, certainly more
radical formally than in Schoenberg's Violin Concerto.

The irony for the traditional conservative picture of Pfitzner
is that the less experimental work for piano is far inferior to
the formally inventive Violin Concerto. The Piano Concerto is
usually described in a language of exaggerated positivism,
which certain features (notably the opening theme) may seem
to encourage.[38] Yet it has its points of contact with the more
reserved side of Pfitzner's nature, and now and again exhibits
some of the chromatic adventurousness (albeit with too many
diminished sevenths) to be found in the cantatas and songs of
the twenties. One problem with the work may be that the two
aspects do not come into any meaningful interaction. The best
movement is the slow third, in which pale reflections of the
night music of *Von deutscher Seele* sound in chorale-like fragments, and in the dotted calls of the horn, which look forward
to 'Scheiden im Licht'; one might even consider it a development from the improvisatory slow movement of the Piano
Quintet, but without the elevating presence of its funeral
march. But in the first movement, when a similar tone sounds
in the contrast theme, the music fails both to take off in
its own right, and to establish any contact with the main
material. This is not to deny the possibility of thematic or
motivic unity; Vogel has provided some instances of connections, which, although relatively tenuous, could be said to
demonstrate some logic.[39] But here analytical proof does not
carry a positive value judgement, for analysis can point to
other weaknesses. Traditionally, Pfitznerians have noted the
renewed influence of Brahms in this work, denying all suggestions of the Lisztian display concerto.[40] The latter point is

[37] Ibid.
[38] See Harold Truscott, 'Pfitzner's Orchestral Music', *Tempo*, 104 (1973), 4–5.
[39] Vogel, Preface to Piano Concerto, pp. vii–viii.
[40] Kroll, *Hans Pfitzner*, 118.

probably true up to a point, though some of the flourishes of the opening seem curiously extrinsic decoration. The most Brahmsian feature is the presence of a scherzo, entitled 'Heiterer Satz', between first and second movements; the parallel with Brahms's B♭ Concerto is obvious. But Pfitzner links this to the first movement by an E♭ alternating in timpani and lower strings, a device of no greater sophistication than the bassoon's B in the Violin Concerto of Mendelssohn (though that becomes the starting-point for something rather more searching than Pfitzner's 'cheerful movement'). Mention of Mendelssohn is not inappropriate. In *Werk und Wiedergabe*, Pfitzner drew attention to 'certain Prestos by Mendelssohn which are precisely only "fast", and otherwise have no peculiarities, absolutely no potential for expression' (*SS III* 213). Alas, it was the fate of the scherzo of his own Piano Concerto to be treated in exactly this manner:

Over the 'Heiterer Satz' of my Piano Concerto I have written 'Rather fast, in constantly breathless motion'. I believe that this direction is clear and unmistakable for everyone who reads this instruction in the light of the appearance of the notes. And yet the legend has already arisen that I wanted this movement taken 'as fast as impossible'. The point here is to be able to read an instruction correctly. 'Rather fast' is not 'very fast', and by 'breathless' I do not mean here so driven that one can no longer breathe, but without pause, without rest, without modification; one can also listen breathlessly, 'breathless lakes' is a beautiful image of Ilse von Stach (in the song 'An die Mark') . . . (*SS III* 215)

The invocation of the Stach setting punctures the complaint, because in the difference between this song and the endless, empty chatter of the 'Heiterer Satz' are measured Pfitzner's best and worst qualities as a composer.

Just as the first two movements are linked, so are slow movement and finale. The two-part structure of the Cello Concerto is recalled, but the parts of the Piano Concerto are more obviously portmanteau structures. In the first part, the notion of sonata form shrivels to two mutually uncomprehending ideas, to which an element of dynamism is applied by the long-familiar device of false recapitulation; the return of the home tonic and the first theme do not coincide. In the finale, the character of the whole is sealed when the traditional cadenza takes the form of a fugue; construction reigns in the improvised, manufacture dictates the structure. Well might one apply the notion of an 'official masterpiece' (as Adorno described Mahler's Eighth Symphony[41]) to this concerto. Its opening octaves reach for an image of the symphonic fashioned after Beethoven, but in the 'after' resides much of the problem. Between the E♭ Concertos of Beethoven and Pfitzner lies Brahms's more meditative and discursive Concerto in B♭; for Pfitzner, the possibility of effecting a new integration of Beethovenian rhetoric with discursiveness proved a mirage.

The qualitative distance between this overbearing work and the Violin Concerto in B minor is not great, since that too seems to imply a symphonic rhetoric of a Beethovenian kind in its first bars, but there the formal context is different. It is subtitled 'in einem Satz', thereby qualifying its notorious reputation: a concerto in which the soloist is excluded from the slow movement. If section is substituted for movement, then the impression may still be misleading, since this is not simply a one-movement work made by stitching three or four traditional movements together. Pfitzner begins his concerto with three themes: a part-motivic, part-virtuosic first theme, a wide-ranging melodic second theme, and a chordal, rhythmically dragging passage in chromatic contrary-motion for brass; all three ideas are labelled numerically. If the first two themes could be regarded as first and second subjects of a sonata-type movement, the third destroys that illusion. The Violin Concerto is as much a hybrid form as *Von deutscher Seele*. The third theme is subjected to seven variations, which take on the aspect of a scherzo in mood; the lack of functional harmonic contrast in the theme results in these variations possessing a largely textural interest, with Pfitzner's orchestration achieving a subtlety in the third variation that contrasts with the dark tones evident elsewhere in the work. As third theme becomes both scherzo and variations, so the second theme is taken up again and developed into the work's lyrical climax: this is the 'slow movement', but in reality, movements have collapsed into episodes. Soloistic treatment is evident here, but for oboe and trombone, not the violin. The first theme then provides a link to another idea, described as 'viertes Thema', which develops into something resembling a finale, with rondo-like returns of the idea. Earlier themes are recalled overtly or (in the case of the third theme at X_1) as the

---

[41] Theodor W. Adorno, *Mahler* (Frankfurt am Main, 1960), 182.

merest suggestions. A similar comment might be made about the 'forms', since variations and rondo are overt, slow movement and sonata transformed into little more than an exposition and an episode. The dwindling of sonata form to a mere thematic contrast is implicit in the first movement of the Piano Concerto. Unlike the earlier work, the Violin Concerto has the courage to draw radical conclusions.

As with the Piano Concerto, Pfitzner's idiom here is less extreme than in 'Abbitte' or Gretchen's scene in *Das dunkle Reich*. The lyrical intensity is couched in diatonic tones at many points, such as to recall here and there the style of the Adagietto of Mahler's Fifth Symphony (particularly at E_1 with its string and harp textures). Where the language grows more chromatic, expression is generated by the 'prose' of the melodic writing. The beginning of the slow section may serve as an example. The twelve-bar oboe restatement of the second theme can be divided into four-bar units, but there is no evidence of conventional periodicity, such as the antecedent–consequent model, or some other pattern based on repetition of phrases (Ex. 7.8); the structure is defined more by the motion of the clarinet harmonies. Within the melody, there is some repetition in sequence, but of a kind that might almost be termed rhetorical rather than structural. The varied repetition of bar 10 a third lower is a local incident. Unifying devices include the interval of a sixth, either direct or as a framing device for arpeggiation (x). Organization is by a number of sub-motivic factors, which accounts for the relatively seamless progress of the oboe solo. Such melody in Pfitzner almost invariably proliferates into counterpoint, as trombone and then orchestral violins enter; the surprised trombonist is reminded to play melodically and expressively in his unaccustomed role—what would Scholz have said about this, Pfitzner may have been secretly asking. The counterpoint fills the full orchestral space, but in a manner more reminiscent of Strauss, perhaps, than Mahlerian *Klangflächentechnik*. Such music rests often in Pfitzner on pedal points, but here the bass is structured largely in chromatic linear motion; the pedals are rather to be found in the variations along with other harmonically static devices such as ostinato.

That the most intense section of the concerto should dispense with the soloist recalls the slightly episodic use of the vocal forces in parts of *Von deutscher Seele*. It is tempting

Ex. 7.8

to conclude that Pfitzner's musical temperament was not suited to the conventionally 'effective'. The impression is strengthened by the manner in which *Palestrina* is structured as a kind of dramatic diminuendo. That the concerto had long ago taken on symphonic mannerisms is a historical truism, and the central place of the orchestra as presenter and developer of symphonically conceived material is not peculiar to Pfitzner. But few composers amongst his predecessors and contemporaries conceived the soloist's part in quite the same kind of dialogue role. The concertos of Bartók and Schoenberg, though quite unmeretricious in their virtuosity, shine a much brighter spotlight on the protagonist than those of Pfitzner. In the best passages of the Violin Concerto, he seems to be writing disguised chamber music, a genre with which he had greater experience. This is apparent in the variations and the slow episode, but also in the diatonic simplicity of the fourth theme: this is the manner of the D major Quartet's finale, or of *Das Christ-Elflein*, folk-like and intimate. Part of the problem with the Piano Concerto is that the intimate sections are overpowered by the attempt to write on a symphonic scale. Not only the Violin Concerto's key, B minor, reminds the listener of Elgar's comparable work. In that concerto, the intimate music of the first two movements is far more distinctive and memorable than the extrovert finale, and much the same might be said of Elgar's Cello Concerto; the compulsion to write the virtuosic play-out is rescued in those works by devices such as the accompanied cadenza (in reality a species of lyrical rhapsody) or thematic recall. Pfitzner incorporates the latter at perhaps a more radical level by his single-movement design, but the need is the same. To mediate between the slow section's chromatic intensity and the dark brass colours in earlier parts of the work, elements are threaded through one another to generate a new and legitimate formal type. Such music repeatedly asks the listener questions about response to structure and genre, but the truth of the matter is that for Pfitzner increasingly all structures were aimed at a private audience for which chamber music was an ideal beyond the symphonic.

To comment on the chamber-music characteristics of Pfitzner's orchestration in the Violin Concerto and parts of the Piano Concerto risks the charge of glibness on two counts. Since the pioneering phase of Mahler studies, chamber-like orchestration has become a cliché of musical writing, more invoked than defined. Since Wellesz's *Die neue Instrumentation*, its presence as a general force in the music of the 1920s has been widely recognized. The second charge is more peculiar to the position of the concertos in Pfitzner's output; within two years of the first performance of the Violin Concerto, he was working on a chamber work, recognized by many as his masterpiece in the genre, which subsequently was arranged as a Symphony for full orchestra. To talk of chamber orchestration may seem an artificial, knowing way of approaching this oddity. The composers of the Second Viennese School of course also arranged chamber works for full or string orchestra, but there was seldom any suggestion that a new genre had been created by the act of transcription. Nor was there any in Mahler's 'orchestration' of quartets by Beethoven and Schubert (though the manufacture of a 'Gastein' Symphony from Schubert's Grand Duo, or Schoenberg's discerning of a symphony in Brahms's Piano Quartet in G minor are parallels of a weak kind). Pfitzner's own explanation for the transcription hovered between act of popularization ('a symphony always has a larger audience') and attempt to throw new light on a work whose 'structure and sound-world...positively call for symphonic treatment'.[42] Whether he explained this to his biographer cannot be said; Abendroth provided a somewhat different explanation which also fitted in with his wish to deflate the reputation of Strauss. Whereas the Straussian tone-poem was essentially a vehicle for orchestral virtuosity, Pfitzner's Quartet/Symphony was a pure 'musical organism', both romantic and classical, expressive and architectonic; Bach's fugues could be played with different forces.[43] The old theme of Pfitzner the 'absolute' musician emerged again, certainly on better ground than in the operas and songs. More recent opinion has tended to vacillate between the bald assertion that 'both versions are equally legitimate'[44] (which leaves the sense of an issue ducked), and the recognition that 'timbral alterations can illustrate relationships', possibly to the extent of altering structures even in a case of 'mere' orchestration: there is virtually no recomposition in the Symphony.[45] The texture of a piece of four-part writing lies underneath Pfitzner's orchestration.

All of this would be a minor question were the work not innately worthwhile. Along with the Piano Quintet and the more extrovert Violin Sonata, the Quartet in C sharp minor is representative of Pfitzner's chamber music at its best. In

[42] Johann Peter Vogel, Preface to Hans Pfitzner, *Symphony [in] C sharp minor*, Op. 36*a* (London and Mainz: Eulenburg, 1987), p. iii.

[43] Abendroth, *Hans Pfitzner*, 378.

[44] Truscott, 'Pfitzner's Orchestral Music', 6.

[45] Skouenborg, *Von Wagner zu Pfitzner*, 151.

certain respects, it almost looks as though Pfitzner was aware of the obvious comparison to be made. The first movement is no fugue, but its intense chromatic contrapuntal writing remembers the first movement of a more famous Quartet in C sharp minor; in the finale, Pfitzner's use of certain driving rhythms also fleetingly recalls Beethoven's far more obsessive finale to Opus 131. But the most striking recollection of late Beethoven in the finale is the use made of the trill. When the slow movement's main motive (Ex. 7.9*a*) appears as a

Ex. 7.9*a*

semibreve cantus firmus, each note is decorated with stabbing trills that recall not merely Opus 131 but even more the *Grosse Fuge* (Ex. 7.9*b*). In this movement too, an important facet of Pfitzner's treatment of rhythm is clarified in a later recall of the same motive (Ex. 7.10). Cross-rhythms were of interest to him in a spirit that recalls Beethoven's tendency to adjust macrorhythm, to create cross-rhythms between phrases. His music frequently draws attention to groupings of bars into larger units: in the Prelude to Act II of *Palestrina*, in variation 7 of the Violin Concerto, in 'Stimme der Sehnsucht'. In the Quartet's finale, the groupings of three bars, each of 4/4

Ex. 7.10

time, are further divided by the implied 6/4 of the cello. Pfitzner's music is indeed fertile ground for Stephan's *Taktgruppenanalyse*.[46] An amusing acknowledgement of this occurs in a group of sketches relating principally to the G major Cello Concerto and *Das Herz*; two systems laid out in three groupings of four bars and two groupings of two bars for some music that was never entered.[47]

In spite of the belief in the quartet exhibited by Pfitznerians, comment on it has seldom been very extensive. Much ink has been spilled on pointing out its superficial features, which by now can readily be seen as general Pfitzner characteristics. Thus the last two movements are joined together, while the first two movements may (!) be linked. Since the sequence places the scherzo second and the slow movement third, the parallel with the Piano Concerto is close. The first movement is, as usual with Pfitzner, closely worked in terms of counterpoint, as is, less usually, the finale; the relaxed conclusion of earlier works is avoided. Yet again the scherzo provokes a commentator to comparisons with E. T. A. Hoffmann, though an even more obvious trait is the manner in which Pfitzner

---

[46] Rudolf Stephan, 'Überlegungen zur Taktgruppenanalyse: Zur Interpretation der 7. Symphonie von Gustav Mahler', *Logos musicae: Festschrift für Albert Palm*, ed. Rüdiger Görner (Wiesbaden, 1982), 202–10; 'Bruckners Romantische Sinfonie', *Anton Bruckner: Studien zu Werk und Wirkung: Walter Wiora zum 30. Dezember 1986*, ed. Christoph-Hellmut Mahling (Tutzing, 1988), 177–82; 'Pfitzner als absoluter Musiker', PLZ.

[47] *D-WÜim*, Mch. f. 730, fol. 13ʳ.

once more avoids a trio section.[48] By now the typical Pfitzner scherzo has become a variation on the second movement of the first 'Rasumovsky' Quartet, in which the traditional scherzo form tends towards a freely developing process, held together by ever more emphatic statements of themes. Thematic transference between movements is rife, with a theme from the first movement as well as the slow movement theme recalled in the finale. That comment has seldom gone beyond this in the English introduction to Pfitzner's music is not surprising;[49] more puzzling is the tendency of German admirers to assume that the work is self-explaining. An exception is the analysis by Vogel in the recently published miniature score of the symphony, which is as penetrating as the limited space permits.[50] But only Skouenborg has really delved below the surface of the work, at least in the first movement, and come up with an interpretation rooted in a systematic view of Pfitzner's music as a whole.[51]

In the last resort, the striking feature of the work is not thematic transference, linking of movements, or architectonic generalizations, but the degree of chromatic freedom which marks the first and third movements. Certain passages verge on a loss of tonality, as Henderson noted, singling out bars 137–8 of the first movement and, to a slightly lesser degree, the beginning of its development for special mention on account of open fourths and fifths alongside non-triadic elements.[52] It is hardly surprising that Skouenborg couches his analysis of the first movement in terms of harmonic features, specifically dissonance, which he categorizes in various ways. His thesis is dependent on a definition of substantiality, which is rooted in the perception of harmony as 'Vierklang' (usually the triad plus the seventh). In Wagner, the degree of substantiality is high, since the seventh is usually well integrated within the harmony in such progressions as perfect and deceptive cadences; secondary sevenths and dominants are the mark of a high degree of substance. In Pfitzner the relationships are of less substance and are therefore more 'structural', inasmuch as secondary dominants are less

[48] Abendroth, *Hans Pfitzner*, 374.
[49] E.g. Truscott, 'Pfitzner's Orchestral Music', 6–7.
[50] Vogel, Preface to Symphony, pp. iii–ix.
[51] Skouenborg, *Von Wagner zu Pfitzner*, 133–53.
[52] Donald Gene Henderson, 'Hans Pfitzner', Ph.D. thesis (University of Michigan, 1963), 96–7.

marked, with dissonance arising from the clashes of the melodic lines; dissonance in Wagner is integrated in harmony, in Pfitzner in line.[53] This is obviously a challenging view of structure that points to a general problem in Pfitzner for the analyst. The conservative Pfitzner was rejected by the conservative Schenker, and with this much good cause. Contrary to Skouenborg's picture of harmonically integrated Wagner, recent analysts have shown that Schenkerian methods are not out of place even in Wagner (or for that matter Mahler and Strauss). The basis of Schenkerian analysis, apart from the obvious *Ursatz*, is the notion that chords, melodies, and part-writing in general may be seen as contrapuntal prolongations of scale degrees and more basic chords. With Pfitzner's music, the impression grows that, as in certain passages in Mahler and Strauss, extensions of Schenker's principles to cover prolongations of chromatic chords may be desirable or necessary. The analyses of Skouenborg seem to imply a different principle in Pfitzner from Wagner, but in practice, analytical systems derived from Schenker already explain dissonance from line in the phenomena of contrapuntally derived chords. In certain passages in the C sharp minor Quartet, a controlling, 'structural' chord may be detected in spite of the chromatic complications. Atonality is not in question when the chromatic lines converge on the dominant to tonic motion in bars 4–5 of the first movement (Ex. 7.11), however much neighbouring notes and passing notes (often in chromatic equal-interval cycles) may disguise the structural motion.

In the passages noted by Henderson, the disguising is carried to an extreme point. From 5 to the establishment of an A minor triad in bar 90, five bars of fluid chromaticism pose the simple question: which chords may be said to possess structural weight, even at local or foreground level, particularly in the progressions of bars 88–9, where even the B♭ minor chord is neither triad nor functional (Ex. 7.12)? Here Skouenborg's curious use of 'substantial' may be endorsed at least metaphorically. That suspended or floating tonality is characteristic of developments is familiar from Schoenberg's theories on harmony. The conservative Pfitzner writes music that here and elsewhere strives to integrate not the dissonance within line or chord but the dissonant chord within a

---

[53] Skouenborg, *Von Wagner zu Pfitzner*, ch. 2, *passim*.

Ex. 7.11

tonal system; his precursor is the Schoenberg who revealed underlying logic in the chromatic chord (and who perhaps had a wider picture of the forms of secondary dominants than Skouenborg). Pfitzner's chromaticism is thus related strongly to Schoenberg's historical dilemma in the first decade of the century. In the first movement of the quartet, in 'Abbitte', and in *Das dunkle Reich*, Pfitzner suggests that post-Wagnerian chromaticism may still be capable of integration, a con-

Ex. 7.12

clusion that not many of his contemporaries would have rejected, even Schoenberg with his concept of a 'return' to tonality. In his music of the 1920s, Pfitzner in a sense made his own riposte to the strident conservatism which he seemed to proclaim in his theoretical works. The German musical tradition was flexible enough to contain new dissonance treatment, and by definition new chromatic prolongations. Of course there was no limit to what might be prolonged once chromatic dissonances came to be perceived as structural. This is a problem which analysis, however, is only now beginning to face. Pfitzner's Quartet/Symphony indeed poses problems which are profoundly to do with relationships among notes; its orchestral form in a sense is an act of analysis, an attempt to turn a spotlight upon abstract problems. It has its didactic side in a slightly different way from the twelve-note sonata forms and suite movements that Schoenberg composed with seeming perversity in the 1920s; the true party was Pfitzner *and* Schoenberg.

In discussing the forms used in the Quartet of C sharp minor, the recognition must be made that Pfitzner follows in an essentially developmental tradition. Here too his music provides clarification of his theoretical writing. The impression there arises that the work may be the artificial product of the *Einfall*, if the latter is seen specifically as the melodic idea. But in fact that more truly indicates Julius Bahle's later position, as described by Wolfgang Osthoff: 'Inspiration to bar 16 and then the hard work begins.'[54] In Pfitzner's best music, the *Einfall* is the whole, and the metaphor of the organic remains as possible framework for its discussion. This has its clearest application in the Quartet in C sharp minor, Pfitzner's most comprehensive attempt to create a work in which integrative principles should dominate. At first sight this may seem strange in the light of an apparent sectionalization of form which seems to spill over from the concertos. The first movement, in spite of the polyphonic web which adheres to everything, clearly delineates its themes. That the opening figure is a motto may be accepted from the manner in which it marks off other ideas.[55] That themes are self-contained enough to return with different structural weight

---

[54] Comment during discussions on Wolfgang Rihm, 'Zur Aktualität Pfitzners', *SPB* 202.
[55] See Vogel, Preface to Symphony, p. vi, for the idea of a motto theme.

recalls the use made of an episode in the development of the D
major Quartet's first movement; it eventually achieved the
status of coda. The triplet theme at *1* in the first movement
of the Quartet in C sharp minor (Ex. 7.13), ostensibly a

Ex. 7.13

transition, achieves a progressive increase in stature, first as
coda to the whole movement, subsequently as participant in
the finale at *49*. Outside the first movement sectional forms
seem to dominate. The slow movement belongs with that
species of double variations familiar from Beethoven and
Bruckner. The contrast of theme and episodes is also a contrast of imitative counterpoint and homophony. But the
relationships between sections may be defined in terms of
continuous motivic extrapolation from certain basic cells;
Pfitzner acknowledges as much, however eccentrically, in his
direction at the end of the first movement: 'The A should be
played if the second movement follows on at once; the G♯ if
the first movement is followed by a pause, which however
should only be very short in order to make the motivic connection meaningful.'[56]

If motivic relationships are clear enough within movements
to prompt talk of 'development forms' and Adorno's concept
of an 'Erfüllungsfeld' in Skouenborg's study, it remains to
enquire how far the quartet's finale can be said to provide a
summing-up.[57] If it is accepted that in this work there should
be little problem in speaking of abstract musical issues, the
ancient question of the 'finale problem' (which was always
first and foremost a problem for hermeneuts) may be pushed

---

[56] Henderson explains the motivic relationship here as bars 195–6 of the first
movement and bar 3 of the scherzo ('Hans Pfitzner', 283).

[57] Skouenborg, *Von Wagner zu Pfitzner*, 108–10.

to one side. There is no question of Pfitzner's quartet being searched for apotheosis, *Verklärung*, or even a 'happy end'. Instead what must be recognized is the manner in which such categories as sonata or sonata-rondo fail to grasp the procedural essence of the movement, which is of a continuous chain of developments from a theme that fuses two distinct motives against an internal tonic pedal (Ex. 7.14). The driving

Ex. 7.14

Beethovenian rhythm is an offshoot of the first of these at *44*, the flowing counter-material after *45* a derivative of the second. Rhythmic development eventually dissolves into an imaginatively impressionistic texture for the return of the first movement's coda theme. Here the contrast between the two versions of the work is particularly interesting. The recalled theme in the quartet is given to the second violin and viola, but in the symphony is allotted to the solo brass instruments for which Pfitzner had an ever greater liking. In the finale, the merits of the orchestral form as far as clarity is concerned are particularly marked, especially in the developmental section which follows *51*. But the quartet version is the more immediate musical experience, in that it more effectively distances all possibility of rhetoric. That developmental section, which effectively removes the form from sonata-rondo into a more through-composed genre related to his scherzo forms, is the protracted climax of the work. The revelation of the connections between motives reaches a peak of intensity controllable only by the melodic means of the cantus firmus, which in turn fragments into cross-rhythms. The work ends in the major mode, a more protracted assertion of C♯ major than that which concludes Beethoven's Opus 131. In the latter, the tensions continue to pulse below the surface of the music almost until the final upsurge. Pfitzner's conclusion is far more valedictory. This is not inappropriate because with the quartet he brought a chapter of his musical life to an end. Valediction of a certain kind becomes the major theme of his later instrumental music, the theme that perhaps made the writing of real but retrospective symphonies possible.

In his life too, a chapter was closed. In the year following the String Quartet Mimi died, and the works which followed are threnodies, none more so than *Lethe*, an orchestral song which quotes from songs associated with Mimi, 'Ich und du' and 'Abbitte', as well as Lukrezia's music in *Palestrina*. Inasmuch as its harmonic and contrapuntal style has provoked comparison with Schreker,[58] it acts as a yardstick for the historical situation which Pfitzner occupied in his music from 1925 to 1929, culminating in *Das dunkle Reich*, his most pessimistic work. The end of this period of purgation is *Das Herz*, Pfitzner's all but unknown last opera, which, however, already points to his last brief period of song-writing and a transformed image of instrumental music.

---

[58] Rolf Urs Ringger, '*Lethe*: Hans Pfitzners Orchesterlied op. 37', *MPG* 43 (Sept. 1981), 97.

8

An Inner Emigration?

HAD Pfitzner's abandonment of composition after Mimi's death and the valedictory *Lethe* proved permanent, his career as a composer would appear remarkably complete. But in practice there were too many ties to music to permit him to remain silent. There were collected papers to be published, and *Werk und Wiedergabe* to be written. *Das dunkle Reich* was another work of valediction, but on a scale to suggest that Pfitzner's career was not over. Life too had an unexpected development, as the 60-year-old Pfitzner to his own surprise fell in love with a pupil nearly forty years younger, Lilo Martin. Most significantly, there came a renewed impulse to write for the stage. *Das Herz* begins a new chapter in Pfitzner's career as a composer, though the resultant style fulfilled itself in instrumental music, the dominant genre until his death in 1949. *Das Herz* and the late instrumental works are the two themes of this final chapter. But it would not be complete without a third, the rise to power, career, and collapse of the Nazi movement. That there might be a connection between Pfitzner's withdrawn late style and a disillusionment with the events of the thirties is a matter that defies simple answers, given that the seeds of this late style were already apparent before 1933 in the last groups of songs. But it is a possibility deserving of some consideration. Only in 1933 did he adopt a posture that suggested solidarity with the regime; subsequently, the closest he came to a prominent Nazi was to the 'sectarian' Hans Frank, of whom it has been plausibly suggested that the Nazis might well have put him to death before the allies finally did so.[1] But equally Pfitzner cannot be classed as an opponent of the Nazis. In comparison with notable figures in other arts, his sympathy with the Nazis' ethos was not as pronounced as that of such initial enthusiasts as Emil Nolde or Gottfried Benn; as a result he never suffered

---

[1] See Joachim C. Fest, *The Face of the Third Reich*, trans. Michael Bullock (London, 1970), 315.

comparable disfavour when even that limited sympathy waned. Like other artists who did not go into exile, he survived by compromising.

The history of *Das Herz* was the initial stage in Pfitzner's retreat into an essentially retrospective style. This is very much bound up with critical reactions to the work, but also with disputes between Pfitzner, his librettist, and those responsible for its first performances. Much information exists as to the circumstances of composition and performance, while the work today is virtually unknown. Complete performances have been non-existent since a staging in Dortmund in 1955. It is consequently almost impossible to verify the work's potential as a 'drama for music', as Pfitzner designated it. A revival is even more urgent for it than for the early operas. This should not be impossible, given the attention lavished in recent years on operas by Zemlinsky and Schreker, composers of comparable stature but of less controversial reputation. But such experiences as Hamburg's much-acclaimed travesty of *Der Zwerg* as *Der Geburtstag der Infantin* offer a warning. Wolfgang Sawallisch provides the information that at least one admirer of the music of *Das Herz* has attempted to write a new book for it.[2] This is not without irony considering that Pfitzner's polemic against the Berlin first production was precisely over the issue of fidelity to the conception. Before surrendering to the tyranny of the opera director, it would be salutary to assess Pfitzner's intentions with a degree of fidelity.

The stages in the composition of *Das Herz* are well documented, from the letter of 21 September 1929 in which a collaboration was proposed to Pfitzner by his pupil Hans Mahner-Mons.[3] Fame of a kind had come to the latter not through music, nor even in his own name, since he was best known as Hans Possendorf, a creator of detective fiction. Abendroth once again provides the significant dates.[4] Discussions were held between composer and librettist in Berlin in January of 1930, but things took a false turn through attempts to derive a libretto from Bürger's *Die Königin von Golkonde*. Only after that did Pfitzner conceive some themes and the central figure quite independently of his librettist, or

---

[2] Gabriele Busch-Salmen and Günther Weiss, *Hans Pfitzner: Münchner Dokumente/Bilder und Bildnisse* (Regensburg, 1990), 92.

[3] Hans Rectanus, 'Materialen zur Entstehung des "Herz"', *MPG* 27 (Apr. 1971), 11.

[4] Walter Abendroth, *Hans Pfitzner* (Munich, 1935), 282–7.

indeed of any pre-existing literary work. The central figure was to be a medieval doctor with supernatural powers capable of invoking his recently dead wife. Essential to the theme was that he should eventually renounce his magic out of respect for the dead and then fall into the hands of worldly enemies. This is hardly the plot of *Das Herz*, but all the details survive in some form into the opera. The personal significance is too obvious to need much labouring: the figure of the wife, renunciation, and the hostility of the world suggest not only Pfitzner's career (as he interpreted it), but also resonances from *Palestrina*. Mahner-Mons eventually placed this group of ideas at the beginning of the eighteenth century in the context of the European witch-craze. Like Grun, he found Pfitzner an impatient taskmaster. Fundamentally he supplied Pfitzner with a scenario, which the composer turned into verse and then composed. The first scene was completed by 27 March 1930, and the whole first act on 31 July; the later acts were completed on 7 November 1930 and 7 January 1931, and then Pfitzner began the orchestration (which was completed on 22 May 1931). By comparison with *Palestrina*, work on the opera was carried through swiftly, mostly thanks to Pfitzner, who found Mahner-Mons an increasingly sluggish collaborator. The libretto that finally emerged elaborated Pfitzner's original ideas into a parable of the black arts that nowadays may pose considerable problems for audiences.

SYNOPSIS. *Act I, scene 1*. Daniel Athanasius is a wandering surgeon of great skill but dubious reputation. When the curtain rises, he and his assistant Wendelin are completing the diagnosis of a young knight's incurable illness. The knight begs him to use magic. When Athanasius refuses, the knight threatens to denounce him as a magician. Athanasius explains to Wendelin that there is a degree of truth in this accusation. He did learn certain black arts in Egypt, and knows how to conclude a pact with a demon at no risk to his soul. The demon Asmodeus requires only the gift of a human heart. When Athanasius draws the demon's sign, three knocks on the door announce the arrival of the curious figure of Asmus Modiger, privy councillor at the court of the local duke. He brings news of the serious illness of the heir, Prince Tankred. Athanasius has been recommended as a doctor by a young lady of the court, Helge von Laudenheim. The councillor clearly desires her in spite of his great age. He departs to inform the duke of Athanasius' willingness to help the prince. Helge now arrives to inform Athanasius of the prince's imminent death and to remind him of an occasion on which he saved her mother's life. Athanasius sets off to meet his destiny with the help of heaven or hell.

Scene 2. In the palace, the duke and duchess watch with horror the death of their son. Helge announces Athanasius' arrival, but he is too late. He insists, however, that the prince is only asleep and that he can save him. The duke is furious but his wife grasps at the doctor's words. When they have left, Wendelin departs for Athanasius' magical equipment. A conversation with Helge, who shares the duke's misgivings, reveals that Athanasius has fallen in love with her. Wendelin brings in a black chest from which Athanasius produces alchemical equipment. He summons Asmodeus with Wendelin's unwilling help, and the demon's face appears. Athanasius asks for the power to restore the dead. The price is a human heart which Athanasius will hold in the black chest for a year. Then Asmodeus will claim the heart and Athanasius must select another to maintain his powers. Asmodeus reveals that in sleep human hearts leave the body and wander in the land of dreams. From a chorus of such hearts, Athanasius selects one at random in the face of Wendelin's protests. As he places it in the chest, Tankred wakens. His parents promise Athanasius due reward. When he turns to Helge, he finds her asleep. On waking, she swears to remain true to Athanasius until death.

Act II. A year has passed and the court is celebrating a masque of the Olympian deities. Athanasius has married Helge and buried the chest where he believes even Asmodeus cannot obtain it. He will not renew the bargain, and has formulas to keep the demon at bay. Wendelin is properly doubtful as to this. Helge sings of her love for Athanasius, but his peace is shattered when Asmus Modiger asks for one night with Helge. When Athanasius refuses in disgust, the councillor denounces him as a sorcerer, and notices that someone seems to be calling the doctor's name. It is Asmodeus himself, who appears and sweeps aside the doctor's feeble spells. Athanasius is forced to give up the heart and Helge collapses dead; Athanasius had chosen her heart. The councillor returns with the ducal couple to repeat his charges, and servants enter with the news of Tankred's sudden death. Armed guards seize Athanasius.

Act III. In a dungeon doctor and assistant await sentence. A prosecutor announces that Athanasius will be burned after torture, but that Wendelin can go free. Athanasius forbids Wendelin to intercede for him, since only a painful death can atone for his crime. The duke enters with a proposition. If Athanasius will revive the prince by renewing the spell, then he will be smuggled out of the duchy to safety. Athanasius refuses, first in the face of the duke's entreaties, then in spite of the enumeration of the tortures that await him. The duke leaves, promising Athanasius an ordeal of unprecedented severity. Athanasius kneels before a crucifix and prays for the heart to be redeemed. The executioners arrive, and are impressed by Athanasius' calm. As they lead him out, they faint. The 'astral body' of Helge appears and shows Athanasius the path to freedom. Asmodeus still holds her heart and her body wanders aimlessly between earth and heaven. Athanasius refuses to escape. The heart suddenly appears in Helge's body. Off-stage voices announce that Athanasius has passed the test. As he touches Helge, she vanishes and he dies. Through the walls of the prison, two spirits can be seen slowly disappearing. The executioners waken in surprise. The prosecutor arrives impatiently, to be told that Athanasius is dead.

Certain moments in Pfitzner's essay, 'Die Entstehung der "Herz"-Dichtung', reflect a defensiveness about this scenario; above all, the reference to a 'Kitsch-novelist ... with whom Hans Pfitzner had sunk so low as to ally himself' suggests an awareness of the kind of prejudice that might result from working with 'Possendorf' (*SS IV* 458). He maintained that all he wanted and got from Mahner-Mons was a certain facility with dramatic structure. In this may be discerned an echo of critical reservations about the often-misunderstood structure of *Palestrina*. But the passage of time has dealt cruelly with Mahner-Mons's libretto. There can be no doubt that Reinhard Seebohm is correct to see (once more) Hoffmannesque traits in the 'Doppelgestalt' of the councillor and Asmodeus (who are sung by the same tenor).[5] But childish play with names (Asmodi = Asmus Modiger) is the stock of popular Gothic film and fiction, and is just as likely to result in echoes of *Rosemary's Baby* as E. T. A. Hoffmann. This development Pfitzner could hardly have foreseen, and he followed in a strong tradition of Hoffmannesque opera, including Busoni's

[5] Reinhard Seebohm, 'Die Tragödie eines grossen Arztes: Die Handlung von Pfitzners letzter Oper *Das Herz* in heutiger Sicht', *MPG* 27 (Apr. 1971), 3.

Die Brautwahl and Hindemith's *Cardillac*. Only a few years before, Busoni's *Doktor Faust* had appeared with baritone hero and tenor demon as in *Das Herz*, and a not dissimilar conjuration scene. But demonic possession and conjuration is nowadays high camp; Asmodeus, Pfitzner's demon, has been played in the cinema in the tradition which embraces both Hollywood and the Hammer film studio. Against such a background, the realism of Mahner-Mons's scenario (as opposed to Busoni's highly stylized conjuration) is almost inconceivable as music theatre. It is doubtful if audiences today can watch even *Der Freischütz* without some degree of stifled hilarity in the Wolf's Glen scene, save in the most imaginative of productions. The tendency to stylize Gothic either into camp or into symbolism was already apparent in Pfitzner's own lifetime. Mahner-Mons and Pfitzner saddled the new opera with a libretto that was paradoxically both unsuited to its potential audience and yet characteristic of the composer, in that it avoided expressionistic extremes and presented its fantastic scenes with sober realism.

Pfitzner's own reaction to the libretto is somewhat puzzling. He 'knew that purely from the theatrical point of view I had to expect that "good" libretto which I had lacked until that time, according to the mediocre judgement of my dramatic works' (*SS IV* 453). This is only partly ironic, since he later speaks of the irrelevance of Possendorf's profession to the ability to invent 'eine gute Fabel'. Effectively that is what Mahner-Mons supplied, since *Das Herz* is a libretto in which characterization by means of reflection is almost non-existent. There is little scope for psychological refinement. Whereas the libretti of Schreker's operas invite close investigation as much with the tools of literary criticism as with musical analysis,[6] *Das Herz* seems to deal with puppet-like figures that again suggest, however improbably, Busoni and the earlier operas of Hindemith. Pfitzner, who spent so much time explaining the motivation of the characters in earlier stage-works, provides hardly any indication as to how he viewed his creations in the two short essays which he devoted to *Das Herz*. By this time in any case, real or imagined slights from critics and false friends had led him to spend more time on the cir-

---

[6] E.g. Peter Franklin, 'Style, Structure and Taste: Three Aspects of the Problem of Franz Schreker', *Proceedings of the Royal Musical Association*, 109 (1982/3), 134–46; 'Schreker's Decline', *The Idea of Music* (London, 1985), 139–60.

cumstances of the work than on the work itself. It is Helmut Grohe who throws some light on the characters, providing the information that Wendelin was the incarnation of the good conscience, and that Helge the innocent had laid herself open to Asmodeus' influence by handing over some of the equipment for the conjuration. This can easily be worked out from the libretto, however, and is less significant than the revelations about Asmus Modiger, who in Grohe's view was apostle, incarnation, and agent of Asmodeus, but not identical with him, nor the possessor of supernatural powers.[7] Given Grohe's closeness to Pfitzner, this explanation may well be authoritative. Neither Grohe nor Pfitzner, however, made any attempt to read the characters with any refinement of detail, nor to unravel the symbolic significance of the plot. The parable of overweening pride and downfall is implicitly accepted as tragedy, the tale of redemption through passive willingness to suffer and through the love of an 'innocent' woman accepted as a norm. Admittedly the tide was running against 'psychological' depiction in the stage works of the *Neue Sachlichkeit*. The baldness and economy of the libretto represented its contemporaneity. Its subject-matter, however, is not merely problematic for today's audience. In its time, horror had taken on new dimensions in the era of expressionism. For that matter war had shown and would show again what real horror meant. It was Pfitzner's intention to accompany the demon's appearance with the sound of a siren, but in a staging of 1939 he was persuaded by Joseph Keilberth to dispense with it for all too obvious reasons.[8] In the last resort, Pfitzner's libretto for *Palestrina* defied dramatic convention and produced something unique and valuable, while the libretto for *Das Herz* accepted dramatic conventions but fell between the stools of different dramatic tastes.

If *Das Herz* is to be revived, its prospects depend almost entirely on the degree to which Pfitzner the composer made good the dramatic defects. Here too Pfitzner reflected in a measure some trends amongst his contemporaries. Hans Rectanus has isolated the tension at the work's heart. Its situations are 'hyper-romantic', compounded of the Hoffmannesque super-

---

[7] Helmut Grohe, 'Hans Pfitzner: *Das Herz*: Der Sinn des Dramas', Programme-book of the Staats-Theater unter den Linden (Berlin, n.d. [1931]).

[8] Seebohm, 'Die Tragödie eines grossen Arztes', 2.

natural and that religiose strain analysed by Schwarz in Pfitzner's whole music-dramatic output.[9] But at the same time Rectanus acknowledges its 'return to the number opera, to apparently classical diatonic theme construction, to simplicity in the harmonic means, and to clearly-articulated cadences'. His conclusions partly stem from Pfitzner's highly limited use of leitmotif in *Das Herz*. Although there are leitmotifs, they do not pertain to every character: Athanasius the hero has no motive, a remarkable departure from Pfitzner's practice in *Der arme Heinrich* and *Palestrina*, whose heroes attracted a variety of musical figures for the purposes of characterization. Admittedly Athanasius is something of an extreme case. Pfitzner seems to have thought habitually in his composition sketches in motivic terms, as has been seen in the case of *Von deutscher Seele*. Once again motives are isolated for use in the sketches for *Das Herz*. One example shows him taking a motive and driving it through a rudimentary melodic sequence that would be meaningless without the attached rubric: 'Asmodi-Mot. sich steigernd bis zur richtigen Harmonie, mit gleichbleibendem Bass'. Thus described, the sequence seems an initial annotation for Asmodeus' final threat in the second act at *66*, though that takes place at a different pitch-level from the sketch.[10] So Pfitzner clearly recognized the continuing presence of leitmotifs in the work. What Rectanus has shown is that these are often subservient as means of organization to the form of the individual scene. Here finally Pfitzner does move from Wagnerian through-composition towards more 'absolute' structures, though even a conventional 'number' such as Athanasius' prayer in Act III lacks tonal closure; its musical language recalls in metre and harmony the contrast material from the first movement of the Piano Concerto—*Das Herz* is no sudden breach with the style of the twenties. But Helge's narration in Act I, scene 3 is far closer to an 'arioso' than anything hitherto in Pfitzner's operas and is, as Rectanus has shown, a rondo that remains in F for virtually its entire length, until the dictates of dramatic continuity deflect it towards F♯ minor after *51*.[11] The first

[9] Hans Rectanus, 'Pfitzner als Dramatiker', *Beiträge zur Geschichte der Oper*, ed. Heinz Becker (Regensburg, 1969), 144; Werner Schwarz, 'Die Bedeutung des Religiösen im musikdramatischen Schaffen Hans Pfitzners', *Festgabe für Joseph Müller-Blattau*, ed. Christoph-Hellmut Mahling (Kassel, 1966), 112–16.

[10] *D-WÜim*, Mch. f. 730, fol. 27ʳ.

[11] Hans Rectanus, *Leitmotivik und Form in den musikdramatischen Werken Hans Pfitzners* (Würzburg, 1967), 168.

scene between Athanasius and Asmus Modiger is rather different in that it is less clearly defined from a formal point of view. In style it is a brittle scherzo, reminiscent of Budoja's music in *Palestrina*, but more relaxed. But formally it may simply reflect Pfitzner's own type of instrumental scherzo, which favoured uniformity of mood and continuity of development without the contrast of the traditional trio. One tonality (D major) is even more firmly in control here than in Helge's rondo.

The deference to the 'number opera' which was prominent amongst Pfitzner's contemporaries is one strand in the work's background. Rectanus draws the obvious parallels with *Wozzeck* and *Cardillac*.[12] But numbers survived also in the Italian opera of Puccini and verismo, and had been domiciled in German opera by d'Albert. In Rectanus' analysis of *Das Herz*, the situation is complicated by the echoes which he finds from earlier forms and traditions: the Baroque 'Lamento' bass in the duchess's mourning for Tankred in Act I, the Wolf's Glen in the conjuration scene.[13] Earlier Schwarz had also noted the funereal sarabande which followed Tankred's death struggles.[14] *Das Herz* is not merely an opera with formally self-contained sections, it also plays against the ghosts of other forms and styles. Some of these are conventional enough from an operatic point of view. The entire dramatic business after Asmodeus' revelation in Act II that the heart belonged to Helge is handled as *stretta* with interruptions, and those quite clearly of a recitative character. The recitatives treat earlier material as reminiscence motives, referring back to the conjuration scene. The *stretta* has its own rapid theme in C minor and triple time, which is also clearly derived from earlier figures associated with the charge of witchcraft. Within the *stretta*, however, it functions as a purely musical organizing force. This seems consistent with the evidence of Pfitzner's sketches here and in other works. The presence of pages of isolated motives, often with directions for their use or order, suggests that motives were often derived, and then treated as material for semi-independent sections. Pages of barely recognizable fragments,[15] are only reconcilable with Pfitzner's aesthetic if the motives are viewed

---

[12] Ibid. 177.
[13] Ibid. 169–70.
[14] Schwarz, 'Die Bedeutung', 115.
[15] E.g. *D-WÜim*, Mch. f. 730, fol. 25ʳ.

as precompositional material, *Tongestalten*, before the operation of the mystical inspiration. The resultant forms,
however, do not always provide such straightforward categor-
ization as prayer, arioso, or *stretta* suggest.

The conjuration scene is a touchstone for analysis. Traditionally such scenes are based less on clear forms than on
looser patterning or on a unifying idea. Thus the Wolf's Glen
scene owes much of its coherence to a key scheme based on
the tonalities of Samiel's diminished seventh (F♯–A–C–E♭).
Busoni's conjuration scene in *Doktor Faust* notoriously contains a set of variations ostensibly without theme.[16] The
former model more accurately reflects Pfitzner's praxis (as
might be expected). The point of contact with *Doktor Faust*
remains, however, if only because forms in *Das Herz* are often
potential rather than realized. The idea on which the conjuration scene is based is the same kind of tonal cipher as
Samiel's diminished seventh, the tritone A♭–D, which is
contained in the name *Asmodi*. This is not so much a matter
of tonalities, however, as of chords and figurations. Scene 8,
the conjuration itself, begins with a progression that uses
juxtaposed dominants of the tritonal opposites as the framework for eighteen bars (Ex. 8.1*a*), before the music settles in

Ex. 8.1*a*

[16] John Warrack, *Carl Maria von Weber*, 2nd edn. (Cambridge, 1976), 220–1;
Anthony Beaumont, *Busoni the Composer* (London, 1985), 332.

Ab minor for the principal Asmodeus motive, the starting-point for later chains of thirds. This is almost immediately contrasted with its free inversion that contains the dominant seventh of a D minor that is not stated (Ex. 8.1*b*). Later D minor emerges in a somewhat veiled manner as the tempo increases. But other keys come to assume prominent roles, notably F♯ and G minors in a pair of linked musical strophes at *106* and *109* respectively. The music here has its own distinct character that depicts the uncanny atmosphere without specific reference to stage events. Only when Athanasius makes the demon's sign is Ab minor briefly restored. The tritonal pairing is thus more an associative force than a structural basis for the first part of the scene. The invocations themselves take it up on a more systematic basis, with a strophe at *112* in Ab minor, which also generates a figuration out of the two triads, Ab minor and D major; almost inevitably Cb major arises as a kind of mediator between the two (Ex. 8.1*c*). The culmination of this strophe is Athanasius' first melisma on 'Oh, Asmodi!'. A new pair of strophes, each con-

cluding with the same melisma a semitone higher, inextric-
ably intermingle elements of D and A♭ in which patterns of
thirds are used as reference points of a motivic kind. The
whole invocation ends on an A♭ minor triad, which thus
opens and closes the section. D minor assumes the function of
a kind of dominant in a three-part structure. Over the whole
passage, the figuration, stemming from the first combination
of A♭ and D minor, grows ever more fantastical, with short
ostinato figures creating local turbulence against the de-
clamations of Athanasius and the brass section.

The demon is finally ushered in by a chromatic paroxysm,
whose starting-point is the two triads. The violent contrary-
motion scale segments culminate in a perfect cadence that
extracts D from a five-note dissonance marking the exact
moment in Pfitzner's directions when the demon's face becomes clearly visible (Ex. 8.2). From here on the means of

Ex. 8.2

organization gradually begins to change. This conjuration
was composed out of two basic ideas, the tritone and chains of
thirds. One sketch page shows Pfitzner simply laying out such
a chain that could be for either Asmodeus' first entry or his
later brief solo beginning 'Du opferst mir sodann ein neues

Menschenherz'. The time signature of the sketch is alla breve, and thus wrong for both sections; the idea of the thirds themselves was all important and may again be described as precompositional.[17] Only at the demon's first entry do the two ideas form the entire basis of the achieved texture, now with A♭ minor as a 'dominant' to D (Ex. 8.3). From here the

Ex. 8.3

[17] *D-WÜim*, Mch. f. 730, fol. 17ʳ.

music begins to assimilate itself more to the style that can be described as Pfitzner's norm, a basic diatonicism in which tonic and relative minor or major coexist. The chromatic tensions that flow from the tritonal pairing recede into the background, emerging in some form usually when Asmodeus sings. With the ninth scene, the chorus of the dreaming hearts, the retreat is almost but not completely achieved. When Athanasius has finally chosen the heart (to Helge's off-stage cry of 'Weh!' on a high B♮), the music briefly returns to the dominant of A♭, just as the later scene with Asmodeus in Act II ends on the dominant of D. In both cases, these are 'potential' dominants without resolution. In both scenes, dramatic considerations are foremost, with form being sub-servient to what Dahlhaus would doubtless have called a form-motive. It is easier to define style than structures, and to this extent Pfitzner distances himself from those composers like Berg in *Wozzeck* who had a more formalized approach to drama.

The chromaticism of the conjuration is its most remarkable feature, since the frenetic rhythms and ostinati could be regarded as an extension of the type of syncopated music of emotional spasm to be found in nineteenth-century opera, par-ticularly as punctuation to arioso. Such chromaticism, with its suggestions of a purely chromatic organization lurking behind tonal norms, is obviously related to the style of the more sombre movements of *Das dunkle Reich* or the String Quartet in C sharp minor. In his book on Busoni, Beaumont sees the achievement of works like the *Sonatina seconda* and the *Nocturne symphonique* as the establishment of 'a basic vocabulary of musical terror, expressly intended for his own *Faust*'.[18] This adequately defines the extent to which in Busoni's career even 'abstract' works were channelled towards one dramatic peak. This cannot be claimed of Pfitzner, since the chromatic language of his supernatural scenes in *Das Herz* is essentially an interruption to a more diatonic norm. The opera is not the climax to a process which had gathered momentum in the twenties, but attempts to place and objectify this process within a language that had never made a specific virtue out of the new and the radical. At the height of the confrontation between Athanasius and Asmodeus, the demon

[18] Beaumont, *Busoni the Composer*, 325.

demands 'Das Herz eines Menschen' to a sarabande-like idea
that eventually comes to stand for Helge's love (Ex. 8.4*a*).
The Prelude to Act II develops out of this music, a prelude
which Pfitzner later extracted for separate performance as
the 'Liebesmelodie'. It is the symbol of Helge's innocent love,
recurs as a duet for her and Athanasius in Act III, and re-
claims the key of D at least from Asmodeus in the opera's
closing pages. The characteristic features of this 'melody'
are a stately, almost baroque rhythm, diatonic dissonance
founded on secondary sevenths, and an elliptical voice-
leading that frequently telescopes tension and resolution (Ex.
8.4*b*). This is the basis for Pfitzner's later style, and to see
it as liberated from the chromatic turbulence of the 1920s in
Das Herz is one valid interpretation that leaves to one side
the extent to which Pfitzner may be said to have fallen from
the ranks of musical 'progress'. But it is also the language
most characteristic of vast stretches of the opera, and is
singularly unsensual as a 'Liebesmelodie'. A chromatic idiom
of emotional reaction is rather sparingly employed throughout the opera, as in the extremely affecting melodic arches

Ex. 8.4*a*

and sequences of Tankred's death (Ex. 8.5). Pfitzner is never more surprising than in the manner in which his most direct portrayal of an amorous passion is realized through simple and chaste musical means. It recalls the nature of the Ricarda Huch song-cycle. Sexual passion is essentially remembered rather than experienced in Pfitzner. No more than Busoni did he subscribe to a music of emotional response, and the history of *Doktor Faust* in performance, a tale of respect rather than acclaim, suggests that *Das Herz*, if revived, might legitimately expect that much but no more. None the less, its music is amongst Pfitzner's most thought-provoking, and suggests that

Ex. 8.5

the work's immediate future may be more in the field of broadcast or recorded music than on the stage.

The history of *Das Herz* after its completion proved disastrous. The librettist and the Intendant of Berlin's Staatsoper, the formidable Heinz Tietjen, made a number of changes to Pfitzner's stage directions that produced an acrimonious exchange of letters and an unpublished polemic from the composer. This was circulated amongst interested parties (including Hans Frank, the Nazis' necessary but despised lawyer; *SS IV* 801). The changes which Mahner-Mons and Tietjen had initiated seem remarkably trivial in relation to the overall effect. Why did Pfitzner think it worth losing the favour of so influential a figure as the Berlin director? Partly it was a reflection of the importance he had come to lay on the composer's stage directions in *Werk und Wiedergabe*. Having had to suffer as a composer from the sloppiness of conductors, soloists, and directors, Pfitzner laid down first principles in his treatise and came close to professional suicide in their defence in the case of *Das Herz*. But the polemic was also a washing of hands. *Das Herz* most generously received a double première in Munich and Berlin under Knappertsbusch and Furtwängler respectively on the same day, 12 November 1931. Pfitzner liked neither performance, and his relationship with both conductors was never easy thereafter. The trifling of Mahner-Mons may have become an opportunity for the composer to absolve himself from responsibility for productions which had failed to find critical approval.

The last remark needs some qualification, inasmuch as the comments of Alfred Einstein and H. H. Stuckenschmidt reproduced by Vogel show that respectful listeners did discern something deeply worthwhile in the opera.[19] But Pfitzner required something more, and there were critics on certain liberal newspapers who failed to respond with sufficient enthusiasm. In Germany, as in Karl Kraus's Vienna, a liberal newspaper often meant Jewish backing, and Pfitzner chose to see himself as the victim of Jewish persecution. At the beginning of the decade, he had come into contact with the Verein zur Abwehr des Antisemitismus, and had formulated some thoughts on anti-Semitism in response to the receipt of their literature:

Anti-Semitism pure and simple and as a feeling of hatred is absolutely to be rejected.

Quite another question is what danger the Jewish spirit [*Judentum*] harbours for German spiritual life and culture. But each race harbours such danger for a culture in a certain manner. (*SS IV* 320)

He went on to make his familiar distinction not between *völkisch* and Jewish, but between 'Jews of such and such a disposition and Germans of such and such a disposition', acknowledging not only the part played by 'educated' Jews in

[19] Johann Peter Vogel, *Hans Pfitzner mit Selbstzeugnissen und Bilddokumenten* (Reinbek bei Hamburg, 1989), 103–4.

Germany's intellectual life, but the nihilism lurking within the *völkisch* mentality. The reception of *Das Herz* now caused him to break off contact with the Verein in 1932 (much to its leaders' distress) at the very moment when the *völkische* elements were nearing their political goal. The repercussions of the 'Herz' fiasco may have played a quite disproportionate part in the chain of events that saw Pfitzner place a symbolic seal of approval on the 'new Germany'.

With that, the question of Pfitzner's cultural-political nemesis can no longer be postponed. The Nazi *Machtergreifung* coincided with a fallow period in which he wrote nothing apart from the arrangement of the Symphony in C sharp minor. Whether the two circumstances were connected is difficult to say. In Pfitzner's career, creativity was often dependent upon a close involvement with other musical activity, from which the outside world was excluded. The beginning of the Nazi period hindered his activities as a conductor, nor would the new masters permit him to be a mere musician. Public gestures of support were required, particularly from a figure whose national credentials seemed proven. Pfitzner made the necessary gestures, and the damage to his living and posthumous reputation was done. How it can be undone, and whether it should be undone, presents problems which cannot be given detailed consideration here. But the student of Pfitzner's music who passed over them in silence would be guilty of cowardice, even if he subscribed to the most rigorous of autonomy aesthetics.

No one has ever suggested that Pfitzner was formally a Nazi. That he never belonged to the party is proven beyond any reasonable doubt. Yet a non-member such as Adolf Bartels, as Wulf noted, was a collaborator to such an extent that the distinction becomes meaningless.[20] In Pfitzner's case the questions that demand an answer are whether he collaborated at an administrative or political level with the Nazis, and whether he shared their cultural outlook and aims. Reference works in many cases maintain a silence that seems to imply that Pfitzner's music is above discussion. On the other hand, it is not hard to find spokesmen for an opposite point of view. As a touchstone may be taken the entry in *Baker's Biographical Dictionary*, in which Pfitzner, 'Being of certified German stock . . . was favored by the Nazi authorities,

---

[20] Joseph Wulf, *Musik im Dritten Reich* (Frankfurt am Main, 1983), 334.

and became an ardent supporter of the Third Reich'.[21]
Phrases like 'moral degradation' hardly suggest the dis-
passionate tone of the dictionary article, but given that it
is applied to Pfitzner's contacts with Hans Frank, it should
not unthinkingly be ruled out of court. At least *Krakauer
Begrüssung* is named in its less than splendid isolation. Among
Pfitzner's compositions after 1933, it alone was written for a
Nazi official (though *Fons salutifer* should at least be noted
as a work written to lines by a poet, Kolbenheyer, who was
quite pronouncedly sympathetic to Nazi ideals; the occasion,
however, seems to have been nothing more dubious than the
dedication of Karlsbad's medicinal springs by means of the
verses of a poet linked through his family to the Sudetenland).
This is an advance on the scattergun charge of David Ewen
that Pfitzner 'wrote compositions honoring Nazis and Nazism'
while 'identifying himself completely with the ideals—artistic
as well as political—of the Third Reich'.[22] To such 'ardent'
support and 'complete' identification should be added the
'enthusiastic endorsement' of Leon Botstein.[23] Pfitzner's
posthumous fame has perished on the points of adjectives.

    In more serious historical works, however, it is still possible
to find a current that judges Pfitzner harshly and implicitly
questions the justice of the Denazification tribunal that
acquitted him. The fact that Denazification was necessary
seems, like the Scottish verdict of 'Not proven', to append
a slur to the character of the acquitted. Thus a respected
historian like Robert Wistrich writes of Pfitzner 'essentially'
subscribing 'to the Nazi creed in his old age'.[24] The tone of
his account, which accepts Pfitzner's complicity in the Third
Reich as a matter of fact, contrasts sharply with his regret
over aspects of Strauss's conduct.[25] Wistrich's article is not as
hopeless a jumble as Ewen's, but Ewen at least implies a shift
in Pfitzner's opinions with the passage of time even if he is
quite at sea with sequence. If *Krakauer Begrüssung* (1944) is to
be taken as a yardstick of Pfitzner's support of the Third
Reich, then can one really say, 'By the time World War II

---

[21] *Baker's Biographical Dictionary of Musicians*, 7th edn., rev. Nicolas Slonimsky
(Oxford, 1984), 1765.
[22] David Ewen, *Composers since 1900: A Biographical and Critical Guide* (New York,
1969), 411.
[23] Leon Botstein, 'Wagner and our Century', *19th Century Music*, 11 (1987/8), 97.
[24] Robert Wistrich, *Who's Who in Nazi Germany* (London, 1982), 233.
[25] Ibid. 304–6.

broke out, Pfitzner and the Nazis had come to a parting of the ways'?[26] The dictionary articles reflect the essentially simplified way in which historical reputations are moulded. Botstein's review shows the problems which lie in the path of 'revision', a word which is particularly difficult in writings pertaining to the Nazi period. 'Revisionist' is a catch-all label that may throw the writer into the company of Ernst Nolte or of David Irving. Botstein's particular target is Bernhard Adamy, an 'apologist for Pfitzner' aiming at the 'sanitizing' of his anti-Semitism. There is a point here, in that Adamy's conclusions are sometimes too charitable, as Reinhard Ermen has pointed out, and have subsequently been qualified by the work of Prieberg and Weiss.[27] But he has presented a substantial body of information showing that Pfitzner's position is hardly to be described as simply that of a Nazi supporter. 'Apologist' has become a term that simply rules out the possibility of discussion.

A major handicap in approaching this whole area is the trustworthiness of the Pfitzner biographers. The books by Valentin and Müller-Blattau would be problematic enough, were the other opinions of their authors not also known.[28] Certain essential information for arriving at a just estimate of Pfitzner is provided by Schrott, who is a prime example of a writer favourably placed in the Third Reich turning critic afterwards. Most problematic is Abendroth. It can be more or less assumed that the denigration of Richard Strauss represents Abendroth's own aesthetic valuation, even if it also reflected a wish to see the nationalist Pfitzner elevated above the successor to the cosmopolitans of the New German School. But he introduced at a late stage many passages to portray Pfitzner in a light sympathetic to the Nazis, while acknowledging the part played in Pfitzner's career by individual Jews. Abendroth's own subsequent career illustrates the perilous nature of the path that he chose. As a deeply conservative critic after the war, he may seem a blinkered reactionary. But

---

[26] Ewen, *Composers since 1900*, 411.

[27] Botstein, 'Wagner and our Century', 97; Reinhard Ermen, *Musik als Einfall: Hans Pfitzners Position im ästhetischen Diskurs nach Wagner* (Aachen, 1986), 14–15; Fred K. Prieberg, *Musik im NS-Staat* (Frankfurt am Main, 1982), 217–20; Busch-Salmen and Weiss, *Hans Pfitzner*, 41–58.

[28] The reference is to Müller-Blattau's first book on Pfitzner (*Hans Pfitzner*, Potsdam, 1940); his role in the cultural politics of the Third Reich is discussed in *Entartete Musik: Zur Düsseldorfer Austellung von 1938: Eine kommentierte Rekonstruktion*, ed. Albrecht Dümling and Peter Girth (Düsseldorf, 1988), 49–55.

the distinct conservative position he espoused as editor of a cultural journal during the war was such as to leave little doubt that the revisions of his Pfitzner biography were the product of a temporary opportunism rather than a deeply felt commitment to a Nazi outlook. Here in all its clarity is the dilemma which faces the researcher. Pfitzner's supporters painted the composer as acceptable to the Nazis in the hope that worldly fame would come to the 'master'. How far Pfitzner approved of this cannot be reliably estimated; what can be said is that he did indeed crave recognition, particularly when he saw a nationalist party come to power. But the need for recognition was a leitmotif of his whole life.

Pfitzner's actions on the Nazis' arrival in power were typically ambiguous. He refused to travel to Salzburg to conduct at the festival, in accordance with Nazi policy towards Austria. He subscribed to a Nazi-backed protest against an essay by Thomas Mann, though it perhaps needs to be emphasized that disagreement with Mann's opinions on Wagner does not turn one into a Nazi; the ominous aspect of the protest against Mann was the manner in which the co-ordinated opinion of the majority was turned against a culturally dissident voice. In such moments Pfitzner appears as solid with official policy. If Pfitzner had not wished to give that impression, then he had the example in the first case of Richard Strauss, who went to Salzburg regardless (while accepting the presidency of the Nazis' Reichsmusikkammer). Later Schrott presented that noisy withdrawal (which was certainly noticed in Austria, and accepted by Pfitzner's fatuously Nazi friend Victor Junk) as virtually enforced by Hans Frank, who in Pfitzner's account to Schrott practically wrote the letter of withdrawal for the composer.[29] Whether this is believable is hard to say without at least a shred of documentary proof, whatever form that might take. Schrott in any case acknowledges that Pfitzner was caught by the mood of 1933 (even if he voted in elections for Hugenberg and Hindenburg).[30] Yet while supporting the general solidarity of the hour, he was writing letters to Hindenburg and to the Nazis on behalf of Cossmann, Felix Wolfes, and Arthur Eloesser. It is an indication of the passions which this issue

---

[29] Ludwig Schrott, *Die Persönlichkeit Hans Pfitzners* (Zurich and Freiburg, 1959), 47–8; Elisabeth Wamlek-Junk, *Hans Pfitzner und Wien* (Tutzing, 1986), 103.
[30] Schrott, *Die Persönlichkeit Hans Pfitzners*, 46–7.

arouses that even his intercessions are capable of being made into a reproach against his conduct.[31] Admittedly the sentiment, 'Every German had his one decent Jew', stands out in a notorious wartime speech by Himmler.[32] But in 1933, Pfitzner's intercession was a not inconsiderable act of courage. He himself could not discern how much worse the regime would become. A letter to Eloesser refers to Pfitzner's inability to 'go along with the way in which the new Germany operates for the time being'.[33] Since Pfitzner was too well known to Eloesser to try to deceive him, his supposition should be taken at face value, that the 'new Germany' would ultimately change its ways, that Dachau would be a temporary stringency. Pfitzner's attitude was outward support, together with an assumption that his name and reputation would count for much in the remedying of injustice. The overlapping annals of resistance and collaboration are full of such morally and intellectually ambiguous standpoints.

In Schrott's account, Pfitzner's experience over the Salzburg cancellation, which cost him financially both in the short term and through his exclusion from Austria for the next five years, led to disillusionment:

After this glimpse behind the scenes of a 'national demonstration', the master later was barely to be moved further by similarly powerful state pressure to make an occasional statement of a general German attitude. I was a witness of the distress under which such a couple of lines were drafted; they proved to be reserved to such an extent that they announced the opposite of sympathy with the Third Reich.[34]

Yet Pfitzner knew such statements for what they were worth and described them in a letter to Lilo Martin as 'Propagandareden für H.'.[35] In 1933 he self-evidently collaborated with the regime. If that is recognized, however, then there can be equally little doubt that disillusionment came rapidly. The same letter to Lilo Martin goes on to record Pfitzner's bitterness over his exclusion from an official function in Nuremberg, where he was to conduct before Hitler on 8 September 1934.

---

[31] Botstein, 'Wagner and our Century', 97.
[32] Speech cited widely, e.g. in Lucy Dawidowicz, *The War against the Jews 1933–45* (London, 1975), 191–2.
[33] Schrott, *Die Persönlichkeit Hans Pfitzners*, 47.
[34] Ibid. 49.
[35] *Katalog 622, J. A. Stargardt Antiquariat* (Marburg, 1981), 230.

There was also the fiasco over the cancellation of 'Zorn' and 'Klage' at the Leipzig lawyers' meeting. Frank as justice minister obviously wished to reward Pfitzner for his support in the Salzburg episode with the invitation, and Pfitzner had no doubt that he was due some sort of financial compensation. Ultimately, as Weiss has shown in his study of the affair of Pfitzner's pension, Hitler himself came to agree with him, but made him wait for it until 1937, quite clearly as an object-lesson.[36] Ostensibly the subject and title of 'Klage' was thought comical for an audience of jurists. But there can be little doubt that the sentiments of both songs were simply not appropriate to any regime dedicated to yea-saying. The cancellation of performances clearly outweighed in Pfitzner's mind the place on the Reichsmusikkammer below Strauss.

The crisis of the Leipzig affair, which drew in not merely Frank (the recipient of another of Pfitzner's polemical outbursts) but also the mayor Goerdeler, fell in the autumn of 1933. The honeymoon period between Pfitzner and the regime did not last long. It was followed by the *cause célèbre* of Pfitzner's pensioning-off by the Munich Conservatory. This has attracted so much attention because it culminated in Pfitzner's widely known clash with Goering. It must be emphasized that financial matters underlay the whole episode, as Pfitzner faced the prospect of loss of salary, lack of reward, and exclusion from his Austrian market. In fact Schrott acknowledged the substantial nature of Pfitzner's income even after the pensioning-off.[37] Ideological matters were only touched on in passing. The clash with Goering (in which Pfitzner was threatened with incarceration) is essentially indicative of the personalities involved. Goering alternated between music critic and bully, Pfitzner blustered, but was torn between real fears and the need to save face with witticisms at the expense of the 'Duke of Oranienburg'. Somewhere in this imbroglio may be the mysterious warning from Heydrich retailed by Schrott.[38] Why the Nazis' most dangerous policeman thought his father's old friend worthy of attention can only really be clarified by going back to the roots of Pfitzner's acquaintance with the Nazis and their leader in the early 1920s.

---

[36] Busch-Salmen and Weiss, *Hans Pfitzner*, 52–4.
[37] Schrott, *Die Persönlichkeit Hans Pfitzners*, 55.
[38] Ibid. 54.

At the heart of this mysterious business lurks a curiously resonant, almost arcane nexus, the interpenetration of German nationalism and Jewish assimilation that bred the tales of the partly Jewish origins of Wagner, Hitler, Heydrich, and others. Pfitzner met Hitler through a personal acquaintance between Cossmann and the founder of the NSDAP, Anton Drexler.[39] There is now no doubt that the two men met at Pfitzner's sick-bed in a Schwabing hospital in February 1923. Hitler recounted his wartime experiences and they discussed Otto Weininger. After the war Pfitzner poured scorn on Hitler's inability to grasp the abstract nature of Weininger's anti-Semitism, and that can well be believed, since Hitler probably knew of Weininger at second hand through the comments of Dietrich Eckhart.[40] The meeting could have been foreseen as a mismatch; even in bed Pfitzner was no captive audience. But later Pfitzner wrote a dedication to 'Adolf Hitler, the great German' in a copy of *Huttens letzte Tage*.[41] That he meant to send it to the imprisoned Hitler is clearly indicated by the accompanying message of sympathy in which Pfitzner specifically reminded him of their conversation in Schwabing. This is the key piece of evidence that presumably lies behind Botstein's belief that Pfitzner endorsed the Nazis in the 1920s.[42] But the matter is by no means as clear-cut as it appears, and rests on a limited reading of the historical circumstances. Pfitzner's dedication is dated 1 April 1924. In the months since the meeting in February 1923, Hitler's career had indulged in remarkable somersaults, of which the most spectacular was his phoenix-like resurgence in the Bavarian courts, assuming the mantle of patriot and 'revolutionary against the Revolution'; in Bullock's words, 'the man who, on 9 November 1923, appeared to be broken and finished as a political leader . . . succeeded by April 1924, in making himself one of the most-talked-of figures in Germany, and turned his

---

[39] Pfitzner's 'Glosse zum II. Weltkrieg', his most comprehensive statement of his attitude to the Hitler regime, was not published in its entirety until *SS IV* 327–43; it is a characteristically abrasive document that exhibits in roughly equal measure Pfitzner's élitist contempt for the Nazis, the extent to which he initially accepted the myth of Hitler the simple soldier, and his growing recognition of the criminality of the regime; it is also quite uncompromising in refusing to accept the notion of the German people's collective responsibility.

[40] J. P. Stern, *Hitler: The Führer and the People* (Glasgow, 1975), 51–2.

[41] Bernhard Adamy, *Hans Pfitzner* (Tutzing, 1980), 300–1.

[42] Botstein, 'Wagner and our Century', 97.

trial for treason into a political triumph'.[43] By exploiting the weakness and confusion of his enemies, Hitler seduced the public opinion that he had failed to carry when a free man, only to lose it again in the obscurity of prison. Pfitzner, the passionate opponent of Versailles, succumbed whole-heartedly to public opinion, and then as Hitler receded into the background neglected to send his gift and the accompanying message. His relationship was towards Hitler the symbol of the hoped-for German recovery, and was as subject to uncertainties and fluctuations as his later relationship to the regime. By the early 1930s, Hitler was a politician for whom one had the choice of voting or not voting; Pfitzner didn't vote for him, but accepted that others close to him could and did.[44]

It later became something of an article of faith among Pfitznerians that Hitler nourished an aversion towards Pfitzner and personally opposed official celebrations of his seventieth birthday in Munich. Schrott's researches led him to the discovery that Hitler 'not only could not forgive the master for his Jewish friendships and particularly his intercession for Cossmann but actually thought him a Jew'.[45] This impression stemmed from 'the unfavourable impression which Pfitzner made on him' in Schwabing. According to Schrott, Hitler remarked, 'He lay before me with his beard like an old rabbi';[46] a bizarre notion about the man whose blond looks had contrasted so sharply with Cossmann in their youth. Yet Pfitzner's letter to Lilo Martin also claims that he had been excluded from the Nuremberg festivities because Hitler thought him a 'half-Jew'.[47] Pfitzner continued to worry about it, as his reaction to Valentin's biography in 1939 shows. Recent research has suggested that Pfitzner had doubts about Valentin's picture.[48] But unpublished letters in the Österreichische Nationalbibliothek are slightly surprising in the light that they throw upon these doubts. Though he may have viewed the contents with something approaching con-

---

[43] Alan Bullock, *Hitler: A Study in Tyranny*, rev. edn. (London, 1962), 114–15; 'On Hitler's thirty-fifth birthday, with the trial not far behind him, the flowers and packages for the famous prisoner filled several rooms' (Joachim C. Fest, *Hitler*, trans. Richard and Clara Windsor (London, 1974), 299).

[44] Adamy, *Hans Pfitzner*, 301.

[45] Schrott, *Die Persönlichkeit Hans Pfitzners*, 61–2.

[46] Ibid. 62.

[47] See n. 35.

[48] Adamy, *Hans Pfitzner*, 313.

tempt, Pfitzner most urgently desired its appearance, and in particular its promised genealogy. His rudest dismissal of Valentin (and the publisher Bosse) came when he feared that the book might not contain the proof of his racial lineage.[49] Earlier his correspondent, Abendroth, had described proof of descent as 'more important today than all proof of sentiment and achievement'.[50] When the book finally appeared, Pfitzner forgave Valentin, in spite of the fact that it contained 'falsehoods' (such as the depiction of Clemens Krauss as an advocate of Pfitzner's music) and inadequacies in the evaluation of his compositions.[51] What mattered was that the story of his Jewish origins was laid to rest. In July 1938, Abendroth had been visited by an emissary from the Reichsstelle für Sippenforschung enquiring about Pfitzner's forebears. Abendroth was left in no doubt that the matter was serious and so confidential that he didn't know whether Pfitzner ought to know of it; that the instigation of the enquiry came from a high quarter was also let slip by the official.[52] The story of Hitler's belief takes on flesh and blood in this exchange, and suggests that the irony of Pfitzner's position in the Third Reich rested on misunderstandings. Pfitzner believed that it was enough to be nationalist in cultural feeling when the Nazi movement embraced a biological ideal against which he was suspected of sinning.

All the indications are that the years immediately before the war represented a potentially dangerous crisis in Pfitzner's dealings with the Nazis. When war finally broke out, Abendroth wrote again, commenting on the 'very notable difference between 1914 and today', and acknowledging that Pfitzner doubtless felt the same.[53] Composer and biographer participated in the sullen national mood of late 1939.[54] What is striking about Pfitzner's reaction to the Nazis is the extent to which he simply shared in the general reaction. He was never an initiator, he shared in no grand collective decisions, but reflected in a measure each shift in general attitude. His rejection of collective responsibility for the German people

---

[49] Letter of 13 Oct. 1939 (copy), *A-Wn*, Pfitzner Nachlass, 288/113.
[50] Letter of 26 Sept. 1939, *A-Wn*, Pfitzner Nachlass, 288/112.
[51] Letter of 22 Oct. 1939 (copy), *A-Wn*, Pfitzner Nachlass, 288/117.
[52] Letter of 19 July 1938, *A-Wn*, Pfitzner Nachlass, 288/74.
[53] Letter of 18 Sept. 1939, *A-Wn*, Pfitzner Nachlass, 288/110.
[54] See Marlis G. Steinert, *Hitler's War and the Germans*, ed. and trans. Thomas E. J. de Witt (Athens, Oh., 1977), 50–1.

after the war is of a piece with the extent to which he passively mirrored its outlook. The wartime report that vouched for his positive attitude to National Socialism, while noting his anti-social character, documents realistically Pfitzner's reluctance to be involved.[55] Perhaps too much faith has been placed in Mann's belief that the First World War had politicized the non-political artist.[56] Pfitzner lacked the inclination to participate in collective activity. What he did not lose was his critical independence. The much-quoted statement which stands at the beginning of his polemic against Wilhelm Rode is no proof of his Nazi allegiance, but a calculated insult of a party favourite, an attempt to hoist a personal friend of Hitler with his own petard.[57] Rode, the intendant of Berlin's Staatsoper, stood accused by Pfitzner of putting on too much Italian opera at the expense of truly national works (such as Pfitzner's own operas, which indeed experienced a slight falling-off in frequency of performance after 1933). The opening and closing quotation of the polemic proclaimed, 'I am a National Socialist and accustomed as such to hit straight back against any attack', and attributed the words with chapter and verse to Hitler (*SS IV* 313–17). Pfitzner clearly meant to frighten Rode and refused to permit the polemic to be published with any palliation; he relied on a journal having the 'Heldenmut' to publish it as it stood.[58] But he also displayed a ridiculous naïvety in sending a copy to Goebbels (rather as he expected Hess to support him against Julius Bahle). There was even talk of attending a reception at the Propaganda Minister's house.[59] From this dream-world Abendroth rescued him: 'A motto by Hitler may stand over an essay only with particular authorization from the Propaganda ministry. In this case the ministry would probably immediately forbid the publication of the essay, which is directed against a state official (and friend of the Führer).'[60] He went on to note that if Pfitzner went to Goebbels' reception, in all probability he would meet Rode there; truly

---

[55] Wulf, *Musik im Dritten Reich*, 340–1.

[56] Thomas Mann, *Reflections of a Nonpolitical Man*, trans. Walter D. Morris (New York, 1983), 312–13.

[57] 'Deutsche Opernkunst in Berlin ausge-Rode-t' remained largely unknown in typescript until Prieberg drew attention to its conclusion (*Musik im NS-Staat*, 224); it has since been published in full (*SS IV* 313–17).

[58] Letter of 16 Nov. 1938 (copy), *A-Wn*, Pfitzner Nachlass, 288/89.

[59] Letter of 18 Nov. 1938 (copy), *A-Wn*, Pfitzner Nachlass, 288/90.

[60] Letter of 19 Nov. 1938, *A-Wn*, Pfitzner Nachlass, 288/91.

the enemy was inside the gates of power. Furthermore, re-ported Abendroth, the Axis and the 'European balance of power' dictated the performance of Italian opera. Whatever Abendroth may have been, he was no fool and could see the irony of the situation. Pfitzner emerged with little credit from the episode but made an important discovery. Outspokenness was no longer possible with the channels to the public securely in Nazi hands.

Pfitzner's contacts with the Nazis after 1933 were marked by mutual suspicion that reflected neither enthusiasm nor outright opposition. The roots of this may also be traced to ideology. If the signs of a 'fascist' outlook are admiration of 'central authority, a planned economy and a one-party state, often joined with a noisy contempt for Western democracy and Eastern communism; of racialism, more often than not; and of military virtue and the heroics of war',[61] then Pfitzner's outlook must be said to overlap uncertainly with the Nazi mentality. He neither bowed to authority nor talked of economic planning; his patriotism respected military virtues but did not make a cult out of war (in this he is quite distinct from Ernst Jünger and the 'aristocratic emigration'). One very important strand in Pfitzner's music, the religious symbolism analysed by Schwarz, was of quite a different kind from the quasi-religious rites of Hitler-worship. There were as a result fears of a boycott of *Das Christ-Elflein* in wartime, at a time when, as Abendroth noted, Schiller's *Wilhelm Tell* was banned for the scene on the Rütli.[62] What was common to all such executive actions in Abendroth's analysis was the secrecy that marked the beginning of 'the action against the Jews'. Secrecy would bar Pfitzner from contesting a ban, since officially a ban would not exist. He had already warned Pfitzner that only unproblematic, 'elevating' works would be tolerated by the authorities (in the letter of 18 September 1939). Now he advised the composer to get a new libretto and title for *Das Christ-Elflein*, perhaps 'an *Antichrist-Elflein*', or 'a *Hitler-Jugend-Elflein*', and sarcastically recalled an essay on 'Die Reichs-Autobahnen—ein religiöses Erlebnis'. Abendroth's gallows-humour, like the anti-Nazi jokes by Pfitzner himself, was the last gesture of protest for men who had once believed the Nazis amenable to their influence. But from this low

[61] George Watson, 'The Literature of Fascism', *Politics and Literature in Modern Britain* (London, 1977), 71.
[62] Letter of 23 Nov. 1941, *A-Wn*, Pfitzner Nachlass, 288/178.

point, Pfitzner's situation improved in a limited extent. His genealogy having been tested, his attitude reviewed, the Nazis improved his financial position and provided him with the opportunity to travel and perform his music.

Of Pfitzner's anti-Semitism, little more can be said other than that it remained consistent. It was not biological racism, though like many contemporaries he could make a gibe quickly enough. In spite of this, to speak of his 'hatred of the Jews' or his 'hatred of Mahler' is the voice of ignorance.[63] His subscription to the 'abstract' racism of Otto Weininger is balanced by a refusal to subscribe to racial bigotry. At the time of the composition of *Von deutscher Seele*, he had to write to the chairman of a Treubund deutscher Musiker und Künstler in Munich which he had joined in the belief that its credentials were above suspicion. Now he threatened to withdraw unless he had an explanation as to how the society had misused his name for its own, possibly racist purposes.[64] Three months later he was still trying to ascertain whether membership of the society was based on racial criteria.[65] The full significance of this episode can be ascertained only with further documentation, but the implication is clear: Pfitzner would not have his name used by racists, though he was willing in his own writings to attack *Judentum* as an abstraction. In this he is quite consistent with his interpretation of Weininger. His outlook was essentially the same as Cossmann's, and words which have been applied to the latter help to define Pfitzner's intellectual relationship to the Nazis:

It is true Cossmann rejected the hysterical antisemitic scenario, according to which the Jews aspired to world domination via 'Jewish war' and 'Jewish revolution.' Cossmann's special kind of antisemitism operated on a 'higher' level, as he was fighting against the so-called 'antinational' ideas of his opponents not because they were Jews but because he deemed them 'traitors.' In the eyes of the Nazis it was one and the same thing, and they naturally rejected any cooperation with Cossmann.[66]

---

[63] Albrecht Dümling, *Gottfried Keller vertont von Johannes Brahms, Hans Pfitzner, Hugo Wolf* (Munich, 1981), 126; this trivial little book is not the serious comparative discussion suggested by its title.

[64] Letter to J. Stolzing-Czerny (copy), 4 Jan. 1921, *A-Wn*, Pfitzner Nachlass, 140/206.

[65] Letter to J. Stolzing-Czerny (copy), 22 Apr. 1921, *A-Wn*, Pfitzner Nachlass, 140/225.

[66] Werner J. Cahnman, *German Jewry: Its History and Sociology*, ed. Joseph B. Maier *et al.* (New Brunswick, NJ, 1989), 107–8.

When the Nazis came to power, Pfitzner took some pains to differentiate his outlook from theirs. Although he signed the protest against Thomas Mann (with published reservations), his critical thoughts on Wagner's anti-Semitism in the essay on the *Sternenfreundschaft* with Schumann clearly were foreign to a *völkisch* outlook. But in fact his 'unfortunate attitude to the Jewish question' had been noted in Munich and reported to Berlin; his contribution to the Verein zur Abwehr des Antisemitismus was particularly singled out. When Hitler ordered the restoration of his full pension in 1937, it was only after weighing Pfitzner's services in 1933 with a manner of communication which 'earlier was not as we might have wished'.[67]

The case of Otto Weininger, whose claim to be a scientist is taken seriously enough by scholars nowadays both in his own right and as a factor in the background of Freud, poses extreme problems for historians.[68] Robert Wistrich's recent account is scrupulous in detailing the extent to which Weininger created a 'feminine' abstraction in the age of Nietzsche and Strindberg to help classify philosophical and cultural distinctions in the field of human psychology and sexual orientation. As an analysis of homosexuality, Weininger's insights seem remarkably free from the hysteria that gripped England and Germany in the Wilde and Eulenburg scandals. Why the Jewish Weininger equated his 'feminine' type with a 'Jewish' ideal type is not entirely clear from his writings, and however much he might have stressed the abstractness of his categories, it is permissible to wonder with Wistrich if indeed this science had roots in Weininger's own psychopathology.[69] In Pfitzner's case, this psychopathological element is not evident in the same degree as with Weininger or even Cossmann. Pfitzner's anti-Semitism is not equatable with the Nuremberg Laws. The most that can be said about his 'ideology' is that he exhibited certain features in common with a whole host of right-wing figures in his society, including some like Spengler who rejected the monster that fed on their image. Eberle's

---

[67] Busch-Salmen and Weiss, *Hans Pfitzner*, 48–54.

[68] See in particular Allan Janik, *Essays on Wittgenstein and Weininger* (Amsterdam, 1985).

[69] Robert Wistrich, *The Jews of Vienna in the Age of Franz Joseph* (Oxford, 1989), 535–6. The full complexity of Weininger's relationship to his own race and tradition emerges more clearly, however, in Steven Beller, *Vienna and the Jews 1867–1938: A Cultural History* (Cambridge, 1989), 223–6.

description of him as 'pre-fascist', a slippery label, is as far as one may go in relating Pfitzner ideologically to the Nazis, and his article is open to all the usual ambivalence that marks arguments *post hoc, propter hoc*.[70] Of the 'pre-fascists' in Cossmann's political circle, some were exploited by the Nazis (with varying degrees of consent), some like Hugenberg were cast aside, and some, like Kahr, were killed.

In the 1930s Pfitzner's personal life lay in ruins, his elder son dead, friends and pupils exiled or imprisoned. Later a breach occurred with his other children which became unbridgeable. His daughter Agnes committed suicide and his estranged younger son was killed fighting in Russia. His house in Munich was destroyed by bombing; his attempt to find refuge in Vienna collapsed with the approach of the Russians. In the circumstances, the 'platonic idea of Germany' (*SS IV* 349) remained as the only durable crutch to which he could turn (though his second marriage provided him with a substitute family which ameliorated the miseries of his last years in the home for the aged near Munich). Amidst this tale of unreason and destruction invitations to visit Cracow from Frank provided the glimpse of official recognition which he had long craved, and he composed a short piece. Here, as ever, Pfitzner retained his capacity to take the researcher's breath away. *Krakauer Begrüssung* was withheld after the war by the publisher Oertel in an act that defies comprehension. What it is, and the circumstances of its composition, have not remained unknown. For the sake of historical accuracy it should have been laid open to inspection. As it is, the sketches for the work are accessible enough in the Österreichische Nationalbibliothek.[71] They show a section based on the emptiest of fanfares, and then astonishingly a polonaise. Is this a tribute to 'the German king of Poland', or to the Poles themselves, revelling in the protection of the Generalgouverneur? Nothing illustrates more clearly Pfitzner's blindness to reality,

---

[70] Gottfried Eberle, 'Hans Pfitzner: Präfaschistische Tendenzen in seinem ästhetischen und politischen Denken', *Musik und Musikpolitik im faschistischen Deutschland*, ed. Hanns-Werner Heister and Hans-Günter Klein (Frankfurt am Main, 1984), 136–43; a more recent essay has presented Pfitzner's ideas as a rejection of all collectivist claims (including both Nazism and collective responsibility). A considerable amount of evidence exists to support this, though the insistence with which Pfitzner presented his own viewpoint partially undermines the argument (Ulrich Mutz, 'Kulturkritik aus dem Geiste der Musik: Kunst und Politik bei Pfitzner', *Etappe*, 2, No. 1 (1989), 48–59.

[71] A-Wn, S.m. 30,462, *Krakauer Festmusik*, op. 54, Skizzen.

a blindness which derived from an increasingly uncontrolled egoism rather than from political commitment. The issue of what Pfitzner saw in Frank, who was fully capable of ordering mass executions as proof of political 'virility' and then preaching the virtues of ruling justly, returns to one of the most long-lasting themes in Pfitzner's career, the need for a patron exhibited in the approaches to Brahms, Bülow, and Bruch, the expectations of 1933, and inversely in the wrath visited upon failed authority figures: Scholz, Tietjen, Goering, and the rest. Frank revelled in the role of patron towards musicians, writers, and even chess players. The world champion Alekhine (who sold his political soul to the Nazis in a way that places Pfitzner's half-hearted gestures in a quite different light) attended tournaments in Cracow and partnered Frank in a consultation game against Frank's adjutant and Ukrainian interpreter (who happened to be Yefim Bogolyubov, one of Alekhine's defeated challengers from the past). In a remarkable display of chess's indifference to politics, this game involving a war criminal and an SS officer was published in the *British Chess Magazine* for 1942.[72] If Pfitzner viewed Frank simply as a Maecenas, he had plenty of fellow travellers. The true slur on Pfitzner's character was his refusal to see Frank for what he was after the war, when the full extent of his criminality was revealed. But Pfitzner's capacity for believing in war guilt had been exhausted in an earlier conflict. He had drawn private conclusions from the murder of the German opposition, but the example of Northcliffian propaganda in the Great War had eroded his willingness to contemplate the true bestiality which hung over the years of Denazification and punishment for war crimes. The Nazis had finally taught Pfitzner the meaning of fear; the four years which remained in 1945 allowed him to raise his voice in angry protest one last time.

From 1935, Pfitzner began again to compose, but with a difference. Songs and music-drama no longer seemed viable. Instead he cultivated instrumental music, including five works for orchestra and two cello concertos. Only during the war did he compose three choral works, of which one, the 'Soldatenlied' of the *Drei Männerchöre*, Opus 53, is explicitly Pfitzner's melancholy reflection on 'this war'; it is the work

[72] *British Chess Magazine*, 62 (1942), 159–60; I must thank Mr Dave Welch of the Liverpool Chess Club for this historical curiosity.

which ought perhaps to be put in the scale to balance *Krakauer Begrüssung*, a lament in August 1944 whether for himself, his generation, his son, or the conservative Germany which had staged its last protest the previous month.[73] Instrumental music was the ideal sphere for a composer who sought no ideological commitment to the regime. But there undoubtedly was another factor in the choice of symphonies, studies, and cello concertos, caught in a half-serious remark to Friedrich Wührer: 'Now I write little things, piano pieces, because no one, no one performs my operas in Germany.'[74] In the 1930s, the reason for the decline in performances of the operas was almost certainly not because of political opposition but because the 'Herz' affair had alienated the composer from some of the most important figures in German musical life. Even before 1933, relations with Fritz Busch had deteriorated to the point where Pfitzner contemplated rededicating the Piano Concerto. Of the conductors who remained in Nazi Germany, Knappertsbusch opposed him with the animus of a conductor who fundamentally disliked rehearsing for a composer who insisted on rehearsing to the point of fanaticism.[75] Clemens Krauss was in the process of committing himself to Strauss, while Furtwängler, as his diaries show, remained deeply divided about Pfitzner, wishing to 'protect the composer from the "thinker"'.[76] Pfitzner was increasingly an oddity in the age of the star conductor, when 'real fidelity to the work' was defined as 'a fight against literal belief... true to its sense'.[77] Given this fundamental discrepancy, Furtwängler's work for Pfitzner's music speaks the more eloquently, particularly since he discerned more clearly than many the real nature of Pfitzner's relationship to National Socialism, the tendency 'forcibly to impose an intellectual picture on to the external world'.[78] Pfitzner the 'thinker' exhibited an affinity of form, not content, with his political masters. But in the compositions of his last phase, the composer offered to Furtwängler (albeit with reservations) something appealing in an age when 'progress' was god, the

---

[73] Johann Peter Vogel, 'Pfitzner's drei Männerchöre op. 53', *Musica*, 41 (1987), 514.
[74] Friedrich Wührer, 'Die Persönlichkeit Hans Pfitzners', *Österreichische Musikzeitschrift*, 14 (1959), 381.
[75] Busch-Salmen and Weiss, *Hans Pfitzner*, 79–87.
[76] Wilhelm Furtwängler, *Notebooks 1924–1954* trans. Shaun Whiteside, ed. Michael Tanner (London, 1989), 132.
[77] Ibid. 75.
[78] Ibid. 168.

quality of 'naturalness', which Furtwängler qualified as the work of the 'highest kind of epigon'.[79]

Pfitzner himself disliked the idea of a 'so-called late style', though he recognized that works like the *Kleine Sinfonie* and the Duo had something in common.[80] The consistency of his outlook from the point of view of form is particularly undeniable, and there are few instances of late works attempting radically new solutions to problems of organization. With one exception, Pfitzner's late orchestral and chamber works are all multi-movement, but attempt to conceal this by various kinds of links between movements; on the whole such links remain within the types found in Schumann and Mendelssohn rather than Liszt. The simplest form of linkage occurs in works which have only the explicit instruction, 'attacca'. The Cello Concerto in A minor is a four-movement work whose only concession to linkage is an attacca between third and fourth movements. In certain cases, the attacca is implicit through the lack of tonal closure at the end of a movement (as in the case of the first movement of the Duo for Violin and Cello and either piano or orchestral accompaniment). At the end of the second movement of the String Quartet in C minor, only the lack of the traditional thick double bar-line suggests that the performers must push on. On the other hand, there is the Symphony in C, whose subtitle, 'Three movements in one movement', points to its unbroken character, while the *Kleine Sinfonie* recalls the Piano Concerto by linking pairs of movements. This is a particularly interesting case, since Pfitzner's original intentions, possibly to write a string quartet, then certainly to write a Moderato and Adagio for orchestra, are shrouded in some degree of obscurity.[81] In accordance with procedures already seen in the Quartet in C sharp minor, a small link connects the first movement with the scherzo: the oboe's triplets anticipate the compound time of the latter. But the motivic links are stronger between the first and third movements, the two parts of the intended Moderato and Adagio. It is preferable to see the scherzo as an intrusion

---

[79] Ibid. 125 ('He [Pfitzner] grasps the spiritual without giving it full expression in a naturally musical way') and 142.

[80] Letter to Walter Abendroth, 20 Sept. 1939 (copy), *A-Wn*, Pfitzner Nachlass, 288/111.

[81] See Peter Cahn, 'Zum Charakter von Pfitzners Spätstil am Beispiel der *Kleinen Sinfonie op. 44*', *SPB* 102–4 (and the comment of Wolfgang Osthoff in response, ibid. 113).

marked by the trumpet's first entry in the work, which is then reconciled by the carefully contrived thematic link between a clarinet figure near the end of the scherzo and the violin melody of the Adagio. Perhaps the most conspicuous example of a motivic link occurs between the second and third movements of the Duo for Violin and Violoncello. The motive of three ascending scale degrees is derived from earlier in the second movement and becomes a cadential prolongation. As an upbeat to a more extended scale figure, it then begins the finale in the cello, while the piano (or orchestra) absorbs the motive into the accompaniment (Ex. 8.6); the link between the fourth and fifth movements of the Sextet is a simpler variant of this technique. But there are cases where movements are designed to follow on as a deliberate intrusion, with the sudden fortissimo chord at the beginning of the finale of the Symphony in C the most obvious instance. In two works, the *Kleine Sinfonie* (third and fourth movements) and *Elegie und Reigen*, cadenzas (for horn and flute respectively) serve as links, providing a reminder of similar moments in *Von deutscher Seele*.

The Cello Concerto in G is the only work of this period that seems to pick up the structure of the Violin Concerto (to which it is chronologically closer than the other late works[82]). As an intimate, lyrical work of little more than a quarter of an hour's duration, it may be seen in a limited sense as a pendant to that most successful of Pfitzner's concertos. Once again, themes are stitched together by such devices as accompanied cadenzas with little concern for completed formal structures. The whole is framed by a lyrical meditation in G on a theme in triple time, as exposition, then as transformed recapitulation; the difference in character is adequately captured by the diffidence with which the theme is launched over a dominant pedal in the opening bars, and the much more secure expansion at *28*. Between these moments come three distinct sections which correspond perhaps to slow movement (*13*), scherzo (*19*), and finale (before *23*). The opening theme is inserted into the latter first in E flat major, after the shortest of cadenzas before *26*. But to use such labels is to recall characteristics of movements past rather than to define living forms. If everything before *13* is a first movement, then it is a

---

[82] The short score was probably finished in Detmold on 25 July 1935 (*D-Wüim*, Mch. f. 730, fol. 11ᵛ).

Ex. 8.6

movement from which contrast has been expunged in the
interests of lyrical unfolding. This type of homophonic triple-
time theme, with accompaniments embracing pedals and
broken-chord figuration, is an archetype for late Pfitzner, and

is found in the Cello Concerto in A minor, as well as the Sextet's first movement and the Duo's finale. It is not always as successful as in the G major Concerto, and the opening movement of the Concerto in A minor is very much a paler reflection, partly because it attempts to do too much with this style. But in the earlier work, it serves an expressive function with complete appropriateness. The other sections similarly hardly have time to do more than make obeisance to traditional forms before pushing on to new material. The 'finale theme' (which achieves its fully realized form at *32*) exists in a symbiosis with the main theme of the whole work. Other late works by Pfitzner (such as *Reigen*) similarly tend to amalgamate material in preference to close thematic working, rather as *Palestrina* ended with a muted transfiguration of leitmotifs. Such amalgamations, often dependent upon combinations of duple and triple time (as in the finales of both symphonies), are closely related to the tendency to abbreviate recapitulations (as in the last movement of the *Fantasie*). The closing gesture of a work is often to be explained as valediction or epilogue. But this is not new in Pfitzner's output; the Piano Quintet had already demonstrated that a whole finale could function as epilogue.

Thematic and formal archetypes sound with particular persistence in Pfitzner's late music. The 6/8 movements in the *Kleine Sinfonie* and the second Cello Concerto may be seen as a retrospective bestowal of substance on the 'Heiterer Satz' of the Piano Concerto. What was lacking there in melodic distinction achieves now a clear profile, particularly in the *Kleine Sinfonie*'s finale. But the thematic profile itself, as Henderson noted, depends on a clear act of self-limitation. The angular contours of the melodic writing as late as the demonic scenes in *Das Herz* yield to the 'restrained, conjunct and symmetrical'.[83] Particular emphasis should be laid on 'conjunct', since even linking motives, as the example from the Duo shows, grow from small linear motions. On a larger scale, Pfitzner manages to avoid the latent monotony in such construction, but a work such as the Cello Concerto in A minor intermittently points to the dangers. The prominence given to scale figures is easily illustrated in moments of climax. Thus the high-point of the first movement of the *Kleine Sinfonie* is

[83] Donald Gene Henderson, 'Hans Pfitzner', Ph.D. thesis (University of Michigan, 1963), 113.

Ex. 8.7

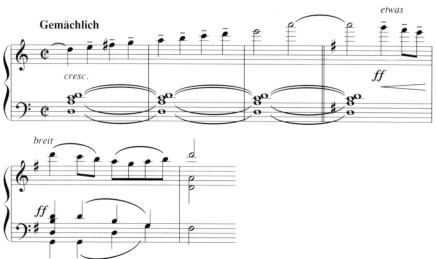

simply an arch formed out of an ascending scale defined by a ninth, a single leap of a fourth, and a descending scale, also defined by a ninth (Ex. 8.7); its effectiveness in part resides in its concealment of the point of recapitulation in a sonata form design. The fact that the accompaniment rests quite motionless for four bars on the dominant seventh of the tonic throws the melodic gesture with its fortissimo peak into the sharpest relief. For other Pfitzner scholars, the movement contains near-quotations from the *Missa Papae Marcelli* section of *Palestrina*.[84] Here the melodic construction is really an assertion of the arch-like ideal that underlies the historical Palestrina's style in general, and as such a statement of belief in traditional musical values.

It is accordingly appropriate that Pfitzner's late music should reveal some of the purest and most classical voice-leading in his output. The primacy of the conjunct rests on bass motions firmly anchored to diatonic scale degrees with relatively mild chromatic inflections. This is not to say that the harmonies are quite without asperities. In *Die neue Ästhetik*, Pfitzner pointed to a moment in Schumann's 'Auf einer Burg' where b, c^1, and d^1 sounded together, yet sounded pleasing and euphonious (*SS II* 227–8). Equally he might in later years have preferred to cite the fifteenth bar of the

---

[84] Cahn, 'Zum Charakter von Pfitzners Spätstil', 107–8; Vogel, *Hans Pfitzner*, 122.

Adagio from his own *Kleine Sinfonie*, where c^1, d^1, and $e\flat^1$ sound together for a moment without compromising the effect of the passage. The voice-leading here is in fact slightly more complex than in the Schumann example, but both depend upon parallel linear motion and a pedal note to explain the seemingly acerbic combination. What tentatively marks Pfitzner's parallel motion as the product of a contemporary of Mahler and Strauss rather than of Schumann is the decoration of a dominant with a chromatic cycle of enharmonic major thirds (Ex. 8.8). In Pfitzner's late music, the analyst

Ex. 8.8

must delve deep into the music to demonstrate its relevance to modernism. The question of the character of Pfitzner's late style as a result depends ultimately on factors of tone and aesthetics. Of purely stylistic consistency from the conjurations of *Das Herz* to the lyricism of the Duo there is evidence enough. Even the antithesis of dominant chords a tritone apart is rendered euphonious at the start of the Duo's brief slow movement. The progression is the reverse of that discerned in Busoni by Beaumont; the language adequate to evil and horror is revealed to be value-free, only a chord progression. It would be modish and probably untrue to say that Pfitzner in his late music deconstructs his earlier style, but perhaps there is some truth in the idea that he deconstructs its more drastic expressive claims. As corroboration, there is the peculiar dearth of expression marks in certain movements, which George Alexander Albrecht saw as a significant departure from the practice of many contemporaries.[85] To Albrecht, this was a problem in performance practice, but it might equally well have some bearing on structure and rhetoric. The G major Cello Concerto sounds like chamber music in the restrictions placed upon its full orchestra. In the even smaller world of the Duo and the *Kleine Sinfonie*, the absence of rhetoric extends to movements which scarcely seem to have expressive climaxes. This is particularly true of the slow movements, which reveal a certain growth in textural complexity, but little sense of self-assertion. This is why the loud return of the finale theme in the *Kleine Sinfonie* with cymbals and trumpet seems so incongruous; the rhetoric held at bay in the slow movement and for much of the finale is suddenly thrown into a lurid spotlight, and then relinquished. Admittedly, the Duo and the *Kleine Sinfonie* belong to a particularly intimate phase even in Pfitzner's late music. But their assertion of musical process above expressive claims is none the less symptomatic. It seems in particular to offer a quite unqualified negative to one speculation of Henderson.[86] The option of performing the Duo as chamber music with piano is consistent with Pfitzner's rejection of expressive show; it is not a reflection of the Reichsmusikkammer's encouragement of chamber music.

It is the virtue of Pfitzner's late music that it leads a persistent aspect of his career towards an overwhelming question (as Prufrock might have put it). Dahlhaus helps to formulate it by his attempts to define the 'metaphorical' nineteenth

---

[85] George Alexander Albrecht, 'Die Problematik der Aufführungspraxis Pfitznerscher Orchesterwerke am Beispiel der *Kleinen Sinfonie op. 44*', *SPB* 16.

[86] Henderson, 'Hans Pfitzner', 44–5.

century. It is indeed 'not immediately apparent from works such as Pfitzner's C sharp minor Quartet...that historical noncontemporaneity must necessarily betoken aesthetic friction', but that arises in large part from the unwisdom of selecting the C sharp minor Quartet and yoking it with Strauss's *Capriccio* as an example of historical noncontemporaneity.[87] Had Dahlhaus picked the C minor Quartet, then the problem would have been immeasurably sharpened. For in listening to it with however much pleasure, one must inevitably wonder with Dahlhaus when (and indeed whether) 'the tradition undermined by Schönberg's emancipation of dissonance became irrevocably hollow and devoid of aesthetic meaning'.[88] To this is linked the curious fact that the 'absolute music' discerned almost universally in Pfitzner by his early admirers becomes most manifest at the historical point when his noncontemporaneity is most marked. The late Pfitzner seems most completely to define a musical conservatism, the cliché that is sprinkled over his whole output with little analytical verification. His concertos and symphonies seem to offer the substantiation of his place not so much as a custodian of tradition as a reactionary in the face of Modern Music.

The tone of Pfitzner's late music initially offers little consolation in the face of such 'aesthetic friction', and indeed can be related to an aspect of his whole career. As Peter Cahn has shown, Pfitzner himself was by no means reconciled to his admirers' attempts to see in his late works 'a mellowed cheerfulness'.[89] This did not correspond to his mental condition since Mimi's death.

I experience this last creative phase as a duty dictated by nature in the sense that the life which still has some way to go in me must pour out, but not accompanied by living joy in creation; rather (and here I can quote again a prophetic line from *Palestrina*), 'What was my highest delight is now weary duty'. (*SS IV* 650–1)

And yet at face value, the 'mellowed cheerfulness' seems to grow out of a persistent strand in his music. Seebohm

---

[87] Carl Dahlhaus, *Nineteenth-Century Music*, trans. J. Bradford Robinson (Berkeley, Calif., 1989), 2; I have preferred 'aesthetic friction' to Robinson's 'a divergent aesthetic' for 'ästhetische Unstimmigkeit' (Carl Dahlhaus, *Die Musik des 19. Jahrhunderts* (Wiesbaden, 1980), 2).

[88] Ibid.

[89] Cahn, 'Zum Charakter von Pfitzners Spätstil', 100–1.

has defined this in terms of Pfitzner's relationship to Haydn (towards whom he claimed to show a closer affection at an earlier age than towards Mozart).[90] Although Seebohm was writing mainly about the two symphonies and their pendant, the *Elegie und Reigen*, he acknowledges that the Haydnesque 2/4 style is apparent in the finale of the String Quartet in D, and in the fourth theme of the Violin Concerto. With its implications for Pfitzner's interest in an often humorous counterpoint and a dance-like strain in his 6/8 movements, Seebohm's argument is very appealing, and renders Cossmann's reference to Pfitzner's cheerful inspirations meaningful (as it obviously wasn't to Conrad Wandrey).[91] And yet the slow movements of the late works intermittently reveal an abyss underlying the Haydnesque positivism that is also apparent in the Eichendorff settings in Pfitzner's last burst of songwriting after *Das Herz*: the relationship between the dominant tone of the late works and their slow movements is foretold in the mysterious setting of the nocturnal wood's shudder amidst the buoyant march rhythms of 'Der Weckruf' (Op. 40 No. 6); in the evening bells of 'Der verspätete Wanderer'; and even in the never-ending spring of 'Das Alter'. Pfitzner's particular genius for the lyric is folded into these late slow movements as much as into the characteristic piano pieces of Opus 47; over the individual movements of the 'absolute' works might stand such titles as 'Ausgelassenheit' or 'Zerrissenheit'. Equally, the instrumental works may also be seen as studies in specific compositional problems, in the same spirit as the Piano Studies of Opus 51, which shun overt virtuosity in favour of investigating figurations marked as much by innate musical interest as digital dexterity. The shrunken scale of the concertos and the *Kleine Sinfonie*, their lack of a true symphonic outlook, reflects the song-writer's habitual range. Historically, Pfitzner may have reached the symphony at a point where German composers (but not Sibelius, as Furtwängler noted) had lost the faculty for thinking symphonically.[92] But his non-symphonic symphonies can hardly be accused of non-contemporaneity on those grounds, inasmuch as Webern the modernist no less emphatically approached the symphony and related forms with a lyric gift, after a period of intense

[90] Reinhard Seebohm, 'Pfitzners Verhältnis zu Joseph Haydn', *MPG* 34 (Oct. 1975), 34–54.

[91] See Ch. 2, n. 26.

[92] Furtwängler, *Notebooks 1924–1954*, 131.

preparation with lyric forms. It is the formally ambitious concertos of Schoenberg that seem to take a traditional genre by force.

But such an argument can only go so far. Ultimately a work like the Symphony in C has not been acclaimed for its 'naturalness', nor has it achieved 'universality'. Pfitzner remains, in Furtwängler's terms, misunderstood.[93] There is a justice in this to the extent that Pfitzner's Symphony is dedicated to his friends (without implying closed doors). Pfitzner found a refuge in withdrawing into a world that made no concession either to popular taste or political pressure. The alternative to the retrospective style of the 'abstract' works is the rather stilted homophony of *Fons salutifer* or the transparent banalities suggested by the sketch of *Krakauer Begrüssung*. What is regularly forgotten in the pronouncements of Pfitzner against his adversaries (whether Goering or Thomas Mann) is the extent to which he was, in Walter Funk's rather scornful words, 'der alte Herr'.[94] The sentiments isolated in the last group of songs metaphorically reflect the composer's mortality, and that of his wife and daughter, with which he struggled intellectually in such pieces as 'Über die persönliche Fortdauer nach dem Tode' and 'Gedanken über Selbstmord'. The sentiments of the first *Männerchor* of Opus 49, and the chromatic homophony with which Pfitzner set them, are the stark, stoically reconciled equivalent in Pfitzner's music of the coda to Mahler's 'Abschied'. When the underlying core is so austere in rejecting the sensuously appealing, it is hardly surprising that Pfitzner's retrospective works have failed to achieve an audience comparable to the hardly less retrospective *Vier letzte Lieder*.

An aspect of the Cello Concerto in A minor adds substance to the belief that these late works are, in their most private moments, meditations on last things. In the foreword to the score, Pfitzner drew attention to a theme borrowed from the early Cello Concerto rejected by Scholtz. This 'greeting' from a late to an early work was inserted into the exposition of the first movement (an interpolation of C minor in an A minor context), into the ingenious duo-cadenza for cello and clarinet of the same movement, and finally into the last movement's coda. But as Wolfgang Osthoff has shown, the Concerto con-

[93] Ibid. 101.
[94] Busch-Salmen and Weiss, *Hans Pfitzner*, 53.

tains a paraphrase of another composition by Pfitzner in the slow movement, which is texturally and melodically related to 'Hussens Kerker'.[95] The implication is of another work of valediction, an elegy in wartime that once again may counsel fortitude (as did Meyer's re-creation of the prisoner's thoughts in the condemned cell). That Pfitzner did not originally include this movement in the concerto, but inserted it and cemented it to the last movement by a piece of metrical modulation, adds to the interest of the associations. It was rare for Pfitzner to submit to the importunities of a performer (Ludwig Hoelscher wanted a slow movement). That he went back to the work and added to it indicates a desire, perhaps, to set a particular personal imprint on it. As Vogel has suggested, Pfitzner's late works may have more than a few associations from earlier periods, though no case is quite so clear as this concerto. This of course had always been a tendency, for various reasons, in Pfitzner's music from *Der arme Heinrich* onwards. What Vogel finds striking in the late works is the persistence of the tendency, and the related echoes of works by other composers, Mendelssohn in the slow movement of the *Fantasie*, Schumann in 'Melodie' (Op. 47 No. 5), and Schubert in the last movement of the Quartet in C minor.[96] If backward glances into a composer's own output are taken as a leading symptom of late style (and Cahn's examination of some sentences of Adorno cast mild doubt on the objective criteria for determining 'late style' in the abstract[97]), then perhaps the echoes of other composers in Pfitzner's last works may be seen as a reflection of a historic lateness that Pfitzner had always feared.

This lateness is not incompatible with gestures towards a more conventional positivism. Indeed the String Quartet in C minor may be seen as Pfitzner's acknowledgement of a tradition characterized by Adorno as 'the positivity of *per aspera ad astra*'.[98] Not only does C minor turn through the subdominant area of the middle movements to C major for a vivacious finale; the presence of certain cells, characterized as much by rhythm as pitch, inevitably suggests the example of Beethoven's Fifth Symphony, but withdrawn to a private

[95] Wolfgang Osthoff, 'Jugendwerk, Früh-, Reife- und Altersstil', *Archiv für Musikwissenschaft*, 33 (1976), 90–4.

[96] Vogel, *Hans Pfitzner*, 121–2.

[97] Cahn, 'Zum Charakter von Pfitzners Spätstil', 110.

[98] Theodor W. Adorno, *Mahler* (Frankfurt am Main, 1960), 180.

Ex. 8.9*a*

sphere of contemplation (Ex. 8.9). Significantly, this quartet makes a deeper impression than the blatant major of the Symphony in C, where the obsessive rhythm suggests a music 'about' C major, rather than a participation in the specific associations of works in that key. It is this factor which makes aesthetic evaluation of Pfitzner's late works ultimately difficult. They walk a thin line between the withdrawn and the reflected, between a personal 'inner emigration' (which might have happened without the Third Reich) and a music composed out of other musics. Pfitzner's last work was to have been a commissioned cantata on Goethe's *Urworte·Orphisch* (in celebration of the poet's two-hundredth birthday), which he left unfinished in fragmentary condition. As the poem extols the apparently predestined law of each life, so Pfitzner remained true to his picture of musical form, intending an orchestral interlude on 'GEDE' (as Goethe's name sounded in his native Frankfurt accent).[99] The work would have been conditioned by the approach established in the cantatas of the 1920s. But as Goethe noted, society and others added an element of chance. It is both the virtue and the vice of Pfitzner's music that it submits to a law which Pfitzner felt in his bones. It is the strongest feature of the Piano Quintet, the first Act of *Palestrina*, and the works from *Von deutscher Seele* to *Das dunkle Reich*. The law is scarcely different from the unconscious inspiration which he extolled in his prose works. The late works, however, like *Das Christ-Elflein* and the later acts of *Palestrina* in their different ways, are much more at the mercy of the chances contingent upon Pfitzner's intellectual intercourse with the composers who made up his ideal tradition. As a result, they seem both retrospective yet characteristic of the 'Zerrissenheit' to which he devoted the fourth of the *Fünf Klavierstücke*. To see the last chapter of his career as inconclusive or melancholy would probably have drawn the reflection from Pfitzner in his more tranquil moments that it was bound to turn out like that anyway (as it did for Palestrina, left with only fragments of themes and improvisations).

Pfitzner's career has yet significantly to be reappraised. If this is to happen, then a number of difficulties must be overcome. In an era of deconstruction, the outlook for him in some ways looks worse than ever. It may not be an exaggeration to say that aesthetics in the light of post-structuralism is poised to flee from the autonomous art-work into the ethical. Pfitzner probably would have recognized the notion, inasmuch as the identity of ethics and aesthetics is an idea which he would have met in Otto Weininger. But by ethical standards, Pfitzner's career and above all his opinions will reveal not excessive inconsistencies but precisely the reverse. It is the

---

[99] Rudolf Hanzl, '"Der Wunsch meine Erdentage in Wien beschliessen zu können...": Hans Pfitzner zum 10. Todestag', *Österreichische Musikzeitschrift*, 14 (1959), 377.

achievement of post-structuralism and deconstruction to nest in inconsistencies and create new contexts with claims to validity that Pfitzner would probably not have accepted, and his outlook may indeed look suspiciously of a piece. But his late works stand in direct contradiction to the near-totalitarian nature with which many of his opinions and theories were expressed. Possibly revaluation should begin with those, since the Cello Concerto in G, the Duo, and the *Kleine Sinfonie* are the most refined statement of a music of gentle reminiscence. If such fine music as *Von deutscher Seele* is to win a wider audience, an act of corporate forgiveness towards his often cantankerous shade must take place, not only from Jews and Israelis, who have the right to feel affronted that their race was taken for an abstraction, but from all people of liberal conscience for whom Pfitzner's strong opinions constitute a stumbling block. Until we can listen to his music as much for its specific qualities as for the intellectual framework he wove round it, he will remain a figure discussed more than performed. Like Schoenberg, to whom he bears such a strong mirror resemblance, he is a composer who provokes thought by the very nature of his often unsensuous music. His songs and *Palestrina*, however, will ensure that his music is always available.

Appendix

Pfitzner's songs with piano accompaniment classified according to poet

❧❧

Songs in square brackets, (1) remained unpublished in Pfitzner's lifetime but are included in the appendix of *Sämtliche Lieder* (2 vols., ed. Hans Rectanus, Mainz, 1979–83), (2) are fragmentary but are also included in the appendix of *Sämtliche Lieder*.

Anon.
    Op. 2/4 'Im tiefen Wald verborgen'
        6/1 'Zweifelnde Liebe'
        — 'Untreu und Trost'
    [Appendix/4 'Mein Liebchen ist kein stolzes Schloss']
    [Fragment/10 'Wär' ich, Geliebte']
Bartels, Adolf (1862–1945)
    Op. 40/2 'Wenn sich Liebes von dir lösen will'
Bartholomew, Mary* Graf (dates unknown)
    Jl./2 'Mir bist du tot'
    [Fragment/9 'Kukukslied']
Böttger, Adolf (1815–70)
    Op. 2/5 'Ich hör' ein Vöglein locken'
Bürger, Gottfried August (1747–94)
    Op. 22/3 'Schön Suschen'
       22/4 'Gegenliebe'
       22/5 'An die Bienen'
       26/4 'Trauerstille'
       41/1 'Auf die Morgenröte'
Busse, Carl (1872–1918)
    Op. 11/5 'Gretel'
       15/1 'Leierkastenmann'
       19/1 'Stimme der Sehnsucht'
       19/2 'Michaelskirchplatz'
Chamisso, Adelbert von (1781–1838)
    Op. 22/2 'Tragische Geschichte'
Cossmann, Paul Nikolaus (1869–1942)

---

* That the Max Graf-Bartholomew given in *Sämtliche Lieder* and all worklists should in fact be Mary Graf Bartholomew is a recent discovery of Hans Rectanus (whom I must thank for informing me of this sex change).

Op. 6/4 'Widmung'
    6/5 'Die Bäume wurden gelb'
Dehmel, Richard (1863–1920)
Op. 11/4 'Venus mater'
    29/4 'Die stille Stadt'
    30/4 'Der Arbeitsmann'
Eichendorff, Joseph von (1788–1857)
Op. 5/3 'Der Bote'
    7/2 'Nachtwanderer'
    7/4 'Lockung'
    9/1 'Der Gärtner'
    9/2 'Die Einsame'
    9/3 'Im Herbst'
    9/4 'Der Kühne'
    9/5 'Abschied'
    10/3 'Zum Abschied meiner Tochter'
    11/3 'Studentenfahrt'
    15/2 'Zorn'
    15/4 'Sonst'
    21/2 'Die Nachtigallen'
    22/1 'In Danzig'
    26/2 'Nachts'
    26/3 'Neue Liebe'
    40/6 'Der Weckruf'
    41/2 'Der verspätete Wanderer'
    41/3 'Das Alter'
[Fragment/11 'Waldesgespräch']
Geibel, Emanuel (1815–84)
Op. 3/3 'Mein Herz ist wie die dunkle Nacht'
[Appendix/5 'O schneller, mein Ross']
Goethe, Johann Wolfgang von (1749–1832)
Op. 18   'An den Mond'
    26/5 'Mailied'
    29/3 'Willkommen und Abschied'
    40/5 'Wanderers Nachtlied'
Greif, Martin (1839–1911)
Op. 40/4 'Herbstgefühl'
Grun, James (1866–1928)
Op. 5/1 'Frieden'
    5/2 'Wiegenlied'
    6/3 'Zugvogel'
    7/5 'Wie Frühlingsahnung weht es durch die Lande'
Hebbel, Friedrich (1813–63)
Op. 11/1 'Ich und du'
    21/1 'Herbstbild'
    26/1 'Gebet'

Heine, Heinrich (1797–1856)

Op. 4/1 'Es glänzt so schön die sinkende Sonne'
    4/2 'Sie haben heut' Abend Gesellschaft'
    4/3 'Es fällt ein Stern herunter'
    4/4 'Es fasst mich wieder der alte Mut'
    6/2 'Ich will mich im grünen Wald ergehn'
    6/6 'Wasserfahrt'
[Appendix/2 'Die schlanke Wasserlilie']
[Appendix/3 'Ein Fichtenbaum steht einsam']

Heyse, Paul (1830–1914)

Op. 7/3 'Über ein Stündlein'

Hölderlin, Friedrich (1770–1843)

Op. 29/1 'Abbitte'

Huch, Ricarda (1864–1947)

Op. 35/1 'Bestimmung'
    35/2 'Ich werde nicht an deinem Herzen satt'
    35/3 'Wo hast du all die Schönheit hergenommen'?'
    35/4 'Schwill an, mein Strom'
    35/5 'Eine Melodie singt mein Herz'
    35/6 'Denn unsre Liebe hat zu heiss geflammt'
    40/3 'Sehnsucht'

Jacobowski, Ludwig (1868–1900)

Op. 11/2 'Ich aber weiss'
    40/1 'Leuchtende Tage'

Kaufmann, Alexander (1821–93)

Op. 2/7 'Verrat'

Keller, Gottfried (1819–90)

Op. 33/1 'Mir glänzen die Augen'
    33/2 'Ich fürcht' nit Gespenster'
    33/3 'Du milchjunger Knabe'
    33/4 'Wandl' ich in dem Morgentau'
    33/5 'Singt mein Schatz wie ein Fink'
    33/6 'Röschen biss den Apfel an'
    33/7 'Treten ein, hoher Krieger'
    33/8 'Wie glänzt der helle Mond'

Kopisch, August (1799–1853)

[Fragment/8 'Historie von Noah']

Leander, Richard (1830–89)

Op. 2/1 'In der Früh', wenn die Sonne kommen will'
    2/2 'Ist der Himmel darum im Lenz so blau?'

Lenau, Nikolaus (1802–50)

Op. 30/1 'Sehnsucht nach Vergessen'
[Fragment/7 'Auf geheimem Waldespfade']

Lienhard, Fritz (1865–1929)

Op. 24/4 'Abendrot'

Liliencron, Detlev von (1844–1909)

Op. 10/1 'Sehnsucht'
  10/2 'Müde'
Lingg, Hermann (1820–1905)
  Op. 2/3 'Lied'
  2/6 'Immer leiser wird mein Schlummer'
Meyer, Conrad Ferdinand (1825–98)
  Op. 32/1 'Hussens Kerker'
  32/2 'Säerspruch'
  32/3 'Eingelegte Ruder'
  32/4 'Lass scharren deiner Rosse Huf'
Mörike, Eduard (1804–75)
  Jl./5 'Das verlassene Mägdlein'
  Op. 30/2 'Das verlassene Mägdlein'
  30/3 'Denk es, o Seele'
Müller von Königswinter, Wolfgang (1816–73)
  Op. 7/1 'Hast du von den Fischerkindern das alte Märchen
    vernommen?'
Petrarch, Francesco (1304–74)
  Op. 24/3 'Voll jener Süsse' (92nd Sonnet)
Redwitz, Oskar von (1823–91)
  Jl./4 'Nun, da so warm der Sonnenschein'
Reinick, Robert (1805–52)
  Jl./6 'Kuriose Geschichte'
Rückert, Friedrich (1788–1866)
  Op. 3/1 'Warum sind deine Augen denn so nass?'
  29/2 'Herbsthauch'
Sallet, Friedrich von (1812–43)
  Op. 3/2 'Herbstlied'
Schack, Adolf Friedrich von (1815–94)
  [Appendix/6 'Ständchen']
Scheffel, Viktor von (1826–86)
  [Appendix/1 'Das ist im Leben hässlich eingerichtet' (*Lied
    Werners aus dem 'Trompeter von Säckingen'*)]
Stach-Lerner, Ilse von (1879–1941)
  Op. 15/3 'An die Mark'
Sturm, Julius (1816–96)
  Jl./1 'Abendlied'
Uhland, Ludwig (1787–1862)
  Jl./3 'Naturfreiheit'
Walther von der Vogelweide (*c.*1170–*c.*1230)
  Op. 24/1 'Unter der Linden'
  24/2 'Gewalt der Minne'

Worklist

❧❦

This worklist does not provide dates for individual movements of multi-movement works. It does provide, where available, the dates of individual solo songs. It has been compiled from various sources, of which the most important are: Karl Franz Müller, *In memoriam Hans Pfitzner* (Vienna, 1950); Helmut Grohe, *Hans Pfitzner: Verzeichnis sämtlicher im Druck erschienenen Werke* (Munich and Leipzig, n.d. [1960]); Hans Pfitzner, *Sämtliche Lieder* (2 vols., ed. Hans Rectanus; Mainz, 1979–83); Hans Rectanus, 'Pfitzners frühe Werke: Bestand und stilistische Anmerkungen', *SPB* 89–98; *Katalog Nr. 288: Hans Pfitzner (1869–1949)* (Tutzing: Musikantiquariat Hans Schneider, 1986).

(a) WORKS WITH OPUS NUMBERS

Op. 1. Sonata in fis-moll für Violoncello und Klavier (1890)
  pub. Breitkopf & Härtel, Leipzig (n.d. [1892])
  ded. Heinrich Kiefer
  1st perf. 21 Jan. 1891, Frankfurt am Main
Op. 2. Sieben Lieder, für eine Singstimme (1888/9)
  pub. by Albert Metzger, Koblenz (n.d. [1893]) then Brockhaus, Leipzig (1898)
  ded. Helene Lieban-Globig
  1st perf. No. 2, 31 May 1889, Frankfurt am Main; No. 4, 7 Mar. 1890, Frankfurt am Main; rest unknown (probably Frankfurt am Main, Hoch Conservatory; also Op. 3–7 and 9)
  1. 'In der Früh', wenn die Sonne kommen will (R. Leander)
  2. 'Ist der Himmel darum im Lenz so blau' (Leander)
  3. 'Kalt und schneidend weht der Wind' (H. Lingg)
  4. 'Im tiefen Wald verborgen' (Anon.)
  5. 'Ich hör' ein Vöglein locken' (A. Böttger)
  6. 'Immer leiser wird mein Schlummer' (H. Lingg)
  7. 'Verrat' (A. Kaufmann)
  Nos. 2, 5, 6, and 7 orch. Pfitzner
Op. 3. Drei Lieder, für eine mittlere Singstimme (1888/9)
  pub. B. Firnberg, Frankfurt am Main (n.d. [1893]), then Tischer und Jagenberg, Cologne (n.d.)
  ded. Baroness Mathilde von Erlanger
  1st perf. unknown

1. 'Warum sind deine Augen denn so nass' (Rückert)
2. 'Herbstlied' (Fr. von Sallet)
3. 'Mein Herz ist wie die dunkle Nacht' (E. Geibel)
Nos. 2 and 3 orch. Pfitzner

Op. 4. Vier Lieder, für eine mittlere Singstimme (Heine) (1888/9)
   pub. B. Firnberg (n.d.), then Tischer und Jagenberg (n.d.)
   ded. Baroness Mathilde von Erlanger
   1st perf. unknown
   1. 'Es glänzt so schön die sinkende Sonne'
   2. 'Sie haben heut' Abend Gesellschaft'
   3. 'Es fällt ein Stern herunter'
   4. 'Es fasst mich wieder der alte Mut'
   Nos. 1–4 orch. Pfitzner

Op. 5. Drei Lieder, für Sopran (1888/9)
   pub. Adolph Fürstner, Berlin (1894)
   ded. 'Herrn und Frau Ravenstein'
   1st perf. unknown
   1. 'Frieden' (James Grun)
   2. 'Wiegenlied' (Grun)
   3. 'Der Bote' (Eichendorff)
   No. 1 orch. Pfitzner

Op. 6. Sechs Lieder, für hohen Bariton (1888/9)
   pub. Fürstner (1894)
   ded. to the memory of Georg Heine
   1st perf. No. 1, 7 Mar. 1890; rest unknown
   1. 'Zweifelnde Liebe' (Anon.)
   2. 'Ich will mich im grünen Wald ergehn' (Heine)
   3. 'Zugvogel' (Grun)
   4. 'Widmung' (P. N. Cossmann)
   5. 'Die Bäume wurden gelb' (P. N. Cossmann)
   6. 'Wasserfahrt' (Heine)

Op. 7. Fünf Lieder, für eine Singstimme (1888/9 and 1897–1900[?])
   pub. Ries und Erler, Berlin (n.d. [1895?])
   ded. Max Steinitzer
   1st perf. unknown
   1. 'Hast du von den Fischerkindern das alte Märchen vernommen?' (W. Müller von Königswinter)
   2. 'Nachtwanderer' (Eichendorff)
   3. 'Über ein Stündlein' (P. Heyse)
   4. 'Lockung' (Eichendorff)
   5. 'Wie Frühlingsahnung weht es' (Grun)
   No. 3 orch. Pfitzner

Op. 8. Trio für Klavier, Violine und Violoncello in F-dur (1896)
   pub. Simrock, Berlin (1898)
   ded. Alexander Friedrich von Hessen
   1st perf. 14 Dec. 1896, Frankfurt am Main

Op. 9. Fünf Lieder nach Gedichten von Joseph von Eichendorff, für
    eine Singstimme (1894/5)
    pub. Brockhaus (1898)
    ded. Anton Sistermans
    1st perf. 15 May 1896, Frankfurt am Main
    1. 'Der Gärtner'
    2. 'Die Einsame'
    3. 'Im Herbst'
    4. 'Der Kühne'
    5. 'Abschied'
Op. 10. Drei Lieder, für eine mittlere Singstimme (1889–1901)
    pub. Brockhaus (n.d.)
    ded. Dr Egon von Niederhöffer
    1st perf. unknown
    1. 'Sehnsucht' (Liliencron)
    2. 'Müde' (Liliencron)
    3. 'Zum Abschied meiner Tochter' (Eichendorff)
Op. 11. Fünf Lieder, für eine Singstimme (1901)
    pub. Brockhaus (n.d. [1902])
    1st perf. No. 5, 18 Dec. 1901, Berlin; rest Munich, 1901
    1. 'Ich und du' (Hebbel) (ded. Mimi Pfitzner)
    2. 'Ich aber weiss' (L. Jacobowski) (ded. Ilse von Stach-Lerner)
    3. 'Studentenfahrt' (Eichendorff) (ded. Ernst Kraus)
    4. 'Venus mater' (Dehmel) (ded. Grete Kraus)
    5. 'Gretel' (C. Busse) (ded. Emilie Herzog)
    Nos. 4 and 5 orch. Pfitzner
Op. 12. *Herr Oluf*, Ballade f. Bariton und grosses Orchester (Herder)
    (1891)
    pub. Bote und Bock, Berlin (1902)
    ded. Karl Scheidemantel
    1st perf. 4 May 1893, Berlin
Op. 13. Streichquartett in D-dur (1902/3)
    pub. Julius Feuchtinger, Stuttgart (1903), then Brockhaus
    ded. Alma Maria Mahler
    1st perf. 13 Jan. 1903, Vienna
Op. 14. *Die Heinzelmännchen*, für eine tiefe Bassstimme und grosses
    Orchester (A. Kopisch) (1902/3)
    pub. Feuchtinger (1903), then Brockhaus
    ded. Paul Knüpfer
    1st perf. 1 June 1904, Frankfurt am Main
Op. 15. Vier Lieder, für eine Singstimme (1904)
    pub. Feuchtinger (1904), then Brockhaus (1906)
    1st perf. unknown
    1. 'Leierkastenmann' (Busse) (ded. Willy Levin)
    2. 'Zorn' (Eichendorff) (ded. Hermann Gausche)
    3. 'An die Mark' (Ilse von Stach) (ded. Johanna Knüpfer-Egli)

4. 'Sonst' (Eichendorff) (ded. Johanna Knüpfer-Egli)
Nos. 2, 3, and 4 orch. Pfitzner

Op. 16. *Columbus* für achtstimmigen gemischten Chor a cappella (Schiller) (1905)
pub. Ries und Erler
ded. 'zum 9ten Mai 1905'
1st perf. 6 Dec. 1911, Strasbourg

Op. 17. Musik für Orchester zu Kleists *Käthchen von Heilbronn* (1905)
pub. Ries und Erler (1905/6)
ded. 'Dem unvergänglichen Dichter als geringe Huldigung'
1st perf. 19 Oct. 1905

Op. 18. 'An den Mond' für eine Singstimme mit Klavier (Goethe) (1906)
pub. Brockhaus (1906)
1st perf. unknown (orch. Pfitzner)

Op. 19. Zwei Lieder, für mittlere Singstimme (Busse) (1905)
pub. Brockhaus (1906)
1st perf. unknown
ded. Otilie Metzger-Froitzheim
1st perf. unknown
  1. 'Stimme der Sehnsucht'
  2. 'Michaelskirchplatz'

Op. 20. *Das Christ-Elflein*, Weihnachtsmärchen (1906)
Poem by Ilse von Stach
pub. Ries und Erler (1906)
ded. Willy Levin
1st perf. 11 Dec. 1906, Munich
revised as
Das Christ-Elflein, Spieloper in zwei Akten (1917)
text revised by Pfitzner
pub. privately (1917), then Fürstner (1918)
1st perf. 11 Dec. 1917, Dresden

Op. 21. Zwei Lieder, für eine hohe Singstimme (1907)
pub. C. F. Kahnt, Leipzig (1907)
1st perf. unknown
  1. 'Herbstbild' (Hebbel) (ded. Grete Eloesser)
  2. 'Die Nachtigallen' (Eichendorff) (ded. Natalie Levin)

Op. 22. Fünf Lieder, für eine Singstimme (1907)
pub. Brockhaus (1907)
1st perf. unknown
  1. 'In Danzig' (Eichendorff) (ded. Johannes Messchaert) [Berlin, Apr.]
  2. 'Tragische Geschichte' (Chamisso) (ded. Johannes Messchaert) [17 Apr.]
  3. 'Schön Suschen' (Bürger) (ded. Rudolf Moest) [early May]

4. 'Gegenliebe' (Bürger) (ded. Fritz Feinhals) [28 Apr.]
5. 'An die Bienen' (Bürger) (ded. Helene Staegemann) [14 May]

Op. 23. Klavierquintett in C-dur (1908)
  pub. Peters, Leipzig (1908)
  ded. Bruno Walter
  1st perf. 17 Nov. 1908, Berlin

Op. 24. Vier Lieder, für eine Singstimme (1909)
  pub. Brockhaus (1909)
  ded. Arthur Eloesser
  1st perf. unknown
  1. 'Unter der Linden' (Walther von der Vogelweide) [Freiburg-Grüntherthal, 6 Apr.]
  2. 'Gewalt der Minne' (Walther von der Vogelweide) [Strasbourg, 21 Apr.]
  3. Sonnett No. 92, 'Voll jener Süsse' (Petrarch) [Strasbourg, Apr.]
  4. 'Abendrot' (Fr. Lienhard) [Strasbourg, 1 May]
  No. 1 orch. Pfitzner

Op. 25. Zwei deutsche Gesänge für Bariton (mit Männerchor ad lib.) und grosses Orchester (1915/16)
  pub. Brockhaus (1916)
  ded. Admiral von Tirpitz
  1st perf. of 1, 14 Mar. 1916, Strasbourg; of 2, 22 Mar. 1915, Munich
  1. 'Der Trompeter' (Kopisch)
  2. 'Klage' (Eichendorff)

Op. 26. Fünf Lieder, für eine Singstimme (Aug. 1916)
  pub. Brockhaus (1916)
  ded. Mientje Lamprecht van Lammen
  1st perf. 10 Nov. 1916, Strasbourg
  1. 'Gebet' (Hebbel)
  2. 'Nachts' (Eichendorff)
  3. 'Neue Liebe' (Eichendorff)
  4. 'Trauerstille' (Bürger)
  5. 'Mailied' (Goethe)
  Nos. 2 and 4 orch. Pfitzner

Op. 27. Sonate in e-moll für Violine und Klavier (1918)
  pub. Peters (1918)
  ded. Royal Swedish Academy of Arts
  1st perf. 25 Sept. 1918, Munich

Op. 28. *Von deutscher Seele*. Eine romantische Kantate nach Sprüchen und Gedichten von Joseph von Eichendorff, für 4 Solostimmen (SATB), gemischten Chor, grosses Orchester und Orgel (1921)
  pub. Fürstner (1921)
  ded. Eva Kwast
  1st perf. 27 Jan. 1922, Berlin

Op. 29. Vier Lieder, für eine Singstimme (1921)
  pub. Fürstner (1922)
  1st perf. unknown
  1. 'Abbitte' (Hölderlin) (ded. Mimi Pfitzner) [11 Nov.]
  2. 'Herbsthauch' (Rückert) (ded. Paul Pfitzner) [8 Oct.]
  3. 'Willkommen und Abschied' (Goethe) (ded. Peter Pfitzner) [3 Nov.]
  4. 'Die stille Stadt' (Dehmel) (ded. Agnes Pfitzner) [7 Oct.]
  No. 3 orch. Pfitzner
Op. 30. Vier Lieder, für eine Singstimme (1922)
  pub. Fürstner (1922)
  ded. Fritz Mayer
  1st perf. unknown
  1. 'Sehnsucht nach Vergessen' (Lenau)
  2. 'Das verlassene Mägdlein' (Mörike)
  3. 'Denk es, o Seele' (Mörike) [10 Jan.]
  4. 'Der Arbeitsmann' (Dehmel) [7 Jan.]
Op. 31. Konzert für Klavier [in] Es-dur (1922)
  pub. Fürstner (1923)
  ded. Fritz Busch
  1st perf. 16 Mar. 1923, Dresden
Op. 32. Vier Lieder nach Gedichten von C. F. Meyer, für eine Singstimme (Bariton oder Bass) (1923)
  pub. Fürstner (1923)
  1st perf. 7 Sept. 1923, Munich
  1. 'Hussens Kerker' (ded. Paul Bender) [25 June]
  2. 'Säerspruch' (ded. Paul Bender) [5 July]
  3. 'Eingelegte Ruder' (ded. Heinrich Rehkemper) [2 July]
  4. 'Lass scharren deiner Rosse Huf' (ded. Heinrich Rehkemper) [1 July]
Op. 33. *Alte Weisen*. Acht Gedichte von Gottfried Keller, für eine Singstimme (1923)
  pub. Brockhaus (1923)
  ded. Karl Erb and Maria Ivogün
  1st perf. 3 Oct. 1923, Munich
  1. 'Mir glänzen die Augen' [22 July]
  2. 'Ich fürcht' nit Gespenster' [24 July]
  3. 'Du milchjunger Knabe' [19 July]
  4. 'Wandl' ich in dem Morgentau' [25 July]
  5. 'Singt mein Schatz wie ein Fink' [26 July]
  6. 'Röschen biss den Apfel an' [20 July]
  7. 'Tretet ein, hoher Krieger' [26 July]
  8. 'Wie glänzt der helle Mond' [26 July]
Op. 34. Konzert für Violine [in] h-moll (in einem Satz) (1923)
  pub. Fürstner (1924)
  ded. Alma Moodie
  1st perf. 4 June 1924, Nuremberg

Op. 35. Sechs Liebeslieder nach Gedichten von Ricarda Huch, für eine Frauenstimme (1924)
pub. Fürstner (1924)
1st perf. 14 Dec. 1924, Berlin
1. 'Bestimmung' [26 June]
2. 'Ich werde nicht an deinem Herzen satt' [26 June]
3. 'Wo hast du all die Schönheit hergenommen'
4. 'Schwill an, mein Strom' [30 June]
5. 'Eine Melodie singt mein Herz' [4 July]
6. 'Denn unsre Liebe hat zu heiss geflammt' [9 July]
Op. 36. Streichquartett in cis-moll (1925)
pub. Fürstner (1925)
ded. Max von Schillings
1st perf. 6 Nov. 1925, Berlin
Op. 36a. Sinfonie in cis-moll für grosses Orchester nach dem Streichquartett, op. 36 (1932)
pub. Fürstner (1933)
1st perf. 23 Mar. 1933, Munich
Op. 37. *Lethe*, Gedicht von C. F. Meyer für eine Baritonstimme und Orchester (1926)
pub. Fürstner (1926)
1st perf. 14 Dec. 1926, Munich
Op. 38. *Das dunkle Reich*, eine Chorphantasie mit Orchester, Orgel, Sopran und Bariton (1929)
pub. Brockhaus (1930)
1st perf. 21 Oct. 1930, Cologne
Op. 39. *Das Herz*, Drama für Musik in 3 Akten von Hans Mahner-Mons (1930/1)
pub. Fürstner (1931)
1st performances 12 Nov. 1931, Munich and Berlin
Op. 40. Sechs Lieder, für mittlere Singstimme (1931)
pub. Peters (1932)
1st perf. 15 Feb. 1932, Munich
1. 'Leuchtende Tage' (Jacobowski) [8 Oct.]
2. 'Wenn sich Liebes von dir lösen will' (A. Bartels) [7 Dec.]
3. 'Sehnsucht' (Huch) [12 Dec.]
4. 'Herbstgefühl' (M. Greif) [19 Nov.]
5. 'Wanderers Nachtlied' ['Der du von dem Himmel bist'] (Goethe) [16 Dec.]
6. 'Der Weckruf' (Eichendorff) [20 Dec.]
Nos. 5 and 6 orch. Pfitzner [with added, partly optional, choral parts in No. 6]
Op. 41. Drei Sonette, für eine Männerstimme (1931)
pub. Peters (1932)
1st perf. 15 Feb. 1932, Munich
1. 'Auf die Morgenröte' (Bürger) [9 Oct.]
2. 'Der verspätete Wanderer' (Eichendorff) [7 Oct.]

3. 'Das Alter' (Eichendorff) [7 Dec.]

Op. 42. Konzert in G-dur für Violoncello und Orchester (1935)
pub. Schott (1935)
ded. Gaspar Cassadó
1st perf. 27 Sept. 1935, Frankfurt am Main

Op. 43. Duo für Violine und Violoncello mit Begleitung eines kleinen
Orchesters oder des Klaviers (1937)
pub. Leuckart, Munich and Leipzig (1937)
ded. Max Strub and Ludwig Hoelscher
1st perf. 3 Dec. 1937, Frankfurt am Main

Op. 44. *Kleine Sinfonie* (1939)
pub. Brockhaus (1939)
1st perf. 17 Nov. 1939, Berlin

Op. 45. *Elegie und Reigen* (1940)
pub. Leuckart (1940)
1st perf. 29 Apr. 1941, Salzburg

Op. 46. Sinfonie in C-dur für grosses Orchester (1940)
pub. Fürstner (1940)
ded. 'An die Freunde'
1st perf. 11 Oct. 1940, Frankfurt am Main

Op. 47. Fünf Stücke für Klavier (1941)
pub. Fürstner (1941)
ded. Walter Gieseking
1st perf. 1941, Berlin
1. 'Letztes Aufbäumen'
2. 'Aufgelassenheit'
3. 'Hieroglyphe'
4. 'Zerrissenheit'
5. 'Melodie'

Op. 48. *Fons salutifer*, Hymnus für gemischten Chor, Orchester und
Orgel (1941)
pub. Oertel (1942)
1st perf. 30 Apr. 1942,[1] Karlsbad

Op. 49. Zwei Männerchöre a cappella (1941)
pub. Oertel, Berlin (1942)
ded. to the Kölner Männergesangsverein
1st perf. 26 Apr. 1942, Cologne
1. 'Wir geh'n dahin' (Hans Franck) [12 Oct.]
2. 'Das Schifflein' (Uhland) [Munich, 13 Oct.]

Op. 50. Streichquartett in c-moll (1942)
pub. Oertel (1942)
ded. Max Strub
1st perf. 5 June 1942, Berlin

Op. 51. Sechs Studien für Pianoforte (1943)

---

[1] Hans Rectanus has informed me that *Fons salutifer* was first performed in
Karlsbad (and not in Munich as other worklists maintain); but there is still a
measure of doubt as to whether it was performed on 30 April or 1 May.

pub. Oertel (1943)
ded. Friedrich Wührer
1st perf. 10 Mar. 1943, Vienna
Op. 52. Konzert für Violoncello mit Begleitung des Orchesters
pub. Oertel (1944)
ded. Ludwig Hoelscher
1st perf. 23 Mar. 1944, Solingen
Op. 53. Drei Gesänge (W. Hundertmark), f. Männerchor mit Begleitung eines kleinen Orchesters (1944)
pub. Oertel (1944)
1. 'Seliger Sommer' [21 Sept. 1944]
2. 'Wandlung' [11 Sept. 1944]
3. 'Soldatenlied' [10 Aug. 1944]
1st perf. 1944, Vienna
Op. 54. *Krakauer Begrüssung* (1944)
pub. Oertel
ded. Hans Frank
1st perf. 2 Dec. 1944, Cracow[2]
withheld by Oertel and replaced by
Op. 54. *Das Christ-Elflein*, revised version
Op. 55. Sextett f. Klavier, Violine, Viola, Violoncello, Kontrabass, Klarinette (1945)
pub. Oertel (1947)
1st perf. 19 Apr. 1946, Berlin
Op. 56. Fantasie für Orchester (1947)
pub. Brockhaus (1947)
ded. Rolf Agop
1st perf. 23 Apr. 1947, Nuremberg
[Op. 57. Kantate nach Goethes *Urworte · Orphisch*, f. 4 Solostimmen, gemischten Chor, Orgel u. Orchester (1948/9)
pub. Oertel (1952); unfinished; sketch realized by Robert Rehan]

(*b*) WORKS WITHOUT OPUS NUMBERS

Sechs Jugendlieder, für eine hohe Singstimme (Sopran) (1884/7)
pub. Ries und Erler (1933)
ded. Gisela Derpsch
1st perf. unknown (probably Frankfurt am Main, Hoch Conservatory, 'Prüfungskonzerte' and 'Übungsabende')
1. 'Abendlied' (J. Sturm)
2. 'Mir bist du tot' (M. Graf Bartholomew)
3. 'Naturfreiheit' (Uhland)
4. 'Nun, da so warm der Sonnenschein' (Redwitz)
5. 'Das verlassene Mägdlein' (Mörike)
6. 'Kuriose Geschichte' (R. Reinick)

---

[2] Whether *Krakauer Begrüssung* was performed on 1 or 2 December is still not entirely clear.

Scherzo für Orchester (comp. 1887)
  pub. Metzger (1893), then Feuchtinger (1898), later Brockhaus (1905)
  ded. Berlin Philharmonic Orchestra
  1st perf. (with orchestra) 23 June 1888, Frankfurt am Main
Der Blumen Rache, für Frauenchor, Altsolo und Orchester (1888)
  poem by Freiligrath
  pub. Ries und Erler (1906)
  1st perf. 6 Dec. 1911, Strasbourg
Musik zu Ibsens *Das Fest auf Solhaug* (1889/90)
  pub. Luckhardt (1903), then Feuchtinger (1905)
  ded. to his parents
* 1st perf. 28 Nov. 1895, Mainz
Der arme Heinrich, Musikdrama in 3 Akten (1891–3)
  libretto by James Grun
  pub. Brockhaus (1895)
  ded. Paul Nikolaus Cossmann
  1st perf. 2 Apr. 1895, Mainz
Die Rose vom Liebesgarten, Romantische Oper in 2 Akten (1897–1900)
  libretto by James Grun
  pub. Luckhardt (1901), then Brockhaus
  ded. Ernst Kraus
  1st perf. 9 Nov. 1901, Elberfeld
Rundgesang zum Neujahrsfest 1901
  poem by Ernst von Wolzogen
  pub. Brockhaus (1901)
  1st perf. unknown
'Untreu und Trost' (Volkslied), für eine mittlere Singstimme (1903)
  pub. in *Im Volkston*, special number of *Die Woche* (1903), then Brockhaus (1917)
  1st perf. unknown
  instr. Pfitzner
Gesang der Barden aus Kleists 'Hermannsschlacht' (1906)
  pub. in *Süddeutsche Monatshefte*, 4 (1907), 120 and supplement, then Fürstner
  1st perf. unknown [1911/12, Strasbourg?]
Palestrina, Musikalische Legende in 3 Akten (1912–15)
  libretto by Pfitzner
  pub. Fürstner (1916), then Schott
  ded. in 1949 to the Vienna Philharmonic Orchestra
  1st perf. 12 June 1917, Munich

(*c*) PUBLISHED ARRANGEMENTS

Undine, Oper von E. T. A. Hoffmann
  pub. Peters (1906)

1st perf. 30 June 1922, Aachen
Acht Frauenchöre von Robert Schumann mit Instrumental-
begleitung
    pub. Universal-Edition (1910)
    1st perf. 12 June 1910, Strasbourg
Der Templer und die Jüdin, Oper von Marschner
    pub. Brockhaus (1912)
    1st perf. of earlier version 20 Feb. 1904, Berlin; rev. version 20
    Apr. 1912, Strasbourg
'Erlkönig' und 'Odins Meeresritt' von Carl Loewe, für grosses
Orchester instrumentiert
    pub. Brockhaus (1916)
    1st perf. 22 Nov. 1916
Der Vampyr, Romantische Oper in 2 Akten von Marschner
    pub. Fürstner (1925)
    1st perf. 28 May 1924, Stuttgart

[Pfitzner also orchestrated a group of three songs by Schumann,
which was performed in Strasbourg on 30 October 1912; these
remain unpublished; a second set of Schumann songs orchestrated
by Pfitzner can no longer be located.]

(d) JUVENILIA, UNFINISHED, UNPUBLISHED, AND POSTHUMOUSLY PUBLISHED WORKS

(i) Works with dates

1880   Geschwind-Marsch
1880   Andante
1880   Stück in e-moll
1880   Zweiteiliges Klavierstück
1884   'Ständchen' (Schack) [Easter 1884]
1884   'O schneller, mein Ross' (Geibel) [24 June 1884]
1884?   'Der Fichtenbaum' (Heine)
1885   'Lied Werners' aus dem 'Trompeter von Säckingen'
        (Scheffel) [8 Apr. 1885]
1885   'Kukukslied' (Bartholomew) [12 June 1885[3]]
1886   Trio in B-dur in drei Sätzen für Violine, Violoncello und
        Klavier [2nd mvt. fragment]
    ed. Hans Rectanus (2nd mvt. reconstructed by Gerhard Frommel)
    pub. Schott (1982)
1886   Streichquartett in d-moll

---

[3] Although this song was published amongst the fragments in *Sämtliche Lieder*, it
has since been published in its entirety by Günter Brosche in 'Der Pfitzner-Bestand
der Musiksammlung der Österreichischen Nationalbibliothek', *Festschrift Rudolf
Elvers zum 60. Geburtstag*, ed. Ernst Herttrich and Hans Schneider (Tutzing, 1985),
85–95.

ed. Hans Rectanus
pub. Bärenreiter (1972)
1887   Trio Es-dur für Violine, Violoncello und Klavier [lost; 26 Jan. 1887, Frankfurt am Main]
1887/8 Trio in E-dur für Violine, Violoncello und Klavier [lost]
1887/8 Rondo für Violine, Violoncello und Klavier
1888   Cellokonzert in a-moll
ed. Wolfgang Osthoff
pub. Schott (1978); min. score Eulenburg (1989)
1943   Unorthographisches fugato für Streichquartett (Vienna, 4 Nov. 1943)[4]

(ii) Works without dates

'Die schlanke Wasserlilie' (Heine)
'Mein Liebchen ist kein stolzes Schloss' (Anon.)
'Auf geheimem Waldespfade' (Lenau) [fragment]
'Historie von Noah' (Kopisch) [fragment]
'Wär ich, Geliebte' (Anon.) [fragment]
'Waldesgespräch' (Eichendorff) [fragment]
Sonatine in c-moll [piano]
Sonatine in F-dur [piano]
Marsch in C-dur für Streichquartett
Quartettsatz in f-moll
Adagio für Violine und Klavier in h-moll
Andante sostenuto in h-moll für Violine, Viola und Klavier
Menuett mit Trio in g-moll/G-dur für Violine, Violoncello und Klavier
Andante und Allegro D-dur/d-moll für Violine, Violoncello und Klavier [fragment]
Triosatz für Violine, Violoncello und Klavier in C-dur [fragment]
Konzertwalzer in a-moll für Klavier

---

[4] As this book goes to press, at least two further songs by Pfitzner, 'Dem Herzallerliebsten' (1884) and 'Ständchen' (4 October 1884, to a text by Bürger), have been discovered by Hans Rectanus; there is also a later setting of Liliencron, 'Tiefe Sehnsucht', which Pfitzner appears to have disowned after using its material in *Die Rose vom Liebesgarten*).

Select Bibliography

❦❦

Details of Pfitzner's own writings may be found in *Abbreviations*. Details of manuscript sources consulted are given in the notes to individual chapters.

Abendroth, Walter, 'Hier spricht die Hitler-Jugend: Hans Pfitzner der Deutsche', *Die Musik*, 26 (1934), 561–5.
—— *Hans Pfitzner* (Munich, 1935).
—— 'Das Missvergnügen an der deutschen Seele', *MPG* 3 (May 1956), 11–14.
—— and Danler, Karl-Robert (ed.), *Festschrift aus Anlass des 100. Geburtstags am 05. Mai 1969 und des 20. Todestags am 22. Mai 1969 von Hans Pfitzner* (Munich, 1969).
Adamy, Bernhard, *Hans Pfitzner: Literatur, Philosophie und Zeitgeschehen in seinem Weltbild und Werk* (Tutzing, 1980).
—— 'Pfitzner und der Verlag Adolph Fürstner', *MPG* 43 (Sept. 1981), 17–63.
—— 'Das *Palestrina*-Textbuch als Dichtung', *SPB* 21–65.
Albrecht, George Alexander, 'Die Problematik der Aufführungs-praxis Pfitznerscher Orchesterwerke am Beispiel der *Kleinen Sinfonie op. 44*', *SPB* 11–16.
—— *Das sinfonische Werk Hans Pfitzners* (Tutzing, 1987).
Ambros, August Wilhelm, *Geschichte der Musik*, ed. Gustav Nottebohm, rev. Hugo Leichentritt (3rd edn., vol. 4; Leipzig, 1909).
Bagier, Guido, 'Hans Pfitzner und die Übrigen', *PVB* 59–60.
Bahle, Julius, *Eingebung und Tat im musikalischen Schaffen* (Leipzig, 1939; 2nd edn. Hemmenhoffen, 1982).
—— *Hans Pfitzner und der geniale Mensch* (Konstanz, 1949).
Berg, Alban, 'The Musical Impotence of Hans Pfitzner's "New Aesthetic"', in Willi Reich, *The Life and Work of Alban Berg*, trans. Cornelius Cardew (London, 1965), 205–18.
Berrsche, Alexander, *Der arme Heinrich: Ein Musikdrama in drei Akten, Dichtung von James Grun, Musik von Hans Pfitzner: Kurze Einführung* (Leipzig, n.d. [1913]).
Blessinger, Karl, 'Romantisches und expressionistisches Symbol', *PVB* 1–8.
—— 'Pfitzners erzieherische Bedeutung', *PVB* 42–5.
Bollert, Werner, 'Pfitzner als Meister des Klaviers', *Musica*, 3 (1949), 176–9.

Brosche, Günter, 'Der Pfitzner-Bestand der Musiksammlung der Österreichischen Nationalbibliothek', *Festschrift Rudolf Elvers zum 60. Geburtstag*, ed. Ernst Herttrich and Hans Schneider (Tutzing, 1985), 73–95.

Busch-Salmen, Gabriele, and Weiss, Günther, *Hans Pfitzner: Münchner Dokumente/Bilder und Bildnisse* (Regensburg, 1990).

Busse, Eckart, *Die Eichendorff-Rezeption im Kunstlied: Versuch einer Typologie anhand von Kompositionen Schumanns, Wolfs und Pfitzners* (Würzburg, 1975).

Cahn, Peter, 'Zum Charakter von Pfitzners Spätstil am Beispiel der *Kleinen Sinfonie op. 44*', *SPB* 99–110.

—— 'Kontrapunktische Züge im Liedschaffen Pfitzners', *PLZ*.

Carner, Mosco, 'Pfitzner v. Berg, or Inspiration v. Analysis', *Musical Times*, 118 (1977), 379–80.

Cossmann, Paul Nikolaus, *Hans Pfitzner* (Munich and Leipzig, 1904).

Danler, Karl-Robert, 'Über die Aktualität Hans Pfitzners', *FHP* 18–21.

Diez, Werner, *Hans Pfitzners Lieder: Versuch einer Stilbetrachtung* (Regensburg, 1968).

Dombrowski, Hansmaria, 'Pfitzner in seiner Meisterklasse', *Musica*, 24 (1970), 62–3.

Dümling, Albrecht, *Gottfried Keller vertont von Johannes Brahms, Hans Pfitzner, Hugo Wolf* (Munich, 1981).

—— and Girth, Peter, *Entartete Musik: Zur Düsseldorfer Austellung von 1938; Eine kommentierte Rekonstruktion* (Düsseldorf, 1988).

Eberle, Gottfried, 'Hans Pfitzner: Präfaschistische Tendenzen in seinem ästhetischen und politischen Denken', in Hanns-Werner Heister and Hans-Günter Klein (ed.), *Musik und Musikpolitik im faschistischen Deutschland* (Frankfurt am Main, 1984), 136–43.

Ehlers, Paul, 'Zu Hans Pfitzners Kammermusik', *PVB* 30–4.

Erhardt, Otto, 'Die Aufgaben der modernen Opernregie', *PVB* 28–30.

—— 'Zum Regieproblem von Hans Pfitzners *Palestrina*', *PVB* 35–6.

Ermen, Reinhard, 'Der "Erotiker" und der "Asket": Befragung zweier Klischees am Beispiel der "Gezeichneten" und des "Palestrina"', *Franz Schreker (1878–1934) zum 50. Todestag*, ed. Reinhard Ermen (Aachen, 1984).

—— *Musik als Einfall: Hans Pfitzners Position im ästhetischen Diskurs nach Wagner* (Aachen, 1986).

Fischer, Gert, 'Am Pult: Hans Pfitzner', *SPB* 155–72.

Fleury, Albert, 'Historische und stilgeschichtliche Probleme in Pfitzners *Palestrina*', *Helmuth Osthoff zu seinem siebzigsten Geburtstag*, ed. Ursula Aarburg and Peter Cahn (Tutzing, 1969), 229–39.

Floros, Constantin, 'Gedanken über Brahms und Pfitzner', *MPG* 49 (Jan. 1988), 68–73.

Franklin, Peter, *The Idea of Music: Schoenberg and Others* (London,

1985; see also *Musical Quarterly*, 70 (1984), 499–514).

—— 'Audiences, Critics and the Depurification of Music: Reflections on a 1920s Controversy', *Journal of the Royal Musical Association*, 114 (1989), 80–91.

Freund, Volker, *Hans Pfitzners Eichendorff-Lieder* (Hamburg, 1986).

Frommel, Gerhard, 'Traditionalität und Originalität bei Hans Pfitzner', *SPB* 175–88.

Furtwängler, Wilhelm, *Notebooks 1924–1954*, trans. Shaun Whiteside, ed. Michael Tanner (London, 1989).

Grasberger, Franz, 'Dokumente zur Wiener Erstaufführung des *Palestrina*', *Österreichische Musikzeitschrift*, 24 (1969), 234–45.

Grohe, Helmut, 'Hans Pfitzner: *Das Herz*: Der Sinn des Dramas', Programme-book of the Staats-Theater unter den Linden (Berlin, n.d. [1931]).

—— *Hans Pfitzner: Verzeichnis sämtlicher im Druck erschienenen Werke* (Munich and Leipzig, n.d. [1960]).

—— 'Im Zeichen Hans Pfitzners zur Geschichte und zum Schicksal zweier Vereinsgründungen', *FHP* 69–83.

—— 'The Miraculous a Possibility: An Account of the Origins of Hans Pfitzner's *Palestrina* from the Historical and Artistic Viewpoints', booklet of *Palestrina* (DG Stereo 2711 013).

Grun, Frances, *Hans Thoma und Frances Grun: Lebenserinnerungen von Frances Grun*, ed. Walter Kreuzburg (Frankfurt am Main, 1957).

Habelt, Hans-Jürgen, 'Hans Pfitzners Lieder auf Texte von Heinrich Heine', *MPG* 46 (Jan. 1984), 3–17.

Halusa, Karl, 'Hans Pfitzners musikdramatisches Schaffen: Eine dramaturgische Studie' (Dissertation, University of Vienna, 1929).

Hans Pfitzner, Vierteljahreshefte des Bühnenvolksbundes, 3/4 (1921).

Hanzl, Rudolf, '"Der Wunsch meine Erdentage in Wien beschliessen zu können...": Hans Pfitzner zum 10. Todestag', *Österreichische Musikzeitschrift*, 14 (1959), 376–80.

Heller, Friedrich, 'Requiem für eine Polemik: Pfitzners Ästhetik in heutiger Sicht', *Österreichische Musikzeitschrift*, 24 (1969), 245–9.

Henderson, Donald Gene, 'Hans Pfitzner: The Composer and his Instrumental Works' (Ph.D. thesis, University of Michigan, 1963).

—— 'Hans Pfitzner's *Palestrina*, a Twentieth-Century Allegory', *Music Review*, 31 (1970), 32–42.

Herzog, Friedrich W., 'Deutsche Studenten feiern Hans Pfitzner', *Die Musik*, 27 (1935), 764.

Hirtler, Franz, *Hans Pfitzners 'Armer Heinrich' in seiner Stellung zur Musik des ausgehenden Jahrhunderts* (Würzburg, 1940).

Hofmiller, Josef, 'Hans Pfitzner', *PVB* 8–10.

—— *Revolutionstagebuch 1918/19* (2nd edn.; Leipzig, 1937).

Katalog Nr. 288: Hans Pfitzner (1869–1949) (Tutzing: Musik-antiquariat Hans Schneider, 1986).

Kindermann, Jürgen, 'Zur Kontroverse Busoni–Pfitzner', *Festschrift für Walter Wiora zum 30. Dezember 1966*, ed. Ludwig Finscher and Christoph-Hellmut Mahling (Kassel, 1967), 471–7.

Klein, John W., 'Hans Pfitzner and the Two Heydrichs', *Music Review*, 26 (1965), 308–17.

Kravitt, Edward F., 'The Joining of Words and Music in Late Romantic Melodrama', *Musical Quarterly*, 62 (1976), 571–90.

—— 'The Orchestral *Lied*: An Inquiry into its Style and Unexpected Flowering around 1900', *Music Review*, 37 (1976), 209–26.

Kriss, Rudolf, *Die Darstellung des Konzils von Trient in Hans Pfitzners musikalischer Legende 'Palestrina'* (publication by the author, 1962).

Kroll, Erwin, *Hans Pfitzner* (Munich, 1924).

—— 'Hans Pfitzner und Oswald Spengler', *MPG* 18 (Apr. 1967), 16–17.

Kunze, Stefan, 'Zeitschichten in Pfitzners *Palestrina*', *SPB* 69–82.

La Grange, Henry-Louis de, *Gustav Mahler* (3 vols.; Paris, 1979–84).

Lederer, Josef-Horst, 'Pfitzner–Schönberg: Theorie der Gegensätze', *Archiv für Musikwissenschaft*, 35 (1978), 297–309.

Levin, Kurt, 'Erinnerungen', *FHP* 58–65.

Lindlar, Heinrich, *Hans Pfitzners Klavierlied* (Würzburg-Aumühle, 1940).

Louis, Rudolf, *Hans Pfitzners 'Die Rose vom Liebesgarten': Eine Streitschrift* (Munich, 1904).

Lütge, Wilhelm, *Hans Pfitzner* (Leipzig, 1924).

Maehder, Jürgen, 'Die musikalische Aura des Meisterwerkes: Orchesterklang als Medium der Werkintention in Pfitzners *Palestrina*', Programme Book of the Bayerische Staatsoper (Munich, 1979), 25–35.

Magee, Bryan, *The Philosophy of Schopenhauer* (Oxford, 1983).

Mahler, Alma, *Gustav Mahler: Memories and Letters*, trans. Basil Creighton, ed. Donald Mitchell and Knud Martner (4th edn.; London, 1990).

Mann, Thomas, 'Zu Hans Pfitzners *Palestrina*', *PVB* 46–9.

—— *Reflections of a Nonpolitical Man*, trans. Walter D. Morris (New York, 1983).

Mayer, Ludwig Karl, '*Die Rose vom Liebesgarten*', *PVB* 16–18.

Mohr, Wilhelm, 'Hans Pfitzners Sextett Opus 55', *MPG* 7 (Oct. 1960), 2–12.

Müller, Karl Alexander von, *Mars und Venus: Erinnerungen 1914–1919* (Stuttgart, 1954).

—— *Am Rand der Geschichte* (2nd edn.; Munich, 1958).

Müller, Karl Franz, *In Memoriam Hans Pfitzner* (Vienna, 1950).

Müller-Blattau, Joseph, *Hans Pfitzner* (Potsdam, 1940).

—— *Hans Pfitzner: Lebensweg und Schaffensernte* (Frankfurt am Main, 1969).

Mutz, Ulrich, 'Pfitzner as a Conservative Thinker', *Salisbury Review*,

5 (1987), 24–8 (trans. Anita Schnell and Roger Scruton from *Criticón*, 16 (1986), 245–8).

—— 'Kulturkritik aus dem Geiste der Musik: Kunst und Politik bei Pfitzner', *Etappe*, 2, No. 1 (1989), 48–59.

Neunzig, Hans A., 'Hans Pfitzner, der streitbare Erbe', booklet accompanying Hans Pfitzner, *Lieder in dokumentarischen Aufnahmen* (Michael Raucheisen Lied Edition, Acanta 40.23 532).

Newsom, Jon, 'Hans Pfitzner, Thomas Mann and *The Magic Mountain*', *Music & Letters*, 55 (1974), 136–50.

Nowak, Leopold, 'Improvisationen des elfjährigen Hans Pfitzner', *Österreichische Musikzeitschrift*, 24 (1969), 224–33.

—— 'Hans Pfitzners Nachlass in der Musiksammlung der Österreichischen Nationalbibliothek, *Österreichische Musik-zeitschrift*, 24 (1969), 252–4.

Osthoff, Wolfgang, 'Pfitzner—Goethe—Italien: Die Wurzeln des Silla-Liedchens im *Palestrina*', *Analecta Musicologica*, 17 (1976), 194–211.

—— 'Jugendwerk, Früh-, Reife- und Altersstil: Zum langsamen Satz des Cellokonzerts in a-moll op. 52 von Hans Pfitzner', *Archiv für Musikwissenschaft*, 33 (1976), 89–118.

—— 'Eine neue Quelle zu Palestrinazitat und Palestrinasatz in Pfitzners musikalischer Legende', *Renaissance-Studien: Helmuth Osthoff zum 80. Geburtstag*, ed. Ludwig Finscher (Tutzing, 1979), 185–209.

—— 'Musikalische Skizzen und Entwürfe Hans Pfitzners in Würzburg', *MPG* 43 (Sept. 1981), 99–103.

—— (ed.), *Symposium Hans Pfitzner Berlin 1981: Tagungsbericht* (Tutzing, 1984).

—— 'Pfitzner und der "historische Materialstand"', *SPB* 115–46.

—— 'Hans Pfitzners "Rose vom Liebesgarten", Gustav Mahler und die Wiener Schule', *Festschrift Martin Ruhnke: zum 65. Geburtstag* (Neuhausen-Stuttgart, 1986), 265–93.

—— 'Hans Pfitzner und München', *Jugendstil-Musik? Münchner Musikleben 1890–1918*, ed. Robert Münster (Wiesbaden, 1987), 40–8.

—— Preface to Hans Pfitzner, *Concerto for Violoncello and Orchestra [in] A minor*, Op. posth. (1888) (London and Mainz: Eulenburg, 1989).

—— (ed.), *Briefwechsel Hans Pfitzner—Gerhard Frommel 1925–1948* (Tutzing, 1990).

Prieberg, Fred K., *Musik im NS-Staat* (Frankfurt am Main, 1982).

Rectanus, Hans, *Leitmotivik und Form in den musikdramatischen Werken Hans Pfitzners* (Würzburg, 1967).

—— 'Die musikalischen Zitate in Hans Pfitzners *Palestrina*', *FHP* 22–7.

—— 'Pfitzner als Dramatiker', *Beiträge zur Geschichte der Oper*, ed.

Heinz Becker (Regensburg, 1969), 139–45.

—— 'Materialen zur Entstehung des "Herz"', *MPG* 27 (Apr. 1971), 11–15.

—— 'Hans Pfitzners Jugendstreichquartett d-moll aus dem Jahre 1886', *MPG* 29 (July 1972), 16–26.

—— '"Ich kenne dich, Josquin, du Herrlicher . . .": Bemerkungen zu thematischen Verwandtschaften zwischen Josquin, Palestrina, und Pfitzner', *Renaissance-Studien: Helmuth Osthoff zum 80. Geburtstag*, ed. Ludwig Finscher (Tutzing, 1979), 211–22.

—— Foreword to Hans Pfitzner, *Sämtliche Lieder* (2 vols.; Mainz, 1979–83).

—— 'Pfitzners frühe Werke: Bestand und stilistische Anmerkungen', *SPB* 89–98.

Riezler, Walter, *Hans Pfitzner und die deutsche Bühne* (Munich, 1917).

Rihm, Wolfgang, 'Zur Aktualität Pfitzners', *SPB* 189–93.

Ringger, Rolf Urs, '*Lethe*: Hans Pfitzners Orchesterlied op. 37', *MPG* 43 (Sept. 1981), 91–8.

Rutz, Hans, *Hans Pfitzner: Musik zwischen den Zeiten* (Vienna, 1949).

Schopenhauer, Arthur, *The World as Will and Representation*, trans. E. F. J. Payne (2 vols.; New York, 1969).

—— *Parerga and Paralipomena*, trans. E. F. J. Payne (2 vols.; Oxford, 1974).

Schrott, Ludwig, *Die Persönlichkeit Hans Pfitzners* (Zurich and Freiburg, 1959).

—— '*Divina Commedia* im *Palestrina*', *MPG* 32 (Apr. 1974), 36–9.

Schwarz, Werner, 'Die Bedeutung des Religiösen im musik-dramatischen Schaffen Hans Pfitzners', *Festgabe für Joseph Müller-Blattau*, ed. Christoph-Hellmut Mahling (Kassel, 1966), 101–17.

See, Max, 'Berührung der Sphären: Gedanken zu einer musikalischen Reminiszenz', *Melos*, 4 (1978), 312–17.

Seebohm, Reinhard, 'Die gotischen Wesenszüge in der Tonwelt Hans Pfitzners', *FHP* 36–57.

—— 'Die Tragödie eines grossen Arztes: Die Handlung von Pfitzners letzter Oper *Das Herz* in heutiger Sicht', *MPG* 27 (Apr. 1971), 1–9.

—— 'Das Rittertum in der Musik von Weber bis Pfitzner', *MPG* 30 (Mar. 1973), 2–13.

—— 'Pfitzners Verhältnis zu Joseph Haydn', *MPG* 34 (Oct. 1975), 34–54.

—— 'Pfitzners Chorphantasie *Das dunkle Reich* op. 38', *MPG* 41 (Apr. 1980), 42–54.

—— 'Der A-capella-Chor *Columbus*', *MPG* 43 (Sept. 1981), 74–7.

—— 'Einheit in der Vielfalt: Beobachtungen an Instrumentalwerken Schumanns und Pfitzner', *MPG* 47 (Dec. 1985), 6–21.

—— '"Eine leichte Art des Ernstes": Betrachtungen zu Pfitzners späten Instrumentalwerken', *MPG* 49 (Jan. 1988), 27–40.

Seidl, Arthur, *Hans Pfitzner* (Leipzig, 1921).

Selig, Wolfram, *Paul Nikolaus Cossmann und die Süddeutschen Monatshefte von 1914–1918* (Osnabrück, 1967).

Skouenborg, Ulrik, *Von Wagner zu Pfitzner* (Tutzing, 1983).

—— 'Die Harmonik Pfitzners mit besonderem Bezug auf die *Eichendorff-Kantate*', *SPB* 207–14.

Smeed, J. W., *German Song and its Poetry, 1740–1900* (Beckenham, 1987).

Stephan, Rudolf, 'Hans Pfitzners Eichendorff-Kantate *Von deutscher Seele*', *MPG* 50 (June 1989), 5–21.

Strub, Max, 'Der Weg zu einer Freundschaft mit dem Meister', *FHP* 66–8.

Toller, Owen, *Pfitzner's 'Palestrina': The 'Musical Legend' and its Background* (London, forthcoming).

Truscott, Harold, 'Pfitzner's Orchestral Music', *Tempo*, 104 (1973), 2–10.

Valentin, Erich, *Hans Pfitzner: Werk und Gestalt eines Deutschen* (Regensburg, 1939).

Vogel, Johann Peter, 'Pfitzners Kompositionen für Solo-Klavier', *MPG* 15 (Mar. 1966), 1–7.

—— 'Annäherung an Pfitzner', *FHP* 11–17.

—— 'Schönberg und Pfitzner', *Musica*, 28 (1974), 225–7.

—— 'Das Lied *Nachts* von Hans Pfitzner: Ein Nachwort zur Kritik Alban Bergs an der *Neuen Ästhetik*', *SPB* 217–31.

—— 'Pfitzner's drei Männerchöre op. 53', *Musica*, 41 (1987), 514–19.

—— Preface to Hans Pfitzner, *Symphony [in] C sharp minor*, Op. 36*a* (London and Mainz: Eulenburg, 1987).

—— Preface to Hans Pfitzner, *Concerto for Piano and Orchestra [in] E flat major*, Op. 31 (London and Mainz: Eulenburg, 1987).

—— *Hans Pfitzner mit Selbstzeugnissen und Bilddokumenten* (Reinbek bei Hamburg, 1989).

—— 'Thomas Mann und Hans Pfitzner', *MPG* 51 (1990), 3–18.

Walter, Bruno, *Theme and Variations*, trans. James A. Galston (London, 1947).

—— *Briefe 1894–1962*, ed. Lotte Walter Lindt (Frankfurt am Main, 1969).

Waltershausen, Hermann Wolfgang von, 'Zur Musik und Dramaturgie von Hans Pfitzners "Armem Heinrich"', *PVB* 10–15.

—— 'Hans Pfitzners Naturgefühl', *FHP* 28–35.

Wamlek-Junk, Elisabeth, *Hans Pfitzner und Wien: Sein Briefwechsel mit Victor Junk und andere Dokumente* (Tutzing, 1986).

Wandrey, Conrad, *Hans Pfitzner: Seine geistige Persönlichkeit und das Ende der Romantik* (Leipzig, 1922).

—— 'Hans Pfitzner', *Völkische Kultur*, 26 (1934), 193–201.

Wellesz, Egon, *Die neue Instrumentation* (2 vols.; Berlin-Schöneberg, 1929).

—— and Wellesz, Emmy, *Egon Wellesz: Leben und Werk*, ed. Franz

Endler (Vienna and Hamburg, 1981).

Wiesend, Reinhard, 'Traditionen der Wiedergabe und Strukturen des Werks: Zu Pfitzners Einspielung der VIII. Symphonie von Beethoven', *SPB* 239–48.

—— 'Pfitzners Beethoven-Partituren', *Die Musikforschung*, 38 (1985), 289–99.

Williamson, John, 'Pfitzner and Ibsen', *Music & Letters*, 67 (1986), 127–46.

Winkler, Gerhard, 'Hans Sachs und Palestrina: Hans Pfitzners "Zurücknahme" der "Meistersinger"', *Richard Wagner 1883–1983: Die Rezeption im 19. und 20. Jahrhundert*, ed. Ursula Müller (Stuttgart, 1984), 107–30.

Wührer, Friedrich, 'Die Persönlichkeit Hans Pfitzners', *Österreichische Musikzeitschrift*, 14 (1959), 380–1.

Wulf, Joseph, *Musik im Dritten Reich: Eine Dokumentation* (paperback edn.; Frankfurt am Main, 1983).

Index

❧❦

Characters and places from Pfitzner's stage works and vocal music are not included in this index, except for the historical figures on whom Pfitzner modelled characters in *Palestrina*; thus Cardinal Navagero is indexed, but Cardinal Novagerio is not; the historical Palestrina is indexed, but the hero of the opera is not.